Robbe-Grillet and Modernity

University of Florida Humanities
Monograph No. 66

photo by Catherine Robbe-Grillet

ROBBE-

GRILLET

AND

MODERNITY

Science, Sexuality,
and Subversion

RAYLENE L. RAMSAY

UNIVERSITY PRESS OF FLORIDA

Gainesville Tallahassee Tampa Boca Raton
Pensacola Orlando Miami Jacksonville

The University Press of Florida is the scholarly publishing agency for the
State University System of Florida, comprised of Florida A & M University,
Florida Atlantic University, Florida International University, Florida State
University, University of Central Florida, University of Florida, University
of North Florida, University of South Florida, University of West Florida.

Library of Congress Cataloging in Publication data appear on the last
printed page of the book.

University Press of Florida
15 Northwest 15th Street
Gainesville, Florida 32611

*To Nathalie
and Kieran*

Contents

Acknowledgments

As I reflect on the origins of this study and on the many people to whom it is indebted, I realize that more than twenty years of intellectual and personal encounters have found their way into the present pages. This book is indirectly a story of my own life. It draws its substance from all those, mentioned or unmentioned, who made the intellectual voyages of these years possible.

From 1968, the first year of my doctoral studies in Poitiers, I retained a desire to deconstruct the subversive new political discourses that were flooding French campuses. My research on the literary subversions in the nouveau roman was also colored by the humanist, British traditions of reading the texts of French culture in which I had been educated in New Zealand. To Nola Leov, an inspiring teacher of literature at Masters level at the University of Otago, I owed the belief in a critical pursuit of the human truths of the texts under investigation, belief from which, in spite of my long subsequent affair with texts of *modernité,* I have never totally parted. In Poitiers I was to be exposed to the apparently equally universal paradigms of traditional French literary criticism, in particular through the mediation of Ida-Marie Frandon, my thesis director, and, to a lesser extent, Michel Raimond (Paris IV), my principal jury member.

But other very different approaches were gaining increasing influence in France in the late sixties and seventies, and new frames of reading were coming into vogue. Jakobson and de Saussure in linguistics, the structuralist theories of Propp, Lévi-Strauss, Barthes, and Foucault, among others, were providing radical new models for reading cultural texts. The *Tel Quel* group, with its focus on language alone, was beginning to exercise a dominance that was inevitably formative.

The personalities and individual destinies of those around me, like my own life experiences, were also having an impact on my receptiveness to new models and to their political implications. I attended lectures by the philosopher Roger Garaudy on reading meaning in art works through their forms at the time he was expelled from the French Communist Party for challenging its orthodoxies. A meeting with a Rumanian student of theoretical physics in Paris, Basarab Nicolescu, focused my interest in the relations between scientific theories of the nature of reality and the sense of science in Robbe-Grillet's work.

The contexts of my intellectual experiences changed in 1974 when I left France for Cambridge University to study linguistics and pursue the reflection on language as an arbitrary sign system that continued to influence my interactions with the nouveau roman. It was not until I returned to New Zealand in 1978 that I become progressively aware of the critical and political need to rethink the field and texts of French literature from other perspectives, interdisciplinary and, in particular, feminist. A small women's group and my own personal experience of separate and gendered worlds, as I attempted to mother two children and simultaneously merit my then relatively rare position as a tenured woman faculty member, fed into my concerns with not only the ideological nature of discourse, including literary texts and criticism, but also with its gender. With the quiet support of a dedicated head of department, Glynnis Cropp, I was able to use a sabbatical leave in Aix-en-Provence in 1984 to begin work on a study of the nature and significance of the thematics of sexual violence in the new autobiographies of Alain Robbe-Grillet, Nathalie Sarraute, and Margerite Duras.

The intellectual climate of Massachusetts, where I moved in 1986, sharpened my focus on the imbrication of the personal and the public, the sexual and the textual. Motivation to write on these questions was intensified by the many forums for exchange provided by the specialized professional associations in North America. Participation in a panel organized by Katherine Hayles at the convention of the Society for Literature and Science kept me in touch with discussion on the implications for literary studies of the new models emerging from chaos theory and from the study of dynamical systems. A conference on feminism and representation held at Rhode Island College and various colloquia on twentieth-century literature provided critical feedback for early sections of the present book. Modern Language Association conventions, in particular those of 1988 and 1990 where I was able to organize special sessions on the nouveau roman, brought me into a much appreciated contact with others in the field (Michel Rybalka, Inge Crosman Wimmers, Lois Oppenheim, Carol Murphy, Tom Broden, Ingeborg Kohn, Deborah Lee, and Martine Motard-Noar, among others). The seminars of the Center for Literary and Cultural Studies at Harvard

University have been a vital resource for keeping in touch with current critical debate on postmodernism and new historicism and for thinking through the implications for women of contemporary theoretical models. Participation in a colloquium on Robbe-Grillet's films at New York University in 1989, organized by Tom Bishop and Annette Michelson, provided valuable feedback on the state and stakes of the debate on the troubling sado-erotic thematics and on the semiotics of sex. The students in my visiting course on the new autobiographies at Brown University in 1991 were a source of useful critical response to my readings.

The reworking of the final text was aided by the informed comments of the initial reader for the University Press of Florida, Raymond Gay-Crosier, editor of the Humanities Monograph Series. My special thanks are due to the two hardworking expert readers of what was initially a very long manuscript. The careful reading and suggestions of Inge Crosman Wimmers, Brown University, her own work on reader response criticism and Robbe-Grillet's *Projet,* and the perceptive, critical input of Ben Stoltzfus, University of California, Riverside, provided the final major shaping of the book.

A Simmons College Faculty Development Grant enabled me to spend three weeks in the summer of 1990 in the rare book room of the Bibliothèque Nationale working on Robbe-Grillet's limited edition collaborative works with Delvaux and Rauschenberg. Alain Robbe-Grillet himself remained unfailingly helpful, courteous, willing to see me whether in Wellington, Toulouse, Paris, or New York and always intellectually generous. Catherine Robbe-Grillet was a warm hostess and interlocutor, allowing me to interview her on her own writing and to intrude into private spaces in the interests of greater understanding. I am most appreciative of my own family's tolerance of my writing projects and thank my son, Kieran O'Callaghan, for his experiments with computer graphics to help with the cover illustration.

An earlier version of chapter 1 appeared as "The Sense of Science in the Work of Alain Robbe-Grillet," *Romance Studies* 9 (Winter 1986). A version of one section of chapter 2 was published as "Chaos Theory, the Work of Alain Robbe-Grillet, and the Female Body," *Language Quarterly* 29, 3–4 (Summer–Fall 1991). Sections of chapters 3 and 4 derive from parts of "The Sadist and the Siren: Modern Myth in the Writing of Alain Robbe-Grillet," *The New Zealand Journal of French Studies*

(May 1986). Short sections of chapters 6 and 9 contain echoes of an earlier article, "The Sado-Masochism of Representation in French Texts of Modernity," *Literature and Psychology* 37, 3 (Fall 1991), and the last chapter reworks some parts of "The Uses and Abuses of Enchantment in *Angélique ou l'enchantement*," *Dalhousie French Studies* 17 (Fall–Winter 1989).

Introduction

Is there subversion in the science or in the semiotics of sex that so distinctively mark Robbe-Grillet's work? This study investigates the nature of the relationships between Robbe-Grillet's avant-garde texts (novels, picto-novels, autofictions, films, and theoretical writings) and new fields emerging at other cultural sites—the new physics, chaos theory, new approaches to myth, new history, linguistics, deconstruction, psychoanalytical theory, and feminist theory—seeking both to clarify the significance of the question and to find replies.

I argue that the analogies between the models appearing in these fields of contemporary inquiry and theory and the forms and content of the writer's work shed light on the origins and meanings of Robbe-Grillet's "scientific" and "revolutionary" practice of writing. Such intersections frame and, I claim, provide responses to some of the major questions posed by the pervasive sado-erotic thematics in the writer's work and, more generally, illuminate the insistent and troubling presence of sexual violence in postmodern texts.

The early chapters analyze parallels between the new narrative forms of Robbe-Grillet's work and modern science (relativity, Heisenberg's uncertainty principle, complementary relations, chaos theory) and investigate the nature and the textual functioning of modern mythologies borrowed from the walls of the modern city and reassembled. They also note the presence in the weave of the text of a biographically and psychically situated scriptor and of the workings of an unconscious. These two approaches—the first entailing an insistence on textuality, the second seemingly grounded in biography and psychology—appear to contradict each other. The recurrent explicitly sado-erotic metaphors and myths that characterize much of Robbe-Grillet's work are read both as manifestations of subversion and modernity and as metaphors of the sexual monsters of the writer's (and the reader's) conscious and unconscious being.

It does seem to be the (postmodern) case that there can be no reality independent of the sign system that describes it. The metaphorical and metonymical orderings of the text, which allow the writer (and the reader) to set out on the track of his/her own compulsions, their play-backs, stills, and fast-forwards[1] of sets of recurring, self-similar scenes, are cut out of a borrowed linguistic and cultural fabric. But are these signs only self-referential, innocent signs of preexisting signs? In the specificity of their selection and the manner of their orchestration, as indeed in their commonplace (places common to all) character, some-thing of real significance may yet be gleaned. The writer, imprisoned in the tower of ready-made language and myth and in the cell of his own phantasies, seeks to investigate his situation and to spin his tale anew for himself and for his reader. The traps are many in his/our detective project, red holes of criminal desire that gleam shockingly between the uneven paving stones. Some are painted the color of blood to make the most critically active or empathetic readers pause in their advance. Yet, it may be just these sexualized holes and gaps in our knowledge that allow the return of the repressed, the irruption between the signs of an unrecognized and largely unknowable "real," for writer and reader alike.

Robbe-Grillet's creative work is not only an assemblage. It is a perilous personal textual adventure through the turbulent zones of the unknown and the aleatory, an unblinking look at the unseen "chaos" in the world and the blind monsters in the self. In this apparently steel-hard intellectual game, the dice of chance call up ready-made positions and generate preset moves. Like the chessboard internally duplicated in the decor of the later works, like the game of nim figured by the male protagonists of *L'Année dernière à Marienbad*, the work is validated and bounded by the play of intelligence and control over the separateness of things. And yet, it is also a game of tarot cards, where meanings derive from shifting contexts and from multiple, unforeseeable combi-nations to form a mobile web, concealing very different drives toward vulnerability, self-loss, and death.

This book traces the trajectories that have been seen as "scientific" and "objective" and as totally subjective, first through a "chaotic" exte-rior world and, later, through "the maze of organs" and an inner desire. My study attempts to sustain, like Robbe-Grillet's work itself, both critical distance from and empathy with the text as it probes the mean-ings of the representations on the walls of the city and the forms of modernity these bring into play and the individuated choices and re-arrangements of signs that evoke the writer's personal universe. But the library of scientific and psychological texts, that is, the sociocultural forms in which our lives are enmeshed, and the threads of personal experience, that is, the individual choices at the crossroads of collective sites (Oedipus, sacrificial violence, resistance to and impulse toward death and self-loss), are inextricably tangled. And personal and sexual politics (both Robbe-Grillet's and my own) turn out to be inevitably imbricated with textual politics (modes of writing and reading).

Robbe-Grillet's staging of the hidden fears and monsters in the topologies or simultaneous layers of the historical-cultural constructs of the Western city, that is, in modern mythologies, is ultimately a mise en scène of his own battle with the (young) sirens and with the angel of death. His "erotic dream machine"[2] generates, from the strangely flattened labyrinths of contemporary urban streets, as from the primitive forest and the faery pools of the fascination of the feminine, those tentacles of seduction and the fear of drowning that give rise to a very specialized set of phantasies of rape, criminal violence, and domination.

Despite readings of his work as postmodern staging of language contemplating and begetting language or as antirealist, impersonal, and dehumanized antinovel, the itineraries through space and inevitably through history, human time, and desire in Robbe-Grillet's texts touch something for which there are no terms other than the "real" and the "self." As the writer has repeated, in the frontispiece of *Dans le labyrinthe* for example, this is, at the least, Robbe-Grillet's own life ("ma vie") and death ("ma mort"). Yet, as a number of critics—Jean Ricardou, Stephen Heath, Bruce Morrissette, Ben Stoltzfus, Inge Crosman Wimmers among them—have shown, such proliferating generative and intertextual devices as *mise en abyme*, assemblage, topological reversal, and infolding, that is, a practice of writing and a set of collective deconstructive procedures structure the narratives. As Robbe-Grillet consciously manipulates the elements of the intrigue to produce, reproduce, and slightly modify phonetic, syntactic, and especially semantic complexes, to create clusters of forms and thematic knots characterized by the recursivity and intertextuality of what has come to be called postmodern generative fiction, any single reading (either essentialist or deconstructionist) is shown to be inadequate.

Robbe-Grillet's project for a revolution, then, if not completely impersonal, is an analytical and scientific one. But in his writing quest the world and the self are mediated both by rule-bound linguistic, semiotic, and thematic operations and by the free play of signifiers. This is no longer the transparent mediation of the "illusion-making" mirror of realist narrative convention but rather the mediation of the semi-opaque, flawed, and deforming "illusion-breaking" surfaces of a new linguistic mirror in which, nonetheless, we may catch a glimpse of the imperceptible asymmetries in the world and the ghosts of the narcissistic gazer's past. The latter magnify through the system to render the voyeur-writer and the world in which he is enmeshed monstrous and (un)recognizable.

The present study brings together the asymmetries and the ghosts in the apparently contradictory pair of science and sexuality, suggesting that there is an important if nontraditional connection between Robbe-Grillet's search for (self) knowledge, the new conceptions in contemporary science of the world as "complementary" and "chaotic," and the sado-erotic character of the semiotics and thematics of the writer's work. That the "complementary" relation in the Heisenberg sense—matter as either wave or particle, continuity and discontinuity, virtual and real according to the measure or kind of intervention—constituted the essential structure of Robbe-Grillet's work was the central argument of my 1972 doctoral thesis on the dislocations of traditional binary logic in Robbe-Grillet's novels and films. Eighteen years later "complementarity" and "uncertainty relations" have become useful literary references for discussion of postmodern texts in general and have not lost their metaphorical or explanatory power in relation to Robbe-Grillet's work. The parallels with models from quantum physics are extended here to other contemporary theories of science and, in particular, to the theory of the "chaotic" structures of the complex objects and dynamical systems of our physical world: the emergence out of randomness and disorder of recursive patterns and statistically predictable order and the movement of ordered systems into disorder and unpredictability through the tiny deviation, the imperceptible flaw, repeated through the recursive structures of the different levels of the system, provide a new model excitingly analogous to forms operating in Robbe-Grillet's text.

Like Noam Chomsky's theoretical model for generative transformational grammar that makes no claim to represent actual linguistic functioning but merely to be one possible model among others, competing for preference on the grounds of its productivity and elegance, chaos theory has limited its epistemological pretensions. The fact that the new non-Newtonian logic and non-Cartesian universes find clear correspondences in Robbe-Grillet's enterprise of (self) knowledge, however, suggests a certain power or generalization of the new paradigms.

The logical contradiction and multiplicity inherent in the new models of the "real" and made aesthetically respectable by the work of the later Barthes, like Robbe-Grillet's own play/pact with the reader, which draws the latter in and out of the text, permit me too, as literary critic and as female reader, to take up more than one investigative position in respect to Robbe-Grillet's thematics of the capture, torture, and suppression of the young and beautiful female body and his violation of the body of the traditional Cartesian text. My apparently distanced critical attention to the textual character of the sado-erotic semiotics of sex coexists with a personal and feminist concern with the hidden meanings of the obsessive sexualizing of text and the thematic importance of the interrogation and suppression of the female body in Robbe-Grillet's work. This does not prevent a "complementary" identification of (and with) the intellectual adventures, risks, and powerful creative happening that Robbe-Grillet's writing represents. Looking at the origins and nature of the voyeur's obsessional gazing and at the feminine figures and sadistic acts that are the objects of his gaze, I too am captured, sequestered inside between the work's mirrors, and yet am outside, framing the political questions of the nature and use of the power of the erotic at work in, or arising from, the text.

If the initial and ultimate question is "Faut-il brûler Robbe-Grillet"?[3] the final chapter argues, much as Simone de Beauvoir did in her study of Sade, that there are both revolutionary literary uses of the body of enchantment (the text/Angélique) and its nonsubversive abuses in Robbe-Grillet's work. Not the least of the former is the arguably subversive textual revelation and transmutation of significant configurations of modernity that this text now proceeds to examine.

Toward the Sense(s) of Science:
Of "Complementarity"

L'avènement du roman moderne est précisément lié à cette découverte:
le réel est discontinu, formé d'éléments juxtaposés sans raison dont
chacun est unique, d'autant plus difficiles à saisir qu'ils surgissent de
façon sans cesse imprévue, hors de propos, aléatoire.

[The advent of the modern novel is linked to just this discovery: the
real is discontinuous, made up of elements juxtaposed without reason,
each of them unique, and all the more difficult to grasp in that they
emerge in an always unforeseen, irrelevant, aleatory way.]
(*Le Miroir qui revient*, 1985, p. 208)[1]

The work of Alain Robbe-Grillet is at the confluence not only of the
literary and artistic movements of his time, most evidently in its intertextuality and its direct interaction with the work of Magritte, Delvaux,
the photographers David Hamilton and Irina Ionesco, and the pop artists
Rauschenberg and Jasper Johns, but also of major new developments
in the scientific world. This chapter explores the relationship between
new models of physical science, in particular of quantum physics, their
concomitant epistemological and philosophical implications, and the
structures and meanings of Robbe-Grillet's creative work.

An insistence on science in relation to Robbe-Grillet's work may at
first appear of little interest. Much of the initial critical reaction to his
writing took the form of an attack on the agronomist-cum-statistician
whose scientific precision and cold objectivity made him inept at writing
"real" novels—warm, human novels of unique individual experience and
expression. The importance of description of objects and the exclusion
of the reflective consciousness in his early novels of the late fifties and
the sixties led to the imposition of the label "chosiste" and to a rather
loose phenomenological interpretation that ignored the intention present
in any act of observation. What was seen as Robbe-Grillet's "école du

regard" was considered to be concerned with the situated existence of the object, its *être-là*, giving primacy to perception cleansed of anthropomorphism. Such an interpretation coincided with popular notions of science. These represented the physical world as a collection of material objects external to ourselves but apprehended by our universal observations and our measures, and ordered by an immutable reason and a universal method, which science called upon to devise observations to test the truth—by which was meant correspondence with an objective reality—of our hypotheses. These notions are in fact those of the positivist science of the nineteenth century, itself inherited from Descartes, Kepler, Galileo, and Newton and barely modified by Maxwell's discovery of electricity and electromagnetism.

The largely materialist-mechanical conceptions of classical science presented nature as a giant mechanism governed by natural laws that ordered bodies in an absolute space, that is, a space seen as independent of the bodies that filled it. The world appeared objective and determined; an ultimate reality existed—the atom. For Newton, time was distinct from space, flowing uniformly and constituting duration, true and mathematical, without reference to anything outside it. Now in one place meant now for the whole universe.[2] For Robbe-Grillet in his early theoretical writing collected in *Pour un nouveau roman*,[3] Balzac's work reflects a similar vision of the world, of the absolute time of linear chronology moving to create related event and causality and to fulfill a destiny. Robbe-Grillet sees Balzac as representing the dominant mode of literary creation even in this century, a mode of imitation or mimetic representation as opposed to the unmaking and remaking that marked the "nouveau roman."[4] The role of Balzacian absolute time was to arouse emotion by creating suspense and to provide the psychological satisfactions of meaning, resolution, and closure in a world considered objective, concrete, but nonetheless in the image of man who projected himself and his meanings by analogy and metaphor on the environment. Governed by immutable social and psychological natural laws (character implied destiny), this literary world reflected the stable, continuous, meaningful, and determined universe of the sciences of its time in both its content and its form.

Roland Barthes's 1954 article "Littérature objective"[5] popularized Robbe-Grillet's writing as "scientific" and "objective." And Robbe-Grillet, seduced, himself wrote in 1956, "l'adjectif optique, descriptif, celui qui se contente de mesurer, de situer, de limiter, de définir, montre probablement le chemin difficile d'un nouvel art romanesque" [the visual or descriptive adjective, the adjective that contents itself with situating, limiting, and defining points the difficult but probable way toward a new art of the novel] (*PNR*, p. 27). Subsequent critical attack led a defensive Robbe-Grillet to repudiate the terms "scientific" and "objective" and to claim in their place passion and subjectivity. In 1961, he wrote: "Le nouveau roman ne vise qu'à une subjectivité totale[. . .] Non seulement c'est un homme qui, dans mes romans par exemple, décrit toute chose, mais c'est le moins neutre, le moins impartial des hommes: engagé au contraire *toujours* dans une aventure passionnelle des plus obsédantes" [The New Novel aims only at a total subjectivity. [. . .] Not only is it a man who, in my novels, for example, describes everything, but also it is the least neutral, the least impartial of men: *always* involved, on the contrary, in a passionate adventure of the most obsessive kind] (*PNR,* p. 148).

Such a swing from objectivity to subjectivity, from science to passion, necessitated a closer examination of Robbe-Grillet's early, self-professedly by cleansed and objective description, and resulted in the discovery of traps carefully concealed in the objective-descriptive style. These traps that were in fact clues enabled Morrissette to give a psychological interpretation of the novels. A number of critics finecombed the text of *Le Voyeur* and discovered Mathias's obsession with the bound and captive body of the precocious adolescent. Mouth distended by gag and legs apart, attached to the pillar of the boat (or to the witches' stake, or to the stakes used to keep the sheep from wandering in the hollow of the hill), the young and vulnerable female body provokes Mathias's subsequent sadistic murder (the naked, tortured body thrown from the cliff). Fragments of this event are relived indistinguishably in memory, delirium, and imagination in the text.

The story of Mathias, a mediocre, antitragic "character" (or the story of the death of the heroic character) has been read as a case study of a schizophrenic sadist or of the working of obsession. Erwan Rault, for example, traces the numerous occasions when Mathias relives and / or attempts to erase the details of his crime, demonstrating the clinical dissociation, inhibition of the flow of thought, and break with the exterior world that characterize the mental illness of schizophrenia, as

well as the care with which the new text must be read in order to extract
its meaning. This is, of course, to read as a search for the hidden
original meaning and to treat the contiguity of very disparate images
and the textual slippages that merge different time frames as indications
of a deranged or obsessed mind.[6] Such a reading does not take account
of the textual nature of such movements or of the conscious semi-
concealment of the obsession by the writer, concealment to which the
text itself continually draws attention. In particular, a coherent psychological interpretation must neglect the flaws in the text, the multiple
and contradictory versions, for example, of the victim or the crime. Is
Jacqueline attached to a column on the boat or to the stake for burning
witches or to the pickets for attaching sheep? There is no way of knowing, no way of differentiating between unconscious phantasy, daydream,
and reality.

Even the red flesh of the well-known quarter of tomato, "la chair
périphérique, compacte et homogène, d'un beau rouge de chimie, . . .
régulièrement épaisse entre une bande de peau luisante et la loge où
sont rangés les pépins, jaunes, bien calibrés, maintenus en place par
une mince couche de gelée verdâtre" [the peripheral flesh, compact and
homogeneous, and of a fine chemical red, . . . of even thickness between
a strip of gleaming skin and the hollow where the yellow, carefully
measured seeds are arranged in a row, held in place by a thin layer of
greenish jelly] (*Les Gommes*, p. 161), a quarter of tomato cut from a
fruit of "perfect symmetry" in the self-service restaurant in *Les Gommes*,
reveals an "imperceptible" imperfection ("un accident à peine visible"
[p. 51]): a raised corner of skin or fatal flaw. In an analogous manner,
the perfect machinery ("La machinerie parfaitement réglée" [p. 23]) of
fate / the crime / the construction of the detective novel will be perturbed
by the slightest chance or fault ("la plus petite faille" [p. 26]). The red
fruit "flesh" will later inscribe sadistic sexual connotations much as the
detective story is already infiltrated by the obscure Freudian quest and
the still canals and dikes are threatened by the "ocean" that unleashes
dark monsters ("le tourbillon sifflant des chimères" [p. 49]). In *Topologie
d'une cité fantôme,* the red flesh of the watermelon with its black seeds,
variant of the tomato, is cut through with a knife, stains, and bleeds.

Barthes's definition of "objective," moreover, was simply "turned
toward the object"; his definition of "scientific" in the work of Robbe-
Grillet was related to what he called the "new physics" rather than to
traditional science:

Sa destruction de l'espace n'est ni onirique, ni irrationnelle, elle se fonde plutôt sur l'idée d'une nouvelle structure de la matière et du mouvement: son fond analogique n'est ni l'univers freudien, ni l'univers newtonien; il faudrait plutôt penser à un complexe mental issu des sciences et d'arts contemporains tels la nouvelle physique et le cinéma.

[His destruction of space is neither oneiric, nor irrational, it is founded rather on the idea of a new structure of matter and movement: its analogical base is neither the Freudian universe, nor the Newtonian universe; one should think rather of a mental complex issuing from contemporary sciences and arts such as the new physics and the cinema.] (*Essais Critiques*, p. 39)[7]

The work of the scientist-philosopher Bachelard on this still unfamiliar new physics and on what he calls the "new scientific spirit" provides an explanation of the apparent contradiction between objectivity and subjectivity that dominated the early discussion of Robbe-Grillet's writing. Bachelard criticizes the limitations of phenomenology as against scientific method on the grounds that: "la phénoménologie donne, comme allant de soi, une primauté au *senti,* au perçu, voire à l'imaginé—précisément la phénoménologie se voue au *primitif . . .* Elle n'aborde guère le *conçu,* le *réfléchi,* le *technique.* Et bien souvent, elle décrit les oeillères de la perception et non pas la ruse essentielle de l'homme de science dans l'utilisation de ses appareils à percevoir" [phenomenology gives, as if this were natural, primacy to the *felt,* to the perceived, even to the imagined—more exactly phenomenology devotes itself to the *primitive. . . .* It is barely concerned with what is intellectually *conceived,* or *reflected* on, or with the *technical.* And very often, it describes the blinkers of perception and not the essential cunning of the scientist in the use of his instruments for perceiving].[8]

To the limitations and confusions of our human sensory perceptions on which Robbe-Grillet's early novels dwell, Bachelard adds the limitations of other "primitive" ways of knowing—"common knowledge" and "the image."[9] Moreover, philosophical traditions of the objective reality of the world of the senses and of the *clarté* of the mind must, affirms Bachelard, be modified by a recognition that experiments and observation give the kind of reply that the theory (the perceiver) expects. The "real" is not an external category that will or will not confirm the body of hypotheses; it *is* the body of hypotheses. "Truth" is thus rather a measure of internal coherence than of conformity to an objective "Real." "Science today," writes Bachelard, is deliberately artificial. "Elle rompt avec la nature pour constituer une technique. Elle construit une réalité, trie la matière, donne une réalité à des forces dispersées" [It breaks with nature to constitute a technique. It constructs a reality, sorts matter, gives a reality to dispersed forces].[10]

The factitious nature of Robbe-Grillet's "science" and the cunning conceptual use of his instruments of investigation become increasingly evident as his work as a writer, and later, as a filmmaker, evolves. We cannot know the properties of things independently of the methods used to observe them; such methods presuppose a human intervention in the observation process. Niels Bohr claims that the physicist is not a spectator but an actor in the theater of life. Robbe-Grillet equally insists on man the actor rather than man the Balzacian "scribe" and on writing as factitious, as a limited human system of interrogation. At the Cérisy conference on the *nouveau roman,* he declared: "Aujourd'hui nous sommes décidés à assumer pleinement l'artificialité de notre travail: il n'y a pas d'ordre naturel, ni moral ni politique ni narratif, il n'existe que des ordres humains créés par l'homme, avec tout ce que cela suppose de provisoire et d'arbitraire" [Today we are determined to fully assume responsibility for the artificiality of our work: there is no natural order, either moral or political or narrative, there exist only human orders created by men, with all that this implies of the provisional and the arbitrary].[11] Like science, writing breaks with nature to constitute a technique, inscribing literary language into nature ("Je ne transcris pas, je construis" [*PNR,* p. 177]).

Abstraction, Bachelard considers, helps scientific psychology escape from the traps of images. The concept of energy, for example, which has replaced the image of force related to human work and thus to common experience, is given as an advance in knowledge. Robbe-Grillet's early detailed account of number, configuration, relative position in space, and his later interest in topology may be considered, then, not so much a phenomenological attempt to know the nature of the exterior (or interior) world, as an abandonment of image and the notion of common knowledge and an attempt to increase, through neutral abstraction, possible relationships with the world. An attempt, also, to distance the obsessive images of nonscientific psychology, the "nocturnal monsters" (fears, sexual phantasies), the primitive forms whose existence, according to Robbe-Grillet's recent autobiographies, played a major role in his decision to write.

Abstraction also constitutes a metatext, that is, a metaphor within the text of the functioning of the text. Language, it has been argued, is a "mapping of reality" in much the same way that scientific theories are attempted mappings of the world into a "man-made medium."[12] From the models of the linguistic relational system as from scientific models—both creatures of our conscious minds—we can make deductions about the corresponding empirical relational system, the "real" world. These deductions cannot be proven but can be considered valid as long as there is no empirical evidence against them. The essential feature of this mapping process is the abstraction that preserves only those attributes of the objects and relations "represented" in the language considered (by shared or learned convention) to communicate and/or store information. This abstraction allows generalization, inductive reasoning, and inference.

In the early novels in particular, the use of geometrical forms in the description of objects played a major role in the process of abstraction. The wharf in *Le Voyeur* is a series of planes, alternately horizontal and vertical. The bedroom described by the husband-planter of *La Jalousie* is a cube whose interior surfaces "se trouvent découpées avec exactitude en minces bandes de dimensions constantes, verticales pour les quatre plans verticaux, orientées d'ouest en est pour les deux plans horizontaux" [are divided with exactness into thin bands of constant dimensions, vertical on the four vertical surfaces, running from west to east on the two horizontal surfaces] (pp. 159–160).

Bachelard postulates a more reliable knowledge by elimination of the personal through abstraction. Robbe-Grillet's early works make people themselves regular and predictable, forms among forms (the boy and the lamppost in *Dans le labyrinthe*, the frozen characters of *L'Année dernière à Marienbad*). The deserted rectilinear streets and the series of identical crossroads could be used by Goldmann, Leenhardt, Dhaenens,[13] and other Marxist critics to support their interpretation of a reification of human beings and of the world and a Robbe-Grillet vision that, by a leap of Marxist theory, was seen to reflect the negative aspects of late capitalist social organization and values. Leenhardt could read *La Jalousie,* for example, as a revelation of the alienation, dehumanization, and exploitation inherent in colonialism, the native "boy" with his "mechanical gait" constituting a clear clue. (As the novel focuses so intensely on the erotic female object A, the thesis of the alienation, dehumanization, and exploitation of women would have been equally as convincing—or unconvincing—in terms of a reading that took account of the whole text.) The neo-Marxists also see these abstract new configurations as struggle at the aesthetic level against bourgeois values.

On closer examination, however, imperceptible accidents and unpredictable changes inevitably encroach on ideal or abstract regularity. Looking carefully at one geometrically shaped plot of banana plants in *La Jalousie,* it is possible to make out the stem that will replace the banana tree cut down a few inches away and beginning to spoil the ideal regularity of the patch. The nature of the terrain also makes the real forms irregular and gives rise to a series of comparisons between hypothetical and actual figures. "La courbure de la rive entre à son tour en jeu à partir de la cinquième rangée: celle-ci en effet ne possède également que vingt-et-un individus, alors qu'elle en aurait vingt-deux pour un vrai trapèze, et vingt-trois pour un rectangle (ligne d'ordre impair)" [The curve of the bank also comes into play from the fifth row on: this row, in fact, also possesses only twenty-one plants whereas a true trapezoid would have twenty-two and a rectangle twenty-three (uneven row)] (pp. 35–36). Mathias's calculations of the ideal statistical sale of watches conflict greatly with the irregular and unpredictable aspects of the real sales. Descriptions of shifting complication increasingly serve as counterpoint to the descriptions dominated by geometry and number. It is rapidly evident that Euclidean geometry is not relevant beyond a certain frame; it is one system of measurement among others (Rieman's geometry, for example), unable to contain the complexity, the changing dynamic nature of phenomena. Bachelard affirms that "il faut penser le noyau de l'atome dans une dynamique de l'énergie nucléaire et non pas dans une géométrie de ses constituants" [one must think of the nucleus of the atom in terms of a dynamic of nuclear energy and not of a geometry of its constituents].[14] Robbe-Grillet notes more generally; "Le souci de précision qui confine parfois au délire (ces notions si peu visuelles de 'droite' et de 'gauche', ces comptages, ces mensurations, ces repères géométriques) ne parvient pas à empêcher le monde d'être mouvant jusque dans ses aspects les plus matériels, et même au sein de son apparente immobilité" [The concern for precision that sometimes verges on delirium (those notions of 'right' and of 'left' that are so nonvisual, those calculations, those measurements, those geometric points of reference) does not manage to prevent the world from moving even in its most material aspects, and even at the heart of its apparent immobility] (*PNR*, p. 160).

Abstraction is only a relative suspension of the most evident subjectivity. The world abstracted is itself a provisional and limited reduction to human order of fragments of a reality that is increasingly characterized by Robbe-Grillet as strange, monstrous, or unassimilable to humankind. On closer inspection, the attempt to attain neutrality or distance from "cleansed" objects or people vies with emotive criminal particularity in these early novels. Already in *Les Gommes* the photo on the identification card of the investigator who turns out to be a criminal prefigures that of the operatic villain ("Turc d'opérette") that Robbe-Grillet sees when he looks at himself in the mirror more than twenty years later at the beginning of his second autobiographical work, *Angélique ou l'enchantement*. Wallas, the detective, turns out to be the "assassin." So also, if indirectly, does Doctor Juard, 11 Rue de Corinthe, who will become Doctor Morgan and the Count of Corinthe. The latter are avatars of their creator and criminals in the later novels and films. In *Le Voyeur* the careful timetable and the innocent itinerary that Mathias establishes conceal the sadistic rape and murder of the young Jacqueline/Violette. The uniform white light that Blanchot saw neutralizing the events of that novel contains shadows; in the green of the sea and beneath the still surface lurks the seamonster. Along with the figure of the sailor perished at sea/in the mother ("le marin péri en mer"/en mère) encountered in *Djinn*, the monster sailor/marine monster that devours little girls ("le monstre marin qui dévore les fillettes") becomes an explicit and ironic alter ego of Robbe-Grillet himself in *Le Miroir qui revient*.

The precise observations of the objects of the colonial house and banana plantation in *La Jalousie*, the mapping of the length of the shadows cast by the pillar and of the progression of the growing banana plants and their harvesting, the description of the gestures and movements of the female A—all conceal monsters, the jealous sexual passion and fears of the narrator/husband. Or do they? For what the narrator/ point of view attempts to conceal is in fact controlled and concealed-revealed by a writer crafting in a very conscious and artificial manner objective-subjective duality and a relationship between writer, narrator, and character. In *Les Gommes* the fragments of garbage bobbing about and reforming on the surface of the water of the canal and contemplated by Garinati and his alter Wallas figure the "grotesque clown face" of both the writer and his characters and the doll victim ("poupée de jeu de massacre" [p. 37]) of their obsessions. Or is it rather "a fabulous animal," a sphinx, "monstre vorace . . . qui avance vers une proie informe" (p. 37)[voracious monster . . . who advances towards a formless prey]—the marine monster again? The personal passions (jealousy, oedipal desires, sadistic sexual impulse) that might dictate choice of detail, the monsters whose imperceptible shapes or traces can just be detected, are cast in the form of stereotypes—the representations of the group (myths, legends) and of the common language (clichés)—that is, of what might be termed an interpersonal subjectivity. In the later novels and films where the experiments with abstraction are much less in evidence, this interpersonal subjectivity constituted by personal choices made from among stereotyped material becomes the very stuff of which the novel or film is made. According to Robbe-Grillet, this material with its violent sado-erotic and mythical and religious elements makes a "grinding sound."[15] These elements draw attention to their status as collective mappings of reality or as the fictions, the elements of a construction, by which we (and he himself) are constituted.

The notion of interpersonal subjectivity is borrowed from science, where the debate on subjectivity and objectivity in a system characterized by abstraction has been central to contemporary thinking. In a series of important Cambridge lectures in the late 1930s, Sir Arthur Eddington claimed, as Bachelard was also to do, that the sensory and intellectual equipment we use to observe and to formulate the results of observation compresses our frame of thought into the available frame of knowledge, thus restricting science to a "selective subjective." This is a kind of interpersonal subjective for Eddington, that is, a general subjective of all good observers and not a personal or individual one.[16] Such a compromise was felt to threaten a tradition, a common belief in the objectivity of the outside world. Oppenheimer, for example, in his popularizing *Science and the Common Understanding,* insisted that where properties of an object and its changes over time can be verified, we must label scientific knowledge as objective and eliminate the arbitrary of the personally subjective.

In *La Nature dans la physique contemporaine* Heisenberg responded to the objectivity-subjectivity opposition by declaring that science must escape from linguistic tendencies to divide and polarize and in particular from the linguistic dichotomies that separate and order as irreducible opposites, mind and world, subjective and objective. As Robbe-Grillet claims, matter itself is at once solid and unstable, at once present and dreamt, both foreign to humankind and ceaselessly being invented in the mind of humankind.

In the course of his extensive critical writing on Robbe-Grillet's work Ben Stoltzfus has identified this interpersonal subjective with the Saussurian notion of "langue," that is, with the shared formulations, the "language of the tribe" of Mallarmé's formulation. "Langue" in its turn would be the "outside" or the "other" in a "dialectical topology" that is not a mutually exclusive or bivalent opposition. Such a topology, whose basic mechanisms Morrissette had described at the Cérisy colloquium as the reversal and infolding analogous to the scientific figures of the Möbius strip or Klein worms, is seen by Stoltzfus as a reversible and interchangeable continuity between the inside and the outside, the subjective and the objective, the reader and the text, and, we assume, between "langue" and "parole."[17] This "dialectical topology" plays a significant role in the later novels where doors, windows, blinds, and the human eye are, as Stoltzfus describes them, mediating agents between two seemingly opposed and irreconcilable spaces. As in Magritte's painting *The Human Condition,* or in the series of paintings entitled *La Belle Captive,* where the painting in the room reproduces that part of the landscape outside the room that the canvas hides, both the picture and the landscape are simultaneously outside the room and inside. These paintings are generators of Robbe-Grillet's recent work.

The disruption of the outside body of "langue," then, might constitute the only space of inside "parole" (or creative cell, or self). This is a space we could characterize, as Stoltzfus does, by the Phoenix, that is, by the disordering polysemic techniques and the play of proliferating generative themes that challenge the outer space, the "falling rock." The rock, a leitmotif from Magritte's work used as a generator by Robbe-Grillet in his picto-roman *La Belle Captive,* could be equated with

Newtonian predictability. In Magritte's work, however, the falling rock hovers above the sea. In Robbe-Grillet's *Topologie d'une cité fantôme,* and *Souvenirs du triangle d'or* the hovering rock subverts chronology and causality by falling repeatedly, but at quite unpredictable intervals ("Et de nouveau ça recommence . . . la pierre qui tombe etc." [And it begins once again . . . the rock falling, etc.] *Souvenirs,* p. 65) to wound, on occasion, a young woman passing along the phantom streets of Pompeii in the shadow of Vesuvius.

Hegelian dialectics take form around the tendency of a notion to move toward its opposition; this conflict between the contradictory aspects of all things, which are nonetheless interrelated, is seen as an instrument for change. Marxist dialectical materialism derives this constant movement not from the Hegelian world spirit or Idea but from material conditions and processes, from practical interaction with social practices and the socioeconomic nature of things. The dialectics of Marx and Hegel generally accept thesis and antithesis to swallow both up in a synthesis that actualizes both. Lévi-Strauss postulates the tendency to conceive of a phenomenon in terms of its opposite and to elaborate whole social systems around such oppositions (between the raw and the cooked, or the overrating and the underrating of kinship relations) as the fundamental principle of primitive cultures. These oppositions, according to the anthropologist, are then mediated by a third category.

Edward De Bono, the exponent of lateral thinking, in his writing on the mechanism of mind,[18] claims that the human memory itself has an innate tendency to divide and polarize the patterns it selects out of the environment. The result of such divisive tendencies in the memory's pattern making, which, according to De Bono, fixes things into discrete categories and makes divisions where none exist—a process reinforced by linguistic labeling and education—is an unjustified arrogance and rigidity of pattern. The memory surface, says De Bono, cannot comprehend that something may be one thing for a while, then the opposite for a while, and then back again. The passive nature of the mechanism of mind means that the patterns, selected out of the environment on the basis of familiarity, tend to be self-perpetuating. The memory records such attention-controlling information and processes it into discrete units; polarizing tendencies then set up extremes, and these opposites can only be entertained separately. As past information controls what happens to new information, the polarizing units help determine what new information is accepted.

Contemporary scientists have been obliged to comprehend that something may be one thing for a while, its opposite, and back again, and to integrate a series of such "opposites" into their theories. The subatomic system has revealed an epistemologically uncomfortable indeterminism wholly at variance with the properties and laws of classical dynamics. In particular, the photoelectric effect—light as both continuous wave and particle—introduces a major discontinuity and contradiction into scientific culture. As the frequency of light shining on a body is altered, the energy of the electrons ejected from the body changes proportionally. This measure of energy in terms of frequency (called Planck's constant) led Einstein to the counterintuitive conclusion that light, known as a continuous phenomenon, propagating from point to point like a wave, is also corpuscular, consisting of discrete packets of energy out of which light waves would somehow have to be constituted. Einstein proved this discrete quality of light by firing photons (particles of light) at a metal surface, causing discrete electrons to break loose from the metal on impact. Further experiment by de Broglie showed that not only the photon but the electron itself will, according to the experiment (that is, whether one seeks to measure the position or to measure the momentum) manifest both the behavior of a wave with continuous propagation and characteristic interference and that of a discrete particle with a well-defined location.

It may be helpful, at this point, to elaborate briefly on the double-slit experiment that set the scene for the theory of "complementary relations" and the debate on the role of the observer/the observation in determining the phenomenon observed. It had been known since the nineteenth century that light is a wave phenomenon. Light passing through an opening smaller than the amplitude of its waves is diffracted and when passed through two slits shows, on a recording screen set up behind the holes, a pattern characteristic of the interference of waves. This was quite unproblematical until light was shown to be also corpuscles. In Heisenberg's ideal two-slit screen experiment, a single photon, rather than a steady beam of light, is fired. A photographic plate behind the dividing screen registers impact. In this experiment, if only one slit is left open, the photon may strike the plate at a point left black when both slits are open. That is, even when there is only one photon to pass through either of the two slits, interference takes place. Any measurement made at the slits to "detect" the passage of a photon appears to actualize a photon from a wave function rather than to measure it. This was, of course, quite contrary to traditional logic or scientific law.

Classical theories permit a phase space representation in which every state is associated with some point and hence with a precise value for each observable. Measures of position, velocity, and acceleration would accurately predict the future state of the object, and strict causality could thus be established. However, in contemporary science, as a consequence of the wave-particle duality of matter, Heisenberg's uncertainty principle makes such complete knowledge and prediction impossible. The uncertainty principle states that the position and the velocity of a particle can be known only with a mutually related uncertainty—a measure of position of a discrete entity preventing an accurate knowledge of velocity of the wave and vice-versa. If there are no atomic situations in which impulse and position can be defined well enough to make the sort of prediction with which Newtonian physics has familiarized us, we have moved beyond Oppenheimer's notion of "common understanding." We are now in a world that allows predictions only of probability. The atom changes from state to state by leaps that can be measured only statistically and may even be considered to be provoked by the measurement itself, producing such logical anomalies as Schrödinger's cat, indeterminately alive or dead—a strange beast who perhaps also calls for a brief explanation.

Disturbed by the implications of quantum theory, Schrödinger imagined an experiment in a closed box or room that would contain a live cat and a phial of poison. The experiment was set up so that there was precisely a fifty-fifty chance that the radioactive material also inside the room would decay in a certain time. Such decay would break the container and kill the cat. For quantum theory, the determination of whether the cat exists or does not exist could only be made "real" by observation. Schrödinger wanted to denounce the preposterous nature of a situation in which the cat could not be said to be either dead or alive unless we look inside the box. However, even the irrationality of his hypothetical cat's situation has been unable to shake the theory that at the subatomic level we cannot observe a phenomenon without changing it. In the atomic world, events cannot be determined by a strict, efficient, or formal cause.

There are, for Rachel Garden, in her study *Modern Logic and Quantum Mechanics,* two fundamental nonclassical properties of quantum states: "The first, their essentially statistical nature and the existence of incompatible quantum observables (wave/particle). The second, the 'jump' which occurs in the state of a system after a measurement is performed."[19] Physicist Niels Bohr initially accounted for the inadequacy of traditional frames to explain these phenomena in terms of the alteration or disturbance of the phenomena by the measurements applied and the impossibility of simultaneously measuring momentum and position. Opposed by Einstein, who was reluctant to relinquish the hope of a unified theory, and anxious to preserve what many considered the naive realism of the continuity, completeness, and determinism of the classical theory, Bohr was obliged to modify this explanation and to claim that we could deduce from quantum theory "complementary" elements of reality. Incompleteness does not lie just in the weakness of the classical theory, or in our ignorance, as Einstein would have it, but in new physical laws, that is, from the superposition of states of the new complementary things that the theory describes. We need, claimed Bohr in 1935, a radical revision of our attitudes toward physical reality. While Einstein refused to abandon his belief that God does not play dice ("Der Herrgott werfelt nicht"), "complementary relations" and the "uncertainty principle" continue to suggest that probabilities are not just produced by measurements. The principle is thus more than an epistemological restriction on human observers. Quantum mechanical reality does not correspond to macroscopic reality, Bohr claims in his *Atomic Theory and the Description of Nature.*

After fifty years of the Einstein–Bohr philosophical differences and differences between classical and quantum logicians (those who insist that subatomic systems and elementary particles must be described using laws of logic drastically different from the laws that govern everyday classical descriptions), no analogue of classical phase space with the traditional properties has been found to generate the probabilities of quantum mechanics and unify theory. One explanation has been provided by the reflection on the nature of our languages, the languages of "common understanding," their categories, limitations, and their relationship with the real world. The descriptions we give are limited by the terms we use. Rachel Garden argues that these terms are particularly unsuited to mapping microscopic systems. The states of quantum mechanics must, she claims, be considered "descriptions" that are not perfect pictures of reality. We cannot assign truth values to all elementary descriptions, and therefore more than one quantum state may be used to describe the same unchanged reality. Her solution, which helps to draw the classical and the quantum logicians together, is, then, that quantum states must be carefully recognized as *descriptions* of reality and distinguished from the real state of affairs themselves.[20]

Robbe-Grillet's recent work seems increasingly to be moving toward a recognition that there are connections between his linguistic constructions and descriptions of reality (or realities), that his texts contain, at the least, "effects" of the real state of affairs. The question of reference is, moreover, continuously and paradoxically posed by the explicit reference to the uncertainties of reference, of memory, and of imagination within the text. Something is touched in his writing. The mirror returns, however ludically. Although this mirror no longer reflects an eternal essence, there are sets of traces, configurations of moving meanings situated in the connections and gaps of the text's elaboration and the processes by which these create a reality. The elements of the text signify not so much a world out there as other constructions of art and of language or their own linguistic and semantic system. Yet, the internal mirrors, posters, theatrical representations, statues, comic strips, and paintings that proliferate in Robbe-Grillet's work suggest the tracing by the experimental text of the complexities of its own internal relationships, functioning, and lacks. And the mirrors also reflect what Roland Barthes would call "degrees" of reality, plural realities, and the search for new or innovative reality hitherto undetected or unwritten.

There are clear analogies between the images produced by the new theories of quantum physics and those that have appeared in contemporary poststructuralist or postmodern literary theory—that is, the body of nontraditional critical thought that came out of and after the modernist and structuralist experiments. In a general theoretical article entitled "Transgressions: A Quantum Approach to Literary Deconstruction," which is strikingly pertinent to my own study of Robbe-Grillet and theories of contemporary science, André Brink cites Jonathan Culler's now classical metaphor of homo ludens in passionate pursuit of Zeno's arrows, used to explain difficult Derridean concepts like "trace" or "différance."[21] The arrow in flight, whose position can be ascertained from one split second to the next at specific points in space, excludes all notion of motion. The only way to explain motion in this context would be to discover in each present here and now state of the arrow, traces of its past and future states; it is a continuous experience of Derridean "différance" (difference and deferment). Although Brink does not make the connection, the preoccupations here, the implications of the impossibility of knowing simultaneously both position and momentum of entities in time and space, are similar to those that derive from Heisenberg's uncertainty principle. Brink's paper reaffirms my own thesis in its unequivocal assertion that if we accept the validity of the proven experiments of Einstein, Bohr, Heisenberg, Schrödinger, and many others in the field of relativity and quantum physics, deconstruction must be seen as the inevitable extension of these discoveries into philosophy and literature.

In general, the irresolvable questions of the relation between a real world and our languages has to be set aside. Stéphane Lupasco, a theoretical physicist, expresses "complementary relations" in terms of relative virtuality and actuality:

L'événement peut se ramasser, tendre pour ainsi dire vers une localisation, obtenir une certaine configuration plus ou moins précise, jamais rigoureuse, par suite de la mystérieuse constante de Planck . . . mais alors, il cesse progressivement d'avoir une quantité de mouvement précise, autrement dit, sa quantité de mouvement se virtualise dans une somme croissante de possibles; et inversement, il peut s'étaler, tendre vers une existence ondulatoire, avoir une vitesse de plus en plus précise qu'arrête encore, avant la précision absolue, la même constante *h,* mais alors sa forme, sa configuration spatio-temporelle remonte, à son tour, vers un nuage de possibles.

[The event may gather itself together, seek, so to speak, a localization, tend towards a certain more or less precise configuration, never exact as a consequence of Planck's mysterious constant . . . but then, it ceases progressively to have a precise quantity of movement, in other words, its quantity of movement becomes a potential for a growing number of possibilities; and inversely, it can spread itself, tend towards an

undulatory existence, attain a more and more precise speed that the
same constant, h stops again, before absolute precision, but then its
form, its temporo-spatial configuration moves, in its turn, towards a
myriad of possibilities.][22]

Uncertainty, probability, and virtuality—Bachelard, for his part,
considers that it is a primitive form of thought that things either exist
or do not—are constitutive elements of Robbe-Grillet's writing. Expressions of uncertainty such as "it is possible," "or else," "either," "as if,"
and "unless" ("il se peut," "ou bien," "soit que," "comme si," "à moins
que") link clauses. Alternatives proliferate: "une fissure dans le plâtre,
ou un fil d'araignée chargé de poussière, ou une trace quelconque de
choc ou d'éraflure . . . ou un simple défaut de l'enduit blanc" [a fissure
in the plaster, or a spiderweb full of dust, or some trace or other of
shock or scratching . . . or a simple defect in the white coating] (*Dans
le labyrinthe*, pp. 135–36; an almost "identical" description recurs on
page 203).
     The intact surfaces that along with abstraction were to protect the
object from metaphorical contamination and humanist depth reveal holes
and gaps in all the novels: there are series of "failles," "fentes," "entailles,"
"échancrures," "fêlures," "fissures," "taches," "défauts," "creux," and
"trous." Beneath the immobile surface of the stream in *La Jalousie*
("comme figée dans ses lignes immuables") there is unseen movement
("le flot s'écoule rapidement"). The predominance of verbs of seeming,
such as "paraître" or "sembler," and adverbs such as "imperceptiblement"
and "sensiblement" suggest the movement below the immobile and
apparently impenetrable surface. The symmetry of the quarter of tomato
is threatened by a scarcely visible accident ("à peine visible"), by a corner
of the skin raised imperceptibly ("qui se soulève imperceptiblement").
The fine vestimentary detail that gives the illusion of the real ("qui fait
vrai") unmakes and remakes the descriptive techniques of Balzacian
mimesis that Robbe-Grillet took to task in *Pour un nouveau roman*: the
button on the doctor's jacket in *Dans le labyrinthe* has been scratched
("entaillé d'une large écorchure") and a tiny strip of leather in the center
is raised by a fraction of an inch ("au milieu de l'arrondi, un lambeau
de cuir . . . [est] soulevé d'un demi-centimètre" [p. 142]).
     The general forms of the novels show an incompleteness and uncer-
tainty similar to the description of objects and the movement of the

description. The circular movement, for example, is a return to the point of departure—or almost. This "almost" in *Les Gommes* literally introduces the curve, present in space-time since Einstein, into the straight line of Newtonian certainty. Einstein had shown that the presence of material bodies in space engenders curves that affect the trajectories of elementary particles. The universe is thus no longer Euclidean, as Euclidean geometry is valid only for a plane surface. With the disappearance of an infinite time, which Newton saw as an attribute of God, the eternal and necessary truths that appeared intuitively natural were revealed to be useful conventions only. In *Les Gommes* the twenty-four hours of classical destiny detected by the most influential of Robbe-Grillet's early critics, Morrissette, and the "mechanically perfect design" that Morrissette traces through the novel correspond to the novel's leit-motif that the "shortest distance between two points is the straight line." However, space-time warps interfere, and such predestination is con-tested by a kind of liberty: The events will "entamer progressivement l'ordonnance idéale, introduire ça et là, sournoisement, une inversion, un décalage, une confusion, une courbure, pour accomplir peu à peu leur oeuvre: un jour, au début de l'hiver, sans plan, sans direction, incompréhensible et monstrueux" [progressively encroach on the ideal order, slyly introducing here and there an inversion, a discrepancy, a confusion, a warp, to accomplish little by little their work: a day, at the beginning of winter, without plan, without direction, incomprehen-sible, and monstrous] (p. 11).

Neither Euclidean geometry nor fate are canceled out—in one frame of reference within the detective novel the assassination of Dupont, the professor, still takes place as ordained—yet, they are contradicted. In *Les Gommes* such slippage comes about by the minute flaw ("la plus petite faille") that haunts Garinati and by the curve ("la courbure") that transforms this assassin into Wallas, the detective. Garinati is the per-fectionist who orders and reorders on his mantelpiece the oedipal objects of the classical story. He is the mechanical assassin whose predestined step mounts inexorably stair by stair toward his victim. Yet his role is incomprehensibly transformed by this tiny flaw. Two missing square millimeters of forehead measurement cast doubt on whether Wallas (avatar of Robbe-Grillet from whom, the writer claims, the "real" meas-urements were taken) is a "real" detective. Like Garinati, he too will

become what the text calls "another." In his case the detective will become
the assassin; Wallas will replace Garinati.

Bachelard does not consider the opposites of continuity and discontinuity to be mutually exclusive or to require a new theory that
would unify them. The movement of scientific thought, he claims, is
towards formulating links between these pseudocontrary notions, not
toward their logical separation. De Bono formulates and promotes a
new kind of thinking that would provide a temporary escape from the
ordered stability of language, which reflects the fixed patterns of a self-
organizing memory system. He proposes acceptance of logical contradictions and of forms that may be definite at one moment but not
permanent, forms that can assume a variety of shapes or change from
one to another and back again. The mind, says De Bono, would be
required to try out a number of alternative approaches to a problem.
Regularity and continuity should be disrupted and reversed to allow
information to re-form into new patterns; disconnected jumps should
trigger off new associations. De Bono called this lateral thinking.

In an interview with Morrissette,[23] Robbe-Grillet refused the terms
of binary opposition and synthesis in his work, preferring to talk of
slippages ("glissements") and of decentralizations. He claimed to create
a shifting order that avoids the Hegelian dialectic. In his earliest critical
writing he had asserted that it is the forms that man creates that can
give meanings to the world (PNR, p. 152); the forms of Robbe-Grillet's
creative work are characterized above all by the coexistence of, and
displacements within, series of antinomies—subjectivity/objectivity,
immobility/movement, precision/uncertainty, perceptibility/impercep-
tibility, reality/virtuality, continuity/discontinuity. As Jean Ricardou
describes the movements in Robbe-Grillet's later novels, the wish for
continuity, for what comes next, is catered to, but what comes next is
"booby-trapped":

> Aux amples descriptions d'objets immobiles jadis à plaisir prolongées,
> se substitue une cascade de péripéties, pleines de rejaillissements impré-
> vus, qui rejoignent ouvertement celle des fictions populaires: romans
> policiers et d'espionnage, érotiques et d'aventures. Davantage: les
> rebondissements, loin d'accumuler les surprises traditionnelles d'une

même histoire, sont à chaque fois, par toutes manières de contradictions . . . comme des segments, plus ou moins voisins, d'histoires
différentes.

[The lengthy descriptions of immobile objects, formerly drawn out at
whim, are replaced by a flood of adventures, full of unexpected recurring events, which are openly those of popular fiction: detective and
spy novels, erotic and adventure novels. Moreover, far from accumu-
lating the traditional surprises of a single story, these vicissitudes are,
on each occasion, by all kinds of contradictions . . . like the more or
less neighboring segments of different stories.][24]

A scene may be developed in detail, reappear hesitantly, to be finally
contradicted, while an initial negation may develop by verbal slippages
into a full-fledged coherent element of a story. Transitions are effected
by a juxtaposition of things seen, which through the series or internal
network they constitute, begin to suggest a subjective point of view or
imagination: the sea gull with its staring eyes, the cord in the shape of
an 8, the iron ring, the burnt-out cigarette, the young girl attached to
the column in Le Voyeur, for example. Descriptions—of a never-ending
native song with recurring elements in La Jalousie and of the labyrinthine
crack in the ceiling in Dans le labyrinthe, among others—constitute a
duplication within the narrative and a metatextual comment on a general
movement of discontinuity made up of unexpected new beginnings
within repetitions, aleatory developments, and a fragmented kind of
continuity, a rhythm created by recursive elements.

Progression of a kind is effected, then, by repetition or serial organization of objects, colors, numbers, words, by the play on the multiple
connotations of words, and by phonetic and semantic slippages or ono-
mastic play. Unity of a kind is constituted by certain "immemorial"
stories, scenes, objects, phrases, and their variants that erupt suddenly
once again ("Une fois de plus, c'est au bord de la mer" [Once again,
we are at the seashore] Un Régicide, p. 11; "De nouveau la pierre qui
tombe, immobile" [Once again, the rock falls, motionless] Souvenirs,
p. 234), and by the circulation of such elements as the objects in a
figure of eight in Le Voyeur, the coils of rope, and the bicycle, as they

appear with ironic or comic effect from work to work. These proliferating elements are "ready-mades," chosen from popular genres (detective, horror, romance, mystery, or pornographic novels), from the writings of Sade and Michelet, from visual art forms (Magritte and Delvaux,
Rauschenberg and Jasper Johns, the photographers David Hamilton and
Irina Ionesco most directly, Duchamp, Mondrian, Man Ray, Bellmer,
and Rosenquist more allusively), and from the general "mythologies,"
in the Barthesian sense, of Western society, (antiquity, tragedy, alchemy,
nature, humanism, seduction and sexual violence, sacrifice, Freudian
psychology, romantic love, and most insistently, woman, inevitably double as angel and as witch, as slave and provocative freedom).

At the same time, stories and elements are plural, discontinuous,
arbitrary, mobile, and self-reflexive rather than progressive. And there
is an apparent contradiction between the highly complex structuring
(particularly evident in *Le Voyeur* and *La Jalousie*) and the apparently
free, creative play of language with cultural fragments (especially in
Topologie d'une cité fantôme, and *Souvenirs du triangle d'or*) designated
by Morrissette as "intertextual assemblage" and as "generative postmodern fiction."[25]

In his major early critical study, *Les Romans de Robbe-Grillet,*
Morrissette set out to investigate Robbe-Grillet's apparently objective
descriptions and to reorder the mythological fragments to find the original order and meaning. In *Intertextual Assemblage* the critic was seeking
the origins of the text in other texts and in the novels' intertextual and
collage-like forms. By "Postmodern Generative Fiction," after twenty-
five years of work on Robbe-Grillet's texts, Morrissette was focusing on
the new generative structures and the subjecting of the narrative field
to infolding, reversal, turning inside out, in the face of the (im)possibility
of determining an origin or original text. This important American
academic intermediary for Robbe-Grillet's work follows an itinerary similar to that of Robbe-Grillet criticism in general.

Robbe-Grillet however, in his recent "autobiographical" *Le Miroir
qui revient,* returns to a preoccupation, expressed often in interviews,
with decomposition, disorder, and death and the corresponding need
to give order, meanings, and permanence to the world and to one's life.
This oscillation seems to him, in retrospect, to have been a major
motivation for his literary and his cinematic work. Ordering, seen as

a general and here a particular human need, is also recognized as being arbitrary, impermanent, necessarily ideological and oppressive. Within his own highly ordered systems, the content creates distortion, improbability, and noise; the overall structures are the new shifting relationships of what I called "multiple complementarity," in a 1972 study of Robbe-Grillet's work.[26]

Similar dichotomies are insistently presented in the work. If probabilities and superimposed virtual states characterize quantum "laws," simple propositions can no longer be logically bivalent (true or false) in all possible worlds. As Robbe-Grillet wrote as early as 1963: "Le *vrai*, le *faux* et le *faire croire* sont devenus plus ou moins le sujet de toute oeuvre moderne" [The *true*, the *false* and the *illusion* have become more or less the subject of all modern works] (*PNR*, p. 163). In *Djinn* little Marie is first in her "lying" class. An assertion generates its negation; a negation generates the state that it denies. Mensonge (Lie / My dream)—as Malcolm Bradbury has called the absent hero of deconstructionist texts in his humorous book entitled *My Strange Quest for Mensonge*—is a blood brother of the real/false protagonist of Robbe-Grillet's work. Like Mensonge, a chameleon-like personage who is at once presence, origin, truth and invention, fiction and untruth (or "social" truth), Robbe-Grillet's characters engage in ceaseless ordering and truth-seeking activities and yet turn out to be contradictory and nonunified.

A number of examples of the "complementary" functioning of traditional dichotomies other than those of order / disorder and true / false are provided by descriptions of oscillation and vibration, phenomena that, as Louis de Broglie demonstrates, pose great problems for scientific description.[27] *Les Gommes* describes the apron of a drawbridge coming to rest, unable to decide on its mobility or immobility:

La descente du tablier n'avait pas pris fin avec l'arrêt du mécanisme; elle s'était poursuivie pendant quelques secondes, sur un centimètre peut-être, créant un léger décalage dans la continuité de la chaussée; une remontée infime s'effectuait qui amenait à son tour la bordure metallique à quelques millimètres au-dessus de sa position d'équilibre; et les oscillations, de plus en plus amorties, de moins en moins discernables—mais dont il était difficile de préciser le terme—frangaient ainsi, par une série de prolongements et de régressions successifs de part et d'autre d'une fixité tout illusoire, un phénomène achevé, cependant, depuis un temps notable.

[The descent of the platform had not ceased when the machinery stopped; it had continued for a few seconds, perhaps moving a centimeter, creating a slight gap in the continuity of the roadway; a tiny upward movement was taking place, which in its turn, was bringing the metal rim a few millimeters above its position of equilibrium; and the oscillations, growing fainter and fainter, less and less noticeable— but whose cessation it was difficult to pinpoint—were framing in this way, by a series of successive prolongations and regressions on either side of a completely illusory fixity, a phenomenon completed, nonetheless, quite some time before.] (p. 158)

In *La Jalousie,* A writes a letter, and the movement of her wrist is described as amplified by her hair. "Bien que le bras lui-même, ni la tête, n'aient l'air agités du moindre mouvement, la chevelure, plus sensible, capte les oscillations du poignet, les amplifie, les traduit en frémissements inattendus qui allument des reflets roux du haut en bas de la masse mouvante" [Although neither the arm itself, nor the head, seem disturbed by the slightest movement, the more sensitive hair captures the oscillations of the wrist, amplifies them and translates them into unexpected eddies that awaken reddish highlights from top to bottom of its moving mass] (p. 212). If such a description suggests continuous wave phenomenon, the word "unexpected" introduces localized if unpredictable movement within undulation. Other descriptions of A's hair do the same, as her head trembles with tiny movements, imperceptible in themselves but "amplifiés par la masse des cheveux qu'ils parcourent d'une épaule à l'autre, créant des remous luisants, vite amortis, dont l'intensité soudain se ranime en convulsions inattendues, un peu plus bas... plus bas encore... et un dernier spasme beaucoup plus bas" [amplified by the mass of the hair they traverse from one shoulder to the other, creating glinting eddies, quickly vanishing, whose sudden intensity is revived again in unexpected convulsions, a little lower... lower still... and a last spasm much lower] (p. 134).

These undulating movements described also as jolting vibrations ("vibrations saccadées" [p. 43]) that disturb the black mass in spite of the apparent immobility of the head sexualize the text, indirectly evoking latent desire and orgasm. Descriptive epithets such as "red highlights" and "moving mass" ("reflets rouges" and "masse mouvante") link A's hair with other sexualized objects and contaminate even the neutral "green mass" ("masse verte") of the banana trees. Erotic vibrations, explosion, and return to equilibrium (or almost) are again present in the text as the narrator / point of view in *La Jalousie* sees / imagines the car, in which A and Franck are returning from their trip to the port, strike the "moving mass" ("masse mouvante") of an erect giant banana tree and come to rest exploding into flames. In another well-known description, the litany of crackling sounds evoked throughout the text— the noise of the brush moving through the mass of hair, or of the centipede, or of the moving feelers of its variant, the crab, or of the crackling flames—brings together movements of oscillation and undulation that suggest at once unmeasurable movement at the heart of phenomena and dangerous sexual attraction. Tiny localized events that may lead to eruptive cataclysm are a constant in the texts of *Topologie,* whose prisons and temples lie in the shadow of Vesuvius.

In *Dans le labyrinthe* the movement of oscillation creates a somewhat different effect; a regular and recurring rhythm evokes an incantatory dreamlike atmosphere. Stephen Heath, in his germinal work on the nouveau roman as a construction of meanings created linguistically in and by the processes of writing, sees opposition as the basic structural principle of this text. The initial movement from inside to outside of the opening lines—"Je suis seul ici, maintenant, bien à l'abri. Dehors il pleut" [I am alone here, now, well-sheltered. Outside it is raining]— from one thing to its opposite, is, for Heath, part of a progression effected by "the substitution of elements in a relation of antinomy the one with the other along the narrative line of the novel."[28] "Dehors il fait froid, le vent souffle entre les branches *noires* dénudées; le vent souffle dans les feuilles, entraînant les rameaux entiers dans un balancement, balancement, dans un balancement, qui projette son ombre sur le crépi *blanc* des murs" [Outside it is cold, the wind blows between the bare *black* branches; the wind blows in the leaves, causing whole branches to swing to and fro, to and fro, in a movement that projects its shadow on the *white* plaster of the walls] (p. 9; my emphasis).

Oscillation serves a further major reflection on dichotomy, on sameness and difference. Robbe-Grillet's earliest texts, "Visions réfléchies"

in *Instantanés,* for example, manifested a fascination with the sameness /
difference of the mirror image and with the semantics of the term
identique. As oscillation creates changes of disposition in space and
time, the reader is brought to ask what, in fact, is sameness. The soldier
walks through the deserted streets,

> avancant machinalement un pied après l'autre, sans même être certain
> d'une progression quelconque, car les *mêmes* empreintes régulières se
> retrouvent toujours, à la *même* place, sous ses pas. Comme l'écartement
> des semelles à chevrons correspond à sa propre enjambée d'homme à
> bout de forces, il s'est mis tout naturellement à poser les pieds dans
> les marques déjà faites. Sa chaussure est un peu plus grande, mais ça
> se remarque à peine dans la neige. Il a l'impression, tout à coup, d'être
> déjà passé là lui-*même,* avant lui.

> [putting one foot mechanically in front of the other, without even being
> certain of any progression, for the *same* regular footprints are always
> there, in the *same* place beneath his steps. As the spacing of the soles
> with their herringbone pattern corresponds to his own stride, the stride
> of an exhausted man, he has begun quite naturally to place his feet in
> the tracks already made. His shoe is a little larger, but this is hardly
> noticeable in the snow. He suddenly has the impression of having
> already passed by here *himself,* before *himself.*] (p. 127, my emphasis)

He looks down "sur les grosses chaussures qui continuent leur mouvement de va-et-vient, comme deux balanciers décrivant côte à côte des
oscillations parallèles, *identiques,* mais *contrariées*" [on the big shoes
that continue their to and fro movement, like two pendulums swinging
side by side, *identical,* but in *opposite* directions] (p. 100; my emphasis).
Later, in the barracks, he catches sight of a "second *identical* door" at
the "*other* end" and notes the windows on the "*other* side" of the street
that are "*identical* to these ones."

The term "identical" is often qualified by an "almost" ("à quelque
chose près," "peu s'en faut"). The apparent contradiction is developed
by the repeated appearance of the mirror reflection (an inversion of left
and right), the double (same and different), and the symmetrical. These
are necessarily both same and different, a same or nearly same reproduced in a different space.

It was principally the reflection on sameness and difference that set the science of linguistics in the twentieth century on new and influential courses. Phoneme theory postulates that meaningful sounds, or phonemes, that is, the sounds that conventionally discriminate meaning by being heard as "same" (or as "different") in the system of a given language are not sounds that are objectively or physically the same (or different), but rather, sounds that are heard as the same (or different). The Japanese, for example, experience difficulty hearing the English phonemes of [l] and [r] as "different." Not only are they not phonemes discriminating meaning in their own phonemic system, but their place and manner of articulation is close to a learned Japanese phoneme that is neither [r] nor [l] but somewhere in between. The "l" sounds in "leaf" and "hell" in English are allophones of one phoneme and heard as "same" although manifestly the "clear" "l" and the "dark" "l" are phonetically different. In Polish, unlike English, both of these sounds can be found in word initial position and distinguish meaning; they are two phonemes of the language and are heard as "different" (*laska* and *łaska* have different meanings in Polish). Hearing "sameness" is therefore less a function of physiology or the character of physical sounds than of learning the conventional and arbitrary set of phonemes of a given language. Meaning is a function of the mentally perceived "difference" between sounds (between the physically similar [p] and [b] in "spin" and "bin" in English, for example) or between words situated in the set of differential relationships between all the words of the language. Because it is constituted only in the network of the relationships between the arbitrary sounds/signs that discriminate meaning in a given language, meaning is not immanent; it is not a given. It is Derridean "différance," that is, both difference and deferral, always at a remove from its object of reference, from the thing itself.

If the binary oppositions of sameness and difference were seen to be somewhat arbitrary in character, the notion of symmetry also posed problems for the new physics. As Katherine Hayles points out in her germinal work on literature and science entitled *The Cosmic Web,* while symmetry was considered by Pauli and by Heisenberg to be a key to unified field theory, traditional symmetries—charge symmetry in which negative and positive particles can be interchanged; parity; the equivalence of left-hand and right-hand mirror images; and time symmetry—

were put into question by the discovery that electrons were emitted preferentially in one direction (pp. 112–15). Discussing symmetry in the new physics in *The Character of Physical Law,* the physicist Richard Feynman explains that although nature does not permit a distinction between right and left (at 99.99 percent), with Beta disintegration, the electrons emitted spin to the left, and the law of the symmetry of the world on the right and on the left can no longer be absolute. (Such a non-absolute symmetry is the stuff of which monstrous antimatter has been made.) The theoretical physicist Stéphane Lupasco asserts in *Les Trois Matières* that where there is energy, there is both system and antagonisms, not just two aspects of a same and single (that is, unified) reality, as an influential school of interpretation of the principle of complementarity would have it, but contradictions. For him, the wave–particle function of Planck's constant is made of just such mutually exclusive contradictions that are constitutive right through the chain of forces and events that constitute a nucleus, an atom, a molecule, a physical object of perception, a solar system, and a galaxy. His principle of antagonism accounts for the discovery that to every kind of particle corresponds an antiparticle; to the positive proton, the negative anti-proton, to the electron, the positron, to the neutron an antineutron, and to the symmetrical molecule, an asymmetrical molecule. Where classical logic claims that a thing may not contain that which contradicts it, where classical physics sought unity, Lupasco postulates necessary contradiction and a dynamic of relative movement between virtual and actual. Pauli's principle of exclusion itself—which states that an electron in an atom or gas occupying a single quantum state excludes any other electron from the same state—postulates difference or nonidentity of electrons within atoms. A force of differentiation of electrons, of het-erogeneity (comparable to the biological diversification of the living cell, of the physicochemical constituents of protoplasm), is opposed to the second law of thermodynamics, which claims that all energy—electrical, kinetic, and chemical—is transformed progressively and irreversibly into sameness, that is, into heat. Such homogeneity, like the homogeneity of biological systems, can be equated with entropy and death.

For Lupasco, the opposed principles do not constitute simple, bal-anced oppositions. Bachelard, too, suggests that a simple dialectic of positive and negative energy is not sufficiently fine to account for atomic phenomena. Nor is there any theoretical reconciliation of these opposites. In Robbe-Grillet's work, such antinomies also reinforce an overall principle not of mediation and unity but rather of multiplicity, virtuality, and movement. Already in "Du réalisme à la réalité," Robbe-Grillet saw that changes in our knowledge of the world affect our relations with it: "D'autre part la connaissance que nous avons de ce qui est en nous et de ce qui nous entoure (connaissance scientifique, qu'il s'agisse de sciences de la matière ou de sciences de l'homme) a subi de facon parallèle des bouleversements extraordinaires . . . les relations que nous entretenons avec le monde ont changé du tout au tout" [The knowledge that we have of what is in us and of what surrounds us (scientific knowledge, whether of the sciences of matter or the sciences of humankind) has also undergone extraordinary upheavals . . . the relations we entertain with the world have completely changed] (*PNR*, p. 173). The writer claimed to be seeking new mobile, multiple, aleatory narrative structures, more in touch with new realities.

The "cosmic web" that is the metaphor underlying Katherine Hayles's ground-breaking study of scientific field models and postmodern literary strategies describes both the dance of particles and the dance of language where meaning and the real derive from ever-changing relations and networks of traces. But the new, open-ended, mobile text referenced by the web necessarily derives from its transgressions of an existing body. As Derrida has pointed out, even in the mobility of transgression, even where a limit is at work, we have to do with a code. The writer, says Robbe-Grillet, in spite of his will to independence, is embedded ("en situation") in a mental civilization and in a literature which can be only those of the past.

The material from which Robbe-Grillet creates is the very body of the conventions of the novel inherited from the nineteenth century and the collective representations, the mythologies, imposed by the society around him, whereas his variable, mobile structures continually contest the material they organize. The relationship here is again as much one of contradiction as of continuity. In an article in *Tel Quel,* as early as 1963, Robbe-Grillet makes this clear. Critics would like to make the public believe that "toutes les nouvelles techniques vont simplement être absorbées par le roman 'éternel' et servir à perfectionner quelques détails du personage balzacien, de l'intrigue chronologique, et de l'humanisme

transcendant; alors que le monde que ces techniques expriment et celui
où vivait l'écrivain au début du XIXième siecle sont, presque en tous
points, antinomiques" [all the new techniques are simply going to be
absorbed by the 'eternal' novel and serve to perfect details of the Balzacian character, the chronological intrigue, and transcendent humanism, whereas the world that these techniques express and the world in
which the writer lived at the beginning of the nineteenth century, are,
almost in all respects, antithetical].[29] The scientist is in a similar situation. As the theoretical physicist Ilya Prigogine writes in *La Nouvelle
Alliance:* "On ne peut ignorer le poids persistant, culturel et théorique,
qui sous-tend la science que nous disons classique. Peu de résurrections
ont été aussi répétées que celles du Phénix mécaniste" [The persistent
cultural and theoretical weight that underlies the science we call classical
cannot be ignored. Few resurrections have been as repeated as those of
the Phoenix of Mechanics].[30]

I would suggest that the relationships between the Balzacian novel
and a work by Alain Robbe-Grillet and that between classical and
contemporary physics might themselves be considered a further example
of "complementarity." Fragments of plot, description, setting, character,
preoccupation with chronology, verisimilitude, the use of tenses and
focalization remain the material of the text, even if unmade by the
general play of the forms. The realistic detail of Balzacian realism was
almost outdone in Robbe-Grillet's early works, to the considerable frustration of their critics and readers.

Robbe-Grillet may have abandoned the search for the Holy Grail,
the perfect mathematical form, the universal ordering key, and the simple
unifying law in a desacralized world as has contemporary science. Yet
the symbolic/ironic figures of the new Golden Fleece, Golden Triangle,
Alchemy, and the Secret Temple or Room dominate his recent work,
Souvenirs du triangle d'or in particular, as the "science" of the occult
makes a major comeback in Western society. Umberto Eco's novel,
Foucault's Pendulum,[31] for example, stages the drama of the meeting of
these very different "sciences" and ages of man. Two Italian intellectuals
of the postmodern era become embroiled in their own rewritings of the
myths and stories of the secret societies of the Knights of the Templar,
the Rosicrucians, Brazilian voodoo, and the secrets locked in the measurements of the great pyramid on a computer that they call Abulafia

(after the medieval cabalist). It is striking that the scientist Ilya Prigogine describes the old science with which his work is in opposition with images remarkably similar to those Robbe-Grillet has used. "L'idée est répandue que dans le Temple de la science, on ne recherche rien de moins que la 'formule' de l'univers. L'homme de science, déjà représenté comme un ascète, devient une espèce de magicien, détenteur potentiel d'une clef universelle . . . d'un savoir optimalement secret" [The idea has spread that in the Temple of Science, we seek nothing less than the 'formula' for the universe. The man of science, already represented as an ascetic, becomes a kind of magician, the potential holder of a universal key . . . of an optimally secret knowledge] (*La Nouvelle Alliance*, pp. 26, 27).

Although its notions are antithetical to those of quantum physics, a slightly modified Newtonian physics is still useful in the world of limited speeds, and the statistical nature of the laws of microphysics are not significant for the gross objects of physical experience, which appear regular and determined.[32] But the solutions of Newtonian physics do not go beyond its concepts and the questions they raise.

Bachelard sees classical physics as valid for phenomena where speed is limited and therefore as a particular case that can be reworked in a system centered elsewhere, but not integrated into a unity. Progress, he claims, is not deductive and linear but recursive; at every stage the previous stage must be rethought to make sure it did not contain a deceptive simplification. Similarly, Robbe-Grillet refuses simply to integrate into his work a "Balzacian" eternal nature and anthropocentrism antithetical to his own conceptions, either as antithesis or in a kind of synthesis. Nor does he deny its influence but rather reexamines the conventions that sustain it within a new system. For Bachelard, too, if there is a unity of the phenomenon, it is a construction and depends on the level at which the phenomenon is studied.

In *The Character of Physical Law* Feynman[33] suggests that any phenomenon is composed of a number of competing and unstable levels, from the movement of a number of protons, neutrons, and electrons, organized in a complex manner, to the notion "crystal of salt," from the property of surface tension to the wave, from nervous impulse to man, evil, and beauty. No one level is privileged or independent. The domain of science, for him, is the structure of the interconnections.

The fissures ("failles," "entailles," and "fentes") in Robbe-Grillet, which we have read as breaches in the surface of things revealing scientific sublayers and structures, at another level link up with the spasmodic movements and rippling oscillations and with a series of open triangles to suggest male sexual preoccupation. At another level the reference seems to be to the sexual overdetermination of all writing. What Ilya Prigogine affirms for the new scientist, Robbe-Grillet might claim for the new novelist: "Nous explorons désormais une nature aux évolutions multiples et divergentes, qui nous donne à penser non pas un temps aux dépens des autres, mais la coexistence de temps irréductiblement différents et articulés" [We are henceforth exploring a nature that unfolds in multiple and divergent ways, which gives us not one time to reflect on, at the expense of the others, but the coexistence of times that are irreducibly different and articulated].[34]

Robbe-Grillet has insisted that his work has several meanings and that these are destroyed by the meanings of the work's overall structure. This structure, which is not a neutralization of opposites, not a unity, and which is made up of the structural interconnections and relations between complex elements and their constituent levels, might be described analogically as "multiple complementarity."

Les Gommes and indeed all of Robbe-Grillet's novels allow a series of interpretations. The novels can be classed as labyrinthine detective story or as self-destructing detective story. They permit a Freudian interpretation (the sublimated oedipal monster lurking in the unconscious of the unsuspecting Wallas), or they can be read as a deconstruction of the Freudian myth. They may be interpreted either as Orphic quests or as antimythological works revealing the stereotyped and cultural nature of myth, as phenomenological texts focusing on the immediate objects of perception and consciousness or metaphysical stories concerned with predestination and free will, as sociological novels, or as psychological tales of love and loss. Robbe-Grillet's novels have also been pronounced by the critic Jean Ricardou a linguistic "adventure of a story" as opposed to a "story of an adventure." Such an interpretation gives meaning to metatextual commentaries within the text on its own events and characters. In *Les Gommes,* for example: "La mort de Daniel Dupont n'est plus qu'un événement abstrait dont discutent des mannequins" [The death of Daniel Dupont is now only an abstract event talked about by dummies] (p. 91.).

For Morrissette this adventure of the text involves an investigation through formal and thematic duplications (that is, above all, the technique common to postmodern generative fiction of mise en abyme) and no longer reinforces the referential meaning of the work by causing the characters to become aware of the message that the author wishes the reader to derive. Instead of strengthening the centrifugal forces leading from the work to the reader, from fiction to life, interior duplication, for Morrissette, "leads in a centripetal fashion back into the work, cutting the work off further from any lines or anchors that the reader may attempt to cast from the book to his real life or daily world. The work becomes self-contained, if not self-productive."[35]

Yet, more recently, Robbe-Grillet himself declared at the beginning of the autobiographical *Le Miroir qui revient,* "Je n'ai jamais parlé que de moi" [I have never spoken of anything but myself] (p. 10). Morrissette, in his study of the evolution of narrative viewpoint, from the relativistic multiple positions of *Les Gommes* to the suppressed or absent I, "Je-néant" of *La Jalousie,* attempts to find an explication for some of the paradoxes of point of view he observes. Arguing, along with Jean Alter, for a *Voyeur* "organised by two perspectives," Morrissette[36] sees these latter as the opposition between the author's outside voice, his "nominal," stylized (scientific?), decor and the inside mind of the protagonist, the psychological tensions and associations of Mathias's psychopathological obsessions. But other critics argue that this "opposition" is itself shown to be arbitrary in the light of the later work and its kaleidoscope of characters and nonjustified viewpoints successively adopted and abandoned by an imaginaire creating his own world.[37] The difference / sameness of author and character remains problematic. Perhaps, once again, complementarity rather than dialectical opposition might provide a better frame for understanding the functioning of the different / same viewpoints of character, narrator, and writer or the "self-production" of the work as opposed to its origins in personal (authorial) and collective obsession. More generally, these works can be seen both as a subversion (and thus a re-production) of the authenticity of the rationally ordered, chronological slice of life of traditional prose fiction, and as an attempt to bring to light new, contemporary, "realisms."

According to the early Robbe-Grillet, influenced by the structuralist theory of the sixties, the multiple meanings are destroyed by an overall structure. Much traditional literary criticism, of course, rejected Robbe-Grillet's work because of this claim for meaning deriving from structural interconnections. The new quarrel of the ancients and the moderns was a general one affecting both the French and the Anglo-Saxon worlds. In the hallowed halls of Cambridge University, a bitter literary quarrel resulted in the expulsion, by those who claim the propagation of eternal human values to be the true task of literature, of a heretical Joycean scholar supposedly wedded to sterile form. Stephen Heath's book on *The Nouveau Roman* (a title imposed by his publisher), designated as *A Study in the Practice of Writing* (his own subtitle), was received with very real suspicion by his colleagues at Cambridge.

One might, with these humanist scholars (who are themselves still painstakingly sifting Robbe-Grillet's text to extract their own gold—myth and symbol of different kinds that might give traditional meaning to the work and the world as it did for the early Morrissette), protest that human beings live above all in the world of the senses, passions, and social experience. Yet, for Robbe-Grillet the latter are, in their turn, part of the network of sociohistorical and psychological interconnections. They have no separate absolute character, except perhaps in the sense that the same emotion, fear, for example, can be produced in different people by administering the same drug. The interconnections in Robbe-Grillet's work are very different from those that link the separate intrigues and the destinies of individuals (who are also representative of types) in Balzac. There, the separate threads illustrate the same general psychological and social laws and ultimately create a continuous, coherent, stable, and unified world. In Robbe-Grillet the interconnections between multiple possibilities are those noted by Lupasco—of dynamic antagonism and attraction of virtualities and actualities, of a discontinuous, noncoherent, nonunified, nonstable work, which paradoxically incorporates the structural coherence both of its own modes of invention and of the language with which it constructs.

Even popular science is beginning to be colored by the recognition that the universe turns out (at both ends—the very small and the very large) to be more complex than we thought or can think. As a popular scientific writer develops this new vision: "Instead of emptiness inhabited by balls of glowing gas and pieces of ice-cold rock, we now conceive of objects undreamed of until recently: pulsars, quasars, neutron stars, black holes the size of an atomic nucleus and objects twenty million light years in length."[38]

From the nuclear where the random is law to everyday physics where the law is never random and surely does not play dice, from the subatomical to the astrophysical, there is a quantum leap. In this universe of limited (localized), relational, and changing knowledge, as we extend by instrument and ruse of mind the range of human senses (us) against a vast backdrop of unknowledge (not us), in the gap between Newtonian predictability and quantum leap, we seem to have little hope of recovering by language full knowledge of an independent observing self or a world out there. The possibility of unified theories seems to be receding despite religious revivals, Stephen Hawkings's search for a grand unified theory, Einstein's non–dice-playing God, and a general nostalgia or demand for order and clarity that Robbe-Grillet to some extent shares.

Ainsi je peux très bien, ému par la douce familiarité du monde, faire comme si tout y portait le visage de L'Homme et de la Raison (avec des majuscules). Et dans ce cas j'écrirai comme les Sagan, je filmerai comme les Truffaut. Pourquoi pas? Ou alors, choqué tout au contraire par la stupéfiante étrangeté du monde, j'expérimenterai jusqu'à l'angoisse cette absence, du fond de laquelle moi-même je parle, et je reconnaîtrai bientôt que les seuls détails qui constituent la réalité de l'univers où je vis ne sont rien d'autre que des trous dans la continuité de ses significaitions admises, tous les autres détails étant par définition idéologiques. J'ai la faculté, enfin, de me déplacer sans repos entre ces deux pôles.

[And so, moved by the comforting familiarity of the world, I can very well act as if everything bore the face of Man and Reason (with capital letters). And in that event, I'll write like the Sagans of the world and I'll film like the Truffauts. Why not? Or else, quite the opposite, shocked by the amazing strangeness of the world, I'll experiment to the point of anguish with this absence, from the depths of which I myself speak, and I'll soon recognize that the only details that constitute the reality of the universe in which I live are nothing but gaps in the continuity of its received meanings, all the other details being by definition ideological. Finally, I am able to move restlessly[39] between these two poles.] (*Le Miroir qui revient*, pp. 212–13)

The "strangeness" that Robbe-Grillet ascribes to the world is the strangeness of the world of the new science as much as it is the strangeness of the sirens of the imaginary and the return of the repressed that Jean-Claude Vareille traced in his psychoanalytical study of Robbe-Grillet's texts.[40] This surrealist "strangeness" of dream, present throughout the work, already dominates the earliest work *Un Régicide* (1949) published in 1978. While in *Les Gommes* the strangeness can possibly be read as the strangeness of the relation between the writing / the writer and the fiction—the pistol shot that killed Daniel Dupont was fired "from another world"—in a television broadcast of "Apostrophes"[41] Robbe-Grillet situated this strangeness in the world. He claimed to explore, in order to know better, that part of the world we do not know; to seek to know "the incomprehensible and monstrous thing that is the world."

The real begins where sense wavers, where dialectical structuring is undermined by the fascinating monsters of complementarity. This is the sense of science in the work of Robbe-Grillet.

Configurations of *Modernité*

The three parts of this chapter pursue the examination of the complex deconstructing and restructuring movements and the modelings of *modernité* in Robbe-Grillet's texts. I use the term *modernité* in the sense that Alain Robbe-Grillet has used it to situate his texts beyond the critical territories marked out by the predominantly Anglo-American signposts of postmodernism and poststructuralism. *Modernité*, like the "postmodern condition," is for me what derives from and comes after modernism and structuralism. These modelings of modernity have striking parallels with major shifts and explorations in other fields of contemporary thought. In the preceding chapter I explored parallels with contemporary physics and proposed the notion of complementarity, in the Heisenberg sense, as metaphor of the new forms that subtend the movements in Robbe-Grillet's work. In this chapter I first look at other sites of twentieth-century scientific inquiry from structuralism to deconstruction, and at models from the new sciences filtering into the general cultural climate that may have indirectly influenced Robbe-Grillet. I subsequently focus on the theoretically fertile emerging science of complex systems that has been designated chaos theory. The question raised is whether these new models drawn from contemporary scientific fields point beyond the double bind of the subject and the object that has locked the postmodern text into narcissistic self-reflexivity and indicated the author's death. Do the new models indicate ways out of the circularity of language and the real? What is the nature (and the gender) of the self that returns in these configurations of *modernité*?

From Structuralism to Poststructuralism

Despite a Kafkaesque strangeness, the early writings and films of Robbe-Grillet projected a strong sense of a search for an objective order in an uncertain and duplicitous world. Such an order was staged in the meticulous description of objects, their geometries, and their physical appearances, the measurement of their similarities and differences one with another in *Les Gommes, Le Voyeur, La Jalousie,* or in the slow insistent movement of the camera over the surfaces of things in the films *L'Immortelle* and *L'Année dernière à Marienbad.* Roland Barthes's reading of *Le Voyeur* as "literal" and "objective"—at least in the sense of being "turned toward the object"—presented these unusual texts as a textual photo-realism that eliminated the subjective. Expressed in a long, parodic pamphlet entitled *La Cafetière est sur la table,*[1] Boisdeffre's derision of Robbe-Grillet's writing was an extreme but historically interesting example of the negative response by the French critical establishment alerted to a threat to their traditional humanist values and hegemony.

As critical paradigms shifted in the sixties, it became accepted and acceptable that Robbe-Grillet's texts were "a practice of writing" rather than of representation. This practice turned on a subversive mise en scène of the old narrative order (linear, logical, causal, closed, and mimetic) and, less directly, on a questioning of the strong realism of traditional science.

Dans le labyrinthe is the story of a writer creating a text using the objects in his room and a painting entitled *La Défaite de Reichenfels* as generators. *Trans-Europ-Express* the story of Robbe-Grillet, filmmaker, and Catherine Robbe-Grillet, script-girl, making a film about diamond or drug smuggling in Amsterdam on the Trans-Europ-Express. Like *La Maison de rendez-vous, Projet pour une révolution à New York,* and the film *L'Homme qui ment* that followed, *Trans-Europ-Express* could be seen to be a new version of Gide's *Les Faux-Monnayeurs,* duplicating and reflecting on the text's production within the text. Yet, these self-conscious new novels and films stage a radical critique of the traditions of novel and film and come to embody new ways of thinking about meaning.

Influenced by the work of Jakobson, de Saussure, Propp, and Lévi-Strauss as the writings of the latter emerged into the general climate of ideas, Robbe-Grillet's texts incorporate the metatextual examination of the dialectical orders that structuralism was making culturally visible. The binary oppositions that were seen to play an important role in the human symbolic systems of language, literary texts, and myth are every-where in evidence in the writer's work. These oppositions designate not only a mechanism of textual functioning but also a ready-made mech-anism of the human mind, which, it has been argued, shapes the world and the self that the mind attempts to describe. The search for new orders through the "practice of writing" is inevitably inseparable from the sub-versive staging of the existing (narrative) orders. The forms of the work can be considered in terms of the Saussurian hypothesis of the split between *langue* (the underlying and unreduced structures of language) and *parole* (the individual use or surface transformations of these deep structures) and of de Saussure's analogous intuition of linguistic binary oppositions in the pair—signifier and signified—that constitute the sign. Robbe-Grillet himself has, if somewhat idiosyncratically, repeatedly used the notion of *parole* in his public lectures to describe his texts, seen as a personal rewriting or subversion of the collective *langue*.

Propp's distinction between character and the (thirty-one) functions that characters perform in his analysis of the plot of the Russian folktale[2] and his elaboration of these functions as finite and identifiable provide a further structural model for approaching the abstract structures that underlie the surface conventions of traditional narrative. Robbe-Grillet's characters no longer have the permanent coherence or continuity of a personality but shed accumulated masks that are often contradictory. Wallas the detective is also the assassin; Jean the King and Boris the Regicide exchange roles; and the male protagonist in *Djinn* (Jan, Jean, Boris, Simon Lecoeur) disappears, while a female of similar description (Jean/Androgyne) is found in his place. Dr. Morgan, healer and sadist, and Marie-Ange/Violette incorporate opposite signs. Names and pro-fessions proliferate, recur, are traversed by other signs, split to decom-pose any fixed identity, and recombine. The sexual sadist concealed in *Projet pour une révolution à New York* is linked to the voyeur himself, to the terrorist, to the omnipresent Dr. Morgan, to the proliferating internal narrator, and finally to the writer. At the same time, critics have been able to construct a character type (or stereotype) from such mobile fragments. A jealous monomaniac can be put together from the discontinuous points of view in *La Jalousie;* a psychopathic or schizo-phrenic sadist can be detected in *Le Voyeur;* and an oedipal parricide reemerges in *Les Gommes*. Stereotypes of women evident in the recent novels—the femme fatale (siren, witch, precocious adolescent) and her opposite, the pure maiden (Blanche, Marie-Ange, Angelica)—have a very old cultural coherence and evoke a complex of related and apparently timeless cultural elements. These heros and villains, witches and maidens in distress, under their many and often interchangeable names and disguises, fulfill roles not dissimilar to Propp's central functions.

Robbe-Grillet's complex plots and multiple skeins of interwoven textual and metatextual event in *La Maison de rendez-vous, Djinn,* and *Projet pour une révolution* and in the films *L'Eden et après, Glissements progressifs du plaisir,* and *Le Jeu avec le feu* move increasingly away from simple diegesis. They may be seen as metatextual staging of the Shloveskeyan hypothesis of difference between the complex, defamiliarizing plot and the simple, linear, chronological story. The deconstruction of the meanings of story with beginning, middle, and end, moving to a resolution and thereby constructing causality and destiny, and of characters simulating presence and unified self, does not completely eliminate time, logic, identity, or story. It does denaturalize these conventions by revealing the hidden Cartesian (rational and metaphysical) system of Western tradition that informs them. The modes of organization of the Robbe-Grillet plot, on the other hand—plot generated from the stock of Western cultural objects and their metaphorical associations and combinations—resemble the new formal linguistic models that were the basis of structuralism. The postulation by linguistics of paradigmatic (simultaneous, similar, metaphorical) and syntagmatic (sequential, different, metonymic) organization along the vertical (associative) and horizontal (combinatory) axes of narrative as the mechanisms that create meaning in their transformations from one mode to the other and back again provides a useful model for an understanding of the combinatory operations of the Robbe-Grillet text.

Lévi-Strauss's central insight that behind the syntagmatic chain of myth sequences that are all partial metaphoric transformations of every other or of a central paradigm there is an underlying abstract pattern (a dialectical organization and a mediation)—which is in fact the meaning of the myth[3]—provides another productive interpretive structuralist model for Robbe-Grillet's work. The recursive surface sequences of the paradigm of the beautiful captive and her transformations (virgin martyr, punished precocious adolescent, sacrificial victim—itself perhaps a variant of incestuous desire) indicate the existence of such an abstract generative pattern. This mythological pattern could also be described psychologically, as a struggle between sexual pleasure and danger or between an ego and an alter or the masculine and the feminine. It is the conflicting desire for, and fear of, such another / (m)other; the drive to power over the other and the desire for self-loss. Or, as Robbe-Grillet puts it ironically in a parody of Marx, it is the "battle of the sexes" that is "the driving force of history" ("La lutte des sexes est le moteur de l'histoire" [Djinn, p. 19]).

The binary oppositions that structure the symbolic systems of language, literary text, and myth are put to play in the Robbe-Grillet text. Black, for example, acquires its meaning in relation to its opposite white, continuity in a formal dance with discontinuity, affirmation with negation, and S with Z in a constant and generative interaction.

In Angélique ou l'enchantement the white knight evokes a black knight; the hero calls up the traitor; the innocent virgin coexists with the dangerous enchantress. Against a background of moving multiplicity, or a recursive central story of the sacrificial female victim in the secret room, a story fragmented and proliferating into complex "polyfictions" for which no clear origin exists, there is a dialectic of old orders and new. At the same time, these binary organizations suggest the redundancy, the lack of information conveyed by the expected. They indicate enclosure; the end is already implicit in the beginning.

Such dialectical mechanisms are self-consciously staged as central to the unmaking of traditional "natural" or "mimetic" meanings and the remaking that will (Robbe-Grillet has not ceased to claim since Pour un nouveau roman) reveal new forms and new meanings in his work. In Le Voyeur, for example, all the clues to the narrator's crime are subsequently erased or disappear in negations. The sea washes traces from the shore; the criminal recovers the candy wrappers and cigarette butts and throws the telltale jacket suspended on the cliffside into the sea; the armless model disappears from the shop window; the cinema poster of the brutal male giant holding a frail young girl by the throat disappears; Mathias leaves the island, and at the end of the novel, as in the initial description, it is as if "no one had heard." The writing appears to return to innocence and equilibrium, but the reader may have caught the writer at his game of making and unmaking, creating and effacing the crime.

In *Dans le labyrinthe* a rhythmic dialectical movement is present in the textual movement of the description, in the slippage between dark and light, the alternating left and right footsteps of the soldier in the snow, and the oscillations of a light swinging to and fro at the end of its cord. As in *Le Voyeur,* this movement is repeated at the more abstract level of the constructing and then striking out or negating of elements and sequences of text. *Dans le labyrinthe* is also the making and unmaking of myths of quest, war, loss, and death, and the text itself is a quest for the (binary) deep structure underlying these myths. The protagonist-soldier, awaiting the arrival of the enemy occupiers, wanders through the labyrinth of self-resembling crossroads in a deserted town, where he seeks to deliver a mysterious/banal shoe-box. He encounters the apparently archetypal figures of a woman and a child. But neither his itineraries, his "mission," his encounters, or his death turn out to have any clearer meanings than the web of spirals and bifurcations figured by the driven and constantly re-forming snow that is the backdrop of his wanderings. The geometry of the labyrinth becomes emblematic of the monsters it "conceals" as the scientific descriptions and the repetitions come finally to serve as metaphors of limitation, imprisonment in analogies, and obsession.

At another level, this novel is the metatextual writing quest of an "I" in an enclosed room, in search of the hidden functioning of the relation of sameness and difference between the objects inside and outside the room (the lamp/the lamppost) and the meanings of the text's own movements and figures. John Sturrock,[4] among a number of other critics, notes the mechanism that operates every time the description touches the heavy red curtains that allow the writer passage from the bedroom to the world outside. Sturrock interprets the curtains as representing the writer's own closed eyelids. In fact, the movement is not clearly that of passage from an inside to an outside reality. As a passage from description to imagination, it may also move from outside to inside. There is a circularity and undecidability in this apparently simple movement from inner to outer and back again, which figures what I call the double bind, discussed later in this chapter. Even in the recent novels, whose use of outside photographic and pictorial generators Morrissette so carefully catalogued in his *Intertextual Assemblage from "Topology" to "The Golden Triangle"* (1979), the binary and yet circular structure of the inner and the outer worlds (quotation and self-quotation, the word and the world) remains ludically and insistently present.

In all the models of symbolic systems mentioned (language, literary text, and myth), as in Robbe-Grillet's texts in general, meaning derives, not, as our common knowledge or common sense suggests, in the relation between a sign or a sequence and an external experiential object (or subject) represented by the sign, but in the internal differential relationships between all the elements and levels of a multilayered, complex system of signs. Awareness of the importance of this network has brought about the most radical of shifts in twentieth-century literary paradigms. Binary relations are subsumed in Robbe-Grillet's work by overlapping ellipses and multiple spirals, forms that appear *en abyme* (internally duplicated) or take the form of physical objects, such as the sinusoidal smoke rings from the incense burner, or the folds in the assassin's cape and the rivulets of blood pooling beneath the victim's breast in "La Chambre secrète," or the spiral staircase in the tower of *Topologie*.

The repetitions and transformations one into another of the binary pairs of Jakobson's "metaphor" (association) and "metonymy" (combination) are subsumed by such metaphors of web or dynamic field. Meanings derive from differential relationships between sets of phonemes or letters (*A* or *V* or *S*, which come to be connoted feminine, as opposed to "masculine" *W* or *M* or *Z*), or occasionally from morphemes. More commonly, in Robbe-Grillet's work meanings derive from basic semantic elements. These are the semantic units, objects, and stories that constitute the cultural "junk" of Western civilization: the accessories found in the attic in *Djinn*, the stage props in the courtyard in *La Maison de rendez-vous*, the artifacts (diary or photographs) in the tin trunk of *Le Miroir qui revient* that recall the Robbe-Grillet past, or Breton legend, fairy tale, and operatic story in *Angélique ou l'enchantement*.

At the metatextual level these representations include the theoretical "constructions" of the various structuralist models themselves. More exactly, the hidden binary relationships and the web of interrelationships that operate within language and that the structuralist theorists have brought within the scope of clear consciousness become, in their turn, the generative material of the text.

What we follow, then, is a "scientific" mind at work, an attempt through careful observation to see the unseen relationships between the orders in the self, in the text, and perhaps in the world, through their interaction. By putting sets of formal orders into play within his creative text, by examining the interplay of the dance of the particles in the cosmic web the writer probes the hidden aspects of their workings.

Robbe-Grillet is a trained agricultural engineer, statistician, and scientific researcher. He astonishes by his passion for and personal knowledge of botanical genera, his careful observation of the detail and the abstract forms of the objects and the theories that surround him.[5] Influenced by the early critical responses to his work and, in particular, by Barthes's articles, to confirm the proclaimed "scientific" aspect of his writings, the writer himself subscribed in his own influential pro- grammatic theoretical writings of the late fifties and early sixties (later collected in *Pour un nouveau roman*) to the conviction that the signif- icance of his work lay in the uncovering in the text of new abstract orders. Some of his claims were later abandoned—the claim that he was cleansing anthropocentric language through the use of the scientific adjective that would measure and situate, for example. His quarrel with metaphor, too, was rapidly forgotten—*La Jalousie,* after all, was based on metaphors of the emotion of jealousy and all language was meta- phoric. Yet, even in his recent autobiographical phase in which the "I" of personal experience is foregrounded, the writer continues to assert that it is the overall form of the work, rather than the material or themes that it manipulates, that creates the meanings of his texts.

This is not, of course, to fall into the trap of the theory of the "text alone," which Jean Ricardou and his ephemeral "nouveau nouveau roman" movement impressed on the thinking on nouveau roman poetics from the sixties on. (Ricardou's movement was most influential in the sixties; buttressed by the work of the *Tel Quel* theoreticians, it wielded some influence until around 1972.) We are not caught with a "geometer," as one early critic would have it, or with a "land surveyor" in an arid web of mathematical calculations as others have claimed. Robbe-Grillet has been set in black and white for the general public, erroneously, as a cleanser of the objects of the world. (A painting by Mark Tansey in the

New York Museum of Modern Art entitled "Alain Robbe-Grillet Cleansing Every Object in Sight," which the writer himself comments on with
humor, represents Robbe-Grillet on his hands and knees attempting to
dust off tiny miniatures of objects including fragments of the Sphinx and
souvenirs of Napoleon.) Nor, however, are we confronted with an impersonal textual deconstruction or a "textual inhuman factory." The textual
machines at work may be producing complex new configurations rather
than traditional "meanings," but these configurations are not gratuitous
and not wholly unmotivated. At times baroque and complex, they may
well be, as Robbe-Grillet himself claims, "necessary."

I suggest that these necessary configurations of *modernité* are themselves individuated metaphoric transformations of collective and changing relations between ourselves and the world in the second half of the
twentieth century. Robbe-Grillet's early professed interest in the hidden
workings of the quotidian text and the mise en scène of the "realities"
this traditional text conceals or generates is doubled by an intellectually
curious investigation of, or indirect relationship with, new texts and
other realities emerging at a number of sites in the culture. Despite the
perils of the term and the baggage of the humanist tradition it still
carries with it, despite the polemical current critical status of the mimetic,
it is possible to argue that, in its transpositions of configurations of
modernité, Robbe-Grillet's work is a new textual "realism"—a "realism"
of its time, a realism that is no longer single or absolute. Within this
new "realism," through games with webs of interrelated characters and
narrative points of view, both the text and the "I" reflect self-consciously
(metalinguistically) on the processes and conditions of their own existence and their relations with other texts and with the world.

The dialectically organized structures of language perhaps linked
to those of the mind, the world we know only through our language
and the instruments that are also an extension of the human mind, and
the mutual implication of the observer and the observed, like the linguistic construction of the real and of meaning, create circularity and
self-reflexivity, traps for the observing, deconstructing walker through
the field. Like Calvino's Marco Polo in *Invisible Cities,* Robbe-Grillet's
traveler moves predominantly through the cities of the mind, in search
of the capture of that naked woman of the imagination, glimpsed fleet-
ingly disappearing around a street corner, in the desire of a dream. And

in the final instance, the construction of a city of desire (Robbe-Grillet's
Secret Room) to prevent the long-haired fugitive from escaping, is per-
haps, "a trap," a web of his own imaginings, in which the writer, like
Marco Polo, is himself caught.[6]

The deconstructing or revolutionary projects in and of the texts,
are vertiginously repetitive (with slight difference) and circular, returning
to (or almost) their point of departure. As the writer's multiple alter
egos attempt to know the world from simultaneous or opposite points
of view, they are led not to a new coherence or totality but to slippage,
recursivity, and incomprehension. The world, like the self, as Robbe-
Grillet declares in *Le Miroir qui revient,* appears largely unknowable,
strange, and essentially outside the limitations of human interrogation,
although this strangeness no longer gives it any metaphysical value or
significance as "absurdity" or "alienation."

The image of the world that takes form in this work is one of a
cosmic web, a cosmic dance or field of exchange between interconnected
knots of force, but constituted rather by the gaps or holes of the
unknown, the discontinuities of the vast spaces that stretch between the
occasional knots as much as by the rare, multithreaded strands of knowledge woven and unwoven uncertainly from knot to knot.

To recapitulate briefly, then, in what Morrissette tentatively called
the second period of Robbe-Grillet's writing, that is, after the phenomenological phase and from the transitional work *Dans le labyrinthe* on,
meanings are self-consciously produced by the differential relations
between the generative elements, much as meaning production was
modeled generally by Jakobson or by Chomsky and Halle in linguistics.
The generators are both the "ready-mades" of Western civilization—
myth, canonical literary representations, advertising, our *lieux communs*
(places common to all), and their references or connotations—and the
forms that the webs of such generators create. These are the multiple
and often contradictory "different" tellings and negations of the "same"
story, the interior duplications (mise en abyme), the repeated embeddings
and repetitions from Robbe-Grillet text to Robbe-Grillet text (intratextual) and from other literary and cultural texts (intertextual).

It was critically argued by Ricardou that self and sense could exist
only within a free, generative, unmotivated play of the "adventure of the
text," its sounds (phonemes), and to a limited extent, its sense. Derrida's

powerful and skeptical analysis of texts postulated that no system of substitution for the object is ever adequate. Imprisoned in signs not independent of mind and language, the object in itself, for Derrida, is always absent, endlessly deferred. Nor can these signs of signs still give a full account of nature for the new theorist of science. For Kuhn, in *The Structure of Scientific Revolutions*, this is because all observation is theory-laden. The observer is part of the observation; the manner of imaging part of the image. In quantum mechanics, as the first chapter of this study pointed out, the measure itself appears to decide the exact state of what is measured. This is not to deny the existence of an outside (history, world) but simply to problematize its knowability.

The most recent phase of Robbe-Grillet's writing, the "autobiographical" fictions or "autofictions" *Le Miroir qui revient* (1984) and *Angélique ou l'enchantement* (1988) that Robbe-Grillet has presented as a new genre by labeling them "romanesques," returns to an exploration of phenomenal or biological orders with which narrative and language might intersect. The "I" returns although the text moves between a first person subject "I" and a third person "he"/Count Corinthe, between the "I" and the "we," the individual and the collective. In a system of complementarity where the first-person subject cannot be disentangled from the third-person object of the gaze, where the individual self is always already there in a system of linguistic signs that is shared by the collectivity, any inner self can only leave traces on the turbulent margins or in the interstices between these zones.

As Robbe-Grillet's work has moved through several modes of experimentation shaped by the antirealist, phenomenological, structuralist, and deconstructionist models and movements of the time, influenced by and influencing the new theory and practice in linguistics, anthropology, science, and literary theory, certain questions appear to have remained constant. These are, predominantly, the question already examined of complementary relations and that of the double bind of object and subject, of language and self. The latter takes us from science to sexuality.

From Science to Sexuality: Beyond the Double Bind?

The examination (fixing) of the phenomenal world through precise objective language, the investigation of the generation of meanings by the text, and the probing of the relation between life and text (or between the individual and the collective) that mark the three phases I label "scientific," "structural," and "autofictional" in Robbe-Grillet's work, do not escape "vertigo." Nor do the orderings effected by the recursivity and symmetry that play a central patterning role in all of these apparently different periods of Robbe-Grillet's work. Interpreted by Genette in his preface to the 10/18 edition of *Dans le labyrinthe* as an objectified (but not objective) "fixing" of subjective "vertigo," the "vertige fixé" that characterizes these textual constructions constitutes a "complementary" pair. In this sense, the characters appear as doubles of the writer seen in a lateral mirror. The writer is the critical observer of the conscious experimental staging and fixing of the less conscious manifestations of a hidden obsessional self. Such doubles reveal the writer's dual nature as readymade "fixed" collective representations and as "vertiginous" mobile passion. The expression "vertige fixé" thus comes to include a set of logically contradictory connotations (of control and of obsession, of objectivity and of subjectivity) in its description of Robbe-Grillet's texts.

Situated in the metaphor of the generative/prison cell, cross-ruled like writing paper in *Topologie d'une cité fantôme,* the writer/investigator is also the uncertain, weary, criminal narrator of the impossibility of cleansing the objects of the world of monstrous subjectivities and limited or obsessional point of view, or of cleansing human language of metaphor and symbolic operation. The perceptual mechanisms, mind, and obsessions of the observer and their influence on the object of observation take center stage as self-reflexivity. Within such a frame there seems little way to decide whether our results are a product of the systems observed or of the observer's intervention.

As Newtonian quantifications and Cartesian rationality (cogito ergo sum) are themselves seen to be the results of an observer's apparatus, the discourse of this scientist loses not only its absolute objective reality but also its innocence and neutrality. The writer/scientist is the detective/assassin following his/my own traces ("l'assassin sur mes propres traces" of a subtitle in *Topologie d'une cité fantôme*), circling to discover, on the double circuit and in minimal difference, his monstrous otherself. In *Un Régicide* Boris, the revolutionary, attempts to assassinate the mad king but somehow is diverted by his own phantasies of erotic domination. The king seems, in fact, to be his other self. Wallas kills Dupont, his father, in an oedipal drama in *Les Gommes*. In *Le Voyeur* Mathias turns out to be a sadistic killer, and the eye/absent I of *La Jalousie* is a murderously jealous voyeur. In *La Maison de rendez-vous* Johnson (inspired by Jasper Johns?) kills Manneret (Man Ray and Manet?), and then he himself is surrounded by British policemen with machine guns in a final scene. Walter Naime is both seducer and bemused victim of Marie-Ange's vampire bite in the film *La Belle Captive*, and the female defense lawyer (Maître David) becomes the victim Nora in the film *Glissements progressifs du plaisir*. The innocent reader, too, is obliged to assume the position of guilty voyeur.

In Robbe-Grillet's work the writer's cell is the secret room of female sacrifice ("La Chambre secrète" of the short story of that title in *Instantanés*), the medieval dungeons of the convent in *Glissements progressifs du plaisir* where young girls are whipped and tortured in sado-mystical rituals, or the prison of classical Pompeii where beautiful young captives or recalcitrant female adolescents are kept sequestered in *Topologie*. The cell is a condensing of the many obsessional secret torture chambers of the writer's sexual phantasies and of previous texts, both a literal and figurative "camera obscura," as Ronald Bogue suggests.[7] In this "dark" or "secret" room, the writer is at once the voyeur-photographer and the object of the photograph, captured by his own voyeuristic machinery. He is both active look and static looked at, he who frames and (s)he who is fixed in frames.

By tiny slippages of the text, or in a play of mirrors where symmetries are imperceptibly inexact, the figure of the writer as scientist and investigator, rigorous orderer of the clues to the crime, first comes to resemble and then becomes the uncertain criminal. He is paradoxically caught in the net of the very language (scientific, investigative, linear in its progression through the organization of subject, verb, and object) through which he seeks escape. Solitary in his "cell," he strains to hear imperceptible absent sounds across the "endless thicknesses of white ice" ("des épaisseurs sans fin de glace blanche," *Topologie*, p. 10) and through vast cotton wool spaces of silence, the strange other, and the unknowable world. What this "guilty" narrator conceals/reveals is not an outside voice, not an absolute truth, but the multiple and circular "truths" of self-reference like the enigmatic statue of *L'Année dernière à Marienbad* (1961), which may as well designate "you and I" as the king and queen or "something other." He is captured in his own textual construction of self. Or, as in Borges's story, "The Circular Ruins,"[8] the writer is perhaps invented, or mirrored by someone other, written himself.

The early texts focused on the "imperceptible," that is, on the strange marginal zones of human sensory limits that binary language describes morphologically as "not visible" or "not audible" (invisible/inaudible) and semantically as indeed (just or barely) perceptible. Such thresholds are analogous to the turbulent, indeterminant, and elusive orders of zones of transition of matter from one phase to another (a solid to a liquid, for example) that chaos theory investigates. They reveal both the limits and the uncertainties of human perceptual mechanisms and the approximations that referential language must use to model these margins. The carefully systematic and precise visual or auditory descriptions that attempted unsuccessfully to be exhaustive or to eliminate the particular subjective situations of the observer (or the discourse) posed the question, central to the current investigations of cognitive psychology, of how things are perceived. What is the relation between the sense experience and the intelligible? For, as Ronald Schleifer argues in a study of the difficulties of a scientific semantic model,[9] what we can "perceive" always has a meaning, always signifies. As a fact of culture, a perception must refer to something else in a relational and cognitive system of information. Robbe-Grillet's passionate charging of the phenomena observed suggests that even if these objects are not just in cognitive mental structures acting on the environment but also in the environment, in a real, out there, their perceived significance is nonetheless an aspect of their existence. Direct and natural perception of invariants in the world, of boundaries that are a function of the world rather than the perceiving process and the material base of perception itself, is problematic. Cognition is inferential and not direct, apparently related to the way in which linguistic structures order experience rather than directly linked with the outside world.

In a similar vein, in literary theory, Stanley Fish[10] argues that we cannot separate our judgments from the contexts in which they are made. Unbiased, objective interpretations are impossible in a world that is essentially rhetorical. Derrida can thus claim, as Schleifer points out, that there is no such thing as perception, which is a concept of an intuition, or of a given originating from the thing itself. Present to itself in its meaning independent of language or the system of reference, synonymous with the origin (the perceiving subject), such a "perception" is, for Derrida, exemplary of the very metaphysics of presence that his critical thought deconstructs.[11] And yet, as Schleifer suggests, structural analyses of discourse

> fail to fully account for the fact that the material which functions arbitrarily in the articulation of meaning is not altogether arbitrary, that it is based—like walking or eating bread—on the material base of the body. . . . In the understanding of the arbitrary signs of the language—the sign level as a whole—the nature of the material by means of which signification is articulated should be taken into account. . . . Just as the mouth, lips, throat, etc. place boundaries on the phonemes which enter into the systems of oppositions for Saussure, so too, the perceptual apparatus places boundaries on the viable contrasts at post-phonemic levels.[12]

Although Schleifer hedges his conclusion ("The problem in this deceptively simple extension of Saussure is that perception itself may involve the very relations we wish to understand")[13] the question of the material or biological base remains a central one for Robbe-Grillet as he puts the most common of human stories, stereotypes, and myths into play and yet makes his own selection among them. The writer examines his prison in minute detail but also works to generate an exit from this cell of reflexivity where he is as much a victim of desire (to embrace/ suppress sexual difference) as of metaphor. Although his status as generator or generated, as origin or simulacrum (Baudrillard's copy of a copy), is undecidable, he continues to write.

Robbe-Grillet's later works pursue his early investigation of the general mechanisms of the mind, which may, in their dichotomous pattern making, select out poles and patterns where in fact none exists. But the mind is seen at work in these later texts not only in dialectical movement but in a linguistic weaving, "differently," of the "same" generative elements (objects, phrases, fragments of old story, names, or points of view and their transformations, paradigmatically and syntagmatically by analogy and juxtaposition) into multiple, moving, surface stories, themselves both familiar and strangely different. The surprises of this difference create noise, which, disrupting the expected, is rich with information. Although new possibilities are suggested for the free-playing metafiction by this theory of information, we are, however, still within the circle. Are we in the domain of the mind or of the text? Is there an escape from the double bind of the real and the represented?

As the recent "new autobiographies" explore the zones between life and text in textualized "memories" of early personal and affective experience, the focus on the sameness and difference which creates meaning has shifted to a focus on the difference that might create an individuated self. These memories include the evocation of what Robbe-Grillet "confesses" in *Le Miroir qui revient* as his sexual "difference" (sadistic phantasies from early childhood and attraction to very young girls). But along with these apparent confessions, there is a very suspect reanimation of formative representations encountered in childhood—a newspaper photograph, for example, of a female Republican captive "spy" in the Spanish Civil War, whose fate at the hands of her "male" captors Robbe-Grillet's parents dwell upon with unconsciously sadistic satisfaction, and an illustration of the ritually sadistic punishment of a young virgin penetrated by a ploughshare in a pseudohistorical work on capital punishment in Turkey in the seventeenth century. Such memories are ironically perverse in all senses of the word. The ploughshare is also part of a series of archaic agricultural implements that recur in many of Robbe-Grillet's texts, popping up, like the voyeur's bicycle, in the most unexpected places as a kind of signature or mark of punctuation. (A prominent juxtaposition of ploughshare and woman occurs, for example, in the "sculptures" of the film *L'Eden et après*.)

Despite the "perversity" of Robbe-Grillet's "memories," it can be argued that in the initial period of his *nouveau roman* the fictive element was produced predominantly by the exploration of the "objective" world as mediated through the relation of subject and object in perception. In a second period it was rather the exploration of the linguistic structures that constitute the text that generated the fiction. In the "autobiographical" texts of the recent period, the story derives more particularly from lived history or from memory in the present of that history. Escape from the double bind of real and represented, the "strange loop" of subject and object, the self as the text of the other, present and past (we cannot recover the past in the present because we know the outcome of the story), is not guaranteed by the body that dominates this last phase in any simple way, yet the significance of individuated bodily experience and choices is no longer excluded. In *La Chambre claire* the later Barthes also slips toward a similar affirmation of a "real" or "self" that, if still under suspicion, is, at the least, passage of light and genetic code, of a "truth" (of the Wintergarden photograph of his mother) that can only be attested by the individual heart.

The sensory and the cerebral modes of perception are influenced by human psychosexual development, collective and to some extent individuated, and so, of course, is narrative itself. As Teresa de Lauretis points out in a study on desire in narrative,[14] Barthes's preface to the 1966 issue of *Communications,* cornerstone for the structural analysis of narrative, ends with the statement: "It may be significant that it is at the same moment (around the age of three) that the little human 'invents' at once sentence, narrative, and the Oedipus."[15] De Lauretis goes on to quote Barthes's later erotic and epistemological discourse on the pleasure of the text, which develops, she claims, from this primary connection between language, narrative, and masculine desire, or the inherent maleness of all narrative movement. "The pleasure of the text is . . . an Oedipal pleasure (to denude, to know, to learn the origin and the end), if it is true that every narrative (every unveiling of the truth) is a staging of the (absent, hidden, or hypostatized) father—which would explain the solidarity of narrative forms, of family structures, and of prohibitions of nudity."[16] The oedipal text, the text as body (of the mother), and analogies between narrative and sexual intercourse with pen as phallus operating on the body of the text have become fashionable in literary theory since Barthes's earlier work, displacing to a large extent the more common nineteenth-century metaphor of the creation of the text as procreation and paternity. Robert Scholes sees the "archetype of all fiction" as "the sexual act" in its "fundamental orgastic rhythm of tumescence, and detumescence, of tension and resolution."[17] But the question that continues to arise is whether this textual body is "masculine" or "feminine," or whether "masculine" and "feminine" might also turn out to constitute a "complementary" structure. (I ask the reader to place the "feminine" and the "masculine" in implicit inverted commas throughout the remainder of this book as referring not to biological sex but to notions or myths or social constructions of various kinds of gender difference.) However, as de Lauretis also points out, femininity and masculinity in Freud's story are "positions occupied by the subject in relation to desire, corresponding respectively to the passive and the active aims of the libido."[18]

The psyche, too, as the psychoanalysts Gear and Hill argue in a study of narcissism,[19] has a bipolar structure. The ego, like the linguistic "I," or subject speaker, which needs a relationship with an alter or a "you" to give it an identity for the linguist Benveniste,[20] requires the movement of a subject (*"actant"*) toward an object (*"actant"*) as in the semantic structures that Greimas postulates. In the texts of Robbe-Grillet, these poles are strongly and traditionally marked (as they are also culturally), on the one hand by "masculine" control and will to power and domination, as pleasure, and on the other by "feminine" powerlessness, will to self-loss and flow, submission to the pleasure of the other.

The sense of Robbe-Grillet's stereotypical, intertextual, often disturbing and excessively "realistic" sadomasochistic thematics and his very conscious traditional dialectical organization of a semiotics of sex around provocative "feminine" frailty, seductive curve, and reactive "masculine" brutality can be situated, particularly in the later period, in confession of personal phantasies close to a lived experience. *Le Miroir qui revient* and *Angélique ou l'enchantement* in a somewhat devious way do "confess" his sexual "difference" (interest in very young girls), and through phantasy and pseudoautobiographical anecdote, as well as in a general reflection on the presence of violent phantasy in Western culture, touch on his own sadomasochistic sexual universe. In an interview with me in 1986 Robbe-Grillet spoke very openly about the personal sexual orientation behind his selections of sado-erotic phantasies. His work can be seen to be an attempt to "know" these impulses better and to "re-write" them in a very conscious way.

When the writer is discussing an incident of real violence in the real world of Czechoslovakia under totalitarian Communist control, however, the whole event appears to be enveloped in cotton wool. While making the co-production *L'Eden et après*, Robbe-Grillet himself was the victim of police suspicion of difference; he was punched in the face, and his teeth were knocked out by a patrolling soldier late one evening on returning to his hotel with the leading actress, Catherine Jourdan. The incident, described in *Le Miroir qui revient,* becomes strangely dreamlike, arbitrary, incomprehensible, and unreal.

More productively than in "confession," or in social criticism, the sense of the hyperreal sadomasochism in Robbe-Grillet's texts can be found in the self-conscious exploration of the content of culturally ready-made (textual) symbols, in particular, the mutually attractive poles of monster and victim, of self-assertion and self-loss marked by opposite gender sign.

The "absent" crimes of sexual violence, oedipal passions (*Les Gommes*), rape and murder of the young Angelica/Violette (*Le Voyeur*), jealousy (*La Jalousie*), which are only covertly present in the selection and organization of the objects of the early novels, become overt and proliferate insistently in the collage of intertextual borrowings and intra-textual fragments that constitute the diegesis or intrigue that frame the later works. The classical myth of the virgin sacrificed to the sea monster in the rites of Spring (allusion to Stravinsky?) in *Le Voyeur* reappears in *Topologie* as the representation of the graceful captive Angélique chained to the rock and rescued from the devouring sea monster by the hero (who is of course himself both the prince and the beast) in a painting by Ingres. The painting is identified as the *Roger délivrant Angélique* that hangs in the Louvre. This romantic and apparently "innocent" representation, itself inspired by Ariosto's *Orlando Furioso*, in turn influenced by the classical myth of Perseus freeing Andromeda, has parallels in Renaissance painting (in Rubens among many others), and in the mythological nineteenth-century British canvases of Richard Leighton, whose representations of women currently stand accused of a certain "misogyny."[21] Another representation of the Andromeda complex is "Roger and Angélique," a 1910 work of Odilon Redon (Museum of Modern Art in New York), in which Roger is a dark indistinct mass on a winged and rearing horse of the same stuff as the sea monster and Angélique a small, white, and exaggeratedly curving feminine figure at the center of the canvas. The significance of the Andromeda complex has become a subject of contemporary feminist reflection. Close cousin of King Kong's frail Hollywood victims, Robbe-Grillet's Andromeda/Angelica reappears as a young and touching prisoner on the executioner's wooden cart, wrists bound behind her back, in the enchanted medieval forest of the autobiographical *Angélique ou l'enchantement.*

The pale (and dangerously emasculating) fiancée of Corinthe borrowed from Michelet's nineteenth-century story, the transformed "Christian" stories of virgin martyrs (Angelica, as martyr, is torn in half), the tortured "victims" of popular s&m or bondage magazines are the flattened pre-texts, which in their transformations in Robbe-Grillet's texts, conceal/reveal the underlying deep structure of the fascination, capture, torture, and will to suppression of the "feminine" other. Designated as cultural representations, much as the early crimes were unraveled as linguistic constructions, these fragments appear to be part of the attempt to bring to clear consciousness the unconscious sadomasochistic orderings at work both in the narcissistic psyche and in our social texts. They might be considered to be an attempt at the recapture of a prelinguistic cognitive or sensory experience or presymbolic truth of the body in the Lacanian sense; to be a reworking of its repressed aspects, beginning with and through its ready-made existence as a fact of culture.

Robbe-Grillet's thematics recall Laura Mulvey's provocative characterization of the narrative as a "forcing" of event or a "battle of will and strength." Mulvey's formula, "Sadism demands a story," is interpreted by de Lauretis as an inference that "sadism," a desire to know, is the "deep structure" or "generative force" of narrative.[22] De Lauretis suggests that the petrifying Medusa and the monstrous Sphinx survived only as inscribed in hero narratives (in someone else's story, not their own,) that is, as topographical and passive projections. These monsters were the limen between the city and the desert, the threshold to the inner recesses of the cave or maze, "metaphorizing the symbolic boundary between nature and culture, the limit and the test imposed on man."[23] In Robbe-Grillet's texts, woman (nature, monster, the unknown in the self) evokes inevitably the battle of strength, the ravishing and suppression of the seductive and dangerous other.

There is, however, in Robbe-Grillet's work, the beginning of a more complex model of psychosexual/textual structures than that of opposition. This model figures reversals and exchanges, "complementarity" between the poles of "masculine" and "feminine," of sexual pleasure and danger, of sadism and masochism, of life and death. If, beyond the deconstruction of monolithic "meaning" and its processes, meanings or senses are produced in these texts, these are no longer a function of a "mediation" between opposites of the kind that Lévi-Strauss finds in the workings of myth or of the Hegelian "Aufhebung" that Robbe-Grillet himself initially adopted to discuss the working of his texts. As the text shifts to form new patterns from old, to draw the inside outside or the outside inside, through keyholes, doors, and windows like the strange topological spaces of Möbius strips and Klein bottles, which take the adventurer through devious twists on a journey back to the point of departure but other or inside out,[24] the reader, initially aggressed, begins to feel that it may be possible to reorder the elements of the binary and oedipal structure and to open new paths of escape.

The meanings of any such new structure would not destroy binary schema of inner and outer, of power and powerlessness, of male and female, of ego and id, shaped overall by the complex differential relations between sets of drives (pleasure, for example), of instincts (will to repeat), and of moral censors (staging of guilt), but these meanings could be reorganized at other levels in a different model, a "field" model, for example, or a "complementary" (contradictory but non–mutually exclusive) form of the kind that quantum mechanics uses to describe the character of elementary particles. In this complementary model, dialectical movement would not be swallowed up in an "Aufhebung" but would proliferate, recursively, symmetrically, to become part of a "chaotic" order.

In her study of scientific field models and contemporary literary strategies, Katherine Hayles[25] asks whether the impossibility of complete knowledge—that knowledge of both position (particle) and velocity (wave) at once that alone allowed us to make traditional measurements—derives from the interference of the process of the observation with the phenomenon observed (Heisenberg's interpretation of the uncertainty relations), whether nature herself is inherently indeterminate and "complementary," or whether the uncertainty results from the necessary exclusion of one pole by the selection of the opposite pole from which to observe (Bohr's interpretation). There seems to be no single or clear answer. What is evident is that as determinist Newtonian paradigms of absolute time and space, like Cartesian rationality, are themselves seen as choices, and as incomplete knowledge becomes inevitable when a single model is selected and others excluded, the discourse of the scientist loses not only its absolute character but also its innocence. Like the writer, the scientist is embedded in cultural and scientific discourses that are only apparently neutral. Enmeshed in ready-made assumptions about objectivity, method, and progress, and the power of science to describe and explain the real, the scientist cannot stand completely outside the object of her/his investigation; he/she must make choices that are not free from situation or status or gender.

Models that allow order and disorder to coexist—e.g., models of "complementary" structures, fields, or chaotic phenomena—are appearing at other sites in the cultural complex. It is increasingly accepted that stable order within the psyche itself arises from conflicts and slippages between a number of levels—from movements between identification with and separation from preferred love objects, between ego and alter or superego, between feminine and masculine. There does seem to be an interconnectedness within the oedipal (Freudian) contradictions of the psyche or its (Lacanian) splitting that is not dialectical. For the later Freud a drive that originates in the biological (such as the tendency to apparently obsessive reiteration of often painful or negative experience) may be in apparent conflict with a drive that functions at the level of psychical representation (such as the pleasure principle). The two coexist much as wave and particle coexist for Heisenberg in energy–matter, that is, as interconnected, contradictory, but not necessarily mutually exclusive entities, somehow determined by the situation of the observer.

These new forms do not, of course, provide immediate answers to the question of the influence of the process of observing on the object of observation, the subject-object bind, but at some level the choices of the elements to be put into play, like the choice of point of view (masculine and feminine pole, sadistic or masochistic preference), will affect the story. Joan DeJean[26] discusses Man Ray's portrait of the "revolutionary" Marquis de Sade, made of exactly the same stones as the Bastille of the Ancien Regime crumbling behind him, as an example of the (self)-defensive "fortifications" that revolutionary or enlightened writers construct in what remain, after all, essentially traditional texts. Like Man Ray's portrait, Robbe-Grillet's textual devices suggest the impossibility of any total "liberation."

The uncertainty and sometimes monstrosity that makes itself felt in many of Robbe-Grillet's apparently borrowed textual cardboard cutouts (legends, paintings, photographs, opera stories) derives in part from the

strange loops of true or false, real and represented, original and simulacrum, writer staging self or text or actor in someone else's text. As
in set theory (the set is included in itself), these projects for a revolution
are part of the whole that they designate; they do not stand outside.
The world, at least to some extent, is a text that is read (Borges's library),
and our lives are like sequential narratives. The postmodern double bind
in which the self is bound by text, like dialectical structuring, is still
everywhere. And yet the text continues to explore the ways in which it
is bound to self. At the simplest level the choices of the elements to be
put into play and the choice of point of view will influence the story.

François Jost[27] sees two antagonistic forces in Robbe-Grillet's texts,
a centripetal force that "tightens all the constitutive elements of the
diegesis" (the "shrinking" in the inaugural sentence of *Souvenirs*:
"Impression, déjà, que les choses se rétrécissent") and frames the fictions
by initial and final door or inside rooms (in *Projet, Dans le labyrinthe,
Topologie, Souvenirs*) and a centrifugal movement to escape, to find an
open window on the sea, a path that "leads to something," a way out
of the room.

In de Lauretis's reading of Lotman's semiotic analysis of mythological
plot-texts as the hero's entry into the closed space (the grave, the house,
the room, the woman) of death and his emergence from it, this rite of
passage is inevitably predicated on the male hero who crosses the boundary as active principle or cultural founder of distinction. The female,
for de Lauretis, is, on the contrary, not susceptible to transformation,
but is a resistance, a matrix of plot-space.

Although such a preference given to the active male principle, to
the conquest of the limen, the founding of distinctions, and to the return
is clearly present in Robbe-Grillet's work, the return (the "Chemin du
retour" in *Instantanés*) is itself threatened by the perilous rising tides,
the encroachment of the sea, the eddying pools that suck men down to
drown in the tentacles of their strange depths. Similar elements are
present in Magritte's painting *La Traversée difficile* [*The Difficult Crossing*] used as a generator in *La Belle Captive*. This figures a ship tossing
perilously on a stormy sea outside a room (or in a painting on the wall,
indeterminately) in which a hand on a table held up by a feminine leg
imprisons a black dove. Both objects are watched over by a phallic but
also somewhat feminized wooden object. Robbe-Grillet's accompanying

text assembles elements and stories that connote masculine sexual reaction to the danger of feminine takeover that recur throughout his work. The sinister ship becomes the one on board which the kidnapped adolescent had been dragged by her ravishers to be raped before being thrown into the sea. It was possibly also the vessel on which David, struck during an attack by the phallic object, was wounded on the temple (a small red wound direct from the sub-title of *Djinn: un trou rouge entre les pavés disjoints*[28] and recurring in the two small red holes on Corinthe's neck).

Jost sees the many doors and windows that delimit the boundaries, the inside/outside spaces in Robbe-Grillet's texts, as providing passage, but we note their uncertain nature. The invented door with its false panel imitating the knots and grain of real wood of *Projet,* with an opening covered by a grid grossly imitating wrought iron, is, claims *Le Miroir qui revient,* the real door of Robbe-Grillet's house of birth in Brest. The black lacquered keyhole-less electronic door that opens *Souvenirs,* the door to the temple, may not even be a door at all. As in Magritte's inside paintings of an outside (where the landscape is both simultaneously inside and outside the canvas), which Robbe-Grillet selected as textual "generators" for his picto-novel *La Belle Captive,* the status of the door/the boundary as real or imitation, inside or outside, is unclear. The question that returns here, once again, is whether we are caught in a "strange" and thus inescapable "loop" as in the formally undecidable propositions that have made the truth of mathematics problematical since Gödel,[29] or whether there are forms that touch the real and offer passage over the limen, catharsis, or escape.

In a discussion of the circular (strange loop) relationship between the law and its transgression (between the imaginary and the symbolic) and the difficulty of envisioning change from "within the conceptual framework of a polarized mythology," Laura Mulvey quotes Juliet Mitchell: "You cannot choose the imaginary, the semiotic, the carnival as an alternative to the rule. It is set up by the law precisely in its own ludic space, its area of imaginary alternative, but not as a symbolic alternative. So that, politically speaking, it is only the symbolic, a new symbolism, a new law, that can challenge the dominant law."[30]

However, Emmanuel Le Roy Ladurie, whose now classic work *Carnaval à Romans* is quoted by Mulvey, sees the reversal effected by carnival not only as a recognition of the law, but as a way to action and as a satirical and lyrical learning experience. Mulvey subsequently argues that although an inversion of dominant codes may indeed fossilize into a dualistic opposition and a restoration of the order cathartically disrupted, it might equally provide a springboard to an unformed language. The liminal moment, like the image of the disorderly woman, could create the turbulence that would facilitate change, thus having political significance. For Mulvey the moment of the "masculine" hero's passage from social order through a "feminine" threshold to another space implies "movement on a linear model, rather than opposition on a polar model."[31] As Derrida had pointed out in *Positions*,[32] even in transgression, we have to do with a code and with a metaphysics. The transgression that takes place across a limit implies that a limit is at work, and this modifies the inside field. It never, however, allows us to settle down, to live elsewhere, never becomes a fait accompli.

It may be that the models of complementary relations or of the liminal moment and the transgression that this involves subvert the processes of interior duplication and intertextuality, that series of self-embedded Russian dolls figuring an infinite Derridean regression, which is already an indefinite skeptical deferring of truth and meaning, always a repetition of the past without possible future. Concealing/revealing analogies or overlap with a more physical "real," these processes may even permit knowledge and change. The question here, as at the heart of the "postmodern" debate, is, once again, that of the double bind.

Although Robbe-Grillet himself has discussed his work in terms of a dialectical movement between order and disorder, the movement from order(ing) to disorder(ing) and back again in his text clearly goes beyond the mise en scène of dialectical mental structures projected in linguistic orderings onto the world. The order(ing) and disorder(ing) are at once much more "complementary" and much more complex. These movements are figured within the texts themselves. The repetitions or repetitions with slight difference, the true and false versions of the text and of the character carry the protagonist far from the beaten track, lured, in *Angélique,* by the enchantment of the siren-songbird into tangled forest and troubled, turbulent waters, or off the straight path into curiously incomplete circles, like the detective who ends his inquiry as the assassin in *Topologie.*

The circles open into spirals that offer promise of violent release. The assassin, black cloak spiraling behind him as he ascends the S-shaped staircase (generated perhaps by Duchamp's famous painting *Nu descendant un escalier*) in *La Chambre secrète*, for example, seems thereby to have an avenue of escape from the scene of his repeated text/ritual crime that is virtually reversible in time. This short story is organized around a whole series of S shapes—the "rose" of the red blood on the victim's white breast, the smoke rising from the incense burner, the curve of the victim's body, a sinuous thread of blood. The inverted question mark in *La Jalousie*, left by the traces of the crushed centipede to pose the enigma and fascination of the violent emotions aroused by the female and figured again by the enigmatic S-shaped curve of a lock of the protagonist A's dark hair, or the curving tails of the erased letters on the sheet of blue writing paper, in what might be seen as an ironic gestalt test for the jealous narrator, the S, become a spiral, promises violent movement even within repetition.

Opposite Z shapes, or masculine configurations that open into zig-zag fractal shapes (straight lines, bipolarity, but also progression in space), such as the iron fire escape in *Projet pour une révolution à New York,* for example, also provide a possible passage between two states, a connection from inside to outside, for both the would-be assassin and the narrator. The only other possible access to the sequestered victim is through the "strange" and closed "loop" of the topological space of the keyhole through which inside becomes outside and vice-versa; in *Projet,* behind the keyhole the victim herself is holding a lurid representation of a victim, that is, the front cover of a popular erotic magazine.

Talking about his own writing enterprise at a colloquium at New York University, Robbe-Grillet described the hole between the uneven paving stones in *Djinn: Un trou rouge entre les pavés disjoints* [Djinn: A Red Hole Between the Paving Stones] as a sign of the "liberating" shock of the "incomprehensible" of "love," in the encounter with the "extraordinary other." As in science fiction, this shock occurs, claims Robbe-Grillet, when two worlds that should not communicate one with another suddenly begin to communicate: "which means that there is a fault in the quotidian world and through it, another world is suddenly visible. This other world functions differently and thus we are thrown into a functioning (both of consciousness and the world), which is not the way with which we were familiar."[33] Beneath the established order ("sous les pavés"), he claims, quoting a popular French song by Renaud, beneath the paving stones, there is this "strangeness" that is "freedom" ("c'est la plage"). The later chapters of this study ask whether it is not a paradox that, as in the work of Sade, freedom and revolution are equated with a "red hole" that is violent and sadistic, and with predominantly "masculine" sexual transgression. The point of significance here is rather that these strange holes, topologically reversible figures, fractal shapes, and spirals are the forms inspiring a new science of chaos that has been developing since the seventies to rethink traditional science and its encounters with an incomprehensible other and to construct a competing model.

The riddle of the real and the represented, of what we can know, has not been solved absolutely or definitively. But the "complementary" and "chaotic" models put into play open up new fields of meanings, new ways of knowing and being, contact with turbulent margins that offer some promise of leap to new orders out of chaos. Besides the model of loss "in the funhouse" (Barth),[34] that is, of play in infinite self-reflexivity, there is, increasingly, an awareness of the turbulence introduced into the text by the sexual body in the writing process, turbulence that points beyond the double bind.

Chaos Theory and the Female Body

Susan Suleiman's germinal essay, "Reading Robbe-Grillet: Sadism and Text in *Projet pour une révolution à New York*,"[35] was the first to offer what she came to call a "feminist deconstructive" approach to the "obvious, provocative aggression of the erotic content of Robbe-Grillet's novels."[36] Suleiman reads Robbe-Grillet as "the combination of the thematics of erotic violence"—rape, mutilation of female genitals, necrophilia, medical experiments on young girls, ritual sacrifice—with a "poetics of anti-realist transgression."[37] Ricardou had argued in "La fiction flamboyante"[38] that the pre-text of *Projet* was the opening description, the penetration of the door with complex and precise patterns on its imitation wood panels, or again the word *rouge*/the color red. For Suleiman, the generator of the text is rather the anatomical drawing or representation of the precise and complicated forms of the female genital organs that figures on a white page toward the end of the novel. The thematics of aggression, like the ritualism and theatricality that also characterize the work, are, for her, aspects of both the subversive intent of the avant-garde text and a textual violation of the mother's sexual parts in a masculine phantasy of self-generation and a will to power.

As the previous section of this chapter suggested, the powerful deconstructing impulse at work in Robbe-Grillet's text is rendered problematic by subjective choices and the material that the text puts into play. Behind the masterly and carefully controlled mise en scène of the factitious conventions of the traditional novel and of the imprisoning commonplaces (*lieux communs*) that direct our readings of the world, there is a strong and intimate sense of imminent threat. Vesuvius, part of the play of the recursive V in *Topologie d'une cité fantôme,* intertextual borrowing from Jensen's *Gradiva,* which itself served as generator for Freud's interpretation of dreams, is conventionally a metaphor of eruption of hidden violence and apocalypse. In Robbe-Grillet's text, this ready-made generator is part of a proliferating series of elements that evoke the violation of the immobilized female body (young and beautiful for eternity) and death. Yet the volcano and the rocks it spews forth to wound vulnerable young females, however doll-like and unreal, is also clearly and ironically individuated, a self-conscious metaphor not only of the inner violence of the text but also of the pain/pleasure of a personal psychosexual sadistic drive.

V in its variant form of Vanadé/Vanessa is the victorious goddess or vanquished impaled butterfly, spirit of disorder or bleeding rose, that calls the fascinated narrator to her interrogation and suppression. As the precocious adolescent Violette (with "le diable au corps" [the devil in her]) of *Le Voyeur,* the seductive sea-siren Aimone of *Un Régicide,* the diaphanous angel/vampire Marie-Ange of Gothic horror stereotype in the 1986 film *La Belle Captive,* or the drowned fiancée Angelica of *Le Miroir qui revient,* her name (purity and provocation, V and its inversion A, golden triangle) is both legion and commonplace.

Yet, according to the writer's most recent autobiography (or "autofiction" to use Doubrovsky's ingenious term), this omnipresent cultural/

textual figure also originates in the writer's personal experience. In *Angélique ou l'enchantement* (1988), there is a lengthy account of the barely adolescent Alain's sexual initiation to games of Roman soldier and slave, his apparently formative "experience" with precocious pubescent Angèle, whose body is subsequently found drowned along the Léon coast of Robbe-Grillet's boyhood. The fate of the young playmate-victim is, provocatively and playfully, a repetition of that of the fictional Violette of the 1955 novel *Le Voyeur*. The text maintains this perverse indeterminism; an unresolved tension between the text and the real. In the margin between the visible and the invisible, between the text and the self, this feminine figure conceals and calls up monsters. Like the dangerous sea of which she is a metaphor, or the variant primal forest of Celtic and Germanic myth, which she haunts in *Angélique* as water nymph and as enchantress, she is the threat and the seduction of feminine disorder and masculine self-loss, the dangerous other in the self, beyond the safety rail of order and control.

The sea, itself a metaphor of the entwining tentacles and proliferating devouring monsters of the forest of metaphor, is also a metaphor of the nonclosure and the chaos of the world, eddying randomly beneath the regularity of its smooth blue surface and giving birth out of this turbulence to strange forms of Venus in the distinctively Robbe-Grillet style. The smooth curve of the white shore, a metaphor of the seductive female body in *Le Miroir*, evokes the night fairy washerwomen of Celtic legend ("les lavandeuses de nuit"), but the fine lace of the delicate feminine undergarments "improbably" drying in the moonlight of Breton legend are, inevitably, both bloodstained and torn in this self-conscious (ironic, subversive, and narcissistic), personally colored text.

Is Narcissus again at risk from drowning in the mirror that the nymphet Echo holds up to him? Or does the subversive irony act as sufficient counterweight? In the film *Glissements progressifs du plaisir* (1974), the sea and the shore are marked incongruously but insistently by objects that recur rhythmically throughout the work, metonymically or metaphorically associated with the capture, violation, and suppression in sexualized paroxysm of the sacrificial victim: the broken bottle, the prie-dieu, the nuptial bouquet, the high-heeled blue slipper stained with red, and the naked, dislocated, white body of the female mannequin tied to the railings of the black iron bed.

Martin Eger points out that for Greimas as for Propp and Lévi-Strauss, myth and folktale narratives seem to operate as a kind of "natural" or basic-level narrative.[39] Defined by a limited number of arbitrary distinctive features, functions, and structures, these tales nonetheless appear to be the most commonly conceived of human stories. The familiar and varied fragments of the "feminine" from Western myth, opera, and folk story that are the generators of Robbe-Grillet's latest works play a similarly double function. They are pre-text and artifice, ready-mades used to construct a brilliant work of art, and yet, like pop art and its predecessors with which they have much in common, they retain connections with general human experience. Similarly, woman's body as conventional metaphor of the object used by the subject, male artist, to help construct his text—the female muse—may not be entirely arbitrary. The female body as basic material object of male desire or interrogation evidently has some degree of referential validity.

Robbe-Grillet's own selection from among available stories or intertexts—a selection that includes the Roman tale of the fatal, "pure" fiancée of Corinthe as retransmitted by Barthes's *Michelet par lui-même* (1954), or the story of the femme fatale Carmen (originally told by the Empress Josephine to Mérimée and subsequently entering Robbe-Grillet's repertoire by way of nineteenth-century operatic tradition and twentieth-century popular culture)—is not without personal motivation. The apparently innocent stories of ecstatic young virgin martyrs and of classical victims of sacrifice to the sea monster for the rites of Spring, like the tales of the enchantments of Robbe-Grillet's *Morgane* (variation on the medieval *Morgan le Fay*, perfidious half-sister of King Arthur), the Breton fairy washerwomen (*lavandeuses*) in all their false-seeming, and the humorously pornographic stories of the sadistic torture of heiressess and prostitutes (Laura, J.R.) in *Projet,* are the instrument and the product of a seduction.

What is not immediately evident is whose seduction this is. In a Freudian scenario, the son's discovery of the doubleness of the mother's asexual or "pure" body or of forbidden desire for the mother may result in a displacement of guilt, onto the figure of the nonmaternal young virgin–whore in this instance. In a more Lacanian reading, the seduction of the body of the mother would derive from a recognition of a splitting and a decentering of the unknown self and the fear of the (castrated/

castrating) other in the self. Or is the seduction, in fact, rather that of the reader held in horror or excitement by the slippages of both the sado-erotic thematics and the slippery body of the text while accepting the alibis set up by the distancing effects (interior duplications, flattening, and fragmentation) of the textual operations? Is the traditional cultural story of dangerous female sexuality subverted or strengthened in Robbe-Grillet's texts?

In every case, the male narrators' projects of objective knowledge ("Je fais mon rapport, un point, c'est tout. Le texte est correct et rien n'est laissé au hasard" [I'm writing my report and that's all. The text is correct, and nothing is left to chance] [*Projet*, p. 189], as a narrator of scenes of torture of the female body insists), their attempts to interrogate and order the world around them, reveal, on more careful examination, and often at the limits of our powers of perception, microscopic discontinuities and imperfections. Tiny fissures, gaps, and hollows, both images of the unknown in the body and inner world of the psyche, and images of the gaps and holes in our knowledge of the universe, lie at the heart of everyday "reality." As in Borges's *Labyrinths* or Barth's *Lost in the Funhouse,* the protagonist's attempt to trace the "labyrinth" to its center, his dead ends and repetitions, simply creates another maze. Theseus escapes the labyrinth by logic, but, as Peter Stoicheff puts it, he cannot in the final instance escape the Ariadne-like labyrinth of his desire.

On close inspection even the apparently objective and scientific character of the early novels (the quarter of a tomato cut "in truth" out of a fruit of "perfect symmetry" and a drawbridge continuing to vibrate imperceptibly as it reached its point of rest in the first published novel, *Les Gommes*) reveals irregularity, indeterminacy of onset or termination, and accident. In the carefully detailed left-right symmetries of the soldier's footsteps in the snow, the oscillation of the light bulb at the end of its cord, and the general binary movement in *Dans le labyrinthe* (1959), there is slight preference for left over right, or a reversal of right and left in space, as in a mirror image. These tiny differences, the unmeasurable oscillations of the drawbridge, which make it impossible to say exactly when the phenomenon begins and ends, leave spaces for disorder, doubt, and fissure, which from infinitely small beginnings are capable of spreading through the different levels of a complex system, from the microscopic to the macroscopic, magnifying their effects, to create unforeseeable distortion and monstrous turbulence. As in chaos theory, a butterfly that displaces the air with its wings today in Peking may cause a hurricane tomorrow in Florida.

In a strict binary system, symmetries, like antimatter, would cancel one another out; indeed Robbe-Grillet himself claimed at the Cérisy Colloquium on his work that such a mutual annihilation was operating for certain of his proper names, the H. M. of *Dans le labyrinthe*, for example.[40] But Robbe-Grillet nonetheless identifies H. M. as Henri Martin, the mysterious "missing" soldier (hero?) of Breton war history, who appears in the novel *Dans le labyrinthe*, and the author of a fictional work he himself found as a child on the shelves of the family library. This work contained a striking illustration of the mythological and ancient Brunhilde, portrayed as an "angelical" young girl tied to the tail of the prancing steed and dragged radiant through the primal forest. Far from being canceled out, both Henri Martin as alter ego of the writer (mysterious hero-traitor) and Brunhilde as hyperbolic stereotype of sadomasochistic phantasy make a reappearance in the autofiction *Angélique ou l'enchantement*. Symmetry, here, appears to play a subversive, nontraditional role, canceling but also, like antimatter, revealing monstrous potentialities in minuscule differences.

Robbe-Grillet's text moves beyond bipolarity and neutralization; his symmetries are at once similar and different, repeating and distinguishing. The tiny initial differences often magnify through the levels of the system to provoke major disruptions. Such a movement where microscopic fluctuations can spread imperceptibly to transform monstrously the macroscopic is remarkably similar to what, in his best-selling work on chaos theory, James Gleick terms "sensitive dependency on initial conditions."[41] As chaos theory looks more closely at the infinitely complex forms of the macroscopic objects that we thought we knew and could predict the behavior of by scientific method—the shifting shapes of cloud, the endless perimeter of a snowflake, the paths of lightning—claims Gleick, it reveals the incompleteness of the linear equations that constitute the order and univocity of our traditional solutions to knowledge of the physical world. This new science looks at the never quite exact repetitions of weather patterns in which the tiniest fluctuation in input can lead to an erratic, unforeseeable, major new output. It examines turbulent flow where vorticity is intermittent and localized and eddies mix with smoothness without homogeneity or without filling the whole space of a fluid.

As Gleick points out, although there are many more non-linear equations without solution than there are solvable equations, the scientific establishment has chosen to exclude the former from its field and to stand firm on ordered ground. Established science, focusing on the knowable, the positive, and the possible in an essentially reductionist frame (what are the smallest particles of the smallest particles) and avoiding the perils of the chaotic and apparently unknowable can only "know" the dangerous other (holes, fractal shapes, and spirals) from within its own limited frames. The emerging awareness of the inadequacy of our traditional "exact measurements" to convey the way in which every part in a complex system depends on the movement of its neighbors—on its differential relations with all the elements of a system, as in structuralist theory—or awareness of the inability to capture the indeterminacy at the heart of matter/energy might find a symbolic equivalent in the "beautiful captive" as emblem of the hitherto suppressed pole of our positivistic scientific establishment. The irregularity and unpredictability in turbulent flow, the incompleteness or inconsistency in number theory that Gödel postulated in his 1931 theorem, and our inability to solve logically "undecidable propositions" and move beyond the "strange loops" that Hofstadter discusses in *Gödel, Escher, Bach* would similarly constitute the visibility of a troubling presence, hitherto suppressed.

As a number of scientists concentrated their investigation on what seemed to lie outside order and the knowable as a result of the emerging interest in chaos, new orders began to appear within the disordered chaotic systems. Between the different levels of complex systems, between the tiny fern frond and the mature plant, in river networks, in microscopic networks of blood vessels and configurations of galaxies, as in the patterns of turbulent flow, there are recursive symmetries. Fractal geometry developed as the study of traditionally unmeasurable, jagged, broken, but self-resembling shapes. Events that appear chaotic, the complex system of the Great Red Spot on Jupiter, for example, demonstrate both turbulence and coherence. The complexity and apparent randomness of the most disordered macroscopic systems—epidemics, economies, ecological systems—reveal strange statistical symmetries over extended periods not unlike the "random" yet highly statistically regular decay of radium in the microcosmic world.

Chaos theory discovers, then, that systems in disorder reveal connections between levels and long-term regularities within indeterminacy that constitute new forms of order. Gleick recounts the story of the scientific suspicion that the visible patterns in turbulent flow or in complex systems, the self-entangled stream lines, spirals, vortices, and whorls that rise before the eye and vanish again must reflect laws not yet discovered. In turbulent flow, for example, eddies mix with regions of smooth flow without homogeneity, without filling the whole space of a fluid. Vorticity is intermittent and localized. "At each scale, as you look at turbulent eddy, new regions of calm come into view."[42] Smooth flow becomes unpredictably turbulent, a swelling round a bottleneck or slower-moving blockage, like the underground travelers swept along the corridors in Robbe-Grillet's *Souvenirs du triangle d'or*.

The dissipation of energy in turbulent flow seemed to lead to a kind of contraction, a "folding" and "squeezing" of a phase space of infinite dimensions. The computer aided the discovery of Lorenzian "strange attractors" whose nonperiodic spirals, never quite intersecting or joining could not therefore simply repeat themselves in a periodic loop. Taking infinitely many paths in a finite space, scope made possible by fractal surfaces, these orbits that are irregular because they do not repeat themselves are nonetheless predictable and reveal hidden symmetries and structures behind their chaotic patterns.

Mandelbrot's work with the self-similarities of fractals and with the strangely beautiful, infinitely spiraling forms that a computer can generate in a finite space from the mathematics of the Mandelbrot set,[43] like Prigogine's interest in nonequilibrium thermodynamics (*La Nouvelle Alliance*), where entropy leads not to death but to new self-organization, or contemporary versions of evolutionary theory suggest that apparent nonlinear disorder can produce self-organization, self-reflexive patterns and organization. While the random possibilities of bifurcation points in physical or biological systems at far from equilibrium states become central, their systematic or probabilistic character is also in evidence. The origins of the universe and of human life itself in the new models are seen to be both indeterministic and the result of a series of probabilities; to show randomness within purposefulness, and to produce new orders out of chaos.

There are striking analogies between Robbe-Grillet's textual trajectories and the forms of chaos theory. The influence of chaos theory may be direct but seems more probably to have been indirect, diffused through the general cultural and intellectual climate. The forms Robbe-Grillet's texts create have much more in common with the hidden currents and unpredictable eddies of turbulent flow behind regular surfaces, with bifurcation points and with intersections or overlap of numerous, often disparate, simultaneously functioning and interacting levels than with traditional movement along the points of a straight line toward a resolution whose meaning is to be found in the sum of the points.

The topologies of Robbe-Grillet's imaginary cities, most particularly in *Topologie d'une cité fantôme* and *Souvenirs du triangle d'or*, deformed by nonlinear twisting and stretching, create a space of complex connection constituted by overlapping, interconnected strata and by knots and holes that paradoxically provide passage from inside to outside. Attempts to incorporate simultaneously branching paths and to model the indeterminacy yet strange predictability that characterizes points of bifurcation seem self-conscious. Such multiple, uncertain, intricate trajectories are figured *en abyme* in the description of a labyrinthine generative crack in the ceiling in *Dans le labyrinthe*, for example, or in the multiple appearances and guises of Angélique-Violette and her adventures with the black and white knights in the forest of the "autofiction" in *Angélique*.

These adventures borrow, multiply, re-begin, and vary the forms of what appears to be an original folk story of female seduction, capture, and death. The reader, constantly encountering contradictory and violent objects or structures already encountered in another space and time (in other cultural texts or in previous Robbe-Grillet works), whose meanings are thus both strangely continuous in their discontinuity and predictable in their randomness, sensed as same behind their difference, feels the ground of linear meaning and of binary organization of meaning slipping beneath her or his feet. The surprises of this "difference," disrupting the expected, create noise that is unexpected and thus rich with information. The pleasure of the text lies partly in this slippage, in the surprises at bifurcation points and in recombination, partly in the recognition of the elements and structures that begin to recur among the infinitely possible variants as new orders establish themselves.

Characters and narrators are made and unmade in a circulation of names, functions, descriptive attributes, and phrases not unlike the bundles of distinctive features that constitute the phonemes or sememes of a language. Their names no longer shore up a metaphysics of presence or an ideology of individuality. It is in the play of the contradictory but recurring characteristics of personae and narrators and in the patterns that emerge from multiplicity and disorder that the moving, multiple, strange, chaotic doubles of the writer, both hero and villain, male and female, narrator and narrated, act out a self. The imaginary autobiographical alter egos of mixed linguistic, literary, mythical, historical, and personal origins are not quite the same as the original. Yet out of a chaotic proliferation of contradictions, the doubles that constitute the self—character/writer, inventor/invented, investigator/criminal, sadist/siren—some sense of coherence or identity emerges that might be seen as individual style or self.

The "new alliance" between nature and science, suggested by the title of Prigogine's work on nonequilibrium thermodynamics and the newly recognized creative possibilities of entropy, once seen as ultimate death of the universe, can be extended and used as a general metaphor for the contemporary metamorphoses of science. This "alliance" of apparent opposites stands in close relation to what the sociobiologist Wilson in *On Human Nature*[44] characterizes as the "grand myth" and to what Martin Eger[45] sees as the "dominant epic." Within this evolutionary epic Eger links Jacques Monod's vision in *Chance and Necessity* (1971) of the purposefulness in mindless molecules as biological feedback mechanisms or microcosmic cybernetics, Eigen and Winkler's arguments in *Laws of the Game* (1975) that such purposefulness of nonliving molecules had to arrive as part of a universal play of chance under the constraint of environmental rules, and Stephen Weinberg's model of the evolution of the universe from the primordial egg (*The First Three Minutes* [1977]). In all these models the chaos of elementary process gives rise to an order. This order may be destroyed at a bifurcation, but the latter may then produce its own new coherence. Hofstadter's devices[46] fit human consciousness into similar feedback models. Prigogine's recasting of the reversibility, determinism, and lawfulness of traditional physics to fit the irreversibility, randomness, and directionality of time of the new evolutionary models and his sought for "new alliance" between the split worlds of subject and object, life-science and science of inanimate things epitomizes for Eger what Kuhn would have seen as a new scientific "paradigm."[47]

The four major aspects of metafictional texts, argues Peter Stoicheff,[48] are precisely the nonlinearity, self-reflexivity, irreversibility, and self-organization that characterize chaotic structures. (Nonlinearity is defined as bifurcation that produces meaning and is understandable at a local level without global or definitive meaning.) These characteristics link the poetics of the new literary texts,[49] and perhaps their politics, to the new scientific paradigm. They indicate clear homologies between science and metafiction. Perhaps, as Stoicheff suggests, both metafiction's consider-ations of the illusions of representational function and the new science's examinations of its own measurements and narratives can be seen as part of a wider movement in contemporary thought. But are these homologies merely metaphorical? Do they touch new aspects of the real? Stoicheff himself seems to be caught in indecision, hesitating between the irony of an antimimetic text that somehow replicates the structures of the newly discovered aspects of a "chaotic" phenomenal world and Borges's view of the world ("The Library of Babel," 1962) as a library, its same volumes repeated in the same disorder, that is, a world constituted by infinite, chaotic, and self-reflexive texts. What is the relation, if any, between Robbe-Grillet's phantasy of the repression of the female body of the text and the aggression and suppression of the biological/sociopsychological bodies of real women?

Eger denounces the possibility of the new epic becoming an authori-tative or canonical final product founded on the old view that the entities of science exist independently, literally, or in a mirrorlike correspondence between the features of the models and a disclosed physical reality. The gap between the objective, scientific, quantitative world and the sub-jective, unscientific, qualitative world that founds the old classical nar-rative, that is, the gap between science and the life-world, would not, he claims, be bridged by an absolute informational model of accident and environmental constraint. An interpretation of the new epic would, for him, require a consideration of the human context (historical, cul-tural, cognitive) out of which it arises. And he too, therefore, sees science caught in self-reflexivity and strange loops between life and text. For at some point in the omniscient, traditional narrative, science comes into being on earth and itself constructs or discovers the grand evolutionary myth within itself. The contained turns out to contain within itself its own container as in an Escher drawing. Which, he asks, is the starting point, the big-bang or its scientific reconstruction?

This interpretation, which sees no way out of the double bind, does not, however, deny the reality and the independence of an external world that plays a role in shaping scientific theories, old and new. But it proceeds from the general recognition that scientific evidence underdetermines the theoretical ontologies out of which descriptions of the world arise. That is: "Empirical evidence can establish with confidence only limited, local phenomena."[50] A metaphorical extension, guided by phenomena, involves the human construction of a larger, symbolic world, embodying the ontology of the models used. This world is neither fictitious nor objective truth. It can, however, for Eger, if it contains within itself the story of this (human) construction, provide a glimpse of the vital margin between the empirical data and the metaphorical extension.

Robbe-Grillet's writing project, which claims to be one of revolution, the "imaginary" speaking, is the human construction of a particular "male" imprisoned in the "symbolic" telling of the story of this imprisonment and investigating the "female" (presymbolic/maternal) chaos of the "imaginary" that opposes it on the margins. At the very least, chaos may provide an alternative law.

The enchantments of chaos, the attraction of "feminine" principles, entropy, are not, as Robbe-Grillet's texts dramatize, without what the poet Gerard Manley Hopkins described as the mind's hidden "cliffs of fall." In a paper that considers the work of Serres, Pynchon, Lyotard, and Deleuze in relation to chaos theory, Eric White[51] concludes that although many contemporary thinkers attribute an emancipatory potential to an unnameable, unimaginable "outside," precisely "chaos" or "noise" as possible source of vitality and renewal, liberation is not a feat that can be accomplished once and for all. Not only, as Eger suggests, do the new models speak with confidence only of limited, local phenomena but, claims White, emancipatory innovations themselves "inaugurate disciplinary norms." Michel Serres's *Le Parasite* (*parasite* means both host creature and static interference in the original French) dreams of presiding over the system it brings into being and putting into play that power that, declares White, quoting Foucault, is inescapably and at once constitutive and repressive. As it is in Robbe-Grillet's fictional practice, the process of making sense, by chance and noise, has to be a never-ending task, because, as White, like Foucault, concludes, power, like desire, is protean and omnipresent. In *Le Parasite*, a text that opposes the fertile, chaotic daughter of the sea, Venus, and the totalitarian Mars, the god of war, Venus (like the parasite), by exerting a destabilizing influence, could, in her turn, come to establish a tyrannous reign.

Escape from culture seems problematic, and as whips, knives, blood, and instruments of torture re-begin in Robbe-Grillet's work their yet more frenetic dance, as the writer's own choice of beautiful captive as generator falls under the same suspicion as the cultural representations he represents, so also does escape from self. Yet from the binary psychical structure of a self (an ego and an opposite alter; masculine opposed to feminine) to its "complementary" possibilities (potentially both controlling ego and threatening other, both subject and object "masculine" and "feminine"), the path seems nonetheless to lead toward the acceptance of a "chaotic" (at once turbulent and potentially coherent) multilayered self.

There are intersections between Susan Suleiman's "feminist deconstructionist" reading and my own conclusions in this chapter. Suleiman's reading sees Robbe-Grillet's work *both* as the subversion of the traditional masculine order that is characteristic of avant-garde writing *and* as the textual violation of the "mother's parts" in a will to power. My reading finds the sexual and the textual imbricated in a similarly "complementary" relation. Further intersecting lines between Robbe-Grillet's work and the texts of chaos theory designate or create a new world of "feminine" disorder. The network of intersections that this chapter has attempted to map does not provide truth, coherence, totality, or single meaning, but its knots, like its holes, are not without significance.

Shoshana Felman[52] argues that the profound significance of the Oedipus story (as of analysis itself) is the assumption of the hero's radical decenterment from his own ego, from his own self-image (that of *Oedipus the King*, the riddle-solver, possessor of a kingdom, of a woman), his assumption of a misrecognition of his story, and an expropriating recognition of the unknown (feminine) other in himself. This

significance, for Felman, lies beyond *Oedipus Rex* and is to be found
in Sophocles' *Oedipus at Colonus* and in Freud's *Beyond the Pleasure
Principle*, that is, beyond the wish for pleasure and in the compulsion
to repeat: "What is, then, psychoanalysis if not, precisely, a *life-usage
of the death-instinct*—a practical, productive usage of the compulsion
to repeat, through a *replaying* of the symbolic meaning of the death
the subject has repeatedly experienced, and through a recognition and
assumption of the meaning of this death (separation, loss) by the subject,
as a symbolic means of coming to terms not with death but, precisely,
with his *life*?"[53] It is in the "constitutive, structural relation between life
and   death: primordial   masochism,   death-instinct,   repetitive
compulsion"[54] and ultimately in a "treating of the real by means of the
symbolic," by a "generative fiction"[55] or founding myth (in science, by
a hypothesis) that this iterative (never definitive) beyond is reached. "To
borrow a metaphor from Physics," concludes Felman, "one could say
that the generative, fictive psychoanalytic myth [and its specimen story
of Oedipus] is to the *science* of psychoanalysis what the Heisenberg
principle is to contemporary Physics: the element of mythic narrative
is something like an *uncertainty principle* of psychoanalytic theory. It
does not conflict with science—it *generates* it—as long as it is not
believed to be, erroneously, a *certainty principle*."[56]

   The knots or coincidences created in Robbe-Grillet's own treating
of his relationship to the "real" female body by a generative fiction,
knots that incorporate chaotic structures, work to effect a similar decentering process. This process involves complicity with but also critical
recognition of imprisonment in Oedipus, the law, the binary, and "masculine" power and an assumption of the misrecognition of his own story,
of the presence of the unknown "feminine" other of the self. Chaotic
structures may work, at least self-consciously, beyond Oedipus, to reinforce this decentering process and the recognition of the other, creating
liberating new orders out of chaos.

The Modernity of Myth: From Oedipus to Andromeda

From imprisonment in received meanings to the openness of new complementary and chaotic structures and from the limits imposed by the signifier to its free creative play and construction of new narrative forms, this study has begun to trace the movement between a number of interrelated, configurations of *modernité* in Robbe-Grillet's texts. In this chapter I seek to define the modernity of myth and look, in particular, at the writer's reconfigurings of the Oedipus story.

The overarching myth of Andromeda/Angelica and its recurrence as the myth of the siren and the sadist at the repeating hollow center of almost all Robbe-Grillet's texts will be discussed separately in the following chapter. As Jean-Pierre Valabréga[1] argues, the feminine cannot be separated from part of its essential content, which is the myth of femininity. The same would be true of the masculine. In this study of myth, both chapters encounter the pressing question of whether the writing of the erotic and the imaginary are imprisonment or liberation in Robbe-Grillet's work.

In his theoretical articles and interviews, Robbe-Grillet makes frequent reference to myth or mythology in the novel and in society. Critics of the writing of his earlier period focused on underlying mythical patterns as a key to the meaning of his works.[2] This critical mapping appeared analytically sound, brilliant even, in the case of Morrissette's early critical writing, but it was disappointingly inadequate as a tool for any real understanding of the work. Is there a more productive approach to the question of the nature and function of the mythological elements in Robbe-Grillet's work—by way of other contemporary reflection on myth, that of Claude Lévi-Strauss and Roland Barthes, for example? Does such an approach provide a more satisfactory explanation of the increasing and problematic sado-erotic character of the

myths of woman, made to appear "natural" by analogy with violent
classical myths or simply ignored in the early interpretations?

A traditional literary understanding of myth might have seen the
latter evolving from a core of historical truth. Euhemerus, for example,
in the fourth century B.C. claimed that Zeus was a Cretan acclaimed a
god in the East, and Euhemerists believed, among other things, that
Ceres was deified for having taught grain farming to the Greeks. More
generally, myth was considered to convey universal human and moral
truths. Jung's psychological theory of a collective unconscious with a
capacity for making images has reinforced such a view. The modes of
functioning of such a psychic substrate that in 1919 Jung named "archetypes" (anima, witch, earth-mother, and their organizing dominants,—
the self, the circle, etc.) "carry forth" the archetypal images that appeal
to primordial emotions in us and provoke an affective shock. Myths are
considered to identify and explain psychic forces; a discovery of Jungian
archetypes and meanings in Robbe-Grillet's texts did not fail to make an
appearance in the critical literature. Jung attributes the division within
modern human beings to their unawareness of their "shadow side" and
their displacement into anonymous units and mass formations. Leigh
Bridge's Jungian reading[3] sees Robbe-Grillet's protagonists in *Djinn*
become the slaves and victims of machines without moral responsibility
like Jung's modern humankind. For Jung, myth, which is the primordial
manifestation of the human spirit, is necessary for individual self-
knowledge; reason alone is inadequate. In *Djinn,* according to Bridge,
there are repeated references to the limitations of reason: "Vous raison-
nez vraiment comme un Français, positiviste et cartésien" [You reason
just like a positivistic and Cartesian Frenchman.] (p. 118). Robbe-Grillet
uses myth very freely: "His sources are Christian (Jean and its variants,
Marie, Joseph); Greek (Oedipus); Nordic (the 'elfe'); Celtic (Morrigan
or Morgan le Fay, the healer); and Persian (Djinn and Jan). . . . The
Larousse Encyclopedia of Mythology discloses that Jann was the father
of the jinns. The entry is illustrated by a representation of the god Zur-
van, who is androgynous, as are Djinn and Caroline."[4]

Bridge asks the obvious question: "Could *Larousse Mythologie* have
been a subsidiary inspiration?" (p. 10). However, claiming that Robbe-
Grillet constantly uses the symbolism of alchemy (this is indeed the case
in *Souvenirs du triangle d'or*) in, for example, the mysterious number

7654321, this critic neglects to take any account of the secondhand nature or overdetermination of most of Robbe-Grillet's "symbols." The "alchemical" number, for example, might just as easily be considered a "serial" number. According to Bridge, and again quite plausibly, the four stages of the Jungian individuation process or journey to self-knowledge can also be traced in Simon's adventures in *Djinn*. At first the hero is dominated by his anima, a state in which, says Jung, a man has a moody and uncontrolled disposition. Then he moves toward the union of anima or unconscious mind and conscious mind or ego-personality (the "coniunctio oppositorum"), and to the death of both and the rebirth of the "new man"—in this case perhaps Marie who survives the death of Jean/Djinn. The meaning of *Djinn*, for Bridge, can thus be found in the universal need it demonstrates in our world for this Jungian "psychic connection."

Such a reading perhaps illuminates elements of the texts, but universality, morality, absolute truth, unity, and self-knowledge are just those absolute terms under suspicion in Robbe-Grillet's writing. There is a similarly suspicious reconfiguring of elements of the Jungian *répertoire* in Robbe-Grillet's recent autofictions or "romanesques." The horse that sees its own mortality in the returning mirror of *Le Miroir qui revient,* for example, could indeed be accounted for by Jungian theory, but the horse as figure of death is omnipresent in Western culture from nineteenth-century painting to Kafka and Claude Simon.[5] A "Jungian" reading that cannot take account of the polysemous functioning of the whole work (and in this instance, the ludic juxtaposing of a classic Jungian image and a classic Lacanian one) may illuminate a critical mise en scène of Jungian mythology but is clearly reductive as an explanation of Robbe-Grillet's work.

Myth has been increasingly seen in our era as originating in individual or collective psychology within the frame of the family romance. Freud read the classical Oedipus myth and the desire for the mother, desire arising from the intensely affective infant bond, as an expression of forbidden and repressed sexual desires. According to Freud, Oedipus feels guilt for killing the father and for his sought knowledge of the body of the mother, and his self-blinding is a symbolic self-castration. In Robbe-Grillet the Freudian reading of the Greek stories in terms of the sexual desires repressed by culture has itself become a myth, a myth of our time, fragments of which are put into play along with Jungian and other stories. Boris, led by the child Jean, plays at being blind in *Djinn*. (At one point, he finds himself in a room completely full of blind men identical to himself awaiting orders from Djinn, with whom he has fallen—blindly—in love.) An old blind beggar makes a number of exaggerated appearances and plays the messenger-prophet (Tiresias) in *Trans-Europ-Express*. We recall the blinding/castrating effect of seeing the Medusa's head in classical myth and that Tiresias lost his sight when he was out hunting and, like Acteon, chanced to see the body of the goddess. The writer's literary alter egos (Jean/Boris, Henri de Corinthe, Henri Martin, Jean Marin) are said to have "péri en mer," that is, "perished at sea" or "been absorbed by the mother." (This is the case for Boris alias Jean in *Djinn*, pp. 38, 46, 93, 119, and for the Comte de Corinthe in *Le Miroir qui revient*, p. 20.)

At the end of the film *L'Eden et après*, Violette, the female protagonist, wades into the sea to fuse with the eternal mother (la mer/mère) in death, that is, in a final dissolve that may be a prelude to a rebirth in a fluid, dangerous, element recalling Kristeva's Chora or fusion with the maternal. For greater cultural or Freudian coherence, it is, of course, the female protagonist rather than a male character who seeks such a dissolution. As early as *Un Régicide* (1949), Robbe-Grillet's male protagonists express, rather, the fear of drowning. The anguish that mounts as the tide rises around the tower that is Boris's refuge and as the stones begin to crumble recurs in the short story "Le chemin du retour," published in *Instantanés*, where the protagonist is cut off by the sea among the deep and dangerous rising rock pools. Yet, paradoxically, even in this first novel, unpublished until 1978, Boris's desire to kill the king or to overpower the sirens seems to be the consequence both of his intense but dimly conscious fears of being swept away or seduced and dominated and of his need to make a connection. In *Un Régicide*, Boris attempts to resist the fascination of Aimone's siren song and the beatitudinous merging with her fluidity in the ocean in which his solitary alter ego, the man on the island, seeks solace. In a discussion of the charms of romantic opera in *Le Miroir qui revient* Robbe-Grillet, in his own critical persona, explicitly discusses and rejects what he calls the "temptation of the West" to meld with this feminine, liquid, emotional universe.

The tradition of the Pre-Raphaelite exotic decadent *femme fatale* also comes to mind in this respect. In the 1887 painting *The Depths of the Sea,* for example, Edward Burne-Jones depicts a dream world in which an ethereal, fragile mermaid triumphantly pulls an inert, sleepwalking male down among tall stone phallic columns in the liquid depths. Variants of such drowning and the analogous theme of entrapment in the tentacles of waterweed / streams of woman's hair take place in the forest in such works as John Waterhouse's 1893 *La Belle Dame Sans Merci.* Here, the knight in armor is drawn down by a gentle flower-fairy who entwines a strand of her hair of similar texture to that of the treetrunks around his neck, not unlike Robbe-Grillet's seductive forest sylphid in *Angélique.* The forest / sea for Robbe-Grillet, as for these painters, is at once a place of danger, nightmare, entrapment by the feminine, death, and evil, and of fascination and even bliss. Marie-Ange dances seductively in her diaphanous white bridal robes on the golden beach against the background of the bright blue Magrittean sea in *La Belle Captive.* Black-clad fascist soldiers erupt at the same site to seize and execute the bemused Walter Naime in a reconstitution of a well-known Goya painting of violet execution. The fiancée of Corinthe, like the beautiful captive, according to Stoltzfus, is spirit of freedom, pure fiancée, unbounded text or "parole." Yet Stoltzfus also presents her as vampire and ready-made text ("the vampiric or Balzacian narrative that is a living death").[6]

Interestingly, it is just such dissolution of self ("drowning" in the sea) or fear of danger (from the forest) that constitutes a central theme in the work of a number of modern woman writers, in the texts of Marguerite Duras or of Jeanne Hyvrard, among others. Such a self-loss in bliss or self-dissolution is not unlike the dispersion among many other conscious awarenesses or memories that Virginia Woolf's protagonists, in *Mrs Dalloway,* for example, sought in death. In Robbe-Grillet's fiction textualization of and play around such a dissolution constitutes, at the least, a humorous designation of the Freudian and artistic stories and their influence as social myth or their importance for the interpretation of his own life.

The oedipal drama, that is the young male's desire for and fear of fusion with the castrated / castrating Mother / Other and subsequent identification with the father, and the young female's identification with the mother and libidinal investment in the father is clearly at issue here. Some feminist criticism has seen the self-conscious textualization of this oedipal drama as a way of knowing, or of bringing to consciousness, and contesting the traditional hero's text of oedipal separation and subsequent virile sentimental and social conquest. I discuss the politics of this textualization of Oedipus at greater length in a later chapter but make no claim, at this point, for thematic textualization in either male or female writing as anything other than very relative "liberation."

Not only the psychological "universals" that Freud and Jung postulate but also the universal experiences that contemporary mythologists catalogue as cutting across mythologies make at least a walk-on appearance on Robbe-Grillet's stage. There has been considerable variation in the elements seen as the most universal. Cassirer presents myth as a "primal language of experience," archaic and vibrant and arising from a (hypothetical and anthropologically improbable) "primitive mentality." Other myth-critics are preoccupied with the detection of the "monomyth" or fundamental mythic pattern. For Joseph Campbell, in *The Hero with a Thousand Faces,* this is the *"rite de passage"*; the mythological adventure of the hero takes the form of separation from the world and penetration to a source of power, that is, initiation and a life-enhancing return. Raglan sees the Dying God as described in Frazer's classic work, *The Golden Bough,* as the "Ur-ritual" behind the monomyth. Eliade favors the myth of creation. For Roheim the nucleus of myth is the death and apotheosis of the Primal Father, whereas Northrop Frye gives the quest myth a central place in literature.[7] It is possible to find traces of Campbell's perilous rite de passage, or initiatory voyage, to the source of power in Robbe-Grillet's short text "Le Chemin du retour" in *Instantanés,* but here it is the process of the dreamlike, anxiety-fraught, difficult return across the turbulent eddying green sea waters of the rising tide and the sudden treacherous holes and pools along the stretch of shore (the dangerous feminine principle) that becomes the focus of the journey. It is not clear that this is a life-enhancing return. Raglan's "Ur-ritual" of the dying God perhaps has some relevance for *Un Régicide* but, here again, the sirens' song and the "hero's" phantasies distract him constantly from his political or Freudian impulses to regicide/parricide. In fact, the king that Boris, the revolutionary, seeks to kill is arguably his own authoritative alter ego,

Jean, or his more shadowy alter ego "Jean Marin" who lives by the sea ("au bord de la mer") in *Le Voyeur* and who has probable connections with both the sexual sadist of that novel and with the monstrous sailor/ the marine monster ("le monstre marin") that devours little girls, ironic alter ego of the writer in *Le Miroir qui revient.*

The death and apotheosis of the Primal Father that is the central myth for Roheim can also be read into *Un Régicide* along with the myth of the fusion with the archaic and fertile mother, but the two are contradictory and over the whole work are generally subsumed by Oedipus. In *L'Homme qui ment,* as Robbe-Grillet himself remarked at Cérisy, Boris is in search of the absent father while Jean clearly participates in patriarchal authority. Two images and sounds mark this tension throughout the work—the sound of marching male boots or of heavy feet pounding the earth and the sound of the axe in the forest cutting deep into the toppling tree, or in *L'Homme qui ment* the sound of the father falling to his death from the collapsing balcony.

Northrop Frye's quest myth is present from the first published "detective" novel and the first complex narrative itinerary in *Les Gommes* but, like the early "erasers," the object of the quest in Robbe-Grillet's work is always missing or derisory. The myth of creation also inflects the labyrinthine paths of the writer in his cell or secret room, yet the end of this creation is always, already, a kind of re-beginning. Robbe-Grillet's works, like Ouroboros, bite their tail but with a subtle difference.

Myths have been explained more generally by similarities in social experience. Bettelheim, for example, sees the need for the child to grow up and, leaving the security of the home, to move forward independently into the dangers of the world as one such powerful common experience.[8] In this century social anthropology has investigated the idea of myth as a modeling, an explanation of the world according to the historical and local organization of the particular group. The laws of the tribe found their own authority in myths, which, at the same time, satisfy the desire of human beings to understand the world and their role in it. Myth could thus be construct rather than revelation, culture rather than nature; its message relative rather than universal. The proper study of myth would be the relation between myth and social context. For Lévi-Strauss,

> Myths say nothing that teaches about the order of the world, the nature
> of the real, the origin of man or his destiny. . . . On the other hand,
> myths tell us a lot about the societies they derive from, they help to
> expose the intimate mechanisms of their functioning, they illuminate
> the *raison d'être* of beliefs, of customs and of institutions whose order-
> ing seemed incomprehensible at first sight.[9]

I argued in the earlier chapters that the new structures of Robbe-
Grillet's work (and this would include the use of myth) were connected
to the new systems of thought emerging in his time. Myth, like language,
could be considered to immobilize the world rather than release the
imagination. Robbe-Grillet's designation of the constructed, relative
nature of myth and its subsequent remaking would be a liberation.

Although versions of the widespread Cinderella myth may ascribe
quite different functions to the "stepmother" in Europe or in polygamous
Africa and may vary in meaning according to the particular social
organization, for structuralist anthropologists, they all seem to contain
a general movement from low status to high, from rags to riches—an
inversion almost invariably operated by moral (socially desirable) qualities. Robbe-Grillet, wary of the humanist connotations of the traditional
notion of "universals," has repeatedly claimed to be concerned primarily
with the "forms" and "movement" of the text, that is, with just such
inversions between binary signs. Feminist criticism has noted, critically,
as we might well also, that in the Lévi-Strauss thesis, the passage from
the state of nature to a state of culture, marked by man's ability to view
biological relations as a series of contrasts (as duality, alternation, opposition, and symmetry), constitutes, for that thinker, not so much a
phenomenon to be explained as immediately given data. Robbe-Grillet
has come increasingly to claim that the "real" emerges necessarily via
the "imaginary," and this imaginary is inevitably his own. In *L'Immortelle*
the ramparts of Byzantium, like the walls of his later "phantom city,"
are "in ruins" at the time of writing. From this "repertoire" of shared
fragments, these places must be reconstituted by the imaginary.

What the structuralist seeks, however, is a general abstract deep
structure behind relationships such as mother/son, father/son, or
father/daughter, and desire. Meaning is to be found not in the individual
elements but in hidden synchronic patterns of relationship between them.

For Lévi-Strauss, the notable characteristic of mythical thought is the organization of things in terms of their opposites (wet/dry, cooked/uncooked, earth/sky, male/female, town/bush, natural/supernatural) and the subsequent need to find a third term to mediate the first two and overcome the contradiction. The interpretation Lévi-Strauss gives of the Oedipus myth functions in these terms. The myth, examined over the whole cycle, gives pairs of antithetical relations—in the stories of Cadmus, founder of Thebes; of Europa and her adventures with Zeus in the form of a bull; of the Spartoï springing fully formed from the dragon's teeth sown in the earth; of Laius and Jocasta; their feared son and heir, Oedipus; and finally of Antigone, the defiant and dutiful daughter. Cadmus seeking out his errant sister and the incest of Oedipus with his mother represent an overrating of kin relations; the Spartoï killing one another and Oedipus killing his father represent an underrating of kin relations.

The centrality of kinship relations in Robbe-Grillet's own life, the mother/son, father/son, and father/daughter relationships, are most evident in the "autobiographical" *Le Miroir qui revient* and *Angélique ou l'enchantement*. In the latter, Robbe-Grillet admits that he imagines his very independent and competent wife Catherine as his child-wife or little girl. However, overrating and underrating (implication in a relationship and resistance to it, particularly in the case of the mother) seem to be inextricably mixed. It would be difficult to find any clear pattern in the fragments that concern Robbe-Grillet's relation with his (dead) mother in *Le Miroir qui revient* and indiscreet, presumptuous, and not particularly helpful to attempt naively to psychoanalyze a writer whose life work, a similar enterprise, is there before us.

At the beginning of *Le Miroir qui revient,* there is an explicit, preemptive, psychoanalytic interpretation of Robbe-Grillet's descriptions of the Jura mountains, where he spent his childhood vacations, and of the dangerous seas of Brittany, where he grew up. These descriptions of formative places, claims Robbe-Grillet, evidently represent the two opposing metaphors of the female sexual organs—the soft green mossy hollow and the dark and dangerous cavern where the octopus (like Ian Fleming's popular *Octopussy?*) lurks. The two could be considered to be a separating out of their original conflation in the deep green sea-hole ("le trou d'eau profond et vert") in *Un Régicide* (p. 31). There are

other somewhat perverse and disconnected allusions to Oedipus elsewhere in this text, including the early memory of the two-year-old child
who, refusing a cup of milk, clamors for mother's milk ("lait Maman")
and the more curious episode of the mother receiving guests, her tame
bat hidden and moving beneath her blouse. Most of these references
are contradictory. In the little boy with long curly hair who "looks like
a girl" there is an intense complicity with the mother, born both of
scientific (masculine?) interest in the small and complex living organisms
of the world around them and the (ironic?) recognition of the mother's
irrational (feminine?) intuition and power. (The mother, for example,
predicts the exact date of her death, date imprinted on her sewing-
machine.) There is a strong identification with this "exceptional" mother
whose voice the writer claims to hear still long after her death. And
yet the writer gives negative accounts of her illness and a certain lack
of energy, of her strange provocations—for example, pushing her children perilously close to the front of a moving bus or removing her son's
head-covering in front of the school principal, apparently deliberately
humiliating and breaking faith with her child whose forbidden long curls
come tumbling down. The mother's tenacious right-wing political con-
victions and refusal to accept the reality of the Holocaust also figure,
touched with some ambivalence.

In the period of the development of his precocious sadistic sexuality
during which, as the writer "confesses" in *Angélique ou l'enchantement,*
two china dolls became the objects of his persecutions, the child experiences a guilty resentment at the disapproving surveillance sensed
behind the heavy red curtains between his bedroom and the living room.
Later, perceived by her now grown-up son as rejecting coarse male
sexuality, the mother is suspected of having had a lesbian attraction to
her close dentist-friend. Although her social roles are essentially limited
to the domestic, and she is a figure of the unknowable Other, the mother
is never lavender and lace. She could be read as a figure of authority
(a phallic mother, denying lack), while the caring father is somewhat
feminized.

Much can be made of this confession and false confession, the
contradictory complicity with and critical distance toward the mother,
but the languages of phantasy and fact, of irony and confidence are
inextricably mixed in *Le Miroir,* and I will not attempt to unravel the

complex, overdetermined knots and risk destroying the texture of the
fabric of the work. Any interpretive enterprise seems better carried out
by a close reading of the forms and of the thematics of all the texts
(and the whole text), together with attention to their distinctive texture
and weave.

Lévi-Strauss finds a second mediated opposition in the Oedipus
myth. The Spartoï suggest the autochthonous origin of man (springing
from the dragons' teeth sown in the earth) while Oedipus suggests
a nonautochthonous origin. Oedipus does indeed turn out (and like
Macbeth, for his woe) to be a man of woman born. Susan Suleiman
reads *Projet* as a drama of the myth of male self-engenderment, or "men
without women." In the later autofictions the mythical, phantastic, generator cum figure of paternity and of historical determinisms, the Comte
de Corinthe, are strikingly central. The mother figure as fertility or
origin or indeed object of sexual desire is hardly present in Robbe-
Grillet's work. Desire is displaced from the maternal to the child-woman,
Salome or Angelica, without any evident reproductive function.

For Lévi-Strauss the elements of myth derive from a limited repertoire constantly rearranged to take on new meanings from their total
configuration, by a technique he terms bricolage, closely related to
Robbe-Grillet's serial and generative organizations of mythological elements.[10] Joan DeJean, in *Literary Fortifications,* a study of the defensive
mechanisms at work in classical texts,[11] argues that such apparently
formal orders as bricolage may not be as neutral as they seem. Bricolage,
like pastiche, which also imposes a new function on an old one, is
always equivocal. Postmodern literary texts may, she claims, themselves
become "classical," that is, enter their own age of the fortress and of
self-defensiveness, protecting by their formal mechanisms material that
might otherwise be put in question. For DeJean bricolage creates the
dissonance and obliqueness seen by Lacanian theory as apt to characterize the defensive displacement of obsessional neurotics. Robbe-Grillet's
writer-investigator, we remember, is situated in the obsessive cell of
generation and criminality. He is himself the mysterious criminal investigating himself; he is "on his own trail."

It was to the writing of Roland Barthes that Robbe-Grillet referred
consistently rather than to that of Lévi-Strauss. In a long essay[12] entitled
"Le Mythe aujourd'hui" that follows the now well-known analysis of

the "mythologies" often fixed in clichés or stereotypes that he sees as
a secondary language (*Mythologies, 1952*), Barthes defines myth as a
"récit," or narrative, a "form," a "message" (the arrow that signifies a
challenge), a kind of "discourse," a "mode of signification," and thus
a part of the science of semiotics. Postulating, as Robbe-Grillet also
appears to, that there are no substantive limits to mythical material and
that everything perceived as such is myth, Barthes too is interested in
the limited historical and social determinations of the myths that can
be found in the most everyday experiences, the principles at work in
their elaboration. ("Le mythe est une parole choisie par l'histoire et il
ne saurait surgir de la nature des choses.")[13] Barthes's study of myth is
synchronic. It includes languages, photography, advertising, ceremonial,
all the sources of knowledge that constitute Western consciousness (and
in particular French consciousness) at a given time. Wrestling, striptease,
fashion, and an advertisement for Astra margarine constitute examples
of contemporary mythologizing and reflect the codes governing their
elaboration. These codes derive from the representation that is constructed by society and imposed on us ("que la bourgeoisie se fait et
nous fait") of the relation between humankind and the world.

Robbe-Grillet similarly insisted that the elements and images his
work presents were taken from popular contemporary mythology, examined ironically, and exposed as representations without depth, neither
natural nor eternal. He claimed that what he calls stereotypes are also
"rétrogradés," that is, that they regress or are broken down, losing their
meaning to become simply the raw materials from which the text is
made, and are given new meaning by the principles at work in the
elaboration of the whole text. While this is clearly true in terms of the
functioning of the text, it is also the case that what Robbe-Grillet calls
stereotypes may be seen as a particular complex of representations
selected from Western society's more underground contemporary mythologies. This complex begins with the very old story of the mermaid
Aimone, in the earliest novel, *Un Régicide,* with Aimone's brown tresses
of aquatic plants slowly swaying after love or Aimone "endormie à portée
de sa main dans une pose abandonnée, étoile de mer oubliée sur la
grève, sans défense, à sa merci" [asleep within reach of his hand in an
abandoned pose, starfish forgotten on the strand, defenceless, at his
mercy] (p. 162). From this provocative sexualized other who evokes the

violence of the slapping waves or the knife of the assassin, to the rape, sawing up, and burning of the genitals of the female mannequins in a waste-lot at the end of *Projet,* and the scenes of incest and sacrilegiously crucified and tortured young communicants in *Topologie, Souvenirs,* and *Le Jeu avec le feu,* the set of mythologies Robbe-Grillet chooses to present is clearly a sado-erotic one.

It is the critique of the "naturalness" of the relationship that Barthes discerns between human beings and the world in contemporary popular culture or mythology that subtends Robbe-Grillet's ironic game with the conventions of the novel and with the mythologies that impose the "representational fallacy" (the claim that language or myth is a mirror of, or parallels, the real world that it expresses). But what is the connection here between myth and choice of mythic complex? Are all myths equal?

In "Le Mythe aujourd'hui" Barthes argued that our historically based culture or mythology presents itself as natural, its organization as necessary, and its human nature as universal. An ideologically based and humanly transformed nature becomes an eternal, unchanging nature. Things are presented as necessarily rational, destined for man. The world provides myth with a historically defined "real"; myth in return constructs a "natural" image of the world. Robbe-Grillet claims that in his work, myth does the opposite, designating constantly its own artificiality and its "nature" as "construct." In "Histoire de rats," a transgressive short text published in the special issue of *Obliques* devoted to Robbe-Grillet's work,[14] a description of a young woman victim, naked, kneeling imprisoned in a cage with rats gnawing at her breasts, a uniformed S.S. officer approaching her from behind, phallus erect, suddenly freezes, releasing the tension of horror and fascination that the reader has been experiencing as the (meta)text designates the story as a page in a sado-erotic sex-shop magazine. Yet this pornographic collective representation or stereotype is both the "construct" of a historically defined period and of a myth-set whose origin is everwhere and nowhere and the choice of an individually situated "constructor" selecting his material.

The *Dictionnaire Hachette* of 1980, prefaced by Barthes, gives the following definition of myth (not under "mythe," but under "mythologie," defined as "a twentieth-century term" and certainly inspired by the title of Barthes's book): "Ensemble de représentations idéalisées d'un objet investi de valeurs imaginaires liées à la mode, à la tradition, aux aspirations collectives, inconscientes" [Set of idealized representations of an object invested with imaginary values connected to fashion, to tradition, to unconscious, collective aspirations]. Barthes situates the inclusiveness of this definition in the richness of mythical signification that has its roots not in the arbitrary or empty nature of the signifier as language does but in a partial motivation of myth by analogy. For myth, he claims, is a metalanguage; that is, myth is elaborated from a preexisting semiological chain composed of signifiers and signifieds. In myth, the sign (which, for Barthes, is a synthesis of the two) is appropriated in a second elaboration of meaning in which it becomes a signifier empty of meaning. One of the two examples Barthes gives of this operation has interesting parallels with the underlying structure of Robbe-Grillet's *Djinn,* in which the peeling away of the intrigue reveals an underlying structure that is that of the progressively complex presentation of the rules of the grammar of French.

Barthes cites, from his school Latin grammar book, a phrase "quia ego nominor leo" [for I am called lion]. A primary semiological system calls upon the open-ended concepts associated with the animal "lion," the meanings of "am called," etc. In a secondary system, however, the sign could be emptied of its immediate linguistic content and "for I am called lion" could then serve as an empty signifier to designate a Latin rule of grammar, the agreement of the predicate. The sign thus regresses to form. The form does not totally suppress the initial meaning but rather impoverishes it, distances it, places it in reserve: "une réserve d'histoire qu'il est possible d'éloigner et de rappeler dans une alternance rapide" [a reserve of story that can be distanced or recalled in rapid alternation]. Could we postulate that an analogous relationship between form and thematic content is at play in Robbe-Grillet's work? The description that follows of the deformation that the myth imposes could be an account of a Robbe-Grillet text:

A la surface du langage, quelque chose ne bouge plus: l'usage de la signification est là, tapi derrière le fait, lui communiquant une allure notificatrice, mais en même temps, le fait paralyse l'intention, lui donne comme un malaise d'immobilité: pour l'innocenter, il la glace. C'est que le mythe est une parole *volée et rendue*. Seulement la parole que l'on rapporte n'est plus tout à fait celle que l'on a dérobée: en la rapportant, on ne l'a pas exactement remise à sa place. C'est ce bref larcin, ce moment furtif d'un truquage, qui constitue l'aspect transi de la parole mythique.

[On the surface of language, something is no longer moving: the use of meaning is there, lying low behind the fact, giving it an appearance of notifying, but at the same time, the fact paralyzes the intention, gives it an uneasy kind of immobility: to make it innocent, it freezes it. For myth is a language ("parole") that has been *stolen and returned.* Only the language that has been brought back is not exactly the same as the language that was taken away: when it was brought back, it was not returned exactly to its place. It is this brief larceny, this furtive moment of trickery that constitutes the frozen aspect of mythical language.][15]

The reader of the Robbe-Grillet text who mistakes the semiological system for an inductive system, who sees the equivalences posed as causal, natural, or factual, is brought up sharply by the sudden freezing of the image, or of the description of narrated event, designated as representation (photo, comic, advertisement, theatrical representation) and subsequently itself often duplicated as a representation of a representation in a process of nesting or embedding. The implicit violence of *Le Voyeur* is explicitly designated as a stereotype immobilized on a film billboard representing a frail young girl threatened by a brutal male giant, in a painting of a young girl kneeling to say her prayers, in a newspaper clipping that recounts a sexual crime, and in an island legend of the ancient sacrifice of a maiden thrown from the cliff to the devouring marine monster for the rites of spring. The stories of *La Maison de rendez-vous,* of call girls and drug runners in Hong Kong, stories generated by a mannequin in the window of a saddler's shop walking a dog on a braided leather leash (the whips in the shop window are a "homage" to, or unknowledged quotation from, *Histoire d'O*), animate from a pornographic comic strip swept up and examined by an old Chinese street cleaner (sweeping up the detritus of civilization), or are tales told by an old actress, Jacqueline, the name of the victim in *Le Voyeur.* The women immobilize into mannequins or into the statue of a "frail" victim carried off by King Kong; the elements of the story are discovered as stage props stored in a courtyard.

In the films *L'Année dernière à Marienbad* and *La Belle Captive* the red curtains borrowed from Magritte repeatedly frame the scenes; "real" stories become spectacle on a stage. The text reveals its own functioning, its construction of meaning at the level of the narration and in the processes of theatricalization and interior duplications. Meanings are momentarily suspended or revealed as sleight of hand in a metaleptic sliding from one level of textual functioning to another. They are a story animated from a scene figured on a character's ring, Barthes's "truquage." Yet, here again, the repeated mirroring effects make the relative limitation and homogeneity of the images chosen more evident. In *Topologie* and *Souvenirs* the mirrors themselves become more complex. These latter have, in fact, never exactly reproduced an original, and now they are formally conceived as a kind of interaction or imaginative game between two creative works (images and texts) that are not constrained in any way to represent or respect the "generating" text. (Delvaux and Rauschenberg were to produce one artwork to be sent to the writer and used to inspire a response; on receipt of a second Robbe-Grillet text the artists were to produce their own idiosyncratic reactions.)

A detailed and systematic examination of the Oedipus myth and its mirrorings through Robbe-Grillet's creative work may be helpful in bringing the functioning and meanings of the practice of "truquage" into clearer focus, although there are a number of other mythic complexes present that we might also choose. Christian stories, for example, appear in various forms. Peter Tremewan[16] has searched out in *Les Gommes* the allusions to myths of the Old and New Testaments. Wallas/Garinati is "a savior" out of the blue or "fallen from heaven" ("tombé du ciel" [p. 37]). Indirect references to Jonas—"Qu'est-ce qu'il attend là? Qu'il passe une baleine?" (pp. 29–30) [What is he waiting there for? For a whale to go by?] and to the Red Sea miracle prepare the way for allusions to the resurrection. Garinati will return to the scene of the crime, freely, "lucid and risen," a modern-day Lazarus ("Il [Garinati] y retournera librement, lucide et ressuscité" [p. 242]). In the later novels and films, scenes drawn from Christian legends of virgin martyrs and from church ritual link the sacrifice of the (feminine) victim and redemption, the sacred and the transgressive, in a sacrilegious deconstructive play with the rites of communion and crucifixion.

But returning to the much more pervasive Oedipus story in the "detective" novel *Les Gommes,* we find numerous clues to the classical tale, as Morrissette demonstrated in his very early study "Oedipe ou le cercle fermé."[17] Most of these fragments of myth freeze to statues and photographs, or they are animated from such reproductions. They are uncertain (the missing letters on the eraser could as easily indicate the word *Didier* as *Oedipe*), or appear, like the hero-investigator-criminal's "swollen feet" (a literal translation of the name Oedipus), as completely contrived. The eraser is, we are told, a "fictitious" object attributed to a "fictitious brand name" ("attribué à une marque fictive" [p. 133]). The text makes its own humorous comments on the myth, for example, on the drinking of the sheep's milk as unhygienic ("peu hygiénique") and alters classical details comically or antiheroically. The "lizard" has not quite the same tragic connotations as the "serpent" it replaces.

The conventions of tragedy are present in the prologue, five acts, and epilogue of the classical tragedy and perhaps in the reference to a perfectly regulated machinery that controls the actions of the protagonists. Destiny makes an appearance in the modified quotation from Sophocles, "le temps qui veille à tout, a donné la solution malgré toi" [time that sees all has found you out despite yourself] and is reinforced by a description of tarot cards that function as generators of events, evocation of hidden meanings, and metaphor of the ludic, random, but predestined, "chaotic" functioning of the text. Oedipus/Wallas, detective, is led from clue to clue in a circle to kill his father/the victim and discover that the mysterious criminal is himself. Morrissette recalls arguments for a close relationship between the psychological and aesthetic bases of the Greek tragedy and the detective novel, both containing the dissimulation of a mystery that the informed reader watches the hero discover, reversals of the situation, recognition, and catharsis.

However, although Morrissette assumes that there is at least the phantasy of an incestuous relation between the desirable Madame Dupont, seller of erasers, and Wallas alias André V.S, and therefore an oedipal content, the Sphinx as an old drunkard, the plague as a series of unmotivated assassinations by a secret (terrorist) organization, the oedipal journey to revelation and self-knowledge as a deceiving of the protagonist by a manipulative text hardly constitute psychological depth. Is there ethical and tragic significance in Robbe-Grillet's staging of fragments of classical tragedy and Freudian myth? Or is there rather another kind of intellectual excitement, a skeptical deconstructive challenge, a new different kind of catharsis in the inversions operated?

The old myths of depth that Robbe-Grillet attacked in *Pour un nouveau roman* ("Les vieux mythes de la profondeur" p. 55) are at least partially displaced by an examination of the functioning of this mythological language and by a work of language on language that integrates the subversion of ready-made mythology (regicide/parricide, incest/the transgressive violence of desire, tragedy, destiny, the gods) and the construction of new mythology. Lévi-Strauss describes this movement of *bricolage:* "Dans cette incessante reconstruction à l'aide des mêmes matériaux, ce sont toujours d'anciennes fins qui sont appelées à jouer le rôle de moyens, les signifiés se changent en signifiants et vice-versa" [In this incessant reconstruction with the same basic material, it is always former ends that are called upon to play the role of means, the signifieds change into signifiers and vice versa].[18]

The functioning of elements from the Oedipus myth as narrative material is not restricted to *Les Gommes.* Europa and Zeus in the form of the black bull find a place in the panoply of sado-erotic images in *Topologie d'une cité fantôme.* Their subversion, or "unmaking," is increasingly operated by humor. In *Djinn,* where the hero's blindness is perhaps also a metaphor of the "scotoma" ("blind spot") that love for Djinn provokes, the references to myth are openly playful and often inexact—gross winks at the reader. "Quant à ma récente tranformation en ce personnage classique d'aveugle guidé par un enfant, elle représentait sans aucun doute une façon d'éveiller la compassion des gens, et par conséquent d'endormir leur méfiance" [As for my recent transformation into that classical character, the blind man guided by a child, it represented without any doubt a way of arousing people's compassion and consequently of lulling their mistrust] (p. 66). Crossing the street with the aid of his white stick, the hero points out his Oedipus complex with humor: "Je dois avoir un sacré complexe d'Oedipe" [I must have a major Oedipus complex] (p. 101). It is hardly a surprise to learn in the epilogue that Dr. Morgan was treating Simon for eye trouble and that: "Morgan, féru de psychanalyse avait tout de suite pensé à un banal complexe d'Oedipe. Le malade s'était contenté de lui répondre en riant, qu'il n'avait rien à faire à Cologne" [Morgan, well up in psychoanalysis had immediately thought of a banal Oedipus complex. The patient, however, answered laughingly that he had no business in Cologne] (p. 145). *Cologne* is evidently *Colonus* and the references to Oedipus humorous.

In an enthusiastic review of *Djinn* entitled "Oedipe à Cologne" [Oedipus at Cologne] Jean-Jacques Brochier places this oedipal figure at the center not only of this work but of all writing projects:

> If we had to make a . . . judgment of what Robbe-Grillet brings us, particularly in this latest novel, it would be the following. First of all, the foregrounding of the character Oedipus, who, at the crossroads of incest, of the murder of the father, of blindness, of prophecy, and of wandering is doubtless the essential character who makes all literature possible. Furthermore, the humor that is not derision . . . forces us to accept that writing is not reality.[19]

The *signifiés* of Oedipus are not limited to those of Greek classical theater and Freudian analysis or even to narrative functions. Barthes sees the story of the anguish of the proud king of Thebes as underscored by the "relation de force" and the general desire to retain personal and political power, rather than by sexual desire. René Girard also moves away from traditional literary criticism of the Greek plays in terms of tragic fatality.[20] Behind Oedipus, Girard discerns the representation of a social mechanism that conceals in myth the truth of an original human violence of which sexual violence is simply a derivative. Girard postulates the existence of a self-perpetuating and undifferentiating chain of aggression and revenge that the social order seeks to break or short-circuit through the sacrifice of a designated victim. This inner violence and this social disorder are situated by myth in the sacred, that is, as exterior to humankind. The plague over Thebes, for example, and the social crisis it suggests are projected outside as divine retribution for the tragic inner guilt of Oedipus. His parricide and incest are exemplary crimes, which, for Girard, in the mixing of blood and of roles that should be kept differentiated, imply the reciprocal violence and lack of differentiation that threaten social order. Order is restored and the group reunified by the collective cathartic transfer of guilt/violence to the one.

Paradoxically, however, as in Sophocles' *Oedipus at Colonus*, the victim is both the harmful element to be driven out and the savior whose sacrifice protects others, both criminal and hero who, in his subsequent exemplary and expiatory wanderings, is dutifully served by the maiden Antigone. Although the early Robbe-Grillet would have rejected the idea of an original, natural, and eternal human violence and its metaphysical implications, his choice of stereotypes in which the combination of the sacred, the sacrificial, the sexual, and the transgressive are predominant is a function at least of a desire to illuminate the hidden social and perhaps psychological mechanisms that operate behind our myths. For Robbe-Grillet as for Girard, Oedipus is a locus of an inversion of signs; he is the anathema and the hero-savior, the criminal and the slayer of monsters (the Sphinx). Robbe-Grillet's figure of the writer-prisoner in the generative cell-prison, seeking to prove his innocence and discovering his guilt, is similarly an exemplary figure: criminal and investigative-hero.

The Freudian myth that derived from the classical story of Oedipus has itself been read as a limitation, a narrowing by a particular social and moral conditioning of a potentially much more powerful discovery. In *L'Anti-Oedipe* Gilles Deleuze and Félix Guattari criticize Freud who discovers desire as libido for maintaining his discovery of the power of sexuality in the overly narrow framework of Oedipus and Narcissus. For Deleuze Freud's belief in the authority and superiority of the father, determined by his time, is at the root of his theories. The Law, Oedipus, and the pleasure of transgression are constructions of Freud's own sub-conscious, and Oedipus is the story of a long-standing error that has blocked the productive forces of the unconscious and the "revolutionary power of desire," imprisoning the latter in the system of the family. "Qu'est-ce qu'Oedipe? L'histoire d'une longue "erreur" qui bloque les forces productrices de l'inconscient, les fait jouer sur un théâtre d'ombres où se perd la puissance révolutionnaire du désir, les emprisonne dans le système de la famille"[21] [What is Oedipus? The story of a long "error" that blocks the productive forces of the unconscious, makes them play out on a stage of shadows where the revolutionary power of desire is lost, imprisons them in the system of the family]. Freud also strength-ened the dichotomy between male and female by associating the mother with sexuality and the pleasure principle and the father with denial, restraint, and authority. For Freud, as Wilhelm Reich interprets him, the id—dark and inaccessible, a chaos or a chasm, a cauldron of exci-tations and a death instinct—is associated with the feminine. Although the femme fatale or nineteenth-century female vampire was imaginatively conceived of as a tyrannical master of the ego, weakening, beheading, or blinding (castrating) the male, paradoxically women were seen as less able to exert that power of the ego over the id that Freud likened to the mastery of a rider over his horse. Variations of such Freudian metaphors find echoes in *Topologie* where the blond equestrienne riding into the water is shot by the hunter-writer.

The Freudian Oedipus, the classical Oedipus of tragedy and destiny, and their shared inability to account fully for violence and desire are made visible in *Les Gommes* in the play of the text, which ceases to point to existing meanings and claims instead to designate its own construction, a construction that can be seen clearly in the author's treatment of the eraser motif. The absent "eraser" that gives *Les Gommes* its name is associated with the psychologically colored adjectives "soft" ("douce") and "crumbly" ("friable"). Recurring in the text at moments when Wallas notices the low throaty laugh or the provocative movement of the hips first of the young "saleswoman" and her "lèvres charnues légèrement entrouvertes" [full, slightly opened lips] (p. 66), then of the "épouse trop charnelle" [too carnal wife], possibly his own mother and fifteen years younger than her husband, the eraser acquires a metaphorical or mythical significance by metonymy and becomes a "sign" of erotic desire. The text insists on this artificial process of the construction of meaning by circulating the adjective "douce" [soft/gentle]. Pauline, object of the aquatic phantasies of the "patron" who frames the story, is described as "la douce Pauline," and as the gentle Pauline, who died in a strange fashion. Setting the scene at the beginning of the novel, the boss attempts to clean away obstinate stains ("taches") and put order into the bar. At the end of this opening scene (and again at the very end of the novel), as he gazes into the murky shadows of the aquarium and remembers, "the boss" is himself dissolved in the kaleidoscope of phantasmatic and watery forms that include the image of the desired, dead Pauline. What is immobilized here, caught in the act (of creating arbitrary meaning), Barthes would claim, continues to have a signifying function.

The "soft" eraser with its "rounded" corners is opposed to the hard paperweight cube with "murderous edges." These two objects, with their adjectives marked respectively by female and male features, have been interpreted as metaphors, representing desire for the mother and the wish for the death of the father. Such early critics as Barthes and the Marxist critic Leenhardt insisted on the material and objective character of the eraser, and the term "corrélatif" was coined by Morrissette to replace "métaphore." Later critics Ricardou and Heath stressed the materiality of the text itself and its generation of meanings. Ricardou argued, for example,[22] that the violent events of Le Voyeur are tricks of metaphorical process generated by the description of the quay as Mathias's boat approaches the quayside ("sans garde-fou qui plonge dans l'eau du port" [without a guard-rail that plunges into the waters of the port] [p.13]) and the coils of rope rolled "strangle-tight" ("serrés à l'étranglement" [p. 10]). For Ricardou, the eraser would be an arbitrary signifiant and not an objective corrélatif.

By applying Barthes's analysis of "myth" to Robbe-Grillet's work, we find the fascination of the eraser in the hovering of the text between primary and secondary meanings. The secondary system does not obscure the primary linguistic system, which is both "eraser" as an arbitrary signifiant and its multiple signifiés (among them, the concept of erasing, which in its turn becomes a metaphor for the functioning of the fiction), but momentarily suspends or distances it.

The erasers of the title on which Wallas's desire is projected or that generate his desire are indeterminately polysemous signs, an unmaking of the Freudian signifié of oedipal desire and the classical signifiés "tragedy" and "destiny" and, on the metatextual level, a reference to the writer's relationship with his text. Other mythic complexes are contained or generated by the title. In a similar interchangeability of container and contained elsewhere in the work, Dans le labyrinthe produces a soldier-Theseus seeking his way in a maze of streets marked by similarity, doubt, and repetition, and evokes a labyrinth that is the central mythological and structural metaphor of the modern and the postmodern writing quests. L'Homme qui ment generates a series of men "who lie"—Don Juan; Boris, resistance fighter who is also Jean, collaborator; Trintignant, the actor who plays Boris; and Robbe-Grillet, the filmmaker-writer himself. L'Immortelle is an enigmatic feminine flower, tulip or forget-me-not (l'éternel féminin) and a symbol of rebirth, the Immortal One or the phoenix rising once again from her ashes in flames, and the victim resuscitated only to die again. L'Eden et après calls upon the biblical myths of Eden and the Fall to produce a student café, L'Eden, and its own problematic Eve and myth of female sexual liberation as Eve/Violette smears herself in ecstasy with a gelatinous red paste that resembles sperm and blood. (For the moment we note in passing that, ravished by Arab horsemen, imprisoned and tortured before she returns to her "initiation" by the blue-eyed stranger/sculptor, Duchemin/Deutschman, Violette's sexual "liberation" poses questions for the female reader who might ask whose liberation this really is.) *Souvenirs du triangle d'or* has suggested a golden triangle that is a mathematical form and aesthetic perfection, a mysterious area of the ocean, and a geographical area where "heroin" is produced, but in the novel the generative metaphor seems to be, above all, the pubic triangle of the sex of the heroine(s). However, the text explicitly replaces the word "sexuel" by "textuel." "Textual" rather than "sexual" faults will be punished. All these readings involve a form of quest myth that both suggests that the answer is already always given (if no longer by fate) and is to be constructed, once again, by reworking the material given or reanimating the representation. The mythic complexes evoked are evidently polysemous and fragmented, classical *and* contemporary, and not continuously coherent. In *Dans le labyrinthe* the labyrinth is the creation of a writer inside a closed room seeking analogies with the outside to enable his text to pass from one to the other, the labyrinth of textual creation, even though the archetypal figures of the wandering soldier with his box, the boy, the woman, once invented by the text, become signs whose presence even their inventor must contend with. These figures accumulate secondary mythical meanings that their immobilization in a painting cannot completely dispel. *L'Immortelle* is a play on the word's meanings, both "flower" and "woman," but it also films a real woman, actress Françoise Brion, whose presence generates meanings. *L'Eden* is the name of a bar in Paris where the action begins; the quest is past, present, and future indeterminately, Eden and after, quest of deconstruction and reconstruction. Its pleasure as in the later films is above all in the slow sliding of sound and sense.

But the question arises once again. Why Oedipus and why transgressive sexuality, recursively, among all the possible originary or generated objects or "correlatives"? Or, why did the "arbitrary" central signifiant just happen to be desire, a desire that becomes an increasingly visible aspect of the narratives? In *Topologie d'une cité fantôme,* the "cité fantôme" is the domain of the imagination and of the Freudian pleasure principle ("l'immense cité des plaisirs—avant de m'endormir" [the immense city of pleasures—before I fall asleep] of the beginning pages), and the text is constructed from fragments taken from Freud's interpretation of the repressions and displacements and fetishistic mechanisms operating in Jensen's *Gradiva* (the curve of the foot of the antique statue, the bird in the cage outside the window of the beloved, butterflies, the buried city Pompeii, and Vesuvius, the smoking volcano).[23]

The writing and the filmic images themselves are increasingly eroticized. André Gardies expresses this with finesse in an article in the volume of *Obliques* devoted to Robbe-Grillet in which the critic coins a hybrid term from erotic and textual, "l'érotuelle," to describe this work. It is Robbe-Grillet's text, he claims, and not his thematics, that gives access to the erotic: "l'érotique du texte, faite de cérémonie rituelle minutieusement réglée, fictionnelle aussi bien que narrative" [the erotic of the text, constituted by minutely regulated ceremony, fictional as well as narrative].[24]

Gardies's interpretation of the text as metafiction and of writing as the real ecstasy and torture has obvious connections with the psychoanalytical thesis of the sexual overdetermination of all writing and Roland Barthes's now notorious claims that the writer plays with (and around) the mother's body ("L'écrivain est quelqu'un qui joue avec le corps de sa mère").[25] We are now back to Oedipus but at a greater distance, or on a "double circuit" like Mathias in *Le Voyeur.* Sex has slipped to text, the writing of torture and ecstasy to the torture and ecstasy of writing.

Discussing the forms of the pleasure of reading/writing, Susan Winnett[26] quotes de Lauretis quoting Scholes (in the closed circulation/ dialectics of names and ideas that characterizes much contemporary critical work and is of the kind staged critically in Robbe-Grillet's work): "The archetype of fiction is the sexual act. . . . For what connects fiction—and music—with sex is the fundamental orgastic rhythm of tumescence and detumescence, of tension and resolution, of intensification to the point of climax and consummation."[27] Winnett argues that the ideology of representation based on the oedipal model of narrative as Peter Brooks articulates this in "Freud's Masterplot"[28] in terms of arousal (incipience), desire or intention (for an end), discharge or return to equilibrium-death is derived from male sexuality. For Winnett the patriarchy, which has "a simultaneously blind and enlightened investment both in the forms of its pleasure and in its conscious valorization and less conscious mystification of them,"[29] obliges the female reader to experience reading pleasure through a homosocial cultural program of pleasure that does not take account of female difference(s). "In the erotics of oedipal transmission, the woman is always a stage (in both senses of the word) for or in the working out of a problem of paternal interdiction, towards the moment of 'significant discharge' when the son frees himself from the nets of paternal restriction and forges a self-creation—however ironized this process may be."[30] In the same volume of essays, however, Richard Levin argues that "the text's masculine project (or phantasy) is always subverted by a feminine subject, often embodied in an absent but omnipresent mother."[31] Barthes, as Suleiman pointed out, gendered the traditional text of beginnings, middles, and ends as feminine in order, apparently, to make its dislocation oedipal. (His "new" text of bliss/"jouissance" was gendered "masculine.") Robbe-Grillet's case is evidently more complex than Winnett's analysis would suggest. His apparently "feminine" text of *modernité* is not a traditional text, and it does not replicate the hypothesized model of male desire, of tumescence and detumescence. Indeed most male-authored postmodern, international literature of literary merit (Salman Rushdie's *The Satanic Verses* and Umberto Eco's *Foucault's Pendulum* come to mind) would, I suspect, also be implicated in what Winnett argues is a "feminine" re-conceiving of issues of incipience, repetition, and closure and be open to subversion of their "masculine" projects by "feminine" figures. Nor is Robbe-Grillet's new text simply subversion of a traditional "masculine" project by "feminine" figures of chaos. In Robbe-Grillet's work these feminine bodies, as I suggested earlier, are the objectified site of the battle of the sexes/texts. The sea for Duchemin or for the narrator of *Topologie* can only be approached by first negotiating the slippery and dangerous steps ("marches glissantes").

This site of attractive feminine fluidity and unpredictable but infinite recurrence, as "it was recounted or as it will be recounted later, I don't know any more" [comme il a été dit ou comme il sera dit plus tard, je ne sais plus] (*Souvenirs,* p. 20), is, at least potentially, complementary to the masculine, oedipal site of conflict with the father's law. The orgastic moment of an omnipotent self-creation may be a temptation, but it too is an ever-recurring need in a text marked by rebeginnings and lack of resolution.

To attempt to draw some conclusions, it appears that although the analogies with the functioning of the Barthesian sign do provide a useful understanding of the *modernité* of the functionings of myth in Robbe-Grillet's texts, the pursuit of the mythologies of Oedipus in this chapter has not been particularly productive of clear meanings. Mathias had often heard the story of his mother's death, his father's remarriage, his aunt as substitute mother and stepmother, but this does not explain his collection of pieces of string or his fascination with little Violet. At every turn this more powerful and pervasive myth—the myth of the siren and the sadist (or Andromeda chained to the rock for the sea monster, sacrificed prostitute, virgin princess, or shepherdess)—seemed to subtend the one investigated. This myth appears in detail in *Le Voyeur:*

La voix basse du narrateur se perdait dans le tumulte . . . Mathias . . . comprit néanmoins, grâce à la lenteur et aux répétitions incessantes du vieillard, qu'il s'agissait d'une ancienne légende du pays—dont il n'avait pourtant jamais entendu parler dans son enfance: une jeune vierge, chaque année au printemps, devait être précipitée du haut de la falaise pour apaiser le dieu des tempêtes et rendre la mer clémente aux voyageurs et aux marins. Jailli de l'écume, un monstre gigantesque au corps de serpent et à la gueule de chien dévorait vivante la victime, sous l'oeil du sacrificateur. Sans aucun doute c'était la mort de la petite bergère qui avait provoqué ce récit.

[The narrator's low voice was lost in the noise . . . Mathias . . . understood nonetheless, thanks to the old man's slow speech and his continual repetitions . . . that he was recounting an old local legend—which he [Mathias], however, had never heard of in his childhood: every year in spring, a young virgin had to be thrown from the top of the cliff to appease the god of storms and render the sea kind to travelers and to sailors. Rising up from the sea-spray, a gigantic monster with the body of a serpent and the mouth of a dog would devour the victim alive beneath the gaze of the sacrificer. Doubtless, it was the death of the little shepherdess that had provoked this story.] (p. 221)

This myth poses a number of questions, particularly for a female reader, not dissimilar to those posed by the nature of the pleasure of the reading of the traditional text. (Why desire? What desire? Whose desire?) Investigating meaning and ideology in *Topologie*, Ronald Bogue[32] puts forward the Barthesian thesis that violence in Robbe-Grillet's work, as in Sade's, functions as an assault on bourgeois complacency and a fracturing of societies' myths of the natural to create a new "parole." Or, as Foucault saw, "at a time when the interiorization of the law of history and the world was being imperiously demanded by Western consciousness as never before, Sade gives voice to the nakedness of desire as the lawless law of the world."[33] The raped virgin, claimed Robbe-Grillet in a somewhat different interpretation in a published interview with Vicki Mistacco, is the gimmick that our entire civilization consumes, from Greek mythology to the popular novels you can buy in train stations. It belongs to all classes and is, for him, "the archetype of the novelistic."[34]

Does the answer to the riddle of the Sphinx perhaps lie not so much in man as in the rape or domination of woman, or in the myths of woman (penetration across the limen, death, compulsion to repeat, self-expropriation) as central object of violent interrogation in Robbe-Grillet's texts? This was already the tentative conclusion of the preceding chapter, which looked beyond Oedipus and the pleasure principle to the compulsion to repeat and the fearful allure of death. The following chapter and the second section of the study of myth, distancing Oedipus-Everyman, at least for the moment (his detective and criminal doubles invariably come rushing back), focuses on this slipping and slippery ground of seduction and sadism to see if, in its turn, it will in fact take us beyond, or return us, once again (but perhaps with a significant difference), to Oedipus.

Myths of Woman, or the Sadist and the Siren

The preceding chapter initiated the cross-examination of Robbe-Grillet's own contention that the myth "woman" is presented fragmented and flat, distanced by humor, exaggeration, and explicit reference to its character of cultural construction.

It is evident that there is a correspondence between the sexualized young girl who figures mythological "woman" in Robbe-Grillet's work and the dominance of the latter in Western representations. Carola Deutsch and Liselotte Steinbrugge,[1] for example, unhesitatingly read the child-woman and the witch, mythological primary objects in *Projet*, as the two poles of the vision of woman presented by contemporary society. They concur with Robbe-Grillet's own contention that such myths are above all an ideological bait; the reader must learn to negotiate the latter to avoid being snared as in a "fur trap."[2]

Indeed, like Barbie dolls, advertising models, and Hollywood heroines, Robbe-Grillet's women are young, beautiful, and virtually interchangeable. None has a stable role or character or even a sustained individual name. A .., the heroine with the painted nails and tightly fitting dress, the object of jealous scrutiny and erotic arousal of the colonial planter-observer of *La Jalousie,* becomes the sexual Lady A, Ava, Eva, in *La Maison de rendez-vous,* or Eve, the dancer in chains in an Amsterdam nightclub in *Trans-Europ-Express.* Joan Robeson, "la belle Joan," JR, red-haired call girl, Irish spy, member of the secret organization, punished on her ironing table by the terrorist-rapist while watching an arousing television documentary on fertility rites in Africa, transforms constantly in *Projet.* On the other hand a single name, "Laura," in the same novel, is used to designate apparently very different young women—the rich captive heiress, the gang leader in the subway, the bored young woman in the apartment overlooking Central Park.

(Earlier, Laura was the political activist of *Un Régicide,* a Laura returns as one of the three seducible daughters in *L' Homme qui ment,* and a Laurette figures among the victims in *Souvenirs.*)

The destinies (or at least the color of the dresses) of Marie-Eve, Violette, Marie, Blanche, and Angelica are in their names. Wild gangs ("bandes sauvages") of adolescent delinquents quite literally run wild. Temple, the rose seller, if one remembers Ronsard's metaphor or Faulkner's heroine in *Sanctuary,* could not but be a "child" prostitute; the aristocratic Lady Caroline (de Sachs/de Saxe) may well be a vampire. Djinn/Jean is an elf, a fairy, an archangel, or a young girl, "as you wish," according to the text. In the novel *Djinn,* "the real young woman is a false mannequin" in the vertiginous game between "real" and "represented" that marks every Robbe-Grillet text.

Analyzing the contemporary mythology of woman in an interview for *Le Nouvel Observateur* in 1974, Robbe-Grillet selected as central the image of the cover girl, young and beautiful for eternity, smooth-skinned, wide-eyed, immobilized.[3] Her enigmatic, inviting, and apprehensive smile is seen as mystery or submission but also as provocation, danger, and perdition. This "woman" is read as multiplicity, instability, falsity, but above all as representation, the subject and object of a discourse, a mythology (at once eternal youth and death), and the inevitable object of textual/sexual violence. At the same time, in this interview, entitled "La Cover-girl du diable," Robbe-Grillet's analysis of the myth "woman" appears to be overtly operating a classical contrast of "signifiés"—Eros/Thanatos, tranquillity/violence, virginity/rape, innocence/crime—of the kind postulated by Lévi-Strauss to be the basic mechanism in the elaboration of myth: "La femme en tant qu'objet mythologique, entretient des rapports secrets avec la Nature (cycle lunaire, grossesse, instinct maternel), mais par malheur, c'est l'animal que sa nature profonde pousse sans cesse à l'artifice: fardée, décolorée, teinte, désodorisée, parfumée, fausse, traîtresse, menteuse, séductrice, elle incarne l'apparence trompeuse dans sa plus scintillante splendeur" [Woman as a mythological object entertains secret relations with Nature (lunar cycle, pregnancy, maternal instinct), but by misfortune, she is the animal that her deepest nature pushes ceaselessly towards artifice: made up, bleached, dyed, deodorized, perfumed, false, treacherous, lying, seductive, she incarnates deceitful appearance in its most sparkling splendor].[4]

At once nature and artifice, she is also both weakness and strength, sea and blood, dark sovereign lady and fair vulnerable angel; "la femme *vulnérable* et *souveraine*, traversée par le flux lunaire du sang, comme la mer" [woman *vulnerable* and *sovereign,* in whom the lunar flux of blood circulates, like the sea] (p. 55). Resembling Sade's favorite victims, she also incarnates "l'esprit vibrant de la vie, de la liberté, de la révolution, du plaisir sensuel" [the vibrant spirit of life, of freedom, of revolution, of sensual pleasure] (p. 55). Marie-Eve/Violette is queen/slave, angel/devil, willing victim/spirit of revolt, instinct/artifice. As object of desire, Woman has the absent, smooth, unchangeable, posed surfaces of the glossy cover girl. As subject, she explores her sexuality in freedom and is a spirit of revolt and of disorder. Attractive, she is fatal: the dark angel of death or spirit of freedom on her motorcycle and the fair captive fiancée of the Comte de Corinthe in *La Belle Captive,* or the perversely innocent little-girl-adult Alice (of Lewis Carroll connotations) in *Glissements progressifs du plaisir.*

Robbe-Grillet incorporates into the "mythologies" at play in his text the oppositions that structuralism saw as those of universal human thought. The contradictions carried by these mythologies of woman—subject/object, angel/devil, nature/artifice, love/death—are again accompanied by dialectical operations in the narrative, passages rewritten (or almost) in the negative or simply negated, a present scene repeated in the past (at the beginning and the end of *Djinn*). The structural organization works to unmake the content carried by these stereotyped thematic elements, claims Robbe-Grillet in an interview with François Jost.[5]

The feminine is marked by such signs as the open triangle of the letter V, by the sinuous S, the diminutive suffix "-ette," and whole paradigms of epithets for smallness: "menu," "petite," "fine," "svelte". Other distinctive features are fragility and vulnerability, ("frêle," "fragile," "tremblante," "ouverte," "offerte"), angelic/diabolical beauty, softness, curve and seduction ("tendre," "charmante," "sinueuse"), and sensuality ("humide," "charnue"). These paradigms are then organized by the text along a syntagmatic axis. Like the early hidden metaphors of the sexual impulse (erasers, figures of eight, A's hair and nails), these feminine signs become insistently overt, proliferate to saturate the later texts, and circulate from text to text. Metaphors of the feminine are

organized from fetishized fragments and poses of vulnerability or provocation that suggest submission to masculine sexual strength: "frail"
nape of the neck, "exposed" or "bent," iron bracelet around the "slender"
throat, the "soft, warm, supplicant" voice, the "slit" skirt, the "pointed"
or "broken" high-heeled shoe, the wrists held behind the back. Adjectives
connote seductive opening—"parted lips," "legs apart," "hair let down"
("lèvres disjointes," "jambes ouvertes," "cheveux défaits")—or, at least,
voyeuristic fascination with opening. Verbs of penetration and dislocation proliferate—"transpierce," "tear," "dislocate" ("transpercer,"
"déchirer," "disloquer")—to contaminate the most innocent description
(of the shapes of clouds, of leaves and of rocks at the beginning of
Angélique, or of beetles flying around a lamp in *La Jalousie*) with a
latent violence. The metaphors of sexual violence cohere or animate to
form glossy, theatrical, or dreamlike tableaux or images in which provocative feminine figures call up the powerful male giant (the King Kong
complex) and his aggressions. From the cultural representations of the
female in Western consciousness, the duplicitous fragility of diaphanous
fairies, teasing water sprites, and sinuous sirens, the danger of powerful
witches (danger seen, for example, in the *Malleus Maleficarum* as originating in carnal desire, insatiable in women) and of beautiful spies and
double agents, Robbe-Grillet constructs a central paradigm of the power
of feminine sexual seduction (the siren) and the masculine violence or
the "war of the sexes" (the sadist) that the siren brings into play. The
Eves, Angelicas, and Lolita-Violettes exert their greatest fascination as
sacrificial young virgin and beautiful captive.

As we have seen, the forms of the work include assemblage, association, and *glissement,* or metaleptic sliding of the text or image
between diegesis and metatext, as well as dialectical opposition.
"Woman" is derived from an assemblage of phonemes, morphemes,
sememes, and elements borrowed from paintings and other representations (Delvaux, Magritte, Rauschenberg) and is associated with other
"mythological" elements (blood, water, viscous material) to generate
multiple and often abstract fictions. Alice paints her body in red (not,
we note, the blue of the original Yves Klein manner) and imprints the
pattern on the white wall of her cell. Violette smears blood (red paint)
mixed with sperm (a bowlful of paste) over herself in a gesture of
liberation. Yet in these quotations and erasures ("gommages" and "hom-
mages," as they have been called), in these abstractions, in the masculine

sequences of struggle and expulsion (that Hélène Cixous would replace by a dynamic, incessant, feminine process of exchange from one subject to another), violence seems necessarily implicated.

The relation of the masculine figure of the investigator to the myths of the feminine is antagonistic. The myths of the masculine turn ineluctably on the fascination of the feminine and the struggle for (sexual) power in Robbe-Grillet's work where secret masculine organizations abound. *Les Gommes* has a terrorist organization for which Wallas, apparently for unconsciously oedipal reasons, unwittingly serves as an assassin; *La Maison de rendez-vous* has its spy, drug, or gunrunning ring and its policeman, among whose compensations are the call girls of the Villa Bleue. In the mythological New York of *Projet* the organization involved in killing presidents also kidnaps and subjugates young women. There are perhaps echoes here of the "real" terrorist organization that captured and broke Patty Hearst. (This group was itself decimated by the police in what turned out to be a major media event creating a new Bonnie and Clyde myth.) The organization fights machines in *Djinn* under the leadership of a beautiful young woman disguised as a man in a trench coat with collar pulled up, hat brim pulled down, dark glasses (like a "policeman of the thirties"), who is, in fact, an androgyne, a cyborg, or a machine invented by Dr. Morgan, much as Morgane la Fay is a creation of the male enchanter Klingsor in the later *Angélique*. In *Souvenirs du triangle d'or* the organization becomes a cabalistic secret society, Knights Templar (like the secret society of Umberto Eco's best-seller, *Foucault's Pendulum*, ten years later) of sexual secrets, specialists in the hunt, with young girls as the deer or hare fleeing before the hounds. Cannibalistic banquet scenes constitute the phantastical and humorous "cruel" finale of these neo-classical hunts, which contain echoes from certain James Bond films such as *Goldfinger*.

Few of these themes and techniques cannot be found in contemporary popular culture. Beyond the subject matter of the sex-shop, there is a panoply of psychopathological video heroes like Freddy Krueger and Jason and a whole genre of TV slasher movies (e.g., the *Friday the 13th* series, *The Hitchhiker*, or *The Exterminator*) that play to the fear/pleasure of the opening or crushing of vulnerable flesh, the thrill of violent power over the other, the fear of death experienced vicariously.

(In the slasher movies male flesh is, however, almost as vulnerable as female.) Video games (which figure the Grim Reaper as defeat or the Beautiful Princess as victory) and a genre of entertainment movie use the monsters of classical myth, fairy tales, folktales, classic novels, and historical legends in new technological and cultural contexts to construct a synchronic reassemblage. This assemblage crunches the distinctions between high and low culture, the real and the imaginary, much as Robbe-Grillet's new texts do. Films by Steven Spielberg are packed with such hybrid monsters of lust as Pizza the Hut. (A Beauty as captive victim is inevitably chained to the Beast even in these often moral and moralizing tales.) The crew of *Star Trek* meets centaurs and cities of Amazon women on its odyssey in space. In *The Temple of Doom*, Indiana Jones, too, must rescue his fair maiden lowered in a cage above a fiery abyss but not before the fear and screams of the nearly sacrificed victim have aroused excitement and created suspense. This hero of the multimillion dollar blockbuster *Indiana Jones and the Last Crusade*, defeats the evil S.S. officers and proves himself a pure knight in order to conquer the power of the Holy Grail, but the beautiful female spy who has seduced both father and son, despite the gallant Indiana's attempts to save her, must be punished for her impurity and venal treachery by her cataclysmic death, swallowed up in the bowels of the earth.

Ricardou interpreted the general abstract themes that link the Belle Jeune Fille (feminine) and the Organization (masculine) —pursuit, being pursued, capture, sequestration, violence, liberation, pleasure—as adventures of the imagination of the text.[6] The latter are not unlike the characterizations Brooks and Scholes give of traditional narrative functioning and that Winnett argues translates a male sexual pleasure. It is, moreover, ultimately a male narrator (or Robbe-Grillet himself) who controls or dictates the narration, that is, the "body" of the text or the "mother tongue."

The elements used in Robbe-Grillet's recent work are quotations from his own previous writing or films, from railway station literature, sex-shops on 42nd Street, or from advertising. They issue from interaction with the work of Sade, Miller, and Bataille, with the romantic photography of young girls by David Hamilton, the neosurrealist paintings of Delvaux and Magritte and their "objects of symbolic function," and the work of American pop artists Rauschenberg and Jasper Johns. The texts of *Topologie* and *Souvenirs* are composed of writings inspired by pictorial work and even titles by the artists mentioned and published elsewhere in "picto-romans": *La Belle Captive* (Magritte), *Construction d'un temple en ruines à la Déesse Vanadé* (Delvaux), *Traces suspectes en surface* (Rauschenberg), *Temple aux miroirs* (Irina Ionesco), *La Cible* (introduction for the catalogue of the Jasper Johns exhibition at Beaubourg in 1981), *Les Rêves de jeunes filles* and *Les Demoiselles d'Hamilton* (Hamilton).

Magritte's immobile falling rock, girl in the net, siren, blue shoe, little man with black suitcase, Johns's light bulb, torch, and cell, for example, reappear in the written texts where they function as generators. Like these pictorial generators from "high" art, the popular images of vampirism, white slavery, lesbianism, incest, inquisition, and black mass in *Glissements* and *Le Jeu avec le feu* are borrowed or reused elements that again insist on the constructed or ready-made nature of Robbe-Grillet's mythologies.

Myths of the feminine, then, are apparently cultural constructions—woman looked at, objectified, and aestheticized to confirm the existence of a subject (male) observer—and not an essence or a whole and knowable person. Could we hypothesize that, rather than being "a (false) revolution against woman's body," as Diane Crowder claimed,[7] Robbe-Grillet's semiothematics work to stage (and thereby to confirm) a feminist thesis? This is the thesis of the construction and cultural imposition of woman as a function of the male's simultaneous attraction to and fear of the alien, powerful, sexual other. In this case Robbe-Grillet's work might constitute a liberating mise en scène of covert male strategies to control or suppress the female threat to their hegemony. Or rather, following Joan DeJean's argument, is pastiche and bricolage, like the undecidability of old repeated myths and the glorification (or subversion) of cliché, a sign of the "defensive" or "fortified" text, protected against the threat of invasion by the reader and complicitous with the order it deconstructs?

In Robbe-Grillet's work Angélique is most characteristically a child-woman and a graceful, compliantly curving prey attached to the stake for the approaching sea monster (or frail prisoner standing wrists bound on the executioner's cart on her way to the block). Presented as complicitous in her helplessness with a voyeuristic, sadistic male sexual pleasure, she is another version of the beautiful, sacrificial victim of the early short story "La Chambre secrète." In the topos of the secret room this short story prefigured the later generative/prison cell of *Topologie*, and in the aesthetic qualities of the chained victim (curves of constrained "milky white" flesh stained with red blood), it anticipates the proliferation in the later work of figures of "La Belle Captive."

In *The Pornography of Representation* Suzanne Kappeler argues for the existence in both high and low culture of a "saturation" of all the processes of imagery and communication by "pornography." This is defined as "the sexual attack on the sex object," "the symbiosis of Thanatos and Eros," and the "extinction" of women as "subjects with human rights."[8] Might Robbe-Grillet's apparently liberating bricolage be a text fortified to protect what Kappeler calls the "feeling of life,"[9] produced in the (male) subject by the conquest of the (female) object, always cast in the role of subjugated victim, whether willing or unwilling. In "high" culture, Kappeler argues, the pernicious character of this pornography of representation is concealed by the prestige of so-called literariness. Kappeler argues against Barthes's pronouncement that "writing is the destruction of every voice, of every point of origin," and disputes Barthes's implication that "great art" and creativity, "immaculately conceived,"[10] are somehow beyond values other than the "literary" and therefore have right of sanctuary. For the "literary," she claims, is always itself embedded in economic and political mechanisms of production and reception, that is, at the least, in the book business. Kappeler, indeed, seeks to enforce the responsibility of the author or the publisher for her or his production.

My earlier analysis suggested that the beginnings of such a responsibility might be found in Robbe-Grillet's deconstructive, subversive staging of "classical" representations, the repressions of the collective unconscious, and his own obsessions. Yet Kappeler insists that even the writer and the critic whose project is to "show up" the nature of these representations, "analyzing, laying bare and reformulating what they have so carefully noted," remain within the literary, nonpolitical, aesthetic, pure "field of desire" that is, for her, "an ideological cornerstone of patriarchal culture." In this extreme frame of sexual/textual politics, Robbe-Grillet's enterprise would not be redeemed from "literary connivance in the pornographic," as Kappeler has defined this, or from the "irresponsibility of authorship"[11] by its deconstructions. Its implication in the "field of desire" would simply be doubly evident in its character of "male" writing.

"To scream/to discharge, this paradigm is the beginning of choice, that is of Sadean meaning,"[12] notes Kappeler, reading Barthes on Sade in *Sade, Fourier, Loyola*. In this case, according to Kappeler, Barthes analyzes the structural mechanisms of the Sadean text "faultlessly" as the binary choice to be resisting victim or consenting libertine. Barthes does not, however, for the female critic, proceed to correct or rewrite Sade's trajectory. Rather, he "replicates" it, analyzing the rhetorical, that is, the world of Sade's words, and not insisting on the real "practices" in which the victim is caught. He pretends unjustifiably, Kappeler protests, that his words are neutral and gender-free.

Robbe-Grillet's texts, too, must speak from gendered positions, but they increasingly insist on the "subjectivity" of this situation and on the problematic of the gap between textual and real practice. The recent autobiographies invite the writer specifically to engage in autobiographical and psychoanalytical modes of reading. Both Barthes and Robbe-Grillet would argue that their analyzing or laying bare (denuding) the representations around them is not only a fascination and a replication but a critical attempt to denaturalize and to "see" differently. Neither writer in the structural organization of his own texts accepts the binary system of victim/libertine or the double bind of subject/object without a struggle. Although I cannot share Kappeler's radical and fixed political reading stance that prevents her from allowing the text to yield its plural meanings, she does see that these texts conceal/reveal, a complicity with the power they re-present and some degree of imprisonment.

From *La Maison de rendez-vous* (1965) on, the reader is submitted to a network of explicit sado-erotic signs that recur from work to work woven in various combinations and permutations into different stories or fragments of story; the reader is forced to ask what it is exactly that is being concealed or revealed. These fragmented, sexual stories of young girls stripped by dogs in exotic entertainment or tied to the stake for the alligator or served up for dinner arouse fascination and horror as they begin to take on a certain density and coherence and move toward a resolution, which, behind the romantic veils and trappings, is usually the violent deflowering of the rose, behind the heroic rescue, the sexual conquest of the helpless heroine, behind the battle of the sexes the torture, sacrifice, or "cruel" death of the precocious adolescent/seductive siren. And yet the diaphanous ondine, self-contained and inaccessible, of *Angélique ou l'enchantement*, the fierce Empress Catherine (an ironic reference to Catherine Robbe-Grillet's new experiences as dominatrix) and her cruel orgies, and the bleeding, chained, impaled female captive are figures of sexual pleasure and danger with whom, the first shock of their explicitness passed, the ludic, flattening effects of the text make any permanent identification difficult. The invitation is predominantly to the intellectual recognition of the intertextual nature of the thematic element and its recursive functioning. Within the texts the breaking down of the distinction between the diegesis (story, intrigue, myth) and the metadiegetic comment on the function of these myths and stories create effects of unreality or slippage between "degrees of reality," to use an expression from Barthes's "autobiography."

As unsettled reader seeking points of reference, I hesitate between suspicion, some resentment at the painful dislocations involved, and seduction. Perhaps I must stop sheltering behind an apparently objective critical third person and take account of my situatedness as a female academic, reading in the nineties, and of the character of my personal interactions with this material. Respectful by training and tradition of what are evidently intelligent and ground-breaking texts and seeking to read empathetically with the grain of an aesthetically powerful writing and its subversive purposes, I am also constantly jolted by the provocatively "masculine" and violent thematics. Yet the first shock and rejection worked through to reach some degree of recognition of intertextuality and familiarity with the material and awareness of its functioning, the brilliant bricolage, and perhaps also the taboo thematic begin to exert an intellectual fascination. What do I recognize here if not of repressed masculine sado-erotic phantasies at least of their other face, feminine "masochistic" imaginings? My secondary, political, response is somewhat different. I do share Joan DeJean's general suspicion that what is present in these texts, beyond a making visible of the nature of the bricks that constructed the monolithic towers of the Old Regime (a deconstruction), is an only dimly perceived personal complicity with the male power invested in these structures (less than a total subversion).

A comparison between Robbe-Grillet's generators and the way in which the writer makes these generative mythologies peculiarly his own appears to justify some of my more pressing doubts. Like Moreau's mystical figures that I consider in another study of Robbe-Grillet's picto-novels, the romantic female figures of the writer and historian Michelet are also "deconstructed" in Robbe-Grillet's text, heavily rewritten yet not completely neutralized. For example, Michelet's 1862 novel, *La Sorcière*, is quoted (without quotation marks, as in the new conventions of intertextual assemblage) in the incorporation and repetition in *Topologie* of the sentence that Robbe-Grillet used earlier in an advertisement written for the Suntory Whisky Company: "Elle boit, de sa lèvre pâle, le sombre vin couleur de sang" [She drinks, with her pale lip, the somber wine color of blood].[13] Through the mediation of Barthes's *Michelet par lui-même*,[14] Michelet's Woman made witch by Nature ("Nature les fait sorcières," claims the latter), who attracts the male by her otherness, her hysteria and madness, her closeness to nature, her weakness, and bleeding wound, is at the center of Robbe-Grillet's film *Glissements*. Barthes stresses the fascination that the woman "in crisis," that is, woman humiliated and observed voyeuristically, rather than possessed, exerts for Michelet. His is "an eroticism of voyeurism, not of possession. . . . Michelet satiated is none other than Michelet voyeur." ("L'érotique de Michelet ne tient visiblement pas compte des plaisirs de l'orgasme, alors qu'il attribue une importance considérable à la Femme en crise, c'est-à-dire à la Femme humiliée. C'est une érotique de la voyance, non de la possession, et Michelet amoureux, Michelet comblé, n'est rien d'autre que Michelet-voyeur.")[15] In *La Femme*[16] Michelet sees woman as eternally submitted to the "sacred crisis" and the "wound of love," a child in sympathy with nature, langor, purity, and grace, tending to sacrifice and martyrdom in the sexual act and in childbirth (the "mal de mère"). Her sexuality is equated largely with suffering and death, while male sexuality is seen as primitivity and sadism.

For Robbe-Grillet Michelet's pale Christian victim is also a vibrant spirit of revolt: "La sorcière de Michelet ressemble par bien des côtés aux victimes favorites de Sade: jeune-et-belle pour l'éternité, à l'image de nos *cover-girls,* ce n'est pas sans un tremblement de tendre volupté que l'auteur la livre à la cruauté des bourreaux. Mais, chez Michelet, elle est quelque chose de plus: à l'opposé des 'anges pâles' que propose la religion, elle incarne l'esprit vibrant de la vie, de la liberté, de la révolution, du plaisir sensuel" [Michelet's witch resembles in many ways Sade's favorite victims: young-and-beautiful for eternity in the image of our cover girls, it is not without a trembling of tender voluptuousness that the writer gives her up to the cruelty of the torturers. But, in Michelet, she is something more: at the opposite pole from the 'pale angels' that religion proposes, she incarnates the vibrant spirit of life, of liberty, of revolution, of sensual pleasure].[17] His own Alice, in *Glissements*, with her taste for nonsense and subversion, claims the writer, is engaged in struggle with the same established order. However, she is a spirit not only of adventure but also of the antinatural, a heroine of an anti-order through her precocious and transgressive sexuality.[18] John Michalczyk's excellent study of the witch in Michelet and Barthes and Robbe-Grillet's Alice in *Glissements* quotes from Michelet's portrait of the Basque sorceresses of 1609 to point out the close parallels with the physical and psychological framework of Robbe-Grillet's protagonist.

> Les femmes, très jolies, très hardies, imaginatives, passaient le jour, assises aux cimetières sur les tombes, à jaser du sabbat, en attendant qu'elles y allassent le soir. C'était leur rage et leur furie.
> Nature les fait sorcières: ce sont les filles de la mer et de l'illusion. Elles nagent comme des poissons, jouent dans les flots. Leur maître naturel est le Prince de l'air, roi des vents et des rêves, celui qui gonflait la sibylle et lui soufflait l'avenir.
>
> [The women, very pretty, very bold, imaginative, would spend the day sitting in the cemeteries on the tombstones, gossiping about the witches' sabbath while waiting to go there in the evening. It was their passion and their frenzy.
> Nature makes them witches: they are the daughters of the sea and of illusion. They swim like fish, play in the waves. Their natural master is the Prince of the air, king of the winds and of dreams, he who swelled the sibyl and breathed the future into her.] (*La Sorcière*, pp. 167–68)

But is this modern, self-possessed witch simply a reincarnation of Michelet's heroines? Michelet's historical portrait paints the witch as a sibyl, image of radical challenge to society and, consequently, society's victim. The sexual implications are more explicit in Robbe-Grillet. Alice's freedom is a fatal attraction; she is a dangerous sexualized vampire, and she calls for punishment and suppression. Significantly, Robbe-Grillet chose to film the white-walled cells of the correctional institution run by nuns for delinquent minors, the main setting of *Glissements*, in the dungeon of the Château de Vincennes where Sade spent seven years of imprisonment. The figure of the witch provides Robbe-Grillet with a pre-text for the staging of sets of sadomasochistic rituals (Sister Maria, kneeling on a prie-dieu, threatened by Sister Julia with a whip, or scenes of the Inquisition in the underground cellars of the prison), as voodoo ceremonies are a pre-text for incising the body of the white-skinned mannequin tied to the black iron railings of the bed cast up on the beach. It is the case that Alice (Anicée Alvina)—the young woman accused of the murder of her friend and lesbian lover, Nora, found with a pair of scissors plunged through her breast—creates social disorder and sexual confusion as she seduces authority figures—the examining magistrate, the female lawyer, and the pastor who are sent to interrogate her. She corrupts the pure Sister Julia to lesbian games, causes the fascinated magistrate to fall ill from sucking glass (and blood) from her bleeding foot, the Protestant minister to fall prey to sexual torment and obsession, and finally seduces and provokes the death of her lawyer Maître David. The latter (Nora's double, played by the same actress), during a simulation of the death of Nora, cuts herself on the broken bottle and bleeds to death. Predictably for a Robbe-Grillet work, when the police inspector arrives to declare Alice innocent of Nora's murder at the end of the film—Nora, it seems was the victim of a male assassin—he finds the body of Maître David/Nora, and the police interrogation (and indeed the film) must begin again.

Yet, this modern-day sorceress rephrases the "possession" that Michelet's heroine manifests physically in the pulsating blood and violent sea of her body. John Michalczyk sees the deceptive/innocent heroine of *Glissements* as corresponding to a particular category of women, Barthes's third category of the witch—the "decadent" stage of the precocious child, innocent and knowing. "La troisième Sorcière procède de la Petite Fille avertie (poupée, bijou pervers) image pernicieuse puisqu'elle est double, divisée, contradictoire, réunissant dans l'équivoque l'innocence de l'âge et la science de l'adulte" [The third Witch derives from the precocious Little Girl (doll, perverse jewel) pernicious image because it is double, divided, contradictory, joining equivocally the innocence of young age and the knowledge of the adult] (Barthes, "La Sorcière," p. 117).[19] In *Angélique*, Robbe-Grillet identifies his own wife Catherine as his "femme-enfant" [child-wife] (p. 186). In both Barthes's *Michelet* and in Robbe-Grillet, the *éternel féminin* is associated with blood—the cardinal substance of history for Michelet—but the red handprint on the nun's white robe or the imprint of Alice's body on the white cell wall is not blood but red paint. The references to surrealist images (a Bunuel-style door opening onto the sea accompanied by Gregorian chant, homage to *Un Chien andalou*, to Bellmer's dislocated dolls, or to Lady Macbeth's "All the perfumes of Arabia . . ." speech) make the game of intertextuality evident. Alice is a spirit of liberation through disorder, and this disorder takes predominantly sexual forms as in Michelet, but these forms are self-conscious, ludic, and of a distinctive (sadomasochistic) character in Robbe-Grillet's work.

The press release for *Glissements* begins with a quotation from an anecdote, the story of the Fiancée de Corinthe in *La Sorcière*, a story that originated at the time of Hadrian (A.D. 76–138) but appeared again in the twelfth and sixteenth centuries. Michelet interprets this story as a sign that the new ideology of virginity and monasticism engendered by Christianity did not correspond to human sexual nature. Echoes of the tale of Corinthe's fiancée will subsequently recur throughout Robbe-Grillet's work. But again, there are marked differences between Robbe-Grillet's fiancée and Michelet's, both in the roles she plays and in the new discontinuous forms of her appearances in Robbe-Grillet. Michelet's story, as Michalczyk tells it, is of a young Athenian pagan who goes to Corinth to meet the fiancée promised to him from his youth. Her family greet the young man in horror; they have converted to Christianity, and the daughter's virginity has been offered to God by her sick mother in exchange for the latter's health. At night, the young virgin, dressed in white, appears to Corinthe (as the spirit Marie-Ange van der Reeves appears to Corinthe in *La Belle Captive*) and tells her tale. Her fiancé begs her to stay with him, and when the mother, alerted by her sensually plaintive cries, enters to interrupt the encounter characterized by Michelet's metaphors of fire and ice, the young woman pleads for a liberation from the living death of chastity, a purification by fire, and a return to the old gods.[20] "Ouvrez mon noir cachot, élevez un bûcher, et que l'amante ait le repos des flammes. Jaillisse l'étincelle et rougisse la cendre! Nous irons à nos anciens dieux" [Open my black cell, set up a funeral pyre, and may the woman in love have the repose of the flames. Let the sparks fly up and the ashes glow red! We shall go to our old gods] (*La Sorcière*, p. 51). There is a certain lyricism of self-immolation in the fiancée's cry.

Other versions of the story suggest that the young woman has died and returns as a spirit to spend the night with her fiancé. In the morning, the young man's hair has turned white, and he begins to suffer from a strange wasting disease. To Michelet's indignation, Goethe makes a vampire of this sexual, life-stirring and life-draining feminine figure who, having exhausted Corinthe, will move on to destroy the others of the young race. Robbe-Grillet's film, too, insists on Alice's dangerous taste for blood and her association with violent death. In a recurring flashback a female lover from her schooldays falls to her death from the cliff, and blood trickles from her mouth. Nora plays at being dead, lying "drowned" among the rock pools. In *La Belle Captive* the pure, pale fiancée, Marie-Ange, inevitably calls up a second and vampiristic self at night in the bedroom. Both Corinthe and Walter Naime become her victims.

Robbe-Grillet borrows and transforms another phrase from Michelet's "La Fiancée de Corinthe," the fiancée's plea to her mother against the mother's denial of passion. "Ne sens-tu pas comme je brûle?" [Don't you feel how I am burning?] With Freud's interpretation of the well-known dream of the burning child in mind, the writer creates a series of scenes that incorporate these or similar words and have evident Freudian reference. This includes the incest scene between Caroline and her father at the Opera in *Souvenirs du triangle d'or* (pp. 205–8) and the burning of Christine in her mahogany coffin in the same novel. As the heavy chandelier falls (stereotype of movies of spiritism and present again above the bed where Marie plays at keeping a candlelight vigil over the dead body of her brother Jean in *Djinn*), setting light to the artificial roses in the coffin, Christine murmurs, "Père, ne vois-tu pas que je brûle?" [Father, don't you see that I'm burning?] (p. 215). In another example of the coming together of recurring motifs that characterize Robbe-Grillet's texts, Christine's pubic triangle is consumed by fire, justifying the suspect character of the half-burned matchsticks of Robbe-Grillet's childhood games in *Le Miroir qui revient* or the cigarette butts in *Le Voyeur*. The burning of the female pubic triangle is, of course, a standard image of a certain kind of pornography. An issue of the magazine *Bête et Méchant* in 1986 used the image of a smoking female "bush" on its cover to comment satirically on the possibly criminal fires alight at that time in the south of France and, indirectly, on the desires plastic cover-girl images themselves may conceal. This image is some distance from Michelet's intense, romantic visions and from Robbe-Grillet's own satirical but very literary and often even lyrical work.

In his analysis of the story of the fiancée of Corinthe, Stoltzfus recognizes that the gap between Michelet and Robbe-Grillet's versions lies in Michelet's choosing the pale fiancée as nature, freedom, and pleasure over the blood-marked vampire that Robbe-Grillet's text seems to espouse. Robbe-Grillet, he concedes, does privilege Goethe's interpretation or the twelfth-century version of the Roman legend in which a statue of Venus, on whose finger a young man puts a ring, comes at night as his devil spouse to claim her due. This perceptive critic explains such a preference in terms of Robbe-Grillet's predilection for the antinatural: "The image of the vampire connotes for him a more virulent state of rebellion against an imposed ideology."[21] Yet, curiously, Stoltzfus goes on to relate the mythical motif of the vampire to a negative metaphor Robbe-Grillet used to speak of the ossified discourse of the nineteenth century. Robbe-Grillet's rejection of this nineteenth-century "vampiric narrative" stems from a deep-seated hostility to all established forces that restrict man's freedom: "He inveighs not only against the prisons of codified narrative forms but also against the dangers of repressed sexuality."[22] While the conclusion drawn remains the positive one that Robbe-Grillet's fascination with vampirism as a folk myth is based on his desire to subvert authoritarian systems, the negative connotations of this figure of the female vampire and its stereotypical character, both directly and indirectly noted (Stoltzfus points out that Luther gives the body of the fiancée the stinking odor of death), are not addressed by such an interpretation. Nor does Stoltzfus come to terms with the fact that in Robbe-Grillet (as indeed in Michelet) the parti pris for the sorceress against the cult of female purity does not prevent veneration from becoming victimization in both cases. He comes closer to the problem when he concludes that the fiancée, like L. (elle), the flower-woman of *L'Immortelle* who seduces Professor N by her beauty but is

nonetheless the beautiful captive of her pimp, is a victim of the duality
of the clichés among which we live. Woman is caught not only in the
proverbial bind but also in the linguistic "double bind." She is either
too natural, in touch with natural rhythms, lunar and menstrual cycles,
life-principle, and therefore a sorceress (Michelet), or not natural, social
code passing itself off as nature, and therefore a vampire (Robbe-Grillet).
In either case, contact with her, as with the nymphet, is illicit and brings
death.

In the film *La Belle Captive* the title refers to the beautiful fiancée,
Marie-Ange, virgin and vampire, to art, and to self. It is the title of a
series of Magritte paintings of an easel in a room re-presenting the sea
and sky outside, that, as Stoltzfus points out in an excellent analytical
article, "calls attention simultaneously to the seascape it purports to
depict and to the painterly object that denies the nature from which it
seems to have drawn its inspiration."[23] The fiancée of Corinthe, for
Stoltzfus, functions as a fable or a figural motif, that is, as an "opér-
ateur." However, Robbe-Grillet's version of the fiancée has a specific
character. Here she is ethereal and fluid rather than incandescent, associated with the sea and its rhythmic pleasures and nightmares, with its
dissolutions, rather than with the rebirth of fire. In *Le Miroir qui revient*
the fiancée is herself a victim drowned off the coast near Montevideo,
the city, as Stoltzfus indicates, of the much admired Lautréamont. The
intratextual and intertextual character of the fiancée reminds the reader
of the specular structures of the text, but Stoltzfus notes with some
consternation the changes that have become explicit in this autobiography: "Contrary to everything that he has said before, Robbe-Grillet
now invites his audience to engage in a psychoanalytic and/or bio-
graphical interpretation of his work. This explains his apparent and
surprising desire to undermine 'nouveau roman' aesthetics—an aesthetics
based on the autonomy of the text and on specular structures that deny
mimesis—and of which he was once (and may still be) the champion."[24]

What is the meaning of this apparent reversal? For Stoltzfus: "It is
no doubt his perverse and customary playfulness that prompts him to
tease his audience and exasperate his critics by blurring the lines between
fiction and autobiography. However, . . . Robbe-Grillet's discourse in
both speaks the complexity of the world, refusing a reductionist acceptance of ready-made values and normative codes."[25] Stoltzfus concludes

by claiming that in its re-creating of material that is culturally repressed while alluding to the intertext (Derrida) or archive (Foucault) of art, history, and the collective unconscious, Robbe-Grillet's work remains, in the final instance, in the domain of reflexive fiction, demonstrating that "all values are man-made" and that "all sign systems oppose nature."[26] While I would not, indeed could not, dispute this premise, I would wish to nuance it. In the preceding chapter, which examined both the discontinuous collective oedipal fragments and the personal autobiographical motifs in the light of Barthes's theory of the functioning of modern myth, I suggested that sense can be found rather in the intersections between metalanguage, that is, meaning or *langue* stolen, reduced to form (Genette's bird of evil omen nailed to the door) and the primary meanings these forms still carry "in reserve." That is, that sense lies in an alternation between contradictory primary and secondary meanings, and not on one side or the other. The final chapter takes up this question again in more detail in a further reflection on the relation between postmodern "constructionism" and what might be called new "essentialisms" or new "realisms" in Robbe-Grillet's work.

Whether or not all languages are man-made and not a reflection of the world, and all sign systems oppose nature (rather than serve it), it seems evident that the choice and recurrence of certain kinds of mythological elements (their forms and their content) within the whole corpus of Robbe-Grillet's texts do point to some kind of historicity and to something that can only be called a self. There are clear differences between Michelet and Robbe-Grillet's re-renderings of the culturally received fiancée/the beautiful captive. The complex if humorously distanced relationship of the Comte de Corinthe with the spirit of his time in the personage of Sarah Zeitgeist is not at all the same as that of the mystical Michelet with his young Muses.

Robbe-Grillet reads an implicit male voyeur-criminal gaze into the images he borrows and indeed suspects Michelet (and Barthes) of being secretly or unconsciously complicitous with the tortures and burning of the witch. While he shares Michelet's voyeuristic fascination, he does not appear, like Michelet, to be drawn by the vulnerability or fragility of the woman to protect her. In *Angélique,* his "suspicion" and fascination is expressed directly in passages that are a curious mixture of self-justification (my sado-erotic phantasies are not, after all, exceptional), rigor of look, and implied personal responsibility. (In this same text Saint-Beuve's discreet reference to the presence of sadism—"une pointe d'imagination sadique"—in Flaubert is picked up and amplified in a reflection on the sado-eroticism masked as historical description of the horrors of the attack on Carthage in *Salammbô*.)

John Fletcher discusses the prevalence of this reflection on the sado-erotic in Robbe-Grillet's work in terms of an attempt to probe "the aesthetic and moral topography of the modern."[27] However, in the light of Robbe-Grillet's rejection of received morality and his attempt to redefine the term, Fletcher's use of the term *moral* (or indeed *modern*) is not particularly useful here. (Whose or what morality or new morality is in play?) It is not at all evident, either, that as Fletcher claims, "the basic seriousness of Mathias's sick condition is not ignored or sidestepped" (p. 35) or that Mathias's crime inspires in us "a sense of terror and guilt" (p. 34). If this were the case, the texts would indeed fit into a frame of conventional "moral" concern. The "crime" in *Le Voyeur* is flattened, revealed and destroyed in and by the process of the writing. The writer himself, it would seem, is both victim of a fascination and agent of a kind of self-liberation, a self-liberation whose characteristics and effects and perhaps, indeed, morality remain to be defined.

The controlling narrative voice, which sets up interior distances between the "pornographic" (sexually explicit) content and the writing process, plays games, often of the cat-and-mouse variety, with the reader. It speculates, apparently innocently, but with tongue in cheek, on the verisimilitude of the details of the repeated, or intertextual, or intolerably sadistic fragments, or on their strange familiarity and intertextual origins. It also directly and humorously designates linguistic details, objects, and metaphors made suspect by appearance in certain earlier contexts, inviting the reader to participate in the textual game. There may certainly be some voyeuristic, mimetic "pleasures" for the reader in the descriptions of the female body and the stories of its sexual domination. There may also be a shock of recognition of his/her own hidden fears, fetishes, and phantasies in the evocation of images of blood, the penetration of the orifices of the body, the tearing of vulnerable flesh, or in the old mythologies of transgression, impurity, and curse. But the text hardly calls for empathy. I have argued that the very excess of this material, the distancing, self-reflexive, fragmenting narrative devices, frustrate any easy continuous identification with the cardboard cutout sexual criminals or with their frail, coerced victims as we recognize their origins in the popular imagination of detective or spy novel, of horror or slasher movie, of Sadean story and "snuff-movie" image, or in the working of an imagination that identifies sexuality with the war of the sexes, violence, Thanatos. The "pleasures" of the text lie in this intellectual activity of deconstruction. The reader is invited into the making of a text: the recognition of its metaleptic slippages, its transgressions, its probing of sense. And yet the invitation has something very aggressive about it. The text can indeed be experienced as a war (of the sexes).

The new text, Robbe-Grillet claims in *Angélique ou l'enchantement,* seeks not mimesis but catharsis. The new writer does not desire the desire of his reader but to open his "blind" eyes and to "kill" the reader. It is less a feminine seduction than a masculine aggression. The hypocritical reader is manipulated into seeing with the eyes of the jealous observer or of the criminal voyeur, forced to accept the role Baudelaire had ascribed her/him ("mon semblable," "mon frère"), and compelled to be a witness to her/his "own" desires. It is in fact unwittingly, by play of narrative viewpoint, that she/he comes to identify with the content of Mathias's psychopathological consciousness. In the later works, an arbitrary play of viewpoints is thrust upon the reader by an all-powerful, mad, creator (King Boris). Many readers have resisted what they sensed to be a coercion in Robbe-Grillet's texts. Others have submitted in admiration to intellectual and textual power or to literary prestige. Most, I suspect, like myself, move uneasily between the poles, between sense of pleasure and sense of danger, resistance and seduction, outside and inside.

In *Angélique* the inevitable beautiful victim (no longer a virgin, because, we are informed, the executioner has fully exercised his pre-execution rights) turns out to be, evidently, only an illustration in a pseudohistorical study of capital punishment in seventeenth-century Turkey. (This "historical" victim does recall the fascination still exerted on the popular imagination by capital punishment that makes tableaux of the latter a major tourist attraction at the London waxworks of Madame Tussaud's and a "historical" film on the execution of Louis XVI a money-making enterprise in Paris in 1990.) It is, again evidently, a very young woman who lies naked on the marble floor in the despotic Turkish-Muslim citadel. The Oriental effects themselves derive most probably in part from the romantic interest in cruel barbarity and the epic despotism/eroticism of harem paintings like Delacroix's *La Mort de Sardanapale*. The young woman's legs are spread, attached to iron rings, while the punishing ploughshare, pulled by two horsemen, approaches the defenseless pubic triangle. We recall the tortured nymphet in *Le Voyeur* attached to stakes in the hollow on the cliff, the supine sacrificial victim of "La Chambre secrète," or Marie-Ange spread-eagled in the form of a swastika on the road in the final scene of the film *La Belle Captive*. In *Angélique* "Un public choisi assiste au spectacle . . . mais tous ces gens sont absents de l'adroite figuration, car ils occupent la place, hors champ, du lecteur aux joues enfiévrées" [A selected public is present at the spectacle, . . . but all these people are absent from the skillful representation, for they occupy the place, beyond the field of vision, of the reader with the fevered cheeks] (p. 54).

The reader—the interlocutor or the dialogic "you" who alone incites the writing "I" to speak, according to the linguist Benveniste—given the role of spectator with the fevered cheeks is unlikely to cooperate without resistance. The curiosity that leads her/him to take a closer look at these forbidden sado-erotic images or to seek new knowledge of self and other and the "lawless law of desire" notwithstanding, the initial reaction is likely to be one of indignation or refusal. The traditional empathetic vulnerability that opens the reader to the seductions of fictional narrative is itself likely to become upset. This might be more particularly the case for women, called to witness voyeuristically aggression against themselves from a masculine point of view. However, as Laura Mulvey, among others, has argued for Hollywood cinematic representations of women, females have long accommodated culturally to seeing themselves as objects of male pleasure.[28]

While the deconstructive strategies may well be both defensive and aggressive, they do expose metaphysical or historical traditions or gender roles whose apparently natural origin—in history or in hidden depths of man, for example—has become untenable, untenable because the origin of an obscurely felt guilt for desire for knowledge and power, for oedipal violence, for desire for the suppression of the body of the other was situated outside any human control.

Robbe-Grillet's metafictional ceremonies constitute a rewriting of the inexorable, blind, and inescapable fate of Greek tragedy, or of the other psychological fate of the "oedipal" psyche, which obliges Jocasta to abandon her child and remain silent and forces sexual crime (incest and parricide, for example) upon the unknowing hero, requiring him subsequently to assume his guilt and expiate involuntary, tragic, but predestined acts. I would suggest that the frustration experienced by the humanist reader, who after a fastidious reading of *Les Gommes* or *Le Voyeur* "discovers" Wallas's unconscious oedipal guilt or Mathias's rape and murder of Violette "repressed" in the text, derives in part from the lack of any guilt and the absence of retribution or resolution in the simultaneous construction and effacing of the clues to the crime, of the crime itself, and ultimately of destiny and tragedy. There is no tortured romantic psychological agony, no white knight in shining armor to avenge the wronged maiden and fight the monster. Rather, as in *Angélique,* the white knight turns out to have a black knight double straight from the texts of Sade, who abuses the heroine in his turn. Perseus is both the sea monster and the liberator. There is no counterviolence by good private investigator or lone avenger or violently tough but straight "lady-killing" cop to make manifest the bad (violence) and oppose it with the good (violence). The story remains unfinished, the text returns to the equilibrium of its beginning, the oedipal or aggressive fragments dance in ever-changing formation but immobile on the apparently moving wave.

Robbe-Grillet's suspicious rereadings of the texts of the feminine in Western consciousness and on display on billboards bear striking resemblances to contemporary feminist readings of our mythologies. His texts reproduce and flatten an ambivalent fascination with the young and beautiful body unmarked by time or death and the desire to control, or silence, or sacrifice, or suppress the fatal attraction of its more hidden orifices. The voyeuristic fascination with, and the visual pleasures provided by, an objectified female other is just that dominant if concealed mode of the responses of Western art to the female body (or the text-gendered female) against which feminism has been reacting.

Perseus or Prince Charming, the slayer of (sea) dragons, is unmasked as himself the monster (Morgan) in the figure of the Comte de Corinthe, designated as the "marine monster" or the "monster sailor" ("monstre marin") who "devours little girls." He is an expert at underwater hunting with a harpoon and joins a series of images of maiden-hunting and target practice on female figures and the piercing of female flesh prevalent in sado-erotic anecdotes in Robbe-Grillet's later work. These are particularly evident in *Souvenirs du triangle d'or,* where Jasper Johns's painting of a target object and the title *The Target* serve as generators of diegesis. The police inspector, lost in the dark subterranean corridor, his flashlight (also inspired by a Johns painting) suddenly extinguished, stumbles across a dislocated wax-model with torn-off limbs and perforations that suggest that the doll has served as a target. Lady Caroline, in the changing shed on the beach, has the impression that she, too, has served "as a target." A final image from the novel portrays the bride derived from Duchamp's *Mariée mise à nu* attached to a target while marksmen cast dice for her and her intimately encrusted jewels. *Topologie* had already staged the hunting and devouring of Nathalie and a tableau in which the occupants of the city of women flee the predatory invading soldiers to become the "gracious moving targets" of their arrows in the blood-reddened sea.

Corinthe, the hunter of the sea-siren is a stereotype, but he is also an avatar of the narrative "I": probably the harpooning assassin of Angélique in the underwater accident of the autobiographical *Le Miroir qui revient* and the "Jean Marin" alter ego of the writer in *Angélique.* Corinthe is also, as we have seen, a borrowing from Barthes's retelling of Michelet's nineteenth-century telling of an old Roman story. In Robbe-Grillet's preferred version of this story, Corinthe, victim of the impure blood of the deflowering of his pure fiancée, is strangely weakened and emasculated. His own attacks on the vampire body appear justified. Angélique/Justine/Temple, vestal virgin, attraction and pure pleasure, is also dangerous siren, impure curse, witch, a medieval Morgane, variation on Morgan le Faye, in *Angélique,* potentially a devouring Juliette. It could be argued that the Comte de Corinthe is an avatar of Count Dracula and a product of Bramstoker's nineteenth-century rewriting of the historical Middle European story of the "real" popular hero Dracula, a strong ruler notorious only for his habit of impaling his enemies. Bramstoker makes Dracula a romantically and dangerously sexualized figure of darkness who by biting at the necks of virgins transforms them into his vampire brides. In Robbe-Grillet's version, however, it is the siren, Angélique, who is (at) the heart or hollow of the story.

What seems to traverse the choice and repetition and modifications of Robbe-Grillet's stories of the Fiancée de Corinthe are echoes of the teachings of St. Augustine and the early Church "Fathers" on the impurity and danger of female menstrual blood (menstruating women were, of course, forbidden to enter a church and are still excluded from the mosque), and the simultaneous attraction to and fear of potentially devouring female sexuality. Absolute identification with the punishing phallic father, Corinthe, against this dangerously emasculating and defenseless nymphet "fiancée" or love-object, while sought after, is never fully assured.

Aware of his own uneasy positioning in his texts, Robbe-Grillet nonetheless claims that the masks his characters at once wear and point to are similar in cathartic purpose to the masks worn in Greek tragedy for the representation of the unspeakable and the otherwise unspoken—that is, the collective and the particular monsters of incest, infanticide, and parricide, the sacrifice of slaves and virgins; and sadomasochistic phantasies. In this sense the goal of the writing project is analogous to the mechanisms in the social ceremonies of the animal world that ethologist Konrad Lorenz investigated. In his book *On Aggression* Lorenz postulates the "redirection" of intraspecific aggression in the ceremonies that establish relations between the sexes and in the "ritualization" of certain aggressive impulses within the mating game. Aggression and sexual drive, for Lorenz, are thus intimately linked. Such phylogenetically adaptive behavior has the positive ends of increasing sexual bonding through the attractive display of fearlessness on the one hand and apparent submissiveness or appeasement on the other, while maintaining the aggressive arousal necessary for the protection of the nest and for the survival of the species.

Human beings are neither fish nor greylag geese, and there is much yet to be said on the relation between biological sex and the social construction of gender, but these redirected and ritualized ceremonies, like the complex greeting ceremony in the greylag, essential for sexual bonding, derive from gestures of aggressive territorial defense, that is, from instinctive drives initiated by brain-stem mechanisms (aggression, appeasement/escape, and bonding) that are essentially the same in all mammals and are perhaps still the impulses at the baseline of much of human behavior, as the biologist Henri Laborit claims.[29] We might hypothesize that mythmaking mechanisms in Robbe-Grillet's work, as in Lorenzian redirection and ritualization, channel sensed aggression into more observable and ludically controlled forms. This would be analogous to the functioning of myth in primitive societies to give form to certain givens clearly related to the body—courtship and reproduction, hunting and feeding, fear and flight, aggression and fight—but also to articulate symbolically, explain, and reinforce, forms of sociocultural organization and hierarchies of power arising out of, but underdetermined by, these biological givens. These forms would be those accessible to the learned, noninstinctual, linguistic, and conceptual investigation that mediates them, an investigation that is itself self-conscious and self-reflexive.

The figures of the sadist and the siren or of the sexually aggressed female body are those of culture (or subcultures), not of essence or nature. But they may still bear "traces" of origins in instinctive drives, in biology and evolution, before they are traces of the transformation of these latter by cultural mechanisms of redirection and ritualization. We recall that the Saussurian theory of the sign is that it stands not for the "thing" but for its image, for a concept, for an imprint or trace of the "thing." It is on such suspect surface "traces" that Robbe-Grillet's text dwells. But we have no clear knowledge of the survival value and function (or maladaptedness to a changed external environment) of the majority of our rites and representations, and perhaps it is also this terrain and its complex strata that the Robbe-Grillet text investigates.

The revolutionary project behind this investigation simultaneously stages self-consciously and mocks through the excesses of its discourse the suspect implications of its attempted involvement in sexual liberation. "Le crime est indispensable à la révolution, récite le docteur. Le viol, l'assassinat, l'incendie sont les trois actes métaphoriques qui libéreront les nègres, les prolétaires en loques et les travailleurs intellectuels de leur esclavage, en même temps que la bourgeoisie de ses complexes sexuels" [Crime is indispensable for the revolution, recites the doctor. Rape, murder, arson are the three metaphoric acts that will liberate the blacks, the proletariat in rags, and the intellectual workers from their slavery, as well as the bourgeoisie from its sexual complexes] (*Projet* p. 153). This revolution would cause "only" a "few" deaths, those of women who were in excess numbers anyway. Mass massacres would be avoided by collective seances of rape and torture to liberate secret passions! A poster reproduced infinitely in the Underground of *Projet* depicts a beautiful young woman lying in a pool of blood on a modern, white, living-room carpet, and again the text is hyperbolic. "Hier, c'était un drame . . . Aujourd'hui, une pincée de la lessive diastasique Johnson et la moquette est comme neuve" [Yesterday, it was a tragedy. . . . Today, a pinch of Johnson's detergent with enzymes and your carpet will be like new] (p. 159). Below the poster someone had written in felt pen, "And tomorrow, the revolution." Elsewhere in the metro in *Projet* a giant graffito represents "un sexe masculin de trois mètres de haut, dressé verticalement jusqu' aux lèvres disjointes" [a male sex organ ten feet high, raised vertically to the parted lips] (p. 173) of a young blindfolded woman. This graffito produces a shock effect in the reader but surely also some incredulity. The narrator as pretended objective investigator of myths in public places is himself subjected to a constant good-humored (self)-interrogation on his complicity with and blowup of the erotic: "Ici encore je vous arrête. Vous employez à plusieurs reprises, dans votre narration, des expressions comme celle-là: 'petits seins naissants,' 'fesses charmantes,' 'cruelle opération,' 'pubis charnu,' 'splendide créature rousse,' 'éclatante plénitude,' et même une fois: 'courbes voluptueses des hanches.' Est-ce que vous ne croyez pas que vous exagérez?" [Here again I must stop you. You use several times, in your narrative, expressions like that: 'little budding breasts,' 'charming buttocks,' 'cruel operation,' 'fleshy pubic area,' 'splendid red-haired creature,' 'wonderful plenitude,' and once even 'voluptuous curves of the hips.' Don't you think you're exaggerating?] (pp. 188–89).

  In the early seventies Robbe-Grillet publicly justified the choice of sado-erotic material in his novels as the use of "sadism against fear." He argued that rather than hiding or suppressing images that do exist in our society and in our literary and artistic forms (popular and cultural topoi, "high" and "low" culture are not distinguished), we should bring them into the open, reveal their superficiality, their lack of "depth," their character as flat, painted images like Cezanne's apples. We should contemplate "our" hidden face in pleasurable and liberating play.[30] The first of the functions of the predominance of this sado-erotic material from popular imagery is, he claimed, often figured ironically in the text itself, in, for example, the proliferation of false "blind" men in *Djinn*.

The writer interprets the recurrence of this oedipal figure for his reader in *Obliques*: "On a toujours tort, pourtant, de ne pas vouloir regarder, les yeux grands ouverts, la société dans laquelle on vit, et ce qu'on a soi-même dans la tête" [We are always wrong, however, not to want to look, with open eyes, at the society in which we live and what we ourselves have in our heads].[31]

This explanation takes no account of the specificity and hyperbole of these cultural stereotypes. Yet there are differences not only of degree (of hyperbole) but also between the kinds of myths among which one lives and what one has in one's head. Earlier in this chapter we concluded that Corinthe's fiancée embedded a patriarchal past in quite different ways in Barthes, Michelet, and Robbe-Grillet's elaborations of the myth. In *Topologie* Vanadé, goddess of a tribe of Amazons (pp. 50–52) in the ancient city of Vanadium, recalls Monique Wittig's feminist rewriting of the classical stories of the Amazons in *Les Guérillères* (1969).[32] Wittig's Amazons are cruel but strong and independent women violently resisting the complicity with men that the race of enslaved mothers has accepted. Robbe-Grillet's own dual Vanadé, vanquished/victorious, her-maphrodite ruler (David/Vanessa) of the city of Vanadium destroyed by a volcano, does not at all resemble the characters of Wittig's rewriting of the myth. Robbe-Grillet's myth, like Wittig's, may be combinatory and constructed out of clichés, but it is predictably a Robbe-Grillet, not a Wittig story. The account of the City of Women, its occupants con-quered by male soldiers and pierced by arrows as they take refuge, bleeding, in the sea and the sequel of a lone young woman survivor taken prisoner to become the victim of rape/revenge on the sacrificial altar carry a distinctive signature.

A long essay by Andrea Cali[33] on the coding of sex in Robbe-Grillet's work dwells on the extended archaeological metaphor put into play by the title of *Topologie d'une cité fantôme,* that of historians or archae-ologists who seek to investigate a series of assassinations of young girls, victims of a rite, their bodies offered "comme sur un autel . . . en travers d'un divan très bas à la romaine" [as if on an altar . . . on a low Roman style divan] (p. 111). Cali observes that this metaphor draws apparently randomly upon a number of generative sources—classical myth, the captured butterfly from Jensen's *Gradiva* interpreted by Freud, metaphor of literary "dig," and variations on the theme of crime against young women existing in previous Robbe-Grillet texts. Cali argues that these multiple sources diminish the possibility or power of any single origin. Vanadé, who comes in variant forms generated partly from a table of anagrammatic transformations of her graphemes or sememes (Gravida, Vanessa, butterfly), also has both an ancient and a modern version. The ancient goddess appears as a hyperrealist sculpture representing a car accident in which a gangster and his mistress perish, that is, as a reference to the myth of Bonnie and Clyde. Cali reads the shifting between synchronic and classical meanings of the mythical material as evidence of Robbe-Grillet's avoidance of any direct confrontation with the sexist material of modern myth:

Or, qualifier les massacres exécutés par des psychopathes de "rites barbares" remontant à une antiquité lointaine, c'est les arracher, de quelque manière, au monde réel des magazines et des reportages télévisés pour les investir d'une aura romanesque, presque d'une légitimité culturelle. En même temps, en utilisant des mythes inventés, Robbe-Grillet exclut la possibilité de lire son texte comme si c'était un compte-rendu de la réalité ou une étude psychologique.

[Now, to qualify massacres carried out by psychopaths as "barbarous rites" going back to a distant antiquity is to extract them, in some fashion, from the real world of magazines and television documentaries in order to invest them with a novelistic aura, almost with a cultural legitimacy. At the same time, by using invented myths, Robbe-Grillet excludes the possibility of reading his text as if it were an account of reality or a psychological study.][34]

Angélique claims an apparently single and "autobiographical" origin for similar stories of the bodies of young girls found drowned or lying assassinated, warm and bleeding in the thickets of the forest. Is this, however, a confession or another defensive pirouette? Cali's attempt to make clear distinctions between real life and cultural stereotype does not seem well founded or sustainable. In *Projet,* for example, the televised documentary ("reportages télévisés") shows fertility rites in Africa that are apparently as ancient and culturally legitimate, but also as exotic and unreal, as the "rites barbares" of *Topologie.* Yet I share the critic's feeling of unease, which seems to derive from the dangers and confusion inherent in the textual sleight of hand (Barthes's "truquage") that operates an incomplete telescoping of the real and the invented, and the *signifiant* or *signifié,* as the text hovers between primary and secondary (mythological) meanings, between exaggerated cultural stereotype and personal selections among these mythologies.

The problems for reading posed by the new mobile web are brought out by Cali's observations on the kinds of appeal to cultural competence that Robbe-Grillet's stories make, appeals that seem to function often very close to a reinforcement of this cultural competence. The "trop charnelle épouse" [too carnal wife] (*Les Gommes,* p. 189) presupposes a sexually faithful wife. A's possible infringement of this code is suggested by her too-tight-fitting dress, her excessive good health, and her energy. Transgression is coded by incestuous family relations in *La Maison de rendez-vous* where Kim and her twin sister are the daughters of Manneret, and Lady A is their mother-in-law, but both Manneret and Sir Ralph have sexual relations with Kim. The "little bitch" (transgressive female sexuality) "deserves the whip" in *Le Voyeur*; the prostitute deserves her "punishment" in *Topologie*. Although Cali concludes that these appeals to cultural competence mobilize and parody the cultural presuppositions of the reader, it is not clear to me that this effect of parody always operates fully for all embedded codes. At metatextual levels the content of myth "regresses to form." And yet even for Barthes, and at this level, there is a residue, a reserve, an alternation, in which the content reasserts itself. Cali herself seems uncertain about the point at which parody or simulacrum ceases to be apparent and distancing or the points at which empathetic modeling through identification with the characters might take place. She observes with concern that the cultural image of revolution as political action or social change is itself "de-natured," as the role of the revolutionaries appears to be to dominate the most "charming" women, and the martyrs of the revolution become the tortured and suppressed JR, the bride, or the young communicants. By the end of her study Cali has in fact shifted the focus of her reading from parody to the discovery of a struggle for power against the feminine in the semio-thematics of sex. Although I share this conclusion in some respects, it is not at all clear how Cali arrived (by a leap of [feminist?] faith) at it.

What is evident is that the woman reader's unease derives also, as Cali's work implies, from the frustration at being prevented from applying a feminist interpretive frame, because the text's games with myths keep insisting on their constructed, or imaginary, or excessive, nature. (A feminist interpretive frame would simply be any frame that takes women seriously or, in this case, that reads Robbe-Grillet's mythologies rigorously as what he has in fact claimed they are: the images in "our," that is in contemporary Western society's, head.)

It is not surprising that critics have taken Robbe-Grillet's work to task, both literally and figuratively. Susan Suleiman's article on *Projet* concluded that despite the recurrent signs of theatricality, what predominates in the work is male aggression aroused by the question of origin. The phantasies played with are those of the rape, torture, mutilation, and murder of the dominated (if textual) female body. These phantasies may relate to a tenacious hatred of mother/nature, as in Sade; the young women degraded may indeed be a stand-in for the maternal body. Or, Suleiman suggests, they may deflect forbidden desire for the mother and keep her inviolate by dividing erotic life into two channels, one exclusively sensual and the other exclusively "tender." Whatever the origin of these unconscious or waking or primal phantasies of the origin, *Projet,* Suleiman concludes, is "definitely a man's book."[35] And despite the constant defusing of empathy (references to machinery and theater, the detached tone, the description of sadistic scenes with the precision of the technical manual, interior duplication), this text arouses and disturbs. Yet, with her usual directness, Suleiman admits that empathy with the ironic game and fascination are aspects of her reading.

John Clayton[36] based a critical moral reading on the opposite premise of the absence of any possibility of empathy (without, however, considering whether this was empathy with the thematics or with the forms of the text). For him, the female victims of cruelty are not cathartic but are turned into aesthetic objects of art; emotional distance routinizes torture and defuses the torturer's (and by implication the reader's) guilt and pain. Clayton reiterates the thesis of domination and abuse, arguing that this aestheticization is simply another aspect of the imagination of control—the imagination of white slavery, prostitution, control by drugs, and sadism.

Diane Crowder concludes much as Cali does that Robbe-Grillet's fiction has an underlying thematic structure based on "a need for power" and "shifting focus from social structures to a psychological revolution by male characters against female sexuality."[37] Like Cali, she examines the conscious fetishization of women's dress throughout the work and the metonymic processes by which the apparently neutral objects of the world are contaminated—the "black mass of the hair" in *La Jalousie* rendering the "green mass of the banana trees" suspect, or the triangular "form of a female organ" of the slit in the automatic vending machine in *Les Gommes* that prepares for the repeated triangles in *Projet* or *Souvenirs*. Paradoxically, the close work of these two critics highlights the way the text constructs feminine, subordinate, masochistic sexuality and masculine dominance, but their political conclusions can take little account of this construction.

Djinn may well have been Robbe-Grillet's humorous response to feminist critics of his work. Djinn and Simon Lecoeur each have "a slighty androgynous face" (pp. 13, 133); and when the young man with blond hair and green eyes disappears, the police find only the body of a young woman of similar description. Djinn gives andro-djinn; the dominator/dominated, male/female become one and the same by the tricks of the narrative and textual analogies. In *Topologie* Vanadé/ Vanessa is bisexual or has a twin brother David, who, engendered out of his mother's rape and immersion in the blood of sacrificial violence, has the body of a woman and a male sex organ.

Androgyny or bisexuality can, however, also be seen as a Barthesian synchronic "mythology," that is, as the mythological material predominant in popular culture at the present moment along with unisex styles of hair and dress, the Jan Morris story and interest in sex change, transvestite entertainment and cross-dressing, the success of Michael Jackson, certain rock band styles, and the general subversion of the traditional heterosexual-homosexual dichotomy. In the eighties, nominations for the Academy Awards in the United States, for example, included a number of portrayals of sexually ambivalent characters such as Dustin Hoffman's portrayal of the "woman" in the "man" in the film *Tootsie*.

These figures also have wide-ranging literary and artistic precedents in Pre-Raphaelite and Decadent art. Much of the literature of the late nineteenth century may be considered pre-texts—Virginia Woolf's *Orlando,* where the narrator is a male in the first part, a female in the second; Proust's Albertine; Genêt's "queen" and the sacrificial violence of his *Querelle* popularized by Fassbinder's film version.

By the end of the seventies Robbe-Grillet was refusing fixed binary sexual oppositions, at least in his theoretical discourse, and in an interview with Germaine Brée,[38] he vehemently opposed the setting up of mutually exclusive male-female poles and the postulation of different male and female imagination and discourse. Recent trends in the theory of gender and writing have envisioned the masculine discourse as based on Freudian repression and control by logical ordering and domination and the feminine discourse as instinctual, diffuse, less controlled and controlling. In the interview with Germaine Brée, Robbe-Grillet states that "there are characteristics that are called 'female' and characteristics that are called 'male,' and that are both present to varying degrees in each individual."[39] But an individual's phantasies, he claimed, may be the opposite of the supposed phantasies of his sexual group. Theoretically masochism is a feminine trait, but a statistical analysis of the number of men who phantasize about being beaten and his own experience of the sadomasochistic universe (which he now admits openly to be the sexual universe he and his wife Catherine share) suggest the contrary.

This argument for masculine and feminine potential in all human beings is itself rapidly becoming an avant-garde doctrine or cliché. And these theoretical stances can be means of parrying attack on his positions at the sadistic pole of sadomasochism. Yet Robbe-Grillet's direct, somewhat perverse, "coming out," the professed staging of his own sexual phantasies in *Angélique*, must also be seen as an ex-posing of skeletons in his closet to view, play, and perhaps debate. Likewise, the processes that place woman as a sign in dialectical opposition to man, implicit in language and culture, are both made explicit and altered by the play of his text.

Susan Suleiman is obviously correct in her pronouncement that *Projet* is a man's book to the extent that the writer behind the narrator behind the masks is Alain Robbe-Grillet himself, and the material he uses is selected out of the mythologies that formed and surround him, and out of his own "life." To what extent is Robbe-Grillet "responsible" for the choice of these images created by society and selected and then used/abused by him? And once again the question arises: Is the "play" of his text in fact the "unmaking," "new organization," and liberation that he claims, or is it the designating of an imprisonment?

Robbe-Grillet commented in an interview for *Le Monde* in 1970[40] that the poetic and aesthetic density his images (or myths) create may be what counters the abstract play of the structures and the language, denies the irony, the humor, the phantasy and makes the critics so uneasy about his designs. As I have argued, form works against the content, but at the same time the content secretes meanings and mythologies that threaten to overwhelm the formal restraints. I conclude once again that the disquiet that this work occasions and its power are best understood in terms of the Barthesian analysis of myth. Nature, humanism, tragedy, crime and punishment, and personal sexual phantasies may be nailed flattened to the door, like the bird of evil omen of Genette's metaphor, ex-posed as harmless representations, but as both Barthes and Genette would argue in their discussions of the function of modern myth, in the process of ex-posure, they have not lost all power. Their meanings are struck out but not erased, they have been placed "in reserve" (or could we also say "under erasure"?) but not destroyed. The text's linguistic confrontation with its own material conditions and semiotic nature and attempted deconstruction of an ideological content (a socially and historically based system of beliefs about humankind and the mythologies that shore up these beliefs suspends, supersedes for the moment, but does not destroy, this ideological content. The content continues to secrete meanings as a function of individual choice, experience, and desire. Perhaps the writer's confrontation with the texts he selects from the discourses that surround him and the confrontation with the hidden origins of his selections offer the only, limited, liberation possible from the monsters that he claims in *Angélique* threaten to invade his waking life.

Robbe-Grillet is both intelligent observer and prisoner of the general mythological network around him and the dialectical processes of its elaboration. His analysis of the myth "Woman" confirms the findings of the feminist studies that have appeared in the last two decades, including work on the prevalence of the Andromeda complex (the ambivalent saving and harming of the fair maiden in distress). And yet the sado-erotic network in which he is personally enmeshed, culturally marked as masculine, is a particularly disquieting one. His work may be an attempt to designate and, to some extent, remake this network through the very language that constitutes it—perhaps his work is not in complicity with it—but such an enterprise, as Robbe-Grillet himself seems to have become aware, is problematic on many levels. Language can neither represent the world nor translate the unconscious:

> Première approximation: j'écris pour détruire, en les décrivant avec précision, des monstres nocturnes qui menacent d'envahir ma vie éveillée. Mais—second point—toute réalité est indescriptible, et je le sais d'instinct: la conscience est structurée comme notre langage (et pour cause!), mais ni le monde ni l'inconscient.

> [First general point: I write to destroy, by describing them exactly, nocturnal monsters that threaten to invade my waking life. But—second point—all reality is indescribable, and I know it instinctively: consciousness is structured like our language (and with good reason!) but not the world or the unconscious.] (*Le Miroir qui revient*, p. 17)

Despite the indescribable character of reality and the invasiveness of language which structures consciousness (or perhaps because of it), as the lived is discovered to be stereotype, myths and stereotypes slip imperceptibly toward the lived. On these margins, at these intersections, perhaps something real is touched. Discussing the autobiographical fragments first published in the review *Minuit*, Robbe-Grillet admits that the stereotypes he denounces and plays with are stereotypes that have formed him, are still present in him, and in whose net he might still be caught.[41]

Postmodern game stumbles against a residue as Robbe-Grillet seeks to make his way through dark labyrinthine underground passages, past barely recognizable dislocated body parts (real or represented?) and the junk of Western civilization. Robbe-Grillet accepts that the choice of myths reveals a constellation that is analyzable. He claims for himself the position of first analyst, but is he, then, both analyst and analysand and what happens to the reader? The following chapter raises these questions of the choice of the complex of the sadist and the siren, of the nature of Robbe-Grillet's "secret room," and of the validity of the cathartic function that Robbe-Grillet claims for his mise en scène of (selected) contemporary mythologies of woman. This study of Robbe-Grillet's films encounters "complementary" and "chaotic" structures in the world and in a sadomasochistic structure that appears to underpin the psyche and that may indicate some of the senses of the sado-erotic thematics and semiotics in Robbe-Grillet's work.

The Sense(s) of Sado-Eroticism in Robbe-Grillet's Films

To begin at the traditional beginning[1] is to begin close to the logos that is origin, meaning, identity, or voice. For signs have reference, and Robbe-Grillet himself claims to be breaking down ("rétrograder") the received meaning of the objects, discourses, narrative structures of our Greco-Romano-Judaic-Christian-Germanic culture. Meanings proliferate in his films, the meanings that are already there in the stories elaborated in the synopses, in the ready-made symbolism of object and scene, in the natural locations, as in the self-conscious metafictional and specular techniques (camera filming within the film, paintings and photographs that animate or generate sequences, interfilmic reference).

In *Trans-Europ-Express* (1966) the narrator is the public personage, film director Alain Robbe-Grillet himself, making a film with script girl Catherine Robbe-Grillet and director Jérome Lindon on the moving train that gives the film-to-be its name. The director, then, is making a film about a drug- or diamond-running ring in Amsterdam and a film about the making of a traditional film. But actor Trintignant (alias Mathias, alias Jean, Robbe-Grillet's literary alter egos) encounters actress Marie-France Pisier (alias Eva, beautiful spy and prostitute, alias Violette, figure of Robbe-Grillet's phantasies). Staging excessive scenes of bondage, rape, and murder, Jean / Mathias ties Eva's wrists to the bedpost in a ritualized scenario, rapes her for her pleasure to the grand romantic air of the bedroom scene with Violetta in Verdi's *La Traviata*, then strangles her. In these scenes, Jean comes to disturb the economy of the projected film of cops and robbers and of the self-reflexive film. This Robbe-Grillet alter ego, is not, as the writer himself points out, the stiff and pedantic Robbe-Grillet-director that the camera films. One Robbe-Grillet can hide another. Nor is he simply an avatar of the self-deluded Gidean narrator as the multiple layers of narrative activity peel away his

145

masks. Jean and Eva derive from the stereotyped underground representations of naked girls tied to the railway track in a bondage magazine,
slipped between the covers of the inoffensive *Express*, that Trintignant
is reading on the Trans-Europ-Express. Actors Trintignant and Marie-
France Pisier are agents of the self-reference of the film about film; they
are also distanced transpositions of the sexual imaginings of the director
and his script girl. The box of string Jean tries so hard to throw away
into the water of the port has many meanings. The montage reverses
temporal order and places the shot in which Jean throws the packet into
the water before the shot in which he is holding it. The box of string
can then reappear providentially as the string in Eva's drawer, which is
used to tie her wrists to the iron bedpost. It also has links to the cardboard box of the young collector that figures in the childhood memories
of the sadistic murderer of Angélique-Violette in *Le Voyeur,* and the box
of the string collection that will appear much later in the childhood
"memories" of Robbe-Grillet himself in *Le Miroir qui revient.*

In the curious sado-erotic lesbian sequence of the punishing of Maria
(avatar of Marie or Marie-Eve) in *L'Homme qui ment (1968),* the young
servant, blindfolded, is forced to bend her head in a slow and erotic
gesture of submission that seems very familiar to a Robbe-Grillet viewer.
A shot of the chopping block precedes Maria's gesture; a sudden fall
of the axe brings the scene to a climax with the cathartic shock of the
image of the axe buried in the empty block and the women laughing
at their own erotic games as at the play of the montage. The fragile
nape of the neck is literally "exposed" in the written texts, in the case
of the frightened waitress with her whipped-dog expression in *Le Voyeur*
and the dancer kneeling over the leather strap of her fine open sandal
in *La Maison de rendez-vous,* for example. The exposing of the fragile
nape of the neck is again given visual equivalence in *L'Eden,* where
Violette, imprisoned and tortured by her male captors, blindfolded,
wrists bound, and kneeling, bends her head to drink from her water
bowl. While these images recur as self-quotation and even as a kind of
humor, it is also the case that desire moves compulsively and obsessively
from signifier to similar signifier in such scenes, from image of submission, fragility, and powerlessness to violent image, in erotic tension,
seeking resolutions but finding no permanent satisfaction.

In *L'Eden et après* (1970) a group of bored students in France in
the sixties overplay flat but transgressive games of the popular press—

the group rape of Marie-Eve, treacherous poisonings, rituals of drinking blood, of penetration with sharp instrument, the terrors of the imagination released in Violette (scorpions, broken glass on vulnerable flesh, torture) by the consumption of a drug, "the powder of fear," or the viscosity of raw eggs, offered by Duchemin. These games are organized around the poles of domination and submission, constraint and liberation, love and violent death.

The heavy machinery of a real, although empty, factory in Bratislava, the huge hooked moving crane of the port, made oneiric and sexualized by lighting, sound, cultural associations ("everyone knows" the locomotives, the motorcycles, the heavy machines, that symbolize virile power!), organizes scenarios of fear and of pursuit. This powerful moving machinery, which also signifies the metatextual machinery of the serial organization of the objects of the film, is thus both sign and referent.

In other kinds of movement (reversal) between real and represented, the gesture (the signifier) creates the feeling (the signified). The stylized repetition of the gesture of a woman's head thrown back and arms raised to protect the face, generated by a painting in the café *Eden*, is a staging of the signs of fear thus made problematic, and opaque; the "real" gesture/emotion is an imitation or simulacrum and not a transparent representation. "Marie-Eve pretends to pretend to be jealous." A dark-haired woman kneels, head back and gun in mouth, immobilized and aestheticized stereotype of thriller and pornography, among the twisted black metal debris of a Rosenquist artwork. But what, in turn, is at the origin of these generators of fear and jealousy?

We are manifestly, as François Jost and Dominique Chateau[2] point out in their work on Robbe-Grillet's films, no longer in a universe of true and false, of real and imagined. The blood we see is at once red paint, element of the composition, codified linguistic meanings, and mental representations. Perhaps we are in one of the worlds of the new semantic logic of the theory of possible worlds, as an article by Chateau suggests,[3] but these elements and events have real referents and psychological implications, however distanced, or held "in reserve."

Whose mental representations are these? Who speaks? To whom? Selection is not completely aleatory or wholly determined by contexts; it suggests an origin in a particular historically situated libidinal and poetic economy that hardly seems to be that of Angélique-Violette. This is true on the simplest level. Robbe-Grillet himself tells the "meanings" of the synopsis of *L'Eden*. In the interviews that followed the film's release he recounts the story of Violette's quest for the Grail through trials and perils as the story of a liberation from the fear of blood and sperm and the taboos of sex. This story of a search for self through love, purification by water, baptism by fire, rebirth by dissolution in the mother/sea (the homonyms mère/mer), repeats age-old elements of female quest. Violet/Violette's (Little Rape) tale is the romantic commonplace of (Sleeping Beauty) waiting for the handsome stranger with the strange pale eyes, experience of more exotic climes, and the authority to initiate the heroine to pain/pleasure, and the cruelty or sexual forcing by her ravishers that is a mainstay of the male genres of thriller and pornography. Robbe-Grillet has insisted that women will always phantasize rape no matter what the changes in their socioeconomic situations.[4] In traditional female romance, as Helen Hazen argues,[5] we see something similar but from the other side: the heroic passive resistance to male brutality and through virtue or self-sacrifice, the ultimate taming, by Beauty, of the Beast. The meanings of liberation that circulate in the thematics and semiotics of sex in *L'Eden* are more probably Robbe-Grillet's own—or, at the least, those selected out of male stereotypes—than Violette's. They might not, in fact, concern her liberation at all.

In *Glissements progressifs du plaisir* (1974) an adolescent Alice is incarcerated in a House of Correction run by nuns. (One of the earliest erotic works to achieve notoriety was the French novel entitled *Venus in the Cloister*.) Alice is interrogated by the police (Trintignant disguised as police inspector in dark glasses and trench coat), carrying out an inquiry into the murder of her friend and lover Nora. The clues to the crime—the broken bottle, the scissors, the dislocated or cut or bloodsplashed mannequin, the blue shoe, archaic agricultural implements—serve as what Robbe-Grillet calls grammatical punctuation in a serial associative organization of the diegetic elements, and their combinations create the violent sexual stories of the film (jagged masculine bottle juxtaposed with feminine blood stained shoe recalling Cinderella's shoe/slipper of fur). The white habit, prie-dieu, cross, candles, and wedding crown, signify purity and the sacred, the chaste and virtuous "Justine" whose defilement is required to construct both impurity and the erotic.

Repetitions of gestures and traces create a countercurrent that works against any linear, causal investigative progression (the detective story) or narrative reading. The young girl's head bending in submission over the prie-dieu cuts to a shot of a head bending over the executioner's block. Two red (vampire) marks link Alice in her white cell with Claudia in her dark cellar and with Maître David (the female investigator who comes to replace the victim Nora in an ironic new "lesbian" version of Oedipus). These feminine figures are linked in their turn with Robbe-Grillet's reading of Michelet's *La Sorcière* and with his own autobiographical alter ego, Count Corinthe, who has the two small red marks on the neck that characterize a victim of the vampire's bite.

The glossy images of *La Belle Captive* (1983) again organize around a fragmented detective story without clear resolution. In the opening scenes, dark Sara Zeitgeist pulses through the night in black leather and white lace, contemporary angel of death and boss of the organization, on powerful motorbike, or the fair Marie-Ange van der Reeves, victim and vampire, dances to seduce the "hero," Walter Naime, in a cabaret. At the end of the story, Walter awakens from his dream to find himself in bed beside his wife (Sara Zeitgeist). But when he walks into the kitchen and turns on the taps, these are no longer working just as in his nightmare. He appears to be living the strange adventures that he has been "dreaming." As Walter sets out from his apartment for work, leaving his wife, Sara, behind him, the bloodstained body of Marie-Ange suddenly looms up once again on the roadway. In a screeching of brakes, Sara Zeitgeist arrives and climbs out of a military vehicle surrounded by militia to arrest the bemused young man. The movement between real and represented, while denying the realism with which the reader attempts to recuperate the text, also becomes disquieting. This "disquiet" does not, I would suggest, reside only in our "recuperation" of the text, that is, in a mimetic reading. The spectator is indeed caught up in the metafictional effects and the often humorous play of visual and verbal references to other works that orchestrate the film—the chained and bleeding young woman victim, the ruined mansion of the secret society, the theatrical red curtains, the thunderclap, the sea and the stretches of strand, the collection of blue shoes, broken glass, pointed nails, bloodstained blue shoe, Marie-Ange looking through the bars of the iron bed, the "voyeur's" bicycle showcased, Inspector Francis and his pile of self-similar postcards, the firing squad from Goya's painting, the death of the Comte de Corinthe from a vampire bite, the sound of dripping water and breaking glass. The strange power of this film derives from the way its forms hold the reader at a distance from this "material" and yet draw him/her aesthetically into the atmosphere of erotic dream.

Complexity and apparent contradiction mark the voices and modes of the narration. One Robbe-Grillet hides another. The synopsis is an inadequate account of seen events. The dialogue fails to comment on the erotic images it accompanies; the image often contradicts the dialogue; the sound track does not always conform to the image but precedes or contradicts or counterpoints it. Narrative control is constantly contested, contradicted, by the look. But who is orchestrating the battles? Whose choice, whose look, is this?

The complex mental universe that organizes the eye seems, in the final instance that of the sadist fixed on the attractive and dangerous power of the other, siren and victim. Her voice is the call to sameness and self-annihilation, and this unacceptable seduction provokes a subsequent "battle of the sexes" for control. It could be argued then that the sense of the marine monster who devours little girls is his striving to erect/protect the patriarchal order and his own position in power against the threat of absorption by the primitive maternal disorder and powerlessness. The very act of rendering visible expresses a capture and a power relation, according to Sharon Willis, and, like Laura Mulvey, Ann Kaplan has argued persuasively that the cinema, in its abstraction of woman, provides only for a male gaze.

And yet seeing in Robbe-Grillet turns out always to be more complex than we thought. We are in a postmythical paradigm of "mythologies," after Adam, Acteon, and Psyche, where seeing and knowing are no longer necessarily loss and death; we are in an Eden after the Fall. Yet the void of self makes the look problematic; the look organized by the sadist to freeze the siren, to know her, is victim of its object, is the object. No one, claims Lacan, possesses the gaze (the Phallus); the look is necessarily castration and lack. Consciousness is constituted, as in phenomenology, as consciousness of its object. And all that is left on the side of the subject-observer is the intentional part of intentional consciousness, intent in this case to maintain distance and separation, resist enchantment.

I situate this "intent" at the juncture between consciousness (of language) and the unconscious drive, and at the intersections of the Freudian pleasure principle and the negative compulsion to repeat, that is, in the postmodern void or vortex of self. This void derives from the lack of any unifying principle, God, or inner self, or humankind, to guarantee a definitive truth or single meaning; it is a space of originary flow and fusion, but also of destructive violence and desire. Intentionality (or authorial intention) is a much debated concept. Is the intent that declared by the writer, or that mandated by a narrator dominating the reader, or that imputed by a reader from a reading of an undeclared author or from a reading of a text? Within the postmodern frame of the polysemous and multilayered text and the decentered self the concept is more controversial again. However, although it might be argued that the intent that I discern is more an effect of my readings than an effect of the intrinsic meanings of the text, I maintain that something exists in the conjunction of these two that I could only call "sense" or "intent." I would want to consider the latter generally as an ethical effect not situated alone in my desire for an author and a morality in the text. Although it may indeed be the case that the manifest intent of an author is of little consequence, it might give some clue to the directions in which the work works.

The omnipresent sea—the noncodified memory of *Glissements*, the restless, tangled web—is evidently also the classical repository of the unconscious. It is the closed primal site of nondifferentiation, the movements of suction and repulsion of the instinctual maternal origin, of fusion and continuity with the mother / other / lover. Locus of a ravishing, of a dissolution of the boundaries of the body or of individuality and separateness, it rolls the pale "ravished" (violated / enraptured) faces of its drowned victims in its eternal waves. The figure of the drowned fiancée is an intertextual borrowing, Shakespeare's Ophelia, or Millais's Ophelia floating among the waterlilies, the faces glimpsed from Rimbaud's drunken boat (*Le Bateau ivre*), or Blanchot's tender fiancée, pale hair entwined in the weeds. But the proliferation of these figures in Robbe-Grillet—Violette wading out dissolving into the sea, Duchemin drowned at the foot of the stone staircase in the Bratislava canal and again in Djerba, Nora playing at being drowned in the pools by the shore, Marie-Ange van der Reeves (the ghostly vampire "fiancée de

Corinthe") drowned on a South Atlantic beach, or Robbe-Grillet's own childhood acquaintance Angélique found drowned along the coast of his native Léon—also creates an intent or sense. There is a conscious mise en scène of the connections of this selection of images with the commonplaces of our culture. Shots of Duchemin's arm and hand stretched out in rigor mortis as he lies in the water are cut to shots of Violette making love and a close-up of her arm in a similar gesture to insist on identity between pleasure and pain, pleasure and self-loss, Eros and Thanatos.

Michel Rybalka explained the presence of such "erotic clichés" in Robbe-Grillet's work as playing in a new mobile construction with the "dull and decadent mythology of the society in which we live."[6] I would argue that the banalized and demystified mythological images in Robbe-Grillet's text are not only simulacra. Suleiman suggests that the mythological female body of Western texts, in its embodiment of the oppositions of the angel and the whore, the maternal and the sexual feminine, life and death, is "the very emblem of the contradictory coexistence of prohibition and transgression, purity and defilement, that characterizes both the interior experience of eroticism *and* the textual play of the pornographic narrative."[7] Transgression, she argues, is (like sado-eroticism) inseparable from a consciousness of the boundaries of the body/text it violates. This is not unlike Susan Sontag's[8] conclusion to her investigation of the "pornographic" enterprise as a sounding of the limits of consciousness/of the text. I would argue also that the choice of these elements has a relation to psychic structures and/or to childhood sexual development. Or rather, it is in terms of the recurrence of the gauntlet that the fascination of alterity (otherness) throws down to integrity (separateness), of the desire to protect individual boundaries, the fear and fascination of fusion or of death in such a desired identification, of loss of the self-possessed self, that I can make the greatest sense of the amorous but violent battle between the sadist and the siren in Robbe-Grillet's films. The writer fights to stay within the symbolic, in control, but at some level, what tempts him is the limen, regression, and loss.

This battle is characterized by what Jessica Benjamin in her study of the master-slave relationship calls rationalized violence.[9] *Rationalized* here refers not to the motive for the violence but to its calculated, ritualized, form of expression. The phantasy of erotic domination and control and of its opposite ecstatic self-loss in absolute submission (even unto death) pervades the texts of our Western culture, the mystico-religious text, the political text, female romance fiction, and the por-nographic. Violence is, for Benjamin, a derivative of the desire to achieve the differentiation that derives from both necessary autonomy and the recognition by the other necessary to achieve this autonomy.

In Benjamin's reading of Hegel's master-slave dialectic, selfhood, existing for oneself, desiring, is an effect of existing for another, of the other's desire, and of being able to affect another by one's acts. To attain this recognition and to obtain the sexual gratification dependent on the other, the self gives up its earliest Freudian phantasy of self, that is, of omnipotence and accepts dependency in return for connection with and recognition from the (m)other or earliest care-giver. Benjamin argues that in an individualistic society the developmental and psychological process of recognizing the other as real, of connecting with another erotic being in order to feel erotically alive oneself, is paradoxically more difficult and can create a sense of isolation and unreality. "Violence acquires its importance in erotic fantasy as an expression of the desire to break out of this numbing encasement."[10] Sadomasochistic ceremonies of the control or devouring of the other are not for her an apology for male violence in general, but an attempt to replay ritually the never totally relinquished desire for omnipotence, or the desire to remain safely autonomous by substituting subjugation of the other for connection. At the other pole, the need for recognition leads to the obliteration of self. "To escape from this conflict, the Hegelian desire for omnipotence (the self-consciousness that wants to be recognized by the other in order to make itself the world) and dependency on the other for recognition," writes Benjamin, "it is all too tempting to imagine that one can become independent without recognizing the other person as an equally auton-omous agent. . . . One need only imagine that the other person is not separate—she belongs to me, I control and possess her."[11] In the novel *Projet*, as Daniel Deneau points out, Laura—the narrator's sequestered "little prisoner" (p. 76), object of "illicit possession" (p. 78), and poten-tially a cause for his destruction, a prisoner whose knowledge of the outside world is filtered through the narrator—is the sexually desirable object of such a common waking daydream: "the man or woman who manages to capture another human being for use as an unwilling sexual object."[12] Laura thinks of her "guardian" as "reassuring" (p. 170) and resists her punishments for disobedience and her "rape" only in a token and ritualistic way.

The body, for Benjamin, stands for discontinuity, individuality, and life; its erotic violation breaks both the taboo between life and death and breaks through our discontinuity from the other. It was in the struggle to the death for recognition through the body's erotic violation that Bataille read the transgression of a fundamental taboo—that separating life from death—in Hegel's analysis of the master-slave relation and concluded that eroticism centers on maintaining the tension between life and death (continuity, nondifferentiation) of self. The rituals of consenting domination and submission serve, as Benjamin sees it, to allow one partner to uphold the limits of rationality and control and allow the other to risk her/his separateness and approach self-loss and psychic death. Some vicarious identification with this limit, visibly experienced in the body by the other, is possible from the position of control. Sexual eroticism, or the phantasy of rational violence, as successors to religious eroticism, offer, for Benjamin, a controlled form of transcendence, the promise of the real thing. Although the story of O is the story of the original failure of differentiation from the mother, repeated in the replay of the roles of subordination and control, Benjamin echoes Nancy Chodorow's recognition that in the present pragmatic socio-politico-historical contexts of power, the roles ascribed the male and female are not the same. Men, says Chodorow, have a psychological investment in difference that women do not have.[13] A similar overdifferentiation figures again in the Lacanian psychoanalytical model of the development of the psyche that must repress the desire for fusion with the original feminine, unify the fragments of the body to come, finally, to see itself as the other (or differentiated self) in the mirror. Indeed, in the oedipal triad, the male seeks recognition (not nuturing) rather from the father, seeks to gain prestige in the violent repudiation of the mother's parts.

The thematic of the systematic sado-erotic suppression by penetration and dismemberment of the female body in Robbe-Grillet's films works to validate a current central paradigm of feminist theory. This is the thesis of the generalized repression, naturalizing, devalorizing, and subjugating of the once powerful mother on whom the infant was so totally dependent (or of the abjection of the disappointing castrated other, or of the flight from the seductive, potentially castrating mother) as the blind spot in our oedipal culture from which everything nonetheless emerges. However oversimplified pronouncements that consider implications in violence to be the province only of the male may be, feminist scholarship is making it evident that, as Susan Suleiman concedes, "there is something in our cultural contexts that endorses and reinforces violence against women" and that this violence "seems to have an origin in deeply ingrained, very old, and essentially masculine attitudes towards sex."[14]

Robbe-Grillet's male is situated in the mainstream of our cultural representations and sociopolitical structures (but not according to Kinsey in actual sadomasochistic sexual practice where male masochism is the most prevalent) at the pole of power. Identification with the powerless or desiring other is carefully controlled so that Robbe-Grillet can, as he himself claims, be *both* the "ridiculously" macho, handsome stranger, or Don Juan operator of the scenarios of domination, *and* the Angélique-Violette, who experiences the pain/pleasure of simulating being swept away or overcome by the masterful other and the "liberation" of humiliation and self-loss. The relation is a complicitous one of mutual dependence where one harms to connect (while maintaining control) or subsequently to console.

And yet, despite this complicity, there is an evident reluctance in Robbe-Grillet's work to extend the forms of "complementarity" developed generally in his work to the thematics and semiotics of gender. The diaphanous angel-vampire is inevitably a woman. Anne-Marie Dardigna,[15] sees the sense of such an omission (only women's bodies are imprisoned and punished in the castles of the French libertine texts in present intellectual vogue) as a complicity, not a rupture, with the dominant ideology, a pseudorevolution of male cerebral control. There is a fixing of poles along gender lines, a distribution of sex roles and phantasies that are the opposite of feminist.

In recovering and rewriting images of female potency, re-membering the feminine body as positive and strong (Suleiman's laughing mother), siren song as call to the new world, and Medusa as laughing in defiance at Perseus's power rather than sleeping through her own immolation

(Cixous), feminist scholarship is uncovering the extent to which these figures (the castrating female look) have provoked repressive anxiety. In a paper with the provocative title "Robbe-Grillet: Sexist or Feminist," given at the New York University Symposium on the Films of Alain Robbe-Grillet in May 1989, Royal Brown argued, much as Robbe-Grillet has done, that it is the feminine figures in the films that impose themselves and come out "victorious." His discourse is, however, couched clearly in the Robbe-Grillet paradigm of the "battle of the sexes" and takes little account of the strange inversions operated in this female "victory." What we have here is no feminist goddess but Robbe-Grillet's goddess Vanadé, victorious/vanquished, who "triumphs in her very violation," as P.R. (homage to Pauline Réage) writes in the preface to Catherine Robbe-Grillet's "classic" sado-erotic novel L'Image.[16] Robbe-Grillet's witch Alice, adolescent principle of explosive freedom and transgressive sexual subversion/perversion, magically outmaneuvering the unwitting and slow moving lawyer, pastor, and policeman armed with the codes of the law, is still a variant of the "monstrous little girl" that Philippe Sollers finds, in Portrait d'un joueur, in the most sophisticated, professionally successful, and autonomous young woman. The same is true for both Marie-Ange unmaking a reviving mystical discourse of spiritism and vampires or the beautiful boss Sara Zeitgeist, black leather and white lace, on her powerful motor-bike. The grace, finesse, and beauty of Alice's mobile body, her independence, and her games may indeed also fascinate a female viewer, but in the final instance, she is an ambivalent creation of a male libidinal economy. She could only be young, small, and beautiful (for eternity), curving, supple, on trial, sociopolitically powerless, falsely innocent, and bound for the stake.

Locus of a collection of the clichés of our society, and of intertextual reference, fatal attraction, witch with the devil in her, vampire, powerful and powerless, Alice, Marie-Ange, and Sara join the immortal L (elle/she) in L'Immortelle with her Mona Lisa smile, the A victim of a persuasion in L'Année dernière à Marienbad, and Eva used and abused (raped and murdered) in sexual games in Trans-Europ-Express. Like Maria, Sylvia, and Laura playing "lesbian" games of queen and slave with whips, blindfold, chopping block, and axes in the attic in L'Homme qui ment, and the blond wounded captive of La Belle Captive, they stage the narrator's choices among masculine obsessions. The young woman is the feminine magnet, the displayed body, that holds the masculine stories together, strangely depersonalized and interchangeable, generator of desire. Jane Gallop, among others (Freud included), has pointed out the pragmatic given of the long tradition of desire for those with less power and privilege, a gravitation toward the child, the woman, the slave.

John Fletcher, who is generally critical of Robbe-Grillet's films and what he calls their "visual monotony," claims that the filmmaker (inimitable prose writer, but lesser visual artist, in the critic's opinion) "has been able in recent years to achieve strongly erotic effects by filming the most beautiful girls that money can hire in provocative situations and poses."[17] There is evidently some truth in this otherwise oversimplistic moral judgment. Yet the actresses (and indeed actors) of Robbe-Grillet's low-budget experimental films have included some of the most intelligent and innovative on the Parisian film scene—Delphine Seyrig and Marie-France Pisier among them. The latter, who plays the prostitute-spy of *Trans-Europ-Express* (turning bound and naked on a revolving platform in a nightclub in Amsterdam), has figured prominently on the scene of feminist action. Again, I would argue, we come close to the situation of pornography or sexploitation and yet remain in a critical position in relation to it. And again the critic (in this case Fletcher) struggles with inadequate, traditional tools to take account of this marginal or double situation.

The meanings at play in the transparent thematics return us, however, inevitably to the primitive, opaque feminine sea—this time as it comes to stand in opposition to the archaic father and to the thematic of the criminal assassin, regicide and parricide, "on his/my own trail," imprisoned in the cell or before the firing squad. In *Powers of Horror*[18] Kristeva anaylzes our age as one of a major demystification of power—of moral, religious, political, and textual authority. Her description of the only ethics possible as the shattering—with play, negativity, and desire—of the codes of social mores before they harden, and the rupturing of the representations of our discourses, dissolving their truths but without losing them, arguably describes the ethos of Robbe-Grillet's texts. But is sexual "perversion" such a clear shattering of codes or demystification of power?

In a study not of sadism but of the more radical male masochism, Kaja Silverman argues that the subversion of established hierarchies operated by perversion can only operate within the structuring moment of the Oedipus complex and the premium this places on genital sexuality: "Perversion always contains the trace of Oedipus within it . . . always represents some kind of response to what it repudiates, and is always organized to some degree by what it subverts" (p. 32).[19] For Foucault, claims Silverman, perversion simply extends "the surface upon which power is exercised."[20] Perversion can thus be both a capitulation and a revolt against hierarchy, genital sexuality, and the symbolic (Father, Truth, Right), disrupting gender, functionality (biological and social), and binarism (pleasure/pain). Perversion, which for Francis Bacon meant "women governing men, slaves governing freemen," will have changing definitions. In our time, it can be seen, for example, as foreplay displacing heterosexual penetration, or deferral outranking end-pleasure.

The fixed positioning of Robbe-Grillet's narrators at the sadistic pole of perversion does not at first sight appear particularly subversive. The male writer's choices conform to Freud's conception of sadism as a desire to subjugate and a combination of cruelty and sexuality in "a serviceable fusion,"[21] considering sadism simply an exaggerated aggressive component of the normal male sexual instinct. Quoting Reik and supported by the work of Krafft-Ebbing,[22] Silverman points out that masochism similarly, is a requisite element of normal female sexuality. While it may stretch the woman's subjective limits, it does not have the shattering qualities it has for the male masochist, who, for Reik, thereby abandons his "self" and passes over into the "enemy terrain" of femininity.[23]

The categories of masochism outlined in Freud's essays "The Economic Problem of Masochism" and "A Child Is Being Beaten" include "erotogenic" masochism, or seeking pleasure in bodily pain/being (beaten) in a passive "feminine" sexual relation to the father; "feminine" masochism, or being "castrated" or copulated with, or giving birth to a baby; "moral" masochism, or pleasure in the ego pain, where the ego is beaten by the superego.[24] Interestingly, even in these Freudian categories the person in the "feminine" suffering position is almost necessarily male. Freud explains the phantasy of being beaten as the phantasy of the incestuous relation with the father which then is repressed to become both punishment and substitute for the forbidden relation. Freud claims that this phantasy appears only in "unwomanly girls" who identify with the father and in "unmanly boys" who identify with the mother, therefore resulting from a (dangerous) negative oedipal complex. Silverman, on the other hand, analyzes the self-display by the male masochist as the exaggerated acting out of the conditions of cultural subjectivity that are normally disavowed and the radiation of "a negativity inimical to the social order." The male masochist loudly proclaims that his meaning comes to him from the Other, prostrates himself before the Gaze even as he solicits it, exhibits his castration for all to see, and revels in the sacrificial basis of the social contract. [He] magnifies the losses and divisions upon which cultural identity is based, refusing to be sutured or recompensed."[25]

In his study of the work of Sacher-Masoch, Deleuze [26] goes beyond Silverman's position radically to reconfigure masochism as a utopian affair between a severe maternal mother and her son, a pact to disavow the father's phallus and the mother's lack and write the father out of his dominant position (in both culture and in masochism). In Freud's explanation of the beating phantasy, boys are being beaten by a male authority figure in the phantasy of the girl—who wants to be a boy— while the figure doing the beating is a woman for the "feminine" and "masochist" boy. But taking as her research corpus accounts of masochistic phantasies and performances since Freud, Parveen Adams concludes, like Silverman and Deleuze, that "something about masochism eludes Freud."[27] For Adams, the masochist of either sex might occupy any of the three positions (the beaten, the beater, and the observer). "The final form of the fantasy is not fixed, either in the sense that there is one form found in women and another in men, or in the sense that the subject occupies only one position in fantasy or in deed" (p. 24). Adams questions whether the terms *passive* and *feminine* are crucial to an account of masochism; she denies that it is the figure of the father who stands behind the figure of the beater and redefines masochism as the participation in a ritual scenario that signifies the abolition of the father in the symbolic and thus also indicates a subversive relation (of travesty) to the Law. At the level of the thematics, Robbe-Grillet's work resists such intersubjectivity and slippage of roles, although this is not the case at the level of his "complementary" and "chaotic" forms.

In Marguerite Duras's writing and film woman is the locus of the contradictions of the pain and pleasure of absolute and unattainable desire; Duras's work portrays the experience of the "ravishing" of the woman (carried away and carried off, enthralled) by love or, as Kristeva puts it in a brilliant article, in self-dispossessing identification with "The Pain of Sorrow in the Modern World."[28] The poetess, whose lost absolute poem celebrates the mystical suffering of her heart pierced by the rays of the sun through a church window on winter afternoons, sacrifices her poetry to love for "the Captain" in the autofictional *Emily L* (1987).[29] Marie Bonaparte, Freudian disciple, quotes Saint Therese's mystical visions of an analogous blade from God, the long golden lance with burning point that penetrates her heart several times and pierces to her entrails, leaving her burning in "the sweetness of that excessive pain" as emblematic of female masochism.[30] (Andromeda's "rescue" as suggested by Ingres is not far away.) Therese's language inspired the Bernini statue of that saint's sexualized mystico-masochistic ecstasy in divine possession that inspired Bataille. Like the "unselfloving" woman investigated in Sarraute's 1990 work *Tu ne t'aimes pas,*[31] the heroines of a number of the most recent female-authored texts of "modernité" are clearly far from affirming active female power. Marianne Hirsch finds in Duras the female sense of connection and receptivity and the self-imagination in which the ego boundaries between self and other/(mother) are exceptionally fluid and undefined that constitute the basis for a distinctive female form of reading.[32] The ground for this "masochistic" orientation may be, as the sociobiological argument has it, in the self-loss and self-sacrifice assumed by or imposed on the childbearing and nursing or caring mother. Kristeva has argued that the feminine role and female creativity are limited by the necessary renunciations of the oedipal daughter.[33] Irigaray, too, after her struggle with the mother in *Le Corps à corps avec la mère*, turned, unexpectedly and disconcertingly, toward an exploration of a mystical fusion of self, not with a fluid female goddess or mother nature, but with a male, bladelike, punishing God. As Emily Apter demonstrated in a perceptive and sensitive paper on female masochism in Irigaray,[34] in her 1982 *Passions élémentaires,* Irigaray collapses the distinction between vaginal and facial lips (as Magritte and Robbe-Grillet do), not, as Apter points out, for the lips to make love with other female lips as in *L'Un ne bouge pas sans l'autre* (1979) and its celebration of the self-sufficient "feminine," but rather to make love with a distinct and overpowering divine male voice. Apter quotes and translates Irigaray. "Ta langue, dans ma bouche, m'a-t-elle obligée à parler? Cette lame entre mes lèvres, est-ce elle qui tirait de moi des flots de paroles pour te dire? Et, comme tu voulais des mots entre autres que ceux déjà prononcés, des mots encore inouïs pour te nommer toi et toi seul, unique en ta langue, tu m'ouvrais de plus en plus loin." [Your tongue, in my mouth, did it force me to speak? This blade between my lips, is it that which took from me the flood of words to say it to you? And as you wanted words other than those that have already been said, words even more wonderful to name you and you alone with, you unique in your tongue, you opened me further and further apart.][35]

Irigaray's text celebrates total self-abnegation, defloration: "This immemorial wound that bleeds only from the invisible pain of nothing, the incrustation of your nothingness on my innocent skin."[36] For Apter, this celebration of abnegation produces a "new *Story of O*/ story of water (*Histoire d'O*/histoire d'eau) with watery poetics of blood, saliva, and sexual discharge, which "shockingly approximates a slave language replete with wounds, lashes and cuts with a knife."[37]

Close as Irigaray's sexualized waiting for God is to Deleuze's theory of "suspense" derived from his analysis of Sacher-Masoch's *Venus in Furs* (erotic postponement and freezing of bodily postures into lexemes of bondage), nonetheless, it is not, for Apter, a simple imitation or travesty of male models. "He takes the form, argues Apter, of what Irigaray, according to Gallop, "wants," that is, as Gallop puts it, "some feminine desire, some desire for the masculine body that does not respect the Father's law."[38] This is similar to the lesbian sadomasochist manifestos[39] of the group "Samois" that imply that women are no longer in bondage, but that it is bondage that is "in drag," Apter prefers, at least provisionally, to consider Irigaray's "protean body-talk" as "a kind of ludic apotheosis, freeing up women to 'play the mistress' or the 'master' as they wish"[40] in a feminist distancing or masquerade of the only discourses we have. The self-negation of Irigaray's story of "I" and her peculiar masochistic pleasure principle, like O's story (in Pauline Réage/Dominique Aury's *Histoire d'O*), nonetheless remains for Apter, choosing her words with irony, "a thorn in feminism's side," "refurbished" but still politically suspect as entrapment.

It is quite evident that women's desires are plural, determined by factors of race, ethnicity, history, and socioeconomic situation. Not all women writers elect, like Duras, Hyvrard, or Irigaray, to pursue a thematics of masochistic female mysticism or self-dispossessing desire— or indeed a life of self-sacrificial childbearing and caring! Men's desires, too, are similarly diverse. Yet the parallel between Duras's writing of hidden feminine masochism and Robbe-Grillet's exploration of underground masculine sadism is striking. Readers and viewers have been unwilling to look too hard and long at these unsettling excavations. In *Le Miroir qui revient*, Robbe-Grillet commented on the scotoma or blind spot of critics unable to see the monsters concealed/revealed in his early texts. While his more perceptive mother found *Le Voyeur* an impressive novel but would, she said, have preferred that the author not be her son, Roland Barthes praised the work as "scientific" and "objective." Large numbers of the establishment's readers attacked it on similar grounds as reifying the world. Blanchot, Robbe-Grillet claims in *Le Miroir qui revient*, was the only critic to observe the "white light" at the heart of *Le Voyeur* where "monsters" lay obscured.

The function of much of the innovative artistic production of our time has been, as Francis Bacon, a painter of notoriously violent and sadistic images, put it, to remove the numerous screens between us and the world and to see beyond appearances by X-raying or distorting the real. This project showcases the vital modern question as being that of the "making" of a reality that is closer to the way things are. Bacon's physically and mentally contorted and suffering bodies resembling animals or bleeding carcasses, and victims of both inner and outer violence, are, however, contrary to Robbe-Grillet's representations, ugly and immediate in their emotional impact. Sexuality in Bacon becomes an animal function, another aspect of the violence and horror of the human condition. In Robbe-Grillet's work violence is sexualized, distanced, aestheticized, and projected onto the guilty/innocent female body, a function less of the human condition or real human relations than of sadistic "masculine" and masochistic "feminine" unconscious desire.

If the feminine signifies freedom and revolution, if feminine masochism can be seen as transgression and masculine sadism as close to the Law, why should the target of Robbe-Grillet's textual aggression and suppression be uniquely the female body? Perhaps the combat with authority is still inextricable from the Freudian myth of the primitive horde. Revolt against that Patriarch's Law is for possession of the Father's women. When the father falls to his death from the crumbling balcony in *L'Homme qui ment*, we hear the sound of a falling tree, linked in its turn to the dull blows of the woodcutter's axe, linked elsewhere in the work to the narrator's beating heart, childhood nightmares, the father working as a sapper in the 1914–18 trenches in fear of the explosion that will bring death (*Dans le labyrinthe* and *Le Miroir qui revient*), the gravedigger's spade, and thus via *Hamlet* back to a Freudian triangle and to the vast lost forest-sea of language and beyond it, the unconscious. Male violence underlies and structures the detective themes and narrative forms, for example, of *Les Gommes* and *Trans-Europ-Express*, where pursuit, murder, knives, and guns displace sex, but erotic violence against the male is a minor mode and brings us back inevitably to the sea, the aggressed female (m)other, the return of the sexually repressed.

René Girard's analysis of classical myth and his study of the ritual texts of pre-industrial societies[41] postulates the ceremonial use of "sacred" violence to purge collective aggressive drives through the sacrificial person of the scapegoat. For Girard the ritualization of violence in classical society served to "purify" the city from a nonrespect of necessary socioreligious differentiations (the incest taboo, the nonkilling of blood relations, for example). Girard postulates the existence of an original self-perpetuating and undifferentiated chain of aggression and revenge that the social order seeks to short-circuit through the sacrifice of a designated victim. Lorenz would locate the origin of this aggression in phylogenetically evolved behavior patterns but also symbolically in the customs and taboos that are themselves for him not arbitrary but, as sociobiologists see it, a complex product of natural selection. Girard's thesis ascribed to the scapegoat of sacrificial ritual, notably in the myth of Oedipus, the curious dual role of the harmful element to be excluded and the savior, criminal other and sacrificial victim/sacred hero, he who takes upon himself the sins of the other. Where Girard's work reads classical violence and social disorder as situated in the sacred, that is, as exterior to man, Robbe-Grillet's work shows this violence as within man (or within his psychosocial constructions) and projected onto the body of the feminized victim/savior. Here too a paradoxical power is ascribed to the scapegoat-victim who promises resolution of tension in transference of criminal guilt. Although Robbe-Grillet's thematics appear to work to stage the sociomythological mechanisms of differentiation and distinction between the sexes that Girard's work argues are central to social survival, it is apparent that they turn predominantly and much more closely than Girard on a fundamentally sadomasochistic structure of psyche.

In a psychoanalytic discussion of the "folie à deux" of the sadist and the masochist William Stekel[42] argued that humiliation and not the phantasy of pain was the essence of sadomasochism. Stekel, like Benjamin, postulated the need for the helpless, vulnerable infant with his frantic desire for the mother's breast to turn the tables on his parent. Although this thesis does not explain the choice of position—reversion to the place of the helpless child or punishment of the imperfect mother—there has been some consensus that the masochist does violence to the self out of rage and guilt and revolt against the mother. Psychiatrist Krafft-Ebbing[43] in the nineteenth century and Havelock Ellis[44] later found perversions in this dialectic of omnipotence and impotence, pleasure in inflicting pain and humiliation, and desire to be the victim subject to the will of a "master" of the opposite sex, humiliated and abused. Havelock Ellis, however, situated the roots of sadistic practices in animal behavior, and his cross-cultural taxonomies suggested that these practices might be instinctual cultural universals. For Freud, too, as we have seen, sadism is a basic psychosexual characteristic, and male aggression is thought to be necessary to overcome the resistance of the sexual object by actions other than mere courting.

In the twentieth century, psychoanalytical theory has considered the sadomasochistic structure to be a universal, interpersonal, and intra-psychic way of dealing with destructive impulses and of avoiding disorganization of the psychic apparatus. In 1905 Freud observed that sadomasochism was a single constellation: "A person who feels pleasure in producing pain in someone else in a sexual relationship is also capable of enjoying as pleasure any pain which he himself may derive from sexual relations. A sadist is always at the same time a masochist."[45] Freud also put forward the thought-provoking hypothesis that when the sexual object is degraded, sensual feeling has free play, resulting in considerable sexual capacity and a high degree of pleasure.

In *Working through Narcissism* the psychoanalysts Gear and Hill[46] claim that narcissism should be viewed as an unconscious bipolar structure that consists of the psychic representations of an ego and an alter organized in isomorphic complementary relations around the opposite poles of sadism and masochism. The structure they hypothesize is very similar to what I have labeled the general "complementary"— contradictory but not mutually exclusive—structure of Robbe-Grillet's work. Sadomasochism, for these two psychoanalysts, is not a restricted perversion but a universal way of dealing with destructive impulse that "takes into account many varieties of submission-dependence."[47] The relation between the ego and the alter, for example, is seen as basically sadomasochistic. The introjected aggression of the subject is used by his superego to blame, torture, and disqualify his ego. The master-servant structure of the superego (that is, the super- or infrarelation of ego and alter) can be explained by the functioning of a competitive pleasure principle that regulates the psychic apparatus, the security and psychic stability of the masochist opting for the pleasure of the other, the lack of security of the sadist opting for his own pleasure. The sadist accepts the masochist's independence but reflects an image of "her" as dependent. The masochist accepts the sadist's dependence on her but reflects an image of "him" as independent. The impulses to seduce and be seduced, to torment and be tormented are irreconcilable but perhaps simultaneous, and the ego cannot satisfy both at the same level. The mirror alone allows the assumption of both positions.

In this narcissistic intra- or interpsychic mirror one partner (or ego) needs the other to see the myth of his/her self-containment. Yet the containment is illusory, and narcissism is essentially a topographical layering of the conscious, preconscious, and unconscious levels of the psychic apparatus and the defensive inversion of conscious representations. Just as perceptual reversal and naming occur in clinical symptoms—the sadist is the torturer who says he/she is tortured by others, the masochist is the cruelly tortured who says he/she is guilty—the martyrs and victims are seen as angels not of mercy but of death. The enchanting siren is the emasculating Salomé in a splitting of the ego, a mechanics of introjection and projection, a change into the opposite and a turn against oneself in repression.

The splitting of the ego in the compulsion to repeat takes one of two directions, sadistic or masochistic. The sadistic child uses omnipotence by identifying with his original other (mother) and actively directing the same treatment at another, thereby repressing his original, dependent, impotent position. The masochistic child achieves this repression by actively seeking a repetition of his passive position in relation to the original other. Parveen Adams has argued that these positions can be reversible and fluid.

Robbe-Grillet's aggressive relation with his spectator, who must be "irritated," "forced" to see and listen, even "killed", according to the writer in *Le Miroir qui revient,* makes this sadomasochistic economy evident. At a symposium on the films of Robbe-Grillet (New York University, 28 April 1989), Tom Conley argued in "The Iconic Text" that Robbe-Grillet's work staged pop-art–style scenarios or enigmatic *rébus* that gave no hold to fixed or definitive meaning or solution. The effect of this, for Conley, was to shut the spectator out, to frustrate every possibility of investigative identification. If one sign simply refers to another, it could be argued that we are in a closed work that renders our interpretive strategies powerless. At the same colloquium, François Jost's paper "Les Eclats de la représentation" ["The Fragments of Representation"]) put forward the more traditional (and opposite) interpretation of an "open" work in the making and unmaking of which, as Robbe-Grillet has always claimed, the reader is invited to participate. And yet, Jost's concluding statement was "Il faut imaginer le spectateur inquiet" [One must imagine the spectator disturbed], which is a play on Camus's existential ethic that Robbe-Grillet's work refuses: "Il faut imaginer Sisyphe heureux" [One must imagine Sisyphus happy]. The pleasure experienced by an off-balance, frustrated viewer might also participate in the sadomasochistic economy.

Such literary questions are not unconnected to the psychopolitical concerns Kristeva articulated after the ground of rationality had crumbled in the age of fascism and of Stalinism. Kristeva sees fascism and Stalinism as manifestations of the deep psychic mechanisms of the human being expressed in the rigid political and religious structures that developed in the thirties and that remain as potentially and no less monstrously dangerous in our time. Her explorations of the contemporary obsession with the repressed psychic spaces connoted "feminine" and her study of what she calls "abjection" (that is, the psychic situation of the borderline subject fascinated with the boundaries between subject and object, with the ambiguous and the mixed, "l'entre-deux," uncertain of an object) express her concern with the volcanic nature of these places. How can the text write such traces? How can the self confront their apocalyptic sense? Kriteva asks whether psychoanalysts can explore and exhibit abjection without confusing their own position with it; Robbe-Grillet's texts may be seeking answers to the same question.

Approaching some conclusion, I situate the senses of the sado-erotic in Robbe-Grillet's films less in the monsters of a specific historical moment than in the recurring spaces of disorder of the void of self (the absence of any organizing principle that gives sense to the world or the self) and the orders that take form from these disorders. Robbe-Grillet's vast forest–sea is a space of the void of self in which the structures of the material world and the monsters of the unconscious meet—and are mediated by—the complex structures of an intellectually controlled linguistic and aesthetic reshaping. Do the "chaotic" and "complementary" structures sensed in the world and the sadomasochistic structure of the psyche that may underpin the person argue for or against the thesis of the eroticization of male domination? There is clearly also a power of the repressed, a power of the erotic, at work.

In the following chapters I examine the premise that the erotic of power and the power of the erotic, like bondage and freedom, are themselves complementary structures in the Heisenberg sense, two contradictory but not mutually exclusive manifestations of the same thing. Locus of the eruption of the unnameable, uncontrollable, powerless anguish of dream behind the apparently free (but, insists Robbe-Grillet, controlled) play in pleasure, pun, and power with conventional meanings (stories, myths, symbols), the sea/the film is simultaneously the site of the emergence and the repression of traces of psychic and historical and still potentially explosive imprisonments. Flooded underground vault and secret sacrificial or inquisitional tower, the cell in its metonymical or synecdochical variations (venetian blinds, barred windows, heavy red curtains) contains not only the immortal beautiful captive but also her captor, his paranoiac resisting attraction to the feminine and his fear of decomposition.

It seems timely to seek understanding of the significant and strong hidden presence, in our culture, of the powers of desire, the desire for power, phantasies of sexual domination and subjugation in male and female alike, to take account of the psychological need to assert independence or to be recognized by the powerful other (a need reinforced in women by representations of their gender as nurturing, self-sacrificing, and seeking connection, or in men in flight from discontinuity and rationality). And yet the inadequacy of these meanings or themes to account for the power of the creative work seems to lead us to a new beginning, as do all Robbe-Grillet's works, not to the senses given by the logos but to the senses suggested by the forms.

In a perceptive paper to which my own reflection is indebted, Alice Jardine[48] discusses the implications of Kristeva's work in terms of its concern for the hidden monsters of the psyche, their relation to historical event in our century, and the work's investigation of the contemporary fascination with repressed feminine spaces. Jardine's paper takes up the question of the political implications of any choice of reading paradigm and of the ideological implications that inhere in the very act of interpretation. It concludes that both the transparent or pragmatic North American feminist reading with its ethical question of the ultimate good of women and the opaque, textual French "postfeminist" reading, which denies the efficacy of traditional frames of meaning and knowledge and ethics, must somehow be simultaneously possible. Perhaps, the sense of the new chaotic and complementary forms of the opaque Robbe-Grillet text and their undecidable meanings must necessarily be read in a complementary relation to the transparent meanings of its thematics and its political contexts. Only so might we approach both a satisfactory academic (critical) and a satisfying feminist (political) reading.

The Eroticization of Power or the Power of the Erotic?

It can be argued that a work of art is characterized by its subversive project: the undermining, by artistic reshaping, of the aristocratic, the bourgeois, or the popular ideologies in power. Sexuality, central complex of taboo and control in all social organizations and cultures, and biological and psychical site of drive and latent energy, would provide privileged material for such subversion. The power of the erotic would be an explosive power for the liberating of our texts and of our social orders. Eroticism would be a humanism. This is the case Robbe-Grillet puts for his sexual/textual revolution.

The Critical Reaction and the Question of Subversion

What if the selections of this subversive material are evidence of a personal imprisonment in the biological and synchronic cultural constructions of the sexuality it puts into play? Feminist views of Robbe-Grillet's creative work and its Sadean inspiration tend to conclude that far from being subversive his work strengthens established (male) power by placing it under the sign of the aestheticized erotic. It writes the erotic of power and not the power of the erotic.

In *Ainsi soit-elle* Benoîte Groult[1] rejects the "pornographic" association of violence and death with sexuality, from Baudelaire's assertion that the unique and supreme pleasure of love lies in the certainty of causing pain to the "snobbish" fashion for Sade, Lautréamont, Masoch, Bataille, and Leiris, for whom the essence of eroticism is defilement. Groult claims that these writers perpetuate the old curse of original sin and the superstitions and taboos of the society they say they are destroying. Their eroticism, she argues, has no place for either the clitoris or for the state of a woman's heart and mind.

Anne-Marie Dardigna's perspicacious study of the perils for the female sex in the contemporary French erotic text[2] argues that the erotic in the works of Bataille, Klossowski, and Robbe-Grillet and the present privileging of the classical libertine writers by French intellectuals constitute a cerebral male erotic of constraint and of the will, not immediate and sensual, and not a liberation. This erotic played out in the French "Castles of Eros" is, for her, the other face of the excessive sublimation and spiritualization operated by courtly love, equally bounded by codes and prescriptions but this time for transgression, a "masculine" erotic in which the flow of "feminine" desire is suppressed.

Although the arguments of Groult and Dardigna are persuasive, we need to know more about the alternatives to a cerebral, controlled masculine erotic and the kinds of "liberating" forms the flow of feminine desire might take before we condemn the former in favor of the latter. As yet "feminine" desires have remained elusive, and it is not clear that they can be defined without reference to the masculine desires in power. Nor is it certain that a separatist or binary division between male and female is desirable. The body of exploratory French feminine writing by such writers as Julia Kristeva, Luce Irigaray, and Marguerite Duras[3] (although these three also demonstrate marked differences) inevitably itself still carries patriarchal traces. Interestingly, the most general movement of these texts is in a dissolution of the powerful subject and search for a new subject whose boundaries are less rigid: "pas un sujet qui pose devant lui en objet. Il n'y a pas cette double polarité sujet-objet, énonciation/énoncé. Il y a une sorte de va-et-vient continu, du corps de l'autre à son corps" [not a subject that poses in front of itself as object. There are not those dual poles of subject-object, enunciation-enunciated. There is a kind of continual movement back and forth from the body of the other to one's own] (Irigaray).[4] This subject may take up a position closer to an apparently traditional (Freudian) and, for some, uncomfortable and politically regressive female masochism. It does allow more slippage between fixed positions (sadistic and masochistic, desiring and seeking to be desired) than is offered Robbe-Grillet's figures of the feminine.

The feminine figures of Robbe-Grillet's texts are most often objects of sadistic desire or repression with little voice with which to express their own (even masochistic) desire. In many cases, they are blindfolded, bound, or gagged, or, at the least, abjured to silence. "Tais-toi, petite idiote" [Be quiet, little idiot], murmurs the intruder-rapist to his apparently willing "victim," Laura, in *Projet pour une révolution à New York*. In the film *Glissements* the same words are recirculated between Alice and her lesbian lover Nora. Their movements are restricted by cords and chains sometimes attached to rings fixed in the floor of the dungeon, prison cell, cathedral, or secret room, where they are held for the pleasure of their captor and, Robbe-Grillet would claim, for the freedom or liberation of their reader. Such combinational freedom to play lucidly and with pleasure with the representations around one, however, may seem a limited form of liberation, especially for a woman.

When it is audible, the voice of the feminine figures utters clichés, signifying indeterminately, as does their enigmatic smile, "everything or nothing." This Mona Lisa smile of promise or of emptiness is, for example, the fixed, mysterious, or absent smile of the opening shots of the fascinating or stereotyped L/Elle (She) in *L'Immortelle*, and the uncertain, fleeting smile of American Jean, the Djinn/Genie of folktale and of *The Arabian Nights*. Djinn is also the leader of the organization and a narrator in *Djinn*. However, the feminine "I" is narrator for only a single chapter in the novel and is not unlike the Jeannie of a popular American TV show, "I Dream of Jeannie," in which immaculately groomed, synthetically beautiful, starlet-genies appear and disappear charmingly at the wave and audible tinkle of the producer's wand. In *Topologie* "Suzanne" briefly becomes the "I," spokeswoman for the dreaming Hamilton nymphets, but her voice is clearly that of the author-in-masquerade. Despite the claims of the writer and filmmaker to have given liberated female narrators a voice more powerful than that of the Law, especially in *L'Eden et après* and *Glissements,* his occasional feminine "I" (Djinn, Suzanne, Violette's narration in *L'Eden,* and Alice's story in *Glissements*) is never completely convincing. "Madame Bovary, c'est moi," indeed, but who exactly is this "me"? A woman or a man? As Luce Irigaray has put it, unless woman is herself producing the images of herself, she may be lost in the two-way mirror that man holds up to her, swallowed up by him in "the abyss of what he does not know of the mother and of woman." "Si elle ne s'image ni ne se sculpte elle-même, l'homme l'engloutit dans l'abîme de ce qu'il ne sait pas de la mère et de la femme . . . Nous sommes volumes rencontrant des volumes,

procréant et créant des volumes. Nous ne pouvons demeurer une énu-
mération indéfinie d'images. Cela ne dure que le temps de dévorer l'autre
ou les autres, de les consommer pour créer l'illusion de chair" [If she
does not produce an image or a sculpture of herself, man swallows her
up in the abyss of what he does not know about the mother and
woman. . . . We are volumes encountering volumes, procreating and creating volumes. We cannot remain an indefinite enumeration of images.
This lasts only the time of the devouring of the other or others, of their
consuming to create the illusion of being flesh and blood] (p. 43).[5]

Jacqueline Lévi-Valensi's study of the feminine figures in Robbe-
Grillet's creative work[6] demonstrates their nature as privileged object,
but as appearance and body without traditional emotional meaning.
She cites the quintessential image of the chained sacrificial victim at the
heart of "La Chambre secrète" as an example of this emotional flattening
in favor of the senses: "Seul, au premier plan, luit faiblement le corps
étendu, sur lequel s'étale la tache rouge—un corps blanc dont se devine
la matière pleine et souple, fragile sans doute, vulnérable" [Alone, in
the foreground, the stretched-out body on which the red stain is spreading, gleams faintly—a white body whose full and supple flesh can be
sensed, fragile, no doubt, and vulnerable] (*Instantanés*, p. 98). In the
subtle exchange between the movement of the crime and the frozen
image, resolved by the final phrase in which the "sinusoidal" movement
of the smoke from the incense burner traces an "irregular curve" [une
sinusoïde irrégulière] "toward the top of the canvas" [vers le haut de la
toile] (p. 109), any embryonic female subjectivity is immediately denied.
The adolescent's smile of hidden secret becomes an "empty" smile in
Topologie. It is "comme si un imperceptible sourire était apparu sur ses
lèvres sans fard, un sourire qui semble le reflet d'un secret ineffable,
lointain, fragile et fugitif, inexistant sans doute, un sourire peut-être
d'innocence et peut-être de complicité, un sourire vide" [as if an imperceptible smile had appeared on her unpainted lips, a smile that seems
to be the reflection of an ineffable secret, remote, fragile and fleeting,
no doubt nonexistent, a smile perhaps of innocence and perhaps of
complicity, an empty smile] (p. 86). Sleepwalker with a "légèreté de
fantôme" [phantom lightness] (p. 87), "danseuse absente" [absent dan-
cer], this "improbable" figure has previously smashed the liquid mirror
of water in her china bowl to obliterate her reflected image and disappeared, leaving the photographer-voyeur David Hamilton alone in an

empty room (p. 79). Mona Lisa's ineffable mystery/emptiness is made and unmade throughout the work in similar passages, and its very redundancy begins to signify.

But what is signified? The dreams and secrets of the absent young convalescent, like the phantasies of the sequestered adolescents, are those of the male narrator. As Vanadé/Suzanne says to her creator: "Mes yeux sont vides. C'est vous seulement, qui posez sur mon corps ce regard trouble" [My gaze is empty. It is only you touching my body with that uneasy look] (*Topologie*, p. 126). For Françoise Bech[7] the female character never acquires an identity; she is trap and prey simultaneously, caught in the tight network of the descriptions that inscribe her in a context calculated by the intellect and influenced by the sensuality of the writer. Valenski's conclusion is that this character is destined to serve only the desires of man. Bech quotes an assemblage of recurring sado-erotic elements that would seem to justify a similar conclusion: "La belle Angélique, condamnée à périr par écartèlement, doit être exécutée le lendemain; Duchamp, suivant une de ses coutumes favorites, a donc ordonné qu'on la lui livre auparavant. . . . Au cours du déjeuner, la jeune fille sera punie de ses inévitables maladresses par divers supplices préliminaires, plus ou moins brûlants ou sanglants, mais n'altérant pas de façon permanente l'aspect extérieur du corps" [The beautiful Angelica, condemned to perish by quartering, is to be executed the following day; Duchamp, following one of his favorite customs, has therefore ordered that she be delivered over to him first. . . . During the meal, the young girl will be punished for her inevitable clumsiness by different kinds of prelimary torture, more or less burning or bloody, but not altering, in a permanent way, the exterior appearance of the body] (*Souvenirs du triangle d'or*, pp. 230–31). Robbe-Grillet's world, says Bech, is a world of crime without object—the vanity of the soldier's death in *Dans le labyrinthe*, the senseless murder of Jacqueline-Violette in *Le Voyeur*, murder as the symbol of a vanished civilization in *Souvenirs*. In this world of void, blood, and death, fixed in its delirium, woman is the idol of a metaphysics of absence as she is the symbol of the absence of metaphysics. She is "the priestess of a destroyed temple."[8] And in this sovereign enterprise the female character remains the prisoner of the writing and of the absolute of phantasies, which, for Bech, are "the reflection of the solitude of the writer reinventing the world according to his own desires,"[9] reflection of a world marked by enslavement and domination, despair, disaster, and neurosis, which refuses to be tragic. The meaninglessness of existence is redeemed only by the aesthetic. Bech situates this text close to concepts of *modernity* in the light of Blanchot's assertion that the task of the work is to liberate thought from notions of value and to open it to new unforeseeable statements. She accepts Blanchot's response to the absence of meaning as an incitation to seek meaning that does not yet exist or is hidden, but in order, in the final instance, to strengthen her own critical feminist reading. Robbe-Grillet's writing is, for her, the gamble of "libertinage" in literature for a new objectification of the latent conflicts of the unconscious that haunt all societies. Its style, she claims, reactivates the problem of feminine emancipation, since its provocations cannot leave one indifferent, and any revolt begins with indignation. The style of Alain Robbe-Grillet has only the value of "the courage of its excess"[10]

In the face of the objectification, capture, and interrogation of the feminine figures, the academic male critics have most often remained discreetly silent. Some have had recourse to the dominant contemporary critical canons that enjoin both good taste and liberal attitudes in sexual matters. In an article cleverly entitled "Bits and Pieces Concerning One of Robbe-Grillet's Latest Verbal Happenings: The Sado-Erotic *Project*"[11] Daniel Deneau reviews the range of these judgments. He passes quickly over the "screeching condemnations" ("pornography of the lowest type" . . . "fictional masturbation") to quote Leon Roudiez as the first critic to suggest that the "obsessions" developed in *Projet* are apparently Robbe-Grillet's own. Roudiez also noted what he called their "bothersome and unpleasant" character.[12] For Deneau this judgment reveals the extent to which the "taboos of Western middle-class culture can still control one's reactions."[13] Antony Pugh "spares" his readers an "anthology" of the countless appearances of the motif of blood, of female genitals, of scenes of rape and torture while finding that these happenings are "essentially therapeutic."[14] Deneau himself echoes Joseph Bentley's claim in *The Perverse Imagination* that "sadism cannot tolerate wit."[15] According to Bentley, comic cleverness and formal artistic complexity function as mediums through which forbidden criminal material can be transmitted to the social world and as a kind of safety valve for the pressure built up by such repressed antisocial material. Deneau's reading of *Projet*'s catharsis is of a series of free-flowing inventions that

express the intimate relation between man's sexual life and his imagination, a kind of permissive waking dream that is controlled and cleverly
self-conscious. "Although the text may remind some readers, as it does
me, of a male's sexual fantasies, ultimately, of course, the randomness
of the text and the subject are controlled by a clever artist, the inventor
of the inventive narrator."[16]

While Deneau attempts to grapple with the sliding between "real"
erotic phantasies and those of pulp fiction, his own taxonomies are
evidently subjective. The disobedient child-woman Laura, as captive
sexual prisoner requiring punishment, corresponds, for him, to "the
serious erotic side of the imagination,"[17] as does the confession of the
false policeman, who states that he will take great pleasure in raping/
buggering and punishing the beautiful, aroused Joan, although the sexual pleasure experienced by the other plays no relevant part in his
personal fixations. This critic categorizes the final scene in the empty
lot with the naked and captive mannequin, JR, astride the saw-blade,
as "game," yet images of red blood flowing in rivulets beneath a door
in the ever-lengthening white corridor, and, behind other doors, the rat
molesting Claudia's dead body and the poisonous spider attacking Sara's
vulva, watched by the voyeur-locksmith—images produced by the perverse imagination that twists together sex, torture, and death—pose a
problem. Deneau accepts John Sturrock's view that the distortions and
humor should put us on our guard against becoming too concerned
with the actual nature of the narrator's obsessions and concludes: "As
I view *Projet pour une révolution à New York,* it is a dynamic illustration
of the unfettered imagination inevitably acting as a creator of erotic and
violent images or fantasies. And let us hope that Robbe-Grillet's witty
book will help its readers to unmask and to smile at their hidden faces."[18]

Does Deneau's conclusion include me, either as a reader or as a
woman critic? Are my hidden faces those of the narrators (or implied
readers) in Robbe-Grillet's texts? Or rather, those of Laura, Sara, or
the mannequin JR? John Sturrock's reading of *Le Voyeur* as rhetorical
"occupatio" (the novel has something to hide and does nothing but draw
attention to the fact that it has nothing to hide) would assume that I,
as female reader, am included in this game of hide-and-seek—but in a
sex-neutral role? Sturrock asserts that the reader "is indeed offered the
part of the analyst, and since the novelist has limited himself to the

more colourful and blatant of contemporary psychoses, this is far from being an impossible part for the reader to play successfully. . . . To treat Robbe-Grillet's fiction as serious psychoanalytical material would be a preposterous mistake. . . . Mathias is . . . everyone's idea of a sado-eroticist."[19]

Morrissette, too, subscribes to the thesis of stereotypes, but, this time, as formal play: "Basically, his theory is this: to choose popular, 'ignoble,' even worn-out fictional situations and themes from porno-graphic novels, detective stories, exotic action films, and Epinal-style engravings of sadoerotic tortures, and structure these by means of generative metaphors, formal interrelationships, correspondences, and *mises en abyme* . . . to produce a radically new kind of novel and film."[20]

Raymond Jean argues in a similar vein that what is important about these stereotypes of sex-fiction is that they "function."[21] Stoltzfus, in his study of *Souvenirs*, sees the stock-in-trade images—fur, blade, blood, door, shoe, fire, etc.—functioning as a "piège à fourrure" or girl-trap set for the reader whose expectations are conventional and who is inevitably lured into recuperating the sexual signifiers in traditional ways.[22] Thomas O'Donnell analyzes a characteristic Robbe-Grillet scene in *Projet* to demonstrate this formal generative functioning.[23] The projector lighting the scene of a naked woman, wrists bound behind her back (an obvious reference to the novel's title, for O'Donnell), generates the theme of interrogation in the tradition of the third degree. The woman's mouth, "indisputably and generously open" [le seul détail indiscutable est la bouche généreusement ouverte] (*Projet,* p. 8), utters a scream of suffering or of terror. But in a juxtaposition of opposites, the "open" mouth is quickly recharacterized as "gagged" by black lingerie. When the text suggests that the woman's tormentor is a doctor, the gag becomes ether-soaked gauze and the "prisoner" becomes a "patient." O'Donnell interprets other baroque transformations—the pen that becomes a hypodermic needle, the long hollow needle piercing the flesh of Caucasian prisoners, and the blood that flows drop by drop through each fine steel tube to become sperm or ink released by a fountain pen—as metaphors of Robbe-Grillet, the writer, becoming the rapist attacking and cutting up doxa. O'Donnell's conclusion retains Robbe-Grillet's own apparently contradictory explanations: the identification of the images of advertising, eroticism, and terror with the repressed imagery of subconscious sexual desire, that is, the thesis that these ready-made images reveal our hidden faces and the designation of a clever generative (inter)textual game where meaning is deferred.

A number of the critics who have justified this game as one of "liberation" have gone to more extravagant interpretive lengths. Historically, claims Bogue, the prison (like the barracks or school or factory with which it is confused in *Dans le labyrinthe*) replaces torture, as, according to Foucault, authorities seek to regulate the body rather than to break it. "Torture within Robbe-Grillet's generative cell then can be read as counter-violence aimed at liberation within confinement."[24] Michael Nerlich finds value in the thematics but in relation to the work's pedagogical worth as a serious study of pornography, a phenomenon to which everyone, he claims, is voluntarily or involuntarily exposed in the modern world.[25] Pornography, repudiated in the realist novel, is "assumed" in Robbe-Grillet's work. Nerlich goes on to make a somewhat inconsistent classical distinction between pornography, as visual or textual doubling of the sexual act, and the erotic, in which the physiological is transformed within a system of signifiers to bring about a new self-consciousness that produces catharsis. Only this artistic "form," he argues, can bring "man [*sic*]" to full sexual liberty in image and in fact in a society where everyone will have the right to the "voluptuous tomorrow" that Robbe-Grillet claims to seek. Nerlich does not address the apparent contradiction between the continuation of an intellectual Enlightenment tradition (cathartic self-consciousness) and the libertine tradition of voluptuousness. Or, for Robbe-Grillet, are the two perhaps complementary? In any case, Nerlich assures us (in good faith?), that the pornographic element is minimal. Curiously, Michel Rybalka, too, found it pertinent to point out that Robbe-Grillet's texts are discreet, and "never describe people making love,"[26] applying a very traditional criterion of "pornography."

Vareille has given the most sustained psychoanalytical reading of Robbe-Grillet's work, accounting for the "mise en cène"/mise en scène" (that is, the cannibalistic feast or mock Eucharist of *La Maison de rendez-vous* [pp. 167–68], which reappears in *Souvenirs* and in the films *Glissements* and *Le Jeu avec le feu*) as symbolic of the oral stage in the child's development. The most primitive and radical means of appropriation by violence of the body of the text/the mother's body, this eating, for Vareille, merges with the ambivalence—mixture of repulsion and fascination, adoration and attack—characteristic of the sadism of the anal stage. While the phallic stage is not greatly in evidence for Vareille, in an inversion, language (the feminine body) begins to devour the male, attracted by dreams of oceanic beatitude; the shell with its delicately furled pink edges becomes a castrating female trap. Vareille does not mention the sponge next to the shell in the same Magritte painting that in the Robbe-Grillet text is described as filled with vinegar and applied sadistically to the soft edges of the shell to make them retract in pain.

For Vareille, eroticism functions as a privileged metaphor of writing exactly because it is a strong figure of protean (Freudian) desire. Only "feminine" language remains, now male and now female, a totality in herself. Yet, victim because she is a goddess, on the side of disorder and movement, like A who stands with the blacks and the colonized in her transgressions of limits and taboo in *La Jalousie*, she is also a statue, immobilized, the object of a cult. Woman is opposites, supple and rigid, undulating and yet symmetrical even in the finest details. ("Au-dessous de la chevelure *mouvante*, la taille très fine est coupée verticalement, *dans l'axe du dos,* par l'étroite fermeture métallique de la robe" [Below the undulating hair, the fine waist is cut vertically, down the line of the back, by the narrow metal zipper of the dress] [*La Jalousie*, pp. 135–36; Vareille's italics].) Vareille quotes from one of *Projet*'s most remarkable passages to insist on the periodicity that marks feminine undulation and woman's uniting of the opposites, freedom and rule, shifting complication and symmetry. This passage describes the call girl, spy, member of the organization, Joan Robeson or JR as a deep-sea fish whose motionless body, half hidden in the ulvae, faintly undulates itself, ready to buckle in sudden violent twists, ready to open in a soft and greedy mouth with "replis compliqués, précis, multiformes, remodelés sans cesse par de nouvelles excroissances ou invaginations, mais qui *conservent en dépit de leurs sinuosités changeantes une constante symétrie bilatérale*" [complicated, precise, multiformed folds, ceaselessly reshaped by new excrescences or invaginations but which preserve, despite their moving sinuosities, a constant bilateral symmetry] (*Projet*, p. 67; Vareille's italics).

Movement behind the frozen statue, as in the paintings of Magritte and Delvaux, beauty cast in stone, woman is threat of disorder ("discohérence" for Vareille, using a term invented by Ricardou), the presence of desire and perverse pleasure in the erotic/textual body. The tortured feminine body only twists harmoniously because it is restricted.[27] Her chain is here to remind us, says Vareille, of a (displaced) guilt and to witness to the fact that freedom is forbidden (aesthetically without efficacy). What Vareille's reading presents as subversion, then, is a movement between text and woman's body so vertiginously and inextricably intertwined (both in Vareille's text and in Robbe-Grillet's) that the questions of where the boundaries are between text and female body or of whose perverse pleasure this twisting under restriction occasions are not noted.

The current literary topos of text as sex, pleasure (Barthes's *jouissance*), and transgression is generally accepted as active and revolutionary. As Stoltzfus puts it, "The artist's pen (poetic signifier for "phallus") opens up *langue* (poetic signifier for "vagina"), pares, thrusts, exposes, reveals and plays . . . violates ideology which is hidden within the folds of *langue* whose vestments are convention—the norms of the establishment. . . . While *langue*, imagery, and establishment codes manipulate the masses, Robbe-Grillet's art (parole) 'plays' with these repressive forces in an attempt to expose and manipulate them."[28]

The Freudian hypothesis of the sublimation of sexual drive to artistic activity has long postulated parallels between writing and erotic activity. Interrogation, penetration, dislocation, and erasing are simply those of the striking out of the seductions of the falsely realist masculine text and its conventions of a linear progression, causality, character, coherence, and moral meanings, in favor of a feminine text of destruction of ready-made meanings, slippage, and pleasure, of bricolage, assemblage, and intertext. The blurb for *Souvenirs*, probably written by Robbe-Grillet, explicitly designates the sado-erotic and incestuous practices of the novels of the seventies, which "not only interrelate but feed off one another." Such incestuousness, says Fletcher, is not accidental, or the result of a shortage of material, but "an organizing principle."[29]

But again, why incest with the daughter? Why the sado-erotic? Might the limitations of this interpretation of text as disruptive and sensuous textual practice conceal the real practices of violence or incest against female bodies in the world? If the traditional text is masculine, why is the target of Robbe-Grillet's textual attack inevitably gendered feminine? We observe the fate, for example, beneath Robbe-Grillet's pen, of the apparently gender-neutral series of hyperrealistic archery or shooting targets, the pop art objects, borrowed from Jasper Johns. These abstract concentric mathematical forms are transformed metaphorically in the writer's text to become naked bodies, sexual "targets" pursued and pierced by male hunter-marksmen and, evidently, female.

Not all male critical readings, of course, have focused on Robbe-Grillet's cathartic or revolutionary premises. In his postface to the 1965 paperback edition of *La Maison de rendez-vous*, entitled "Un écrivain non-réconcilié," Franklin Mathews, while sympathetic to the strength of the artistic innovation, claims to hear a voice of anguish and fear behind the hardness and certainty of the flat surfaces that recall the pop art of Rosenquist and Lichtenstein. He reads the work as unresolved tension between the distanced fixing of the object of desire and the invulnerability of the flesh to extravagant torture, and the violent irruption of subjectivity. In particular he notes the contradiction of the "faultless glossy sentences" and "the increasing madness of the narrative."[30]

There has been male condemnation. For John Fletcher, "Robbe-Grillet's view of women's sexuality seems at best misleading and at worst sadistic and perverse." Robbe-Grillet, claims Fletcher, has implicitly compared himself with the men in Turkey who stare at Western women and "follow with motionless intensity, the outline of their bodies under their summer dresses, down to their unfettered ankles, and pursue an inward dream which would make them captive, chained up within a magic circle" (Robbe-Grillet, *Obliques*, p. 228). "Such a notion on the part of a citizen of a civilized country that protects women as far as possible from male violence might seem merely harmless frivolity; but I think that, were I a woman, I would consider it not only nonsense, but dangerous and pernicious nonsense."[31]

While it is indeed what Nancy Miller has called "the violence of the silence of theory from which all traces of the body have been erased"[32] that motivates my own suspicion of certain critical readings, my criticism of Fletcher's book, on the contrary, is that it has obliterated any gap between the imaginary, sociohistorical reality and phantasy, between text and life. The literary and the real have simply been telescoped. Fletcher's argument here links him with certain practices of the Women against Pornography movement caught in a similar simplification. Apart from the intellectual difficulties I have with positions of censorship, Fletcher's apparently innocent little phrase "were I a woman" also raises a number of questions. Fletcher's work succeeds, however, in foregrounding the sociohistoric traces of the real body, under erasure, both in theory, as Miller claims, and in real practice. At the 1990 Modern Language Association convention in Chicago Christie McDonald read a paper about the massacre of fourteen female engineering students in Montreal the previous year by a young man who subsequently committed suicide. In the year-long police silence that suppressed/repressed the killer's written note explaining his action as a so-called justified reaction to "women taking power," she saw an insidious further act of violence against women. Robbe-Grillet's text may well help to break such silences on both real and imaginary violence. This does not, of course, exclude the possibility that gender may play a less than entirely subversive role in the manner of the writing of this violence. But perhaps Robbe-Grillet's aggressive ex-posing of the socially and sexually repressed may be seen as a significant first subversive step.

Cultural Subversion

Beyond the thesis of self-contained sexual text of pleasure or that of the aesthetic playing out of the de-dramatized male passions of fear, will to domination, and solitude, critical canons and reader sensibilities are also influenced by the conscious, post-Freudian sociohistorical "liberation of love": the interest in the sexual "pleasure bond" in which Western society is immersed. In France the literary rediscovery of the classical and eighteenth-century libertine writers, already revived by the surrealist interest, presented the latter as freedom writers. This was the judgment of the editor of the "Libérateurs de l'amour"[33] and the assessment that Robbe-Grillet's theoretical writings have shored up in the face of the recent publication of the complete works of the "divine Marquis" (de Sade), the rediscovery of Restif de la Bretonne, the return to favor of Choderlos de Laclos (in Vadim's film version of Les Liaisons dangereuses in the early sixties, in the Renaud-Barrault theatrical production, and in the successful 1989 and 1990 Hollywood remakes of the work), and the fascination exerted by the cruelties of Lautréamont, Artaud, Genêt, and even Beckett. The excesses of Bataille and Klossowski, like the popular success of Histoire d'O, could be interpreted as intellectual curiosity about what might lie behind or beyond social or religious limits and repressions or behind an arbitrary law. It might inscribe a recognition of taboo as enmeshed in symbolic orders or an interest in the power generated by the effraction of this taboo. This is the sense in which Lacan interprets the Freudian dream of the burning child and the child's words— "Ne vois-tu pas père (que) je brûle?" [Don't you see, Father. I'm burning]. The figure of the young woman burning watched over by the father and the phrase itself, recur in Robbe-Grillet's texts and films. Like the general "liberation of love," this phantasy, in the Lacanian interpretation, represents the attempt to repossess the power of repressed desire, power that might be released in the effraction of sexual taboos.

Or is the expression "freedom writers" a misnomer, a blind, or a political inversion like the analogous expression "freedom fighters" used repeatedly by former President Reagan to designate the Contra rebels in Nicaragua in the attempt to make the term seem natural and self-evident? For John Clayton the pretended objective distance and aestheticization of women's bodies in Robbe-Grillet is an attempt to routinize their torture and pain and to "stop the world dead."[34] Robbe-Grillet's own diatribe against contemporary feminism in Angélique ou l'enchantement would seem to lend weight to this hypothesis. For all their liberatingly "perverse" sexual practices, such contemporary libertine works can indeed be read as emanating from a deep fear of feminine takeover and an attempt to stop the contemporary history of women dead.

How then would we situate the sadistic, pedophiliac, homosexual phantasies of cruelty in Hervé Guibert's "new novels" (L'Image fantôme [1981] or the later "Vous m'avez fait former des fantômes [1987], whose title is taken from Sade's epistolary reproach to his exemplary wife), tales of young adolescent boys abducted, kept naked in sacks in a cave, tattooed and heads shaven, their vocal cords cut, and trained for the sport of their (sexual) masters?[35] What can be said about the phantasies of captive and tortured sexual slaves or of young boys sitting on rows of pointed stakes in Tony Duvert's homosexual work? Or of the often monstrous Amazons or warrior women, the warfare, cruelty, and bestiality of Les Guérillères (1969) in Monique Wittig's first lesbian work? The women on leashes in the inner circles of hell and the masochistic weeping mothers who must be liberated by violence from complicity with an old violent order, guided by the ferocious woman Manstabal before a new order can perhaps come to pass, are similarly problematic in the 1985 novel *Virgile, Non*. One scene, not unlike a Robbe-Grillet scenario in *Souvenirs*, takes place in the circle of the shooting galleries where female "souls" with their chests cut open serve as targets for amateur sharpshooters trying to hit the exposed heart. In *Le Corps lesbien* Wittig's female body is both concrete in its obstinate presence (sex) and shows the phantastical properties of the imaginary and abstract (text), much as in Robbe-Grillet's work. Here the lover-reader must forget tenderness or affection and undergo a violent decomposition or violation in a sado-masochistic relation with the writer in order to be remade; this violence, too, is presented as offering liberation. It can be argued that Wittig's discourse, so similar to Robbe-Grillet's, is in fact a perverse imitation (travesty) and appropriation of the phallocratic discourse. Yet is it possible to say that Wittig's recuperation of the "male" paradigms for her own revolutionary literary and feminist purposes are acceptable inversions while similar operations on this material of her male counterparts are unacceptable offense?

The premise of the subversive and liberating power of unbounded sexuality and the searching of the limits of the range of human sexual feelings and experience in an essentially materialist modern Western world links the literary fashions with the currents and the climates that are producing the present sociosexual revolution. Stemming partly from the technological society and the availability of contraception, this is ultimately a revolution in ways of thinking. The desocializing of sexuality (sex as individual human desire, need, or pleasure, not necessarily linked to family, procreation, and inheritance) and the desacralizing and deregularizing of sexual relations like the insistence on the fulfillment of the individual body, its unique needs for pleasure here and now, are major breaks with the classical Greco-Roman philosophies and the precepts of the Judaic and Christian revealed religions that have formed the traditions of Western civilization. Freud saw the repression of energies of the libido as necessary for the investment of energy in social and artistic enterprises and the inhibition of destructive instincts as necessary for the creation of civilization. Marcuse argued for struggle against hidden sexual images and impulses (of the collective and personal unconscious) as a valorization of consciousness.

Robbe-Grillet claimed that his work sets in motion what he considers to be the "lieux communs" [places common to all] of the synchronic set of representations of general Western consciousness (or, alternatively, of the collective unconscious). The fires, the black thief or rapist (like the "Willie Horton" propaganda of Bush's presidential campaign), and the terror in the subway of *Projet* or the virgin exposed to Zeus's shower, to arrows, or to the stylet of the artist that generate *Souvenirs* would constitute such "commonplaces" as would the dangerously mysterious feminine figure dragging the curly mane of the extinct auroch behind her along the shore. But, as attitudes around him modified, theory changed, and he himself grew braver, the writer conceded that his texts were also speaking of an individuated inner self. It is the lines between stereotype and self, so very difficult to draw, that complicate the situation. For a post-Freudian generation, it is hardly a surprise that sexuality or the concealed obsession with the body of the other (originally, of the mother) should appear as the driving force behind these "commonplaces." And the belief that the female body is a disorder and thus a dangerous seduction for the rational male with a fully developed superego, called to moderation in his pleasures through concern for his self-image, his social standing, and his power, has been with us since the Greeks, as Foucault demonstrates in *Histoire de la sexualité*.[36] *L'Usage des plaisirs* discusses the sexual temperance prescribed in the Greek writings of the fourth century B.C. as a moral ethic for the elite of free adult males. Such an ethic advocated male self-mastery and thus deserved mastery of others and the avoidance of the dangerous realm of sexual pleasure. In *Le Souci de soi,* which studies the texts of the first two centuries of our era, Foucault shows the prevalence of the concern that sexual pleasure is potentially dangerous, costly, and difficult to master, related to the illness of the body or to evil, and to be contained in the conjugal relation and its reciprocal obligations.

"It was Beauty killed the Beast," still, twenty-five centuries on, in the final lines of the twentieth-century Hollywood success *King Kong*. Movies of primitive or brutal superior male strength capturing (and captured by) the little woman are still a significant feature of contemporary Hollywood romanticism.

In its attack on classical Idealism and Greek canons of sexual temperance, socioreligious (Judaic-Christian) regulation of pure and impure sexuality, and Christian (virginal) grace and (deadly) venal sin, Robbe-Grillet's literary subversion of the sexual status quo could be considered analogous to aspects of the movement for women's "liberation." But how exactly does the social/textual subversion of the Law through libertinism, "crime," Sadean debauchery and torture (particularly of female victims), or through "monsters" of the female sex like Madame de Merteuil and Juliette, created by male authors, fit into the emancipation of women? Robbe-Grillet's recent tendency, we noted, has been the public "confession" that stories of crime and sexuality are at the center of his work. In a 1978 interview,[37] *Souvenirs* is described as the story of a man in prison for a sexual crime attempting to protest his innocence by describing his cell meticulously, or of a doctor performing textual experiments on young girls in a luxury house of prostitution, or of a corrupt policeman falsifying his own report to hide his (sexual) collusion with the criminal. While such interpretations are multiple and contradictory, they do reveal some coherence. All these parodic figures of the writer show him caught by errors of judgment in the trap of his own images, criminalized by his very effort to prove his innocence. In the light of this recurring thematic do Robbe-Grillet's theoretical claims need to be nuanced? The writer justifies the presence of collective male phantasy and situation of power as self-conscious and scandalous:

> Je ne l'impose pas, je le mets en scène. L'imaginaire de l'homme ayant toujours été au pouvoir, je suis au pouvoir comme n'importe quel homme . . . L'hégémonie du pouvoir masculin est beaucoup plus battue en brèche par la mise en scène que je fais que par la façon dont il passe surnoisement inaperçu dans la plupart des oeuvres. . . . Le viol et le fantasme de cruauté est montré, encadré, souligné, désigné, comme un événement qui n'est pas naturel mais scandaleux.

> [I do not impose it, I stage it. As man's imaginary has always been in power, I am in power like any other man. . . . The hegemony of masculine power is breached more by the staging I effect than by the way it passes slyly unnoticed in most works. . . . Rape and the phantasy of cruelty is shown, framed, underlined, designated, as an event which is not natural but scandalous.][38]

A long literary tradition that includes Prévost, Restif de la Bretonne, Laclos, de Nerciat, and Sade himself justifies what censors might find scandalous or immoral material with the argument that this material is an accurate depiction of the manners and morals of the time. Their representation is thus edifying, a means of changing such manners. But a morally indignant Robbe-Grillet, defender of a feminist cause against scandalous violence, is not completely convincing. The avant-propos of *Projet* (p. 3) claims that the work integrates these stereo-traps of violence into a living discourse, which, refusing to submit to their constraint, reinvests them with the writer's own imagination. I have argued rather that the fetishist shoe, the hollow needles, the sadistic priest, the themes of cruelty, penetration, and humiliation borrowed from the divine mar-quis, are, in fact, selected as a function of the writer's imagination, and that this imagination reinvests apparently inoffensive images of Moreau, Michelet, Johns, and Hamilton, with something much more immediately "perverse."

In the wider context there is the question of whether, in a scientific, self-aware, materialist society, the emergence of repressed raw material of sexual drive to power or of its partner, impulse to fusion or self-dissolution, traditionally filtered through romantic sublimations of the power of love, is necessarily a liberation. The recognition that human relationships are developed in social contexts of power imbalance or in the context of conquest by sex or love may not help solve the conflicts that this situation provokes. The display, however distanced, of our underground texts may be more dangerous than cathartic. It is possible that the images that reveal the centrality of male voyeurism or male exercise of power on the body of the (female) other at the heart of our representations of sexual relations (or Lacanian absence of relation) might still fall into the contemporary bind of representing and thus reinforcing or modeling what they wish to critique. Similar questions are posed by the representation of the multiple-rape scenes in the film *The Accused*, the antipornography documentary *Not a Love Story*, or even the much-in-demand U.S. Government *Report on Obscenity and Pornography*, with its verbal accounts of such "classics" of the genre as *The Devil in Miss Jones* and *Deep Throat*. (The report was, in fact, republished by Bantam Books.)

There is no political intention in Robbe-Grillet's work to transform the sexual representations taken from the public scene, the pubic "Golden Triangle" or new Golden Fleece, for example, from alienating to positive. This was what Judy Chicago sought to do with her tri-angular-shaped exhibition of embroidered place settings and ceramic plates, *The Dinner Party*, celebrating women's talents and achievements. Her representations of female sexual organs, butterfly-like, infinitely repeated on dinner plates, like Georgia O'Keeffe's paintings of flower vulvas or Cixous's laughing and beautiful Medusa, struggle against the negative cultural current to re-create and revalorize the female body from within. Robbe-Grillet's project for a subversion is neither from within the feminine nor clearly its re-creation. The common-places of Western patriarchy and its (en)gendering of women are reused but perhaps abused in complicity as much as re-created. Red-winged butterflies marked by violet/little rape ("aux ailes rouges marquées de violet") are verbal play, humor, recursive generators, but not a revalorization.

There is, however, a significant coincidence between Robbe-Grillet's content—triangles, butterflies, shells, and female sexual organs—and the material represented in O'Keeffe or Chicago's feminine rewritings. Suzanne Kappeler would argue that this is evidence for the impossibility of attempting to transform "pornographic" representations of women from within existing culture, even by altering the roles or the context of the content, as do Chicago and Cixous. Kappeler's thesis is an indict-ment of any complicity with the material of oppression.

And yet, encouraging those who have been looked at through the one-way mirror to look critically back, and casting white light on the shadowy images hidden in our culture and ourselves, seems an essential starting point for any change. The history of representation may well be "the history of the male gender representing itself to itself," as Kappeler claims,[39] but, she too can only begin to suggest or explore this by writ-ing. In her thesis of the sexualization/animalization of woman dispos-sessed of her subjectivity and energy by a male-constructed culture, Kap-peler develops the apparently extreme argument that women in history, like the animals or raw materials with which they are interchangeable, have been processed as "food" like manufactured commodities. Robbe-Grillet constructs stories of similar excess. They too provoke by leaving the reader halfway between uncomfortable laughter and disbelief at the processing of Angélica von Salomon in a salmon factory and her com-mercialization in cans labeled "la belle sirène." In *Sade, Fourier, Loyola*

Barthes links the sadist, the utopian idealist, and the priest by character-
izing all three as subversive through their excesses.[40] Does such "excess"
give Robbe-Grillet and/or Kappeler the political or critical efficacy, the
subversive power, that this work by Barthes would predict?

Already beguiled by the traps and pleasures of intertextual reference
and the constant, self-conscious dance of traditional feminine figures
(Morgan le Fay, Angelica, Justine, Salome), the (feminist) critic seeking
to respond to Robbe-Grillet's work finds her/his path mined by such
correspondences. Not unlike the spectator of the popular culture movie
Spaceballs, a pastiche and reassemblage of the *Star Wars* trilogy among
other major box-office successes of the end of the eighties, the Robbe-
Grillet reader moves between the comedy of the outlandishly exaggerated
adventures and recognition of their origin as intertexts and an almost
involuntary empathy with the quest of the hero and his saving of the
captured princess; the reader vacillates between ironic distance and the
habit of identification with the romance.

As the objects and figures of Robbe-Grillet's texts are increasingly
marked by a specialized sado-erotic construction of the feminine, however, the majority of the narrators and characters are evidently proliferating fictions of their "author." The latter traces and appears to write
against the old mythologies of the writer—to pastiche the omniscient,
omnipotent father-creator (Balzac), the Faustian investigator who risks
damnation for knowledge, or the Baudelairean seer who plumbs the
depths. Yet it cannot be discounted that this modern wielder of a phallic
pen, sexual deviant or sacred monster, may be seeking new authority
as much as cathartic knowledge by re-presenting his relations with his
muse and that his reader might become the victim of his persuasion.

The Pornography Question

The democratization of a previously censored and essentially male
Hades (the "enfer" of the Bibliothèque Nationale, for example), of a
repressed "demonic" or "decadent" or "libertine" aesthetic of frenetic
self-gratification and an id not subject to the control of any social
superego, might be more analogous to what we could call the popular
pornographic revolution than to a feminist revolution. My own working

definition of pornography after research and reflection on the question is "sexually explicit representations designed to arouse for profit." (I define the word *pornography* as neutrally as possible, given the negative social history of the term over the last two centuries.) The official legal definitions in the Western world are a function of synchronic and local sexual mores and taboos. For example, in the United States sexually explicit material must not appeal to "prurient" interest or violate "community standards" or be without "redeeming social value" in a given community.

The "pornographic" revolution has mainstream, peripheral, and hard-core manifestations. The precursors of the main stream include such older French traditions as striptease and can-can girls. Its more modern forms in the West are the artificial seduction and curvaceous gyration of the commercial nudes of the *Playboy* or *Penthouse* enterprise, and the generally repetitious, glossy, smiling, naive, sometimes aesthetically pleasing transgressions of the old censorships of sexual explicitness or full frontal nudity. On the *Playboy* cable television channel the reclining and "objectified" female "playmates" of print become the mythological copulations of interchangeable subjects, body beautiful, in panting pleasure, for the watching eye. For the most part, and weighed against the implications and current dangers of moral and religious censorship and limitations of women's control over their bodies and their choices, these aesthetisized and sanitized nudes and often soft and soapy TV "porn" have been seen to be relatively harmless and even in some cases therapeutic. Despite the political pressures for increased censorship of explicit materials, the attorney general's "Commission on Obscenity and Pornography" of 1970 came out with a clear verdict that no demonstrable social harm resulted from pornography.[41] The recent French television imitations of American *Playboy*-style programs, *Folies Sexy*, for example, are generally seen as silly or as simple entertainment rather than as harmful. The 1970 United States commission confirmed, if somewhat regretfully, what Simone de Beauvoir had concluded in 1952 in her long and intelligent essay, "Faut-il brûler Sade?": rapists do not read Sade's work. (Robbe-Grillet attacked de Beauvoir's essay inaccurately and with a surprising personal vehemence as a feminist denunciation of Sade's work.) What seemed to characterize the sexual criminals investigated by the commission was their sexual ignorance and late exposure to pornographic materials. While Nixon vituperated politically against the report he had commissioned—"I have evaluated that report and categorically reject its morally bankrupt conclusions"—the work of social scientists indicates that given the nature of pornography and the state of scientific inquiry into pornography in the sixties, despite conservative political pressures, there was simply no other possible conclusion the commission could have drawn.

The report of a similarly conservative commission led by Edwin Meese in 1985 was somewhat more uncertain in its findings, especially in respect to the general increase in violence in the pornographic product and the modeling and desensitizing effects or reduction of inhibition that might result from this increase. It was only when sexuality was linked with violence that social science research found any statistical correlation between exposure to pornography and increase in aggressive or harmful sexual behavior. One of the social scientists whose work was used to justify the 1985 commission's decision to tighten censorship has expressed concern at the misunderstanding of his results. Donnerstein exposed one group of males to a violent film, another to a film where the violence was sexual and directed at women. He subsequently set up a "game show" that permitted the administering of punishment (apparent electroshocks) to a confederate of the opposite (female) sex for an incorrect answer. He points out that the correlations between a male player's preparedness to inflict shocks after exposure to a violent film and after the viewing of violent pornography were similar.[42] In the same way, the positive correlation shown by the commission between the consumption of *Playboy*, *Penthouse,* and similar material from state to state and the rate of reported rapes was no higher than the relationship between the purchase of male hunting and shooting magazines like *Field and Stream* and *The American Rifleman* and sexual crime. The hypothesis could be put forward that crimes of sexual aggression correlated with certain constellations of "macho" values rather than with sexual explicitness. A 1981 study of the covers of 1,760 "adult" magazines, for example, yielded 17.2 percent of representations of bondage and domination, while 76 percent of the covers of detective magazines depicted domination and 38 percent domination and bondage. A *Clockwork Orange* may be at least as dangerous to the social fabric as *Emmanuelle.* Research also showed that sexual arousal to violence was greatest to scenes of "consenting" rape.

In the light of such research and of changes in social attitudes,[43] the British Film Board has abandoned its former policy of cutting scenes of forbidden sexual positions, acts, or camera angles, and adopted a policy of cutting only scenes that show violent sexual acts with positive outcomes. The final scene of *Emmanuelle*, for example, where the rape of the heroine by the anonymous occupants of an opium den is seen as a necessary part of her sexual emancipation, and in some way effected with her "consent," was an object of this new definition of harmful pornography that should not be shown. The United States has not yet made this move and the National Endowment for the Humanities is struggling with a legal body for whom obscenity or pornography seems more closely correlated with the disturbance "deviance" still creates and with the moral taboos on the erotic depiction of "deviance" than with the depiction of violence. In 1990, for example, charges were laid against a Cincinnati art gallery director for exhibiting Robert Mapplethorpe's allegedly pornographic photographs of children or of homosexuals, and the owner of a record store that sold the lyrics of the rap group *Two Live Crew* went on trial for disseminating criminal "obscenity." (Both were acquitted.)

In the light of the shifts in European attitudes, it is evident that even if Robbe-Grillet's work does not obtain its impact by traditionally pornographic sexual explicitness, as Rybalka hastened to point out, the work is still not outside the realm of the potentially harmful. In its repetition of images of violence against a sexualized female body with a positive or, at the least, neutral outcome, it could be seen as desensitizing the reader further and destroying inhibitions against rape. The fact that Robbe-Grillet's work refracts images of sexuality that move between female angelism and male criminality, male redemption and female sacrifice, thus making sacrificial violence a correlative of innocence (recalling writers like Dostoevski, and a whole romantic and literary tradition of victims and self-sacrificial or expiating dying heroines from *Manon Lescaut* to *La Dame aux camélias*), would, for mainstream current social science theory, effect a classic conditioning of gender association. Are these conclusions still valid, however, when such a pairing is intellectual, pedagogical, or self-displayed?

It has been suggested that the romantic sexual images of the earlier part of this century, the sentimental virtue of certain true romances and family sagas, and the bridal myths of purity were limiting, even harmful. The grandiose symbols of sexual contact in the cuts to pounding surf and triumphant rockets, the final and climactic marriage-ever-after kiss of Hollywood tradition, and the modern stories of Snow Whites and Sleeping Beauties waiting for the prince were probably, in terms of their refusal to accept or to examine the hidden and darker sides of our emotions and sexual impulses, at least as pernicious as much contemporary pornography. They may, of course, have been much more successful in regard to the social control of sexuality through the shoring up of the institution of heterosexual marriage. The real questions of inequality and struggles of power in *Gone with the Wind* stay hidden; the angelism of *The Little House on the Prairie* passes for reality. In a Robbe-Grillet text the diaphanous young female "elf" Angélique, "tender" breasts and pink nipples concealed/revealed by her translucent robe, pure angel of light, is not only a romantic (or erotic) phantasy. The inevitable staining of her white body with red blood stages the suspicion of a hidden desired potential violation or, at the least, the battle between a drive toward death and destruction and an impulse toward love and life or between the competing pulls of ego, superego, and id for dominance, of the kind that Freud postulated. Archaeological excavation beneath the fascination she exerts exposes the many-layered desire concealed in our innocent classical texts and traditional sexual myths. But violence derives also from Robbe-Grillet's own perverse manipulations of these texts and of his reader. The resulting sado-erotic phantasies have complex resonances for me and, I suspect, for most women.

The question of pornography split the feminist movement in the eighties. The Women against Pornography and Obscenity movement supported the Andrea Dworkin and Catherine MacKinnon ordinances that attempted to make pornography illegal to protect women's civil rights. The Anti-Censorship Taskforce argued that even the material of a sexist culture should be available for discussion. It was not always clear whether what was at issue was a conservative attempt to mandate moral homogeneity and morality by suppressing sexually explicit representations or a revolutionary stand to limit violence against women. A number of ideologically fierce works, Andrea Dworkin's *Men Possessing Women* and *Take Back the Night*, Kathleen Barry's *Female Sexual*

Slavery, and Mary Daly's *Gyn/Ecology*, presented pornography as part of the global plot by essentially violent men to continue to disempower and dominate women. *Caught Looking: Feminism, Pornography, and Censorship* argued, on the opposite side, that mutual desire was sometimes operating even in the strangest and most degrading pornographic phantasies.[44] This latter work, with which my own intellectual sympathies are most closely aligned, expressed concern about any attempt to sanitize or cover over deep and complex sexual feelings or to mandate forms of behavior and desire consistent with any "correct" feminist politics. (Subsequently the Supreme Court declared the ordinances unconstitutional.)

Evidence from recent social science research (and the increase in male strippers) suggests that as male bodies are also increasingly displayed as objects of sexual pleasure and as mainstream pornographic material is produced for a new female clientele, the voyeuristic pleasures of this unromantically explicit and visual mode of physical sexual representations, at present considered to be generally male territory, can be physically arousing to the female as well as to the male. Christine Pickard shows from her research on female physiological response to such depictions[45] that although women have generally reported verbally that they found these visual physical representations unattractive, objective tests measure noticeable physiological response. As female conditioning and notions of purity, modesty, and propriety are modified, the relations of women to pornography (pornography itself) appear open to change.[46] Susan Sontag's now classic article "The Pornographic Imagination" argued that both sexes feel, at least in phantasy, the "erotic pull of physical cruelty" and an "erotic lure in things which are vile and repulsive."[47]

The sexual revolution of our time includes not only explicitness but also, at its margins, the ambiguous violence of the young, tough, overtly sexual, and apparently socially transgressive punk rock and heavy metal scenes, where groups with names like "Sid Vicious," "The Sex Pistols," "The Pointed Stick," "The Wounds," "Scorpion," and "Poison" produce music that physically aggresses the listener to excite him/her. Paradoxically, the singers often adopt "feminized" garb (long hair, open shirts, gold chains, and earrings) and allow their voices to enter the more characteristically female range. The curiously dual Madonna, bride doll and virgin, material girl and whore, sex-object but also assertively anarchic and constantly changing subject playing with stereotypes she represents, may similarly embody at once an imprisonment within original scenes of sexual aggression and submission and some deconstructive staging of these codes.

The sexual "revolution" also extends, somewhat more disturbingly, to the growing multibillion-dollar industry of "hard-core" product: peep show, dial-a-porn, and video, the greater immediacy of image or comic predominating almost completely here over printed word. Innocent and guilty, pure and secretly licentious, Justine plays a greater role in this pornography than Juliette. The feminist documentary film *Not a Love Story* and the attorney general's 1985 Commission on Obscenity and Pornography concur completely in their portrayal of this increasingly visible hard-core pornography as turning on the "deserved" violation and humiliation of the female body. In the extreme and somewhat mythological "snuff" movies, this violation becomes physical destruction.

While there are striking parallels between the thematics of this hard-core pornography and the themes of the Robbe-Grillet texts, there are also evident differences. Robbe-Grillet's films may be aestheticized representation or revelation of the hidden content of the erotic, exotic stereotypes of the industry, but they are evidently not produced for commercial gain. Indeed, they provoked uncomprehending restlessness and, in Italy, riot, among cinema audiences with expectations of familiar and reassuring pornographic entertainment. The scenes that constructed connections between the sexual and the violent—A's persuasion by X in *L'Année dernière à Marienbad,* the strangulation of Eva, informer/prostitute, in the mythological Amsterdam of diamond and drug smuggling and red-light girls in *Trans-Europ-Express,* the lesbian games of queen and slave, with axe, chopping block, and whips as accessories in *L'Homme qui ment,* Alice's games in *Glissements* met none of the audience's expectations and left fury or unease. Sex in Robbe-Grillet's work is less an activity of the sexual organs than sex filtered through the imagination, an activity of the mind.

Excessively slow or overlong scenes, shots taken at the margins of light possibilities, and hand-held camera leaping make the scenes of Violette's interminable dance around the fire and her tumultuous horseback "ravishing" or her labyrinthine adventures in the course of her overplayed sexual "liberation" in *L'Eden et après* disconcerting even to the most ardent neophyte of experimental cinema. Yet the thematic material that serves the new forms—the medieval dungeons and female wards of the punishing religious sisters; the ever-present dressmaker's dummy tied to the railings of an iron bed "once again at the edge of the sea" in *Glissements;* the fair, wounded, chained victim of the Secret (Vampire) Society; and the dark motorcycle angel of control and death in *La Belle Captive*—extends and repeats interminably the repertory of power and powerlessness, of fascination with and self-defense against enchantment. The wave unfurls, once again, over the enchanting sea anenome of the very earliest work *Un Régicide*, the mermaid Aimone, daughter of the sand and of the sea-spray, but already potential siren "at his mercy."

Robbe-Grillet's re-presenting of this material situates itself outside the moral and political concerns that preoccupy both the feminists and the "Commission." His concern is not to assess the potential current social harm of depicting rape and "rape myths" (that is, the representing of female enjoyment of, or complicity with, the "deserved" violence used against women) but to explore these myths as texts functioning to produce meanings. For some critics, as we saw earlier in this chapter, this exploration has not only a literary but also a moral or revolutionary purpose. As Rybalka paraphrases Robbe-Grillet's declared purposes, exploiting not women's bodies but "exploiting, serially, erotic clichés, Robbe-Grillet wanted to shed light on the phantasms, on the dull and decadent mythology of the society in which we live."[48] It is this implication of moral purpose that seems, at the least, debatable.

For the claimed "dullness" of this mythology does not preclude the vertiginous repetition of a very specific cluster of images unlikely to be labeled "decadent" by a writer whose only declared moral war has been on traditional "virtue." Repeatedly emerging from behind the partial demise of the old censorship and repression in the still somewhat underground and visual modern world of pornography are the same apparently timeless mythologies of the dark female continent—of the fallen angel, Eve, temptress of Adam, requiring punishment and control; of the insatiable, tempting-tempted, fatal witches of affective power; dark angels of death; or fair sirens of disorder, whose bodies must be tamed and suppressed in the battle of the sexes. Within these myths Europa's complicity with her rape by the Olympian bull, Leda's entwining with her divine Swan, and the chained Angelica/Andromeda with her shining savior whose heroic feats require the entry of the devouring beast suggest that "the sweet tears" or cries of the "feminine" victim are an inevitable or natural or universal aspect of the order. The most evident pleasure in textual construction is the capture and control of the pure/impure body of the other; the subject writer or artist takes as the site of his investigation the object female body. The most evident pleasure in destruction is, as in Sade, that of the rape and humiliation of a (falsely) angelic or insatiable female and the victim's underlying complicity with this punishment, his pleasure in her pain, her scream, his "discharge." In mainstream movies erotic footage precedes and contrasts with carnage or film gore. Shots of the young woman undressing in the soft haze of the bedroom or in the sensuous shower cut to the assassin approaching; images of her fear precede the stabbing knife.

Robbe-Grillet's little-documented collaborative adventures with a number of experimental texts, close enough to commercial pornography to have been confused with it, increase my uneasiness as a female critic of his work. These lesser-known texts both illuminate and complicate the debate. The photo-novel *Temple aux miroirs* (1977), for which Robbe-Grillet wrote the text, using Irina Ionesco's photos of her pubescent daughter in seductive poses as generators, sufficiently resembles commercial pedophilia for the *Brigade des moeurs* (the vice squad) to have interrogated its indignant writer. Although these photographs show a very young woman posing as object of the voyeur's gaze, defined by symbols of seduction (boa feathers, pearls, garters, lace and roses), there is, however, both intellectual and aesthetic exploration and subversive intent in this work, perhaps not dissimilar to that of Cindy Sherman's photographs of herself as Hollywood vamp or Madonna's self-presentation as a virgin. But, as in the latter, the line between irony and imitation, betwen re-presentation and representation, or between the opening up of significant questions of child sexuality and child abuse, is fine and difficult to trace.

Obliques published a disconcerting Robbe-Grillet fragment that had previously appeared in the journal *Minuit* and would later be reprinted in Jean-Jacques Brochier's biographical-critical sketch of Robbe-Grillet.[49] None of these publications contain critical comment on the choice of this text or on its disturbing and excessive content. In the story, entitled "L'Ange gardien," a little girl is killed ritually by a stilet and goes to heaven to intercede for her (beloved) killer and soothe away the weariness and grief of his life. Is this a parody of a little-known literature of pedophilia? Is it an ironic text ex-posing a false angelism in representations of little girls in Western society and a false mysticism surrounding their deaths? Or is it proselytism? In one sense, as a variation on the mise en scène of the Andromeda theme—the sacrificial young virgin whose shed blood redeems and restores purity—it is perhaps also an example of intertextuality. At the end of *Crime and Punishment*, for example, the murder (and rape?) of a little girl not only reveals the obscure dark passions hidden in the heart of man but seems somehow to have a generally cathartic and redemptive function in the denouement of the novel, much as Sonia's self-sacrificial love may redeem Raskolnikov's violent crime and rescue that negative hero from the void. (Robbe-Grillet has claimed a serious debt to Dostoevski.)

In an interview at the Editions de Minuit in Paris in 1985, I asked the writer why the pure young girl in his work generally and in "L'Ange gardien" precisely seems always to evoke her own suppression. His answer, which was that he simply did not know, appeared more honest than evasive. But it was also thought-provoking. If the writer did not know, the task of the critical reader was all the more significant. My own initial response to "L'Ange gardien" was one of perplexity and refusal of what appeared to be played out in this text. On the most direct narrative level, this was the indulgence in a sexual phantasy of the sacrificial murder of a child accompanied by the narrator's sexual arousal, reaching paroxysm with her death, and resolving in her absolution of, and intercession for, the beloved killer. The shock of the thematics blocked out the immediate awareness of any internal distances or play of critical metatexts. Yet as scenarios of child abuse and incest, Western society's last taboo, emerge in astonishing numbers from the darkness into a social space that is by no means occupied only by the ignorant or the economically impoverished, it may also be the case that the apparently extreme marginality of these representations and the impulses that lie behind them is deceptive. Mary Daly argues in her celebration of the distinctively or essential "feminine,"[50] that it is the young adolescent's wholeness of mind and body, of thought and feeling, and the fact that her sexual feeling has not yet been shaped by culture that calls for her suppression in patriarchy. This follows, Daly's thesis contends, her refusal to be extinguished as a human being in order to be fulfilled as a sexual being.

In literature, where these questions can be investigated more subtly, Duras's *Agathe* and *L'Amant de la Chine du nord* and Marguerite Yourcenar's passionate but soberly classical *Anna Soror* have joined the film *Souffle au coeur* as explorations in our decade of the intense mother-son or brother-sister bond. The libertine interest in incest and, in particular, Restif de la Bretonne's preoccupation with incestuous relations in the stories of the discovery of long-lost fathers and brothers are being rediscovered. Indeed, like Laclos, Restif de la Bretonne has suddenly become canonical.

The short text "'Histoire de rats' ou La vertu, c'est ce qui mène au crime," which appeared in *Obliques,*[51] describes a young woman, kneeling naked in a cage, breasts gnawed by rats, and imminent victim of sexual assault by a uniformed SS officer. The description freezes to an illustration in a sadomasochistic pornographic magazine moving the reader from inside the story to outside and attempting, through this use of metalepsis, to eliminate depth and vertigo. The caged woman or beautiful captive and the rodent is a recurring intratextual motif; she also has a number of intertextual sources and variants. In *Les Chants de Maldoror* Lautréamont raves lyrically in the register of cruelty around the phantasy of the tearing and wounding of the body's most secret and vulnerable inner parts. (This phantasy proliferates in contemporary popular television series like *Freddie's Nightmares* or movies like *Friday the Thirteenth, Halloween,* or *The Terminator.*) A passage entitled "Empusae Raptus" brings together a rattrap, the sewing machine, and the umbrella in proximity to the dissection table that will reappear both in Magritte's work and in *Topologie.*

> Il est beau comme la rétractilité des serres des oiseaux rapaces; ou encore comme l'incertitude des mouvements musculaires dans les plaies des parties molles de la region cervicale postérieure, ou plutôt comme ce *piège à rats* perpétuel, toujours retendu par l'animal pris, . . . et surtout comme la rencontre fortuite sur une table de dissection d'une machine à coudre et d'un parapluie.

[He is beautiful like the retractability of the talons of birds of prey; or again like the uncertainty of muscular movements in the wounds of the soft parts of the posterior cervical region, or rather like this perpetual *rattrap*—always reset by the trapped animal, . . . and above all like the unexpected meeting of a sewing machine and an umbrella on a dissection table.] (My emphasis)[52]

In another short Robbe-Grillet text entitled "Pour Sibylle Ruppert" and written to accompany that artist's limited edition artwork[53] *Dessins pour Lautréamont*, illustrating Lautréamont's texts, the obsessive nightmare phantasies of death, cruelty, and the vulnerability of the body reappear along with structural forms now familiar to a practiced Robbe-Grillet reader. Advancing apprehensively and with difficulty along a crowded underground passage, through alternating bright light and darkness, precision of the representation ("le tracé sans bavure d'une pointe aigue") and ambient uncertainty, at once inside and outside the text (Ruppert's, Lautréamont's, and his own), the writer has the impression

qu'il doit y avoir là une grande quantité de chevaux éventrés, . . . avec des herses, et des crocs de boucher, et des socs de charrue, avec aussi des femmes nues aux formes splendides mêlées au carnage. Je pense à la mort de Sardanapale, évidemment, mais la scène qui m'entoure se situerait plusieurs minutes après l'instant fragile immobilisé par Delacroix où toutes les courbes du désir sont encore rangées à leur places diurnes. Tandis qu'ici, . . . ce qui s'offre aux sens révulsés ce sont les hontes secrètes de l'anatomie: les orifices écartelés, les entrailles répandues, les sécrétions, les pertes. Une pointe aigue, ai-je dit. Oui le gluant et l'acéré semblent maintenant s'engendrer en cercle l'un l'autre, le fin couteau du supplice appartenir au même monstre que la chair ignominieuse qui s'entaille (se déborde), les sexes s'invertir, insidieusement, et s'invaginer l'arme du crime.

[that there must be a great number of disemboweled horses, . . . with harrows, and butcher's hooks, and ploughshares, also with naked women splendidly full-formed mixed up in the carnage. I think of *The Death of Sardanapale*, evidently, but the scene that surrounds me would be situated a few minutes after the fragile instant immobilized by

Delacroix in which all the curves of desire are still ranged in their day-time places. While here, . . . what are offered to the senses in revulsion are the secret shames of the anatomy: the orifices torn open, the entrails spilling out, the secretions, the waste products. A sharp point, did I say? Yes the viscous and the steel-hard seem now to engender one another in a circle, the fine sacrificial knife to belong to the same monster as the ignominious flesh which is cut into (spills out), the sexes to invert, insidiously, and the murder weapon to invaginate.][54]

The sharp steel point is engendered by the soft ignominious flesh. The criminal knife/weapon/phallus has invaginated, or turned in upon itself, and the torturer become the victim. But touching the infamous sticky substance, the writer discovers in the final lines that, once again, "tout cela est en métal, poli, sec, luisant mais dur et froid comme de la glace" [all this is made of metal, polished, dry, shining but dry and cold like ice]. Lautréamont as seen by Ruppert and Ruppert as seen by Robbe-Grillet may have resulted in a wavering of sense and sex, but Robbe-Grillet has not really renounced the hard masculine domain of invulner-ability or his own domain of intertextuality, of complementarity, and of self-conscious sado-erotic thematics.

Amateur of less obviously cruel or perverse labyrinthine and inter-connected plots in his early "detective" novels, Robbe-Grillet also wrote a preface for a photo-novel (or rather a meta-photo-novel) appropriately called *Chausse-trappes*.[55] In this text, entitled "Pour le photo-roman," Robbe-Grillet insists on the ludic possibilities of the new photo-novel genre and its potential for effects of "illusion" ("truquage") in the mech-anisms of reversal and slippage between the real and the remembered and phantasized. These permit the elimination of a whole sequence of the story (the murder—or is it just the phantasy of the murder—of the husband, run down on the road to make way for a new lover). This scene subsequently comes to appear imagined and unreal in spite of the paradoxically detailed presence of the image. Indeed, as the image reveals unsuspected uncertainties, its status as real or imagined becomes undecidable. It is, Robbe-Grillet claims, the contraction and elongation of time, the paradoxical spaces and branching paths, and the various tremblings of the real that catch and hold the imagination of the writer and reader rather than the stereotyped content of the thriller comic.

The big black limousine reappears a second time, toward the end of the photo-novel, stopping, this time, to let the husband cross the road instead of running him down and thereby placing all the heroine's earlier crimes, murders, and adventures with her new lover in imagination or under "erasure."

Once again, however, it may not be without significance that the story of this banal thriller in the Hadley Chase mode is one of unsentimental sex, crime, feminine betrayal, loss, and death from which only literary "truquage" provides escape. Robbe-Grillet's preface also contains comments on the constitution of an identity, interesting in the light of our concern with the respective roles of masculine and feminine narrators. The writer claims that the husband takes on an objective position only when it is in fact he who "sees": "N'étant plus désormais 'vu' par l'héroïne (c'est au contraire lui qui la voit) il prend aussitôt une existence objective" [No longer "seen" by the heroine (it is on the contrary he who sees her) he immediately takes on an objective existence] (p. iii). Robbe-Grillet himself uses a similar banal love triangle in a synopsis for a prospective film, Le Magicien,[56] in which a husband-director pushes the wife he loves into the arms of another (an actor). The risk he takes brings voyeuristic agitation and pleasure (he sees), but he then finds that his wife has come too close to the other man. In the end the wife shoots her husband, but not, of course, for real—"le réel réduit au réalisme, quelle misère" [the real reduced to realism, what poverty], Robbe-Grillet writes in the preface to Chausse-trappes (p. ii). The final images are those of the actors and actresses of the film, resuscitated like Eva and Jean (Marie-France Pisier and Trintignant) at the end of Trans-Europ-Express.

Robbe-Grillet also wrote the preface for a more controversial photo-novel (perhaps better called comic-strip) version of Sade's Justine.[57] The intellectual or artistic import of this production of transgressive images initially, at least, seems marginal, especially as the comic-book style of flattening the image and reducing the text to cliché makes the work virtually indistinguishable from the texts sold in the hard-core sadistic sections of the sex-shop. Yet the preface is a curiously theoretical plea for Justine's legitimacy as active subject, conscious witness, and narrative voice ("parole narratrice"). Sade's ambiguous claim to be Justine ("Mademoiselle Justine, c'est moi") is not interpreted as a physical identification with the victim but rather, Robbe-Grillet argues (somewhat speciously?), as scriptor, the victim becomes the aggressor. "Nouvelle Alice au pays des Merveilles, sa présence qui dispose en un ordre calculé événements, situations et commentaires, marque dans l'oeuvre la place du scripteur. L'antagonisme qui oppose son destin d'esclave et sa fonction organisatrice, c'est la contradiction même de Sade, maître de mots dans sa prison" [New Alice in Wonderland, her presence, which disposes events, situations, and commentaries in a calculated order, marks the place of the writer in the work. The antagonism that opposes her destiny as a slave and her organizing function is the very contradiction of Sade, master of words in his prison].[58]

It is meaning that is made to tremble, not flesh, in the antihumanist, anti-Christian work of Sade, claims Robbe-Grillet, and this is perhaps also one of the modern vocations of the comic-strip album. The writer's theories, however, come close to being a rationalization of his own literary projects as much as being an exploration of the repressions these effect. Robbe-Grillet justifies the comic-book version of Sade's project as a proving of innocence by the cleansing of the text and the creating of a perfect form.[59] The encounter between Sade and Robbe-Grillet seems to be less a dislocation than an empathetic imprinting of Robbe-Grillet on a Sade laid out carefully and amorously on a very narcissistic dissection table.

Robbe-Grillet's preface was obviously intended to lend this album of doubtful worth a certain literary respectability and authority. Similarly, when Catherine Robbe-Grillet published L'Image[60] under the pseudonym of Jean de Berg (a character of Topologie and an allusion to Robbe-Grillet's collaboration with the inspirational figure of Rauschenberg), the work included a preface signed P.R., the presumed pseudonym of the author of Histoire d'O whom Robbe-Grillet had early identified in an interview as Pauline Réage. At the least, the preface of this work, which is an assemblage with little literary merit of the clichés of the sadomasochistic universe, although it has become a classic or exemplary work in its genre, seems to have been written by Robbe-Grillet himself. John Fletcher suggests that "Pauline Réage" may indeed have had a hand in the writing along with a group of Robbe-Grillet's friends, but I can find no stylistic or even thematic evidence for this. On the other hand, Fletcher argues that one section of L'Image contains characteristic Robbe-Grillet stylistic "thumbprints" such as the use of "soi," where standard syntax would give "lui" (in phrases like "devant soi" [in front of oneself/himself], for example), and it seems probable that the writer helped and encouraged his wife in what they both describe in conversation as a liberating venture. Catherine Robbe-Grillet has since claimed to be the author of both *L'Image* and of a subsequent work entitled *Cérémonies de femmes,* on her opposite experiences as a dominatrix, and published under the feminine pseudonym of Jeanne de Berg.[61]

The authorship or encouragement of such texts is not an indictment either of Robbe-Grillet's person or of his work. The major erotic or transgressive texts of our culture have almost all been suspect, objects of fear, disgust, and outrage, or banned as "pornographic," at some time. We recall *Madame Bovary* on trial and, in this century, not just the work of Henry Miller and D. H. Lawrence but also James Joyce's *Ulysses* and Rushdie's *The Satanic Verses.* Other highly respected writers or poets have left underground texts that could be accused of being sexually self-indulgent if not of being pornographic—Apollinaire's *Julie ou la rose* and *Les Cent mille verges* or Vian's recently published *Ecrits pornographiques,* for example—that have, at the least, the merit of bringing to light both the fascination of the feminine and the phantasies and fears this feminine evokes. Vian's texts make explicit an obsession with a toothed or dangerous vagina that clearly has connections to Robbe-Grillet's more distanced, playful, or metatextual interest in a feminine fur-trap. ("Piège à fourrure" is the title of one of his unfinished films.) Even homosexual work such as Fassbinder's film adaptation of Genet's *Querelle* does not escape the dialectics of masculine and feminine and of domination and submission, or the symbolic power of the link between sex and violence and sacrificial death.

Yet the nagging doubts as to whether the intellectual positioning of this work as "liberation of love" is a self-protection or blind for the writer's personal complicity with his own sexual preferences or a manipulation of the (female) reader are not assuaged. Like Barthes's rereading of Sade and his argument that the calculations and computations of encyclopedic libertine excess is boring as content but a great and liberating performance as narrative, the argument for pornography as liberation is never entirely convincing. I share Joan DeJean's concern that the totalizing vision and the attempt at mastery of secrets inherent in Sadean listings may take over the reader's space. Nor is the question of the advisability of giving detailed re-presentations of the sado-erotic clichés or tableaux answered in any way. Once again, do the texts of transgression indeed "exceed" in their excess the bourgeois language and the censorships in which we are caught as a means of changing them, as Barthes claims in his preface to *Sade, Fourier, Loyola*, or are they themselves caught in collusion? Does the critical or metatext become implicated in what it re-presents in spite of its metaleptic acts of disculpation?

The flat, calibrated, geometrically ordered surfaces of objects in Robbe-Grillet's text, like the meticulous detail and careful quantification of sexual/textual acts and of taxonomies of the gastronomic dishes served at table in the writings of Sade, conceal a hidden face. Behind the insistence of the masculine camera eye and the apparent immutability of the blue expanse of feminine sea, obsessions, anomalies, currents, eddies, and monsters of the deep leave their suspect trace. There is, in this work, no averting of the gaze, but the fear of castration has not been exorcised. "Chaotic" feminine disorder exerts a fascination, attracts a self-defensive violence to control the dangerous body of seduction. The chapter on myth traced the struggle between the siren (fair, vulnerable, angelism of beauty and youth but also dark, powerful, angel of death) and the sadist (the god of storms, who in the legend of the island will only ensure the safe passage of travelers and sailors if the virgin is hurled as a sacrifice into the sea). This is a struggle that leads to the imprisonment of the male in the camera obscura/the bounded "secret room," like his victim, and not to his liberation in the boundless sea. In the light at least of the secondary texts, Dardigna is partially right in her thesis that a masculine cerebral erotic caught up in the structures of sexual power is not a liberation.

The Uses and Abuses of Enchantment

This final chapter considers the question of the meanings of the configurations of modernity in Robbe-Grillet's work, in particular their
sexual politics. More generally, the study of the nature of Robbe-Grillet's
intergeneric experiments is part of that cluster of contemporary theoretical interrogations that enters the domain of the "postmodern debate."

The Postmodern Debate, *Modernité,* Difference

Many eminent scholars have sought to find a shared definition of
the *postmodern* (a term popularized by Lyotard's essay "La Condition
postmoderne") or to distinguish the latter from Derrida's skeptical enterprise of the "deconstruction" of the "logocentric" intellectual traditions
of the West, or again, to set it apart from the more clearly historicized
term *poststructuralism.* I have also used the general term *metafiction*
to refer to Robbe-Grillet's deconstructing and self-conscious texts. For
the most part, however, this study has preferred to adopt the writer's
own use of the term *modernité* to designate the new configurations with
which he works. Modernity, as Françoise Gaillard sees it, in an essay
that investigates postmodernism as the "angst" or "agony" of modernism, is not a historical period. "Since every period enmeshes it in a
different web of significations and functions,"[1] modernity is, in fact,
equally as vague and slippery a notion as the postmodern. Nonetheless,
two things characterize what is generally understood as artistic modernity for Gaillard—autonomy and a will to break with tradition. Robbe-
Grillet's conception of literary modernity is more radical, including the
"subversion" and the "revolution" that characterize the avant-garde.

The postmodern encompasses a wide cultural area. Gaillard herself, writing particularly of architecture, quotes Colomb to give some idea of this range. "The philosophers who reject the master thinkers implicated in totalitarianism; the architects who seek to reintroduce the imagination, even the irrational, into an art which had been totally invested with modern rationalism; the painters and musicians who yield to the subversive pleasures of eclectic citations and mocking historicism: all these are subsumed under the category of 'postmodernism'" (p. 8).

Gaillard agrees with Lipovetsky that the postmodern is the cool, blasé phase of modernism. It is "cold" or decontextualized symbolism accompanied by technical precision and the development of fluid structures geared to the individual and her/his desires. Chaos theory and other new configurations in myth, history, literature, and science, discussed in earlier chapters, share many of these apparently contradictory characteristics of the postmodern—precision and fluidity, for example. The questions that the "postmodern debate" would have us ask in relation to Robbe-Grillet's work are whether modernity has, in fact, been overtaken by postmodernity and, whatever the label attributed, what Robbe-Grillet's particular style of rupture with the past might signify ideologically and politically. Gaillard characterizes the overtaking of modernity by the postmodern as the burnout of modernity and the death of subversion, the forgetting of the ideological and political meaning or critical function of the gesture of rupture with the past, in a cool consensual liberal society. The postmodern has imprisoned us, Gaillard argues, in aesthetic effects (the invention of forms), in facades and surfaces "where cultural imprints and the appeal to memory no longer open any window onto a beyond of signs" (p. 11) and questions of meaning are irrelevant. Seen from the Right, postmodernism can thus be criticized as a moral and aesthetic decadence or resistance to values in which "anything goes"; from the Left (Jameson), as a dehistoricization and lack of political commitment; for feminism, as the absence of a place from which to resist oppression.

Is Robbe-Grillet's banalization of aesthetics indeed an aesthetics of banalization? Is his irony mere pastiche? Are the resurgence of myth and symbol in his work simply an indication of an emancipation so great that, as Gaillard would put it, its use entails "no risk of regression"?

Can we say that the questions of meaning and of freedom, as of hierarchy, in his work indeed become irrelevant? Further, if the postmodern
is "the cult climate" we bathe in, the "cool" culture of hedonistic indi-
vidualism without transcendence and the mediocre images of desacralized, platitudinous, commercialized surfaces against a backdrop of the
death of ideology and of author, as Gaillard suggests, do we respond
to Robbe-Grillet's citations in the same way that we receive mass media
images?

I would argue that Robbe-Grillet's reproductions of a pornographic
magazine cover, for example, like the Allighiero or Boeti reproductions
of magazine covers that Gaillard discusses, or his interactions with the
work of contemporary artists and with pop art in general, are not
merely stylistic eclecticism or a deculturizing and a decorative effect
"empty of emotional or phantasmatic punch." Although they deconstruct
themselves, that is, use specular structures to deny the realism with
which we try to recuperate their meaning, they are renegotiated, replen-
ished, by their new contexts and the artist's ironic intent, reinvested
with meanings by textual strategies such as metaleptic slippage that
erase the old and inviolable boundaries. This dissolution of the sacred
distinctions between narrative levels (the world where one narrates, the
world narrated), and in the real world, in *Projet,* for example, between
white and black, Paris and New York, the subterranean and the public,
as Deborah Lee suggests,[2] constitutes subversiveness. I would also argue
that the origins of these texts in the banal and the popular, and their
subsequent slippage between, and breaking down of, the hierarchical
levels of high and low culture and of the boundaries between individual
and collective mythologies infuse them with an ultimately political
power.

Despite his early flirtation with Ricardou (repudiated at Cérisy),
Robbe-Grillet has consistently, if somewhat intuitively as much as theoretically, situated himself between modernity and the postmodern. As
in the work of Sarraute or Duras, there is something in his texts, carried
by language, that is not language, an abyss that opens up behind words
suggested by the thematics of violence. To bind this inexpressible something in language and interrogate it might be to destroy it, but nonetheless it may be approached by language even as language deconstructs

itself, doubled by sign systems, imperfectly, uncertainly, glimpsed fleet-ingly in turbulent margins between *langue* and *parole*. Meaning is not absent from this enterprise.

Reader reception, too, participates in these movements. "Deprived" of all basic narrative functions to which she/he is accustomed and "provoked" by the text's "unnatural" subject matter, as Inge Crosman Wimmers points out in her germinal text on Robbe-Grillet and the aesthetics of reception,[3] the victim, also called to be active reader, is both intellectually curious about the possible meanings of the new slip-pages and implicated in the project of catharsis of unacknowledgable desires. (Such, in any case, is my own response.) The affective reaction of flight or fight to the aggressive assault the content makes on the reader's cultural conditioning and the greater or lesser intellectual seduc-tion by/resistance to the assemblage game (the backwards scanning, the recognition of disguises, the juxtaposition of different frames) that Crosman Wimmers discusses implicate the reader in a "complementary" movement between irreconcilable opposites. She/he oscillates between the intellectual distancing of a critical, self-conscious reading that takes pleasure in the chaotic recurrences (strange new orders within unpre-dictability, an erotic of self-similar forms) and the emotional shock and stimulation of being manipulated into voyeuristic sexual aggression against women. The reader, like the writer, is drawn from the outside and the hardened, glossy surfaces of cliché inside, to touch, momentarily, the soft vulnerable orifices of the unnameable and analogies with her/his own life.

Simply to refuse to nail Robbe-Grillet to the door with any single label (postmodern) that might put meaning or life under erasure, pre-ferring to overlap this with his own general use of *modernité*, does not provide a completely adequate response to a difficult question. Despite her nostalgic and pessimistic reading of postmodernism, Gaillard aligns the "superannuated" values of revolt designated by "modernity" with "a pale and flabby modernism" (p. 6) of the past. She sees the project of real centrality to our epoch as the understanding of the (postmodern) processes of insignificance and of the elimination of order and meta-physics. However, the earlier chapters of this study found an implicit exploration of just such processes as the apparent elimination of order and metaphysics and single meaning in the configurations—complementarity, chaos, mythologies holding meaning in reserve, the powerful erotic, and the sado-erotic structure of the psyche—that it labeled as those of *modernité*.

Susan Suleiman, in her work on what she calls "subversive intent" in the French "avant-garde" movements of the twentieth century[4] (the latter come to subsume the postmodern for Suleiman), argues that the postmodern play of forms does indeed have ethical and political effects and thus political significance even where these are (in much surrealist work) sapped by a nonrevolutionary or sexist politics. Suleiman cites the political furor, repression, barbarous death threats, and fierce passions directed against Salman Rushdie's *The Satanic Verses*. Far from provoking indifference, such passages in this ludic work as the scene in which the names of the Prophet's wives are projected onto the village prostitutes who function ironically as simulacra aroused violence.

While the question of the validity of readings is central here— Suleiman claims from within the postmodern logic that all readings, including a fundamental Muslim reading, are theoretically equal—I would suggest that the forms of Rushdie's work, at least for the (post)modern reader, stand in a complementary relationship to their content. The ironies in the staging of the phantasies of male desire and the ludic subversion of certain mythologies of Islam are evident to a reader educated in the (postmodern) paradigm within which Rushdie is creating. I have argued elsewhere in a study of critical readings of Nathalie Sarraute's "new autobiography" *Enfance* that there are some criteria for critical validity.[5] These range from attention to the actual physical properties and material content of the work (the integral reading that was omitted by, or not possible for, the majority of Rushdie's critics) to concern for the overall structures of the work and awareness of the paradigm (the frames of reference) within which the text operates. Readings that do not attend to the whole text and its contexts could be seen as perhaps politically valid but not as critically valid.

My own reading of Rushdie's parody as of Robbe-Grillet's pastiche is that the ludic scene, the phantasy in borrowed clothing, the masquerade, is again like Genette's bird of ill-omen or Barthes's mythology, that is, at once the designation of a myth (fear/enchantment) and of a liberation. The sign/the myth for Robbe-Grillet, as for Barthes, is not only sign of a sign but sign of an imprisonment. Robbe-Grillet, Barthes, and Rushdie are not involved uniquely in the reduction of ideology, its emptying to language. Rushdie, the hybrid, citizen of the West and former Muslim, marginal in both cultures, can write only out of what he once loved or feared and what still haunts him. Like Robbe-Grillet the sadomasochist, he writes out of a love-hate (if self-conscious and intelligent) relationship with history/his own past and with his own present. The flattened myth or simulacrum both serves as an ethical effect or a liberation from past and ideology and retains something of that "emotional or phantasmatic punch" that Gaillard would deny post-modernism. It contains a certain "difference" deriving from the historical situation and the traits, often related to gender, that make each writer's situation specific and differentiate one production from another. This difference, which is meaning, derives from choice, from local contexts, and from combinations. In a serial production, it may reside, in the work of Warhol, for example, in the choice of motifs—the electric chair, Campbell's soup can, Marilyn Monroe and Mao Tse Tung faces—or in the juxtapositions (of a sensual Marilyn and a sensuous Mao), or in the minutest of changes in a precisely drawn cold image from one frame or photo-image to another.

Individual difference (what makes Robbe-Grillet and Duras, for example, or Rauschenberg and Warhol, distinguishable) emerges through a manifestly intellectual filter, and its character and origins in affect are difficult to isolate and analyze. However, individual difference is inextricably mixed with the "phantasmatic punch" that comes from the repetition and ritualization of violence (at once against difference and to preserve necessary distinctions of difference, according to René Girard's thesis), a ritualization also operated in popular culture.

The Ritualization of Social Violence

In an entertaining and mind-moving study entitled *Preposterous Violence: Studies of Fables of Aggression in Modern Culture,*[6] James Twitchell argues that the endless loops and the repetitive rehashes of apparently gratuitous violence in the "junk" of mass media "circuses" present an uncorrupted view of the phantasy life of male adolescents and of their transition from individual and isolated sexuality to pairing and reproductive sexuality. Because this transition is "fraught with unarticulated anxiety," it is "ripe for the resolutions of violence" (p. 15). According to Twitchell, "in those fantasies is the lore of the ages, the unutterable concerns of the race, the deepest commands of the species" (p. 4), and although we outgrow childhood tastes, we still continue throughout adult life to be interested in the mysteries and inductions we first came across in adolescence. Repetition in popular culture, Twitchell argues, is ritualization, and ritual is both a key to what is "privileged" information and a deflecting force or fence around socially dangerous aggression or retributive or retaliatory violence.

Twitchell suggests provocatively that the central sign system of "preposterous" violence in Western popular culture is the Passion and Crucifixion of a Christ refigured from a medieval stoic mystic to the suffering, flagellated, pierced, and bleeding human victim of the Renaissance, sexualized by images of nursing or of circumcision. Women, he claims, are traditionally rarely involved in violence except as victim and reward, but it could be argued that the Christ figure is feminized. The young, sexually innocent, female victim or Christ-like martyr has, however, according to Twitchell, been replaced in comics, detective and pulp novels, splatter or stalk-and-slash movies by a victim who has victimized others and who can become the target of the forces of social order pointing an ideological message in a Manichean world of good-guy/bad-guy. But the essential mechanisms remain the same. "Without a victim, there can be no violation, and without violation there can be no violence, and without violence there can be no retributive vengeance, and without vengeance, there can be no preposterous violence" (p. 100).

While this includes, for Twitchell, both violence against the female "for whom males must battle" and, as in the Gothic, violence to protect the female whose induction into the sexual is imminent, his scenarios are more general, less gender-specific, and less sado-erotic in character than those in Robbe-Grillet's work. Twitchell's study argues that, historically, mass-produced images of violence (Punch and Judy, fin de siècle Gothic novels of the Frankenstein monster, Dracula, or Dr. Jekyll, in which repressed or impossible sex—sex with a monster—settles instead for violence and in its turn creates the reader's or society's revenge on the violent villain) have appeared as other forms of real violence have disappeared (dueling, bear- and bull-baiting, cock-throwing and cock-fighting, public executions). Printed pictures and texts, he claims, transferred the voyeuristic thrills from real to artificial texts. The role of these texts "is finally not escape, but return, a return to our 'natural' selves, a safe return to levels of contained aggression" (p.47). In this respect, a new definition of catharsis is called upon:

> In arguing that popular culture does the work of the judicial system and organized religion by providing a cohesive system for mythologizing aggression, I realize that I am dangerously close to arguing for its cathartic value. In no way do I wish to suggest any Aristotelian sense of catharsis in which the audience is purged of passions. Preposterous violence is not made up of tragic or purgative rituals and these rituals do not arouse terror or pity, nor do they cleanse. They excite, incite, becalm, delay, and defuse aggression. It is worth noting that prior to Aristotle, *katharma* was synonymous with *pharmakon* in signifying at once poison and remedy. (p. 46)

This definition of catharsis—a complementary inciting and becalming, exciting and defusing of aggression—could describe the effect induced in the reader by Robbe-Grillet's writing project.

Harlequin's Gold Eagle Books division, Twitchell notes, is making a fortune with male action/adventure books with titles like *The Avenger* and *Cutthroat Cannibals,* selling 500 million copies of five leading men's adventure series alone in 1987. For this critic, analogous movies such as *Aliens, The Fly,* or *Halloween 4,* or Stephen King's sadistic cine-matographic novels are successful because they "translate popular culture into prose, seamlessly" (p. 104). Thomas Pynchon and Donald Bar-thelme, however, like Robbe-Grillet, do this much more self-consciously. The generative mechanisms of the latter produce a seam, an alert, a discomfort, a distance, what Robbe-Grillet has called "a grinding sound."

Robbe-Grillet's texts function in a similar fashion to Pynchon's and Barthelme's or even to those of popular culture insofar as they panto-mime phantastic popular scenes too traumatic for actual experience. Yet it is around a specific story within this paradigm, the recurring def-loration and ritual sacrifice of the virgin and potential vampire, that

Robbe-Grillet's work turns. In Bram Stoker's nineteenth-century version, the virgin Lucy, tainted by Dracula's attack and thus dangerous, is destroyed. Arthur Holmwood must drive a phallic stake through the heart of his fiancée as Ben Mears will kill Susan in an orgy of blood, fluids, revulsion, and pain in Stephen King's contemporary story. In other versions, the Dracula myth plays out the primal horde scenario (the reclaiming by the sons of the women carried off by the father). In the stories of the Frankenstein monster, the mad scientist or criminal doctor is introduced to the scene.

Robbe-Grillet will distance, aestheticize, freeze-frame, and flatten these mythical, monstrous events and characters. But, in his work, preposterous violence will inevitably be acted out against the young female victim/whore, however deceptively or anxiously the pin-striped suit and bowler hat of the scientist and perfect gentleman sit on Frankenstein, Dr. Jekyll, Dracula, or the assassin borrowed from Duchamp, Delvaux, or Magritte, or indeed on Dr. Morgan, Robbe-Grillet's own fictional alter ego. The difference is that Robbe-Grillet's dramatizations of retribution or of what Twitchell calls "dream work made visible" (p. 262), unlike those of popular culture, do not reestablish the order that they break to enact fables of socialization and "the final establishmentarian doctrines of maturity" (p. 262). The moral order reasserts itself in popular culture, even while allowing a space for the vicarious experience of the amoral and of disorder: "These fantasies of aggression are neither for violence nor against it. What they abhor is unmediated and uncontrolled revenge. Such fables all reiterate the moral—get back in line—while at the same time they vouchsafe the vision of a life out of line, a life out of order" (p. 262).

In the sense that Robbe-Grillet engages in both a "pharmakotic" (poisoning and remedying) staging of the images he re-presents and enjoys these representations themselves (taking pleasure in looking at what he is criticizing), there is a parallel to be made with the images of popular culture. As Twitchell concludes for these representations— that this violence is not real but its multiple and complex effects and perhaps its origins in dreamwork are—so might we for Robbe-Grillet's representations.

The controlled and ordered surfaces of Robbe-Grillet's texts are those of the mise en scène of collective mythologies of Andromeda and

Medusa, of the Siren combing her serpentine hair, and of the Monster-Minotaur. The smooth-skinned cover girl, unwrinkled myth of timelessness and eternity in our culture, is the surface of a fiction, a simulacrum, a consumer product, and a collective phantasy of which Robbe-Grillet himself is a self-conscious prisoner. Although the subject positions open for adoption may be "always, already," constituted, to use a Derridean expression, the writer chooses among them. His choices not only reflect or react against the dictatorship of history and narrative but are also a function of his personal history/story. Positioning himself close to the set of sado-erotic representations as a result of his own experiences, Robbe-Grillet turns his relation to those myths and phantasies that have seduced him into a masquerade. Is this, as the writer claims, a masquerade of our social constructions? Or is it also a masquerade of his own essential difference? In the last section of this chapter I will suggest that the relation between social construction and essentialism is complementary, chaotic, and undecidable, that the postmodern frame of autonomous language is inadequate. Meanwhile, the texts' embedded traces give us more reliable evidence than the writer's statements of intent.

The Ritualization of Sexual Violence. Difference in Robbe-Grillet's Fictions

From the earliest work the fine sinuous curve or S-shaped spiral that at the level of the textual functioning threatened the straight line of control and certainty, the monstrous movements behind the surface traces, the dark seduction of Medusa that slips toward its opposite pole, the fair helplessness of the victim Andromeda in her pose of mixed abandon and constraint were concealed/revealed in the metaphorical processes of Robbe-Grillet's language. Surfaces, cultural and linguistic, both mask and suggest the imperceptible movement, the imperfection or fault, the trap, the hole, the hollow of the crime, the chaos in the order of the sociocultural fabric and behind the ordering of the text.

In the earliest work *Un Régicide,* Boris, like Camus's protagonist Mersault, is strangeness, monstrosity, and void, opposed to Laura who represents direct contact with real existence and political activism.

Laura, however, is progressively replaced in the thoughts of Boris by Leila or Aimone, daughters of the foam, imaginary and poetic sirens of desire and of a possible reconciliation of the apparent opposites of domination of the other and self-loss, of void and plenitude. The young siren on the seashore tells Boris that despite his difference, his solitary and frightening visage, she has been waiting for this man whose head has already marked the hollow in her shoulder, whose gray eyes reflect the image of hers, and whose calloused palms find the contour of her hips "all by themselves" (p. 144). This optimistic vision of harmony with the sylphides shifts to focus on its dangers. The bard Malus declares to the daydreaming narrator that the sirens singing his name are monsters, "terrifying human fish descending from warm seas, who seek only our death here" (p. 142), a vision apparently of oedipal conflict and intensified battle of the sexes.

Les Gommes (1956), as we have seen, reassembles ludically the elements of Oedipus, both the classical myth of destiny and its Freudian, sexual retellings. Wallas, the detective, kills the victim (his father) and desires the victim's ex-wife (his mother); yet at the end of his circle round the city and the monstrous twenty-four hours of his quest, this modern-day Ulysses, weary and swollen-footed, still remains oblivious of the nature of his impulses and the incestuous motivations behind his acts. The crime is manifest / concealed in names and metaphors. The relation with the father can only be begun to be unraveled in the objects of the world and in language, in the cube of the paperweight with its "murderous" corners, the desire for the mother's body in the "soft," "friable" erasers "with rounded corners" that Wallas seeks throughout his wanderings. Direct contact with the world and self seems impossible as language and imagination impose overlays. Yet, paradoxically, this imagination and this language form the blocks, the paving stones, through which the red hole of hidden desires gapes and gleams.

The general movement of the text, however, is the attempt to neutralize tragedy, depth, and destiny and the universal "romantic heart of things" of humanism behind these mythological representations and to suggest the chaotic (dis)orders in the world that defeat the detective's orderings. This movement includes both the designating of the operations of phantasy and the flattening of the hidden anguish and half-light of the patron's violent aquatic sexual phantasies or of the oedipal enigmas of self and hidden impulse or "tragic" flaw.

The reader is pressed into a deconstruction, an unraveling of the workings of hidden metaphor, and a detective game. He / she is required to interrogate the "clues" to the representations within which Wallas and we ourselves are caught. Such a game offers no certainty of resolution or escape, or moment of insight for narrator or reader or writer. The weary criminal Wallas who prepares to leave the labyrinthine town unconquered behind him, the patron obstinately repeating "le patron c'est moi" [I'm the boss] (p. 265) at the end of the novel while dissolving in the kaleidoscope of moving watery shapes, and the literary critic Morrissette's "keys"[7] to the underlying classical intertexts that he later discovers to be "absence of key,"[8] figure the lack of unified solution or self at the center of this work. But the writer's refusal to let Wallas ride off as a hero into the sunset or to settle the "patron's" identity is not vain. The work takes up a position against settling down in the meanings of the already constructed and in favor of the quest for the imperceptible and the uncharted—through the new sciences as through the waking dream.

In Le Voyeur the hole at the heart of reality and the gap in the text that conceal the phantasized rape and murder of the little girl on the boat in a graceful attitude, hands behind her back, is the consciously hidden center of the work, but it is as if no one is quite aware of the implications of this situation. "C'était comme si personne n'avait entendu" [It was as if no one had heard] (p. 9) or as if the villagers, anxious to suppress the disruptive sexual freedom of the socially subversive anarchic adolescent, are silent accomplices to the violent suppression of her disorders or her sacrifice to social order. Theirs is the moralizing retributive violence that Girard and Twitchell postulate in their different ways. But Mathias's hidden desires, perhaps also his crime of suppression of the fatal attraction of the anarchic feminine, are already suggested by metaphoric process and ready-made cultural clue; the overheard lieux communs of the fishermen, "Elle mériterait le fouet, cette garce!" [That little bitch deserves the whip!] (p. 141); the mother's words, "Elle a le démon au corps, cette gamine!" [That child has the devil in her!] (p. 83); the ancient myth of the virgin, sacrificed at Spring to the sea monster; the crushed frog on the road, "cuisses ouvertes, bras en croix" [its legs open, its arms crossed] (p. 91); or the parapet on the quay without safety-rail that "plunges" into the water of the opening description. Citing this last example seemed to give weight to Ricardou's interpretation of a pure generation of text by the signifiers alone—that is, a generation of rape and murder by language or by discursive practices (social construction) ungrounded in any essential reality—but the choice of clues and metaphors is never "innocent" or entirely fortuitous. It reflects both social attitudes and a choice made by a consciousness in situation (a narrative subjectivity) whose obsessions direct him to identify with given linguistic forms. It may be that the subjective positions the writer, narrator, or character takes up (latent sadomasochism close to an O or void that in *Angélique* seems to be gendered feminine) is itself a ready-made cultural construction. Yet it too has a historical, textual, and even experiential specificity. *Le Voyeur* is grounded in Robbe-Grillet's own gendered and sexed body and in the unsayable of a specific sexual and phantasmatic experience of the world and also, inextricably, in the stories and collective representations of his time.

In an article on unraveling *Le Voyeur*[9] Ruth Holzberg argues that Mathias is the scapegoat of a complicity that the text develops between writer and reader. The text, she says, does "accuse," as all efforts to show Mathias's innocence finish by convincing of his guilt. Holzberg does not raise the vital question of who exactly is accused, but she suggests both the self-conscious, metatextual control with which the writer enters into his game of complicity with the reader and the anomalies or gaps in his discourse in the following citation: "Malgré cela, l'ensemble du discours conservait—en apparence du moins—une architecture cohérente, si bien qu'il suffisait de l'écouter d'une oreille abstraite pour ne pas s'apercevoir des anomalies qu'il présentait" [In spite of this (the sailor's contradictions) the general tone of what he said retained— in appearance, at least—a coherent structure so that it was sufficient to listen distractedly in order not to notice the anomalies involved] (*Le Voyeur*, p. 152).

These anomalies are the gaps, the holes in the world, the difference in the self that Robbe-Grillet has identified as reality. In *La Jalousie*, although the narrator spies on the smallest movements of the heroine with whom he is jealously obsessed, her sexual difference keeps her impenetrable and unknowable. Valenski wonders whether it is just this impenetrability, this smoothness, that provokes aggression. In spite of the unreliability and limits of perception and the problems of difference, the reader is given some indications for an understanding of the heroine, but these are curiously limited to phrases with connotations of capture and dominance—the overheard words that might be "savoir la prendre" or "savoir l'apprendre" [know how to take her / know how to teach her], for example.

Projet's "revolutionary" and often humorous acts emerge from the narrator's imagination at work on the artificial wood grain of the entrance door from which appears the naked woman captive, wrists bound behind her back, mouth open in a scream. These acts of violent imagination and violation, of "illegal entry,"[10] are again curiously limited to a self-similar sadomasochistic set, culminating in the penetration by sharp instrument, medieval torture with saws, and chains, and pulleys, and destruction by fire, of the naked white bodies of female mannequins on a waste lot in New York. Bright red blood (paint) splashes virginal white as in Robbe-Grillet's films; black (print) threatens white (page) in a hyperbolic play with the mythologies and hidden fears of that city that, the preface claims, are the writer's own. Generative play of linguistic elements and their free associations, JR, the beautiful Joan (Jean) Robeson (son / daughter of Robbe-Grillet), revolutionary member (and victim) of the authoritarian organization (the omnipresent conspiratorial myth of the contemporary political world), is a redhead. Her name generates (or is generated by) a scene where, ironing the folds of her sinuous, sexualized, green silk dress ("robe") while watching a television documentary on primitive, sadistic, fertility rites in Africa, she inadvertently, in her arousal, burns a hole in the dress at the level of the groin. The scorched dress ("grillée" / Grillet) calls up the rapist-assassin (à l'aine / Alain Robbe-Grillet), disguised as a policeman, and leads "evidently" to the torture of Joan's "oluptuous ulva" (ulve oloptueuse) on her ironing table. Illegal entry and aggression link JR with the other female protagonist, Laura, captive heiress listening breathless in fear and in anticipation for the step on the stair of the assassin / brother who will also act out a scenario of complicitous sadomasochistic rape-game. The final scenes replay what are recognizable and yet unpredictable scenarios. Twelve young girl communicants kneel blindfolded in a church, mystically fervent before a sacrificial host. This is, in fact, the bleeding body, limbs, breast, and pubis torn off, of an ecstatically smiling red-haired victim. The watching "I" who "has no time to waste" must, however, return to the "fragile adolescent" in the small white interrogation cell to which M, the vampire, and Dr. Morgan are now returning, having finished their sandwiches. M pulls at his mask to try to erase the lines of his real face underneath. Morgan recognizes, with stupefaction, the face of the narrator, and the scene cuts to a blank. Then, unexpectedly, the action begins again with the "I" descending a metal staircase, carrying a young girl's body in a blanket, "as if to save her from the flames." The I / narrator closes the door behind him. Laura raises her head as she listens in fear. The text rebegins at its ending in a pirouette between personal confession and analytical staging of collective stories of heroism and sadism. The dialogues imitate hard-boiled detective fiction; the humor is hyperreal, but Robbe-Grillet's themes and the modes of their combination are distinctive.

In *Djinn* the murder of Djinn / Jean and the blood between the uneven paving stones ("pavés disjoints") appear mysterious and romantic and not explicitly as sado-erotic. The female body is not persecuted, and Jean and Marie, if somewhat unusually adult or perverse children, play engagingly childlike roles. Marie, in particular, charmingly retells traditional children's stories. These, however, are tales of being carried off by gypsies, forced to work in the circus, locked up in the lion's den for punishment, and finally discovered by their long-lost father. (In *Projet* Laura had watched the black children from the neighboring school playing cruel and mysterious games.) The underlying thematics of rape, domination, and incest are never made overt, nor is the fear and violence present in the "innocent" tales of dangerous Soviet agents, sabotage, poisoned candy, or industrial pizza. In an article on the narrative codes in *Djinn,* an otherwise perceptive critic[11] wrote that the lack of explanation of the repeated semantic unit of the uneven paving stones brings us to conclude that this "theme" has been included as a sign of literary gratuitousness. That is, says Dufy, that one can write sentences that mean absolutely nothing! But the selection of this "theme," like that of the charming, innocent little girl Marie, daughter of Djinn / Jean (Jean, we recall, is one of Robbe-Grillet's pseudonyms) is clearly, in the context of the whole of Robbe-Grillet's production, perverse. The uneven paving stones are a transformation of the "parted lips" (lèvres disjointes"). Illegal entry to the feminine in *Djinn* again takes the ludic and veiled form of incestuous relation.

In *Souvenirs* a poster of a bride animates inevitably to a *Mariée mise à nu* in the Robbe-Grillet or the Bataille rather than the Duchamp style, the virgin "lamb" bound for the sacrificial altar. (Laure Adler's studies of nineteenth-century marriages and marriage manuals[12] would argue that this metaphor of marriage was grounded in reality.) Robbe-Grillet's textual associations recall Bataille's linking of sensuality to the violence of death and desire, and to a vision in which sacred institutions that sanction transgression of the taboo against sex (ritual violence, marriage, war, prostitution) control this violence without denying it.[13] In Robbe-Grillet's text, as in Bataille's, once a marriage is consummated, the bride's function as an object of transgression is usurped by the prostitute. As Bogue points out, all these institutions of transgression appear in *Topologie* in hybrid forms, which "force an awareness of their kinship" (p. 38).[14] The prisoners in the cell of the phantom city are religious prostitutes, officiants at sacrifices, delinquent courtesans, ("rule-bound transgressors of rules") promised to exemplary punishment. The crown of the bride is a "crown of sacrifice" for a "cruel ceremony" (*Topologie,* p. 103) and when the police find the fourth sacrificial victim in the dress shop window (two Magritte-inspired mannequins dressed as bride and groom), the bride is standing in a pool of blood / red paint, her white dress marked over the groin with a red triangle in which the word "hymen" is inscribed.

Bogue suggests that Bataille's *L'Erotisme* may in fact serve as secondary generative material in Robbe-Grillet's work. I would argue rather that these mythical motifs are again deconstructed in the Barthesian sense ("rétrogradés"). Although Robbe-Grillet rejects the metaphysical, mystical, and dark currents in Bataille's incandescent texts, evident complicity and perhaps serious investigative intent remain in this homage by selection. In both *Topologie* and *Souvenirs* the symbolic networks of sacred religious imageries and their links with violent, sacrificial suffering are constantly the object of a literal, explicit, deliberately desacralizing aggression as the most sacred Western rituals and symbols are incorporated. Travesties of female Christian saints and their ecstatic martyrdoms or of the crucifixion itself become a dominant material of the text. The victim is not now a "feminized" Christ but a female innocent—Christine, nailed to a cross or waking in her coffin of roses, literally a mortuary chapel lit with tapers ("chapelle ardente") that surround the coffin, and Freudian heroine who will resurrect as the legendary Phoenix. Dr. Morgan is now, "evidently," the demonic, Sadean-inspired, subversive priest who forces lit church candles up the vaginas of the young girl "brides" taking their first communion and crucified upside down in "cruel ceremonies."

Distancing its transgressions as corrosion of the traditional religious paradigms of the sacred and the obscene, the pure and the impure, as intertextual reference to the texts of Sade or Bataille, and as literal play with metaphor, *Topologie*'s text rushes breathlessly on in a sadistic, incestuous, sacrilegious virtuoso excess. This simultaneously fascinates and aggresses its readers (or, at the least, me) in an attempted ravishing (both a carrying away and an overcoming). The female, expiating, as sacrificial victim, both her own provocative body and perhaps the collective violence of the group, as René Girard's thesis would suggest, is hunted, wounded, and served up at a ceremonial dinner. "Man is the hunter, woman is his game," as Tennyson puts it lyrically in *The Princess,* and, in *Souvenirs,* as Ben Stoltzfus demonstrates,[15] the multiple threads of this commonplace hunting paradigm are again pursued ludically. Woman as wild animal or, like the goddess Diana, able to turn man into an animal, is figured by the young girl dragging the skin of the mythical auroch along the sea shore. The equestrienne rides into the sea moments before she is shot; hunter and writer are one, as the two halves of the black book entitled *Propriétés secrètes du triangle* come together with the sound of the shot, and the girl's cry blends with that of the wounded Phoenix.

While the myth of man, the hunter of the woman, is a commonplace of humanist culture, it also has its inversions. Diana takes revenge on Acteon's spying on her bathing by turning the huntsman into a deer to be devoured by his own hounds. In Lawrence's *Renard the Fox* the male fox is killed to provide gratification for the female. But Robbe-Grillet does not focus on this aspect of the myth, which gives the female an active role, although he does figure woman as a vampire or a Salome.

To write is in fact to hunt for gold, claims Stoltzfus. This critic traces the complex weaving of the interconnected ideograms of gold and triangle through the shape of an inverted triangle enclosed in a circle and the atomic number for gold (79), the nine rings of an archery target, the recurring fetish object of the woman's blue shoe, the green apple, the rose, the fur, and the beggar-girl or prostitute named Temple associated now with the number 7. Stolzfus, however, does not comment on the inevitable fate of these feminine symbols in the "surrealist" text that also brings into play "themes" or phrases from other Robbe-Grillet texts:

> Et à présent, Carolina se baisse pour ramasser un autre débris: sa seconde chaussure bleue, dont le cabochon en miroirs a été arraché avec des tenailles, laissant dans le cuir tendre une large blessure ouverte, qui s'étend depuis le centre jusqu'a la pointe du triangle constituant la partie antérieure de l'empeigne. Cela forme une sorte de bouche, entaillant le bout du soulier selon son axe longitudinal. Et il y a du sang qui s'écoule entre les deux lèvres disjointes; mais l'épais liquide paraît noir, sous les rayons funèbres de la lune.

> [And now Caroline bends over to pick up another piece of debris: her second blue shoe, whose ornamental stone inset with mirrors has been torn out with pliers, leaving a large open wound in the tender leather that stretches from the center to the point of the triangle constituted by the front section of the shoe-upper. This forms a kind of mouth piercing the end of the shoe along its longitudinal axis. And there is blood flowing between the two parted lips; but the thick liquid appears black, beneath the funereal rays of the moon.] (*Souvenirs*, p. 194)

In *Souvenirs* the gaping pubis, the red hole or stain and the sadistic character of the representation of women, has its origins in a child's picture book entitled *Belles et bêtes*, which is recounted by Lady Caroline née de Saxe. The origin of these figures in fairy tales is one among a series of possible origins given—stories of virgin Christian martyrs, of the classical Andromeda-Angelica, or of the Germanic Griselda:

> J'ai trouvé l'histoire de la fille aux chiens dans un vieux livre d'images, au grenier, quand j'étais tout enfant. Il y avait aussi le supplice de Blandine, emprisonnée nue dans un filet à larges mailles pour être livrée dans l'arène au grand taureau noir, dont les cornes ont été spécialement aiguisées à son intention; et celui d'Angélique enchaînée au rocher, tout en bas de la falaise, attendant vêtue de la seule écume des vagues, le squale géant qui va venir la dévorer vivante; et celui encore de Griselda,

ou Brunelda, ou Brunetta, jeune reine aux lignes très pures de déesse
antique, attachée par les pieds à la queue d'un cheval sauvage, que les
soldats lancent à coups de fouet à travers la forêt originelle; la chair
éblouissante de la victime illumine tout le sombre sous-bois, tandis que,
derrière elle, son immense chevelure flottante s'écoulant en cascades
ressemble à la rivière de l'Eden.

[I found the story of the girl and the dogs in an old picture book, in
the attic, when I was a little child. It also had the torture of Blandine,
imprisoned naked in a loosely meshed net to be delivered in the arena
to the great black bull, whose horns had been specially sharpened for
her; and the story of Angelica chained to the rock, right at the bottom
of the cliff, waiting, clothed only in the sea spray, for the giant shark
who will come to devour her alive; or that of Griselda, or Brunelda,
or Brunetta, young queen with the very pure lines of a classical goddess,
attached by her feet to the tail of a wild horse, that the soldiers whip
into motion through the original forest; the glowing flesh of the young
victim lights up the whole somber undergrowth, while, behind her, her
immense crown of floating hair, cascading in waves, resembles the river
of Eden.] (pp. 162–63)

Most of these "legendary" variants of Beauty contribute their own
connotations to a single tale. Bettelheim has elaborated the hidden messages in the fairy tale, the psychoanalytic secrets of existence, and the
sexual foundation that ground the figures of Beauty and the Beast(s).
The myth of Eden, too, has powerful psychosocial and sexual referents
from Judeo-Christian to (anti)feminist. In Robbe-Grillet's text, however,
these stories have become idiosyncratic sado-erotic reinventions, nailed
to the door and transformed by their (humorous, self-conscious, intertextual) contexts but carrying a latent personal charge.

Robbe-Grillet's claim that he is reworking the synchronic collective
representations of our society, of interest for a feminist analysis in itself,
confirming as it does that the war of the sexes and the symbolic suppression of the female is at the core of these representations, must, it
seems, be modified by an account of the individual qualities of this
literary voice—of choice and of transformations of these representations.
Just as the shops in 42nd Street divide their material into categories for
different tastes in pornography, so Robbe-Grillet constitutes a distinctively sado-erotic set. As de Lauretis has affirmed, the very work of

narrativity is the engagement of the subject in certain positionalities of meaning and desire. This subjectivity is not only engaged in the codes of narrative but is to some extent constituted in the relation of narrative meaning and desire.

The lifelong, carefully guarded-against sexual interest in very young girls, and the sadistic phantasies that accompanied adolescent and adult sexual arousal that Robbe-Grillet confesses with apparent candor in *Angélique* constitute an evident "origin" for the writer's engagement in certain sexual / textual positionalities. These "confessions" operate, however, within a text that undermines the "truth" of traditional confession and the possibility of the knowing of "a man in all the truth of his nature" that was Rousseau's professed project in his prototypical *Confessions*.

At the end of the autofictional *Angélique,* which is a textual exploration in the present of memories of the past and of past and present phantasies, the book presents itself as deriving from the writer's childhood encounter with the pubescent Angèle. In this final confession or provocation, Robbe-Grillet tells the apparently moving story that he claims he previously told to his publisher and friend Jérome Lindon. Could this, then, be the "key," the formative childhood sexual experience with a precocious adolescent that is the "real" experiential model for Angélique-Violette? Are we, the readers, disquieted and enthralled, finally within the original "secret room" of the writer's imaginative text?

The narrator evokes the twelve-year-old boy's emotion as his older playmate Angèle plays sexual games apparently with all the "sincerity" and "truth" that Lejeune's theory of the traditional "autobiographical pact"[16] requires. This young adolescent asks her partner to lie on her, to kiss her, to touch her body, then threatens to denounce him to her mother. A later meeting in a barn where the pair have taken refuge from the rain and Angèle has removed her wet clothes leaves the pubescent boy again fascinated, aroused, but mistrustful as she proposes games of Roman soldier and female slave.

The memory of the writer-narrator appears to erase the fifty-four intervening years without the slightest difficulty as the first-person narrative in the present tense continues to take a dramatically personal but strangely familiar shape. In subsequent encounters Angèle demands that Alain tie her up. This then was the origin, "evidently," of Mathias's suspect childhood rope collection in *Le Voyeur* that Trintignant is still trying comically and unsuccessfully to dispose of in the film *Trans-Europ-Express*. And yet, the confessed childhood passion for collections and the original shoe-box of pieces of string that Robbe-Grillet claims in *Le Miroir qui revient* were part of his childhood are no more clearly the "true" origin of the rope—or of the iron rings or the bedposts with which it comes to be associated by metonymy—than any of the recursive representations of female bondage in the fictions and films.

Apparently seeking to make the young Alain take responsibility for a transgressive sexual experience by being made a prisoner, Angèle, once tied up, invites the male to introduce a finger into her vagina. The story reaches its "climax" with his fascination, fear, and intense emotion as blood stains the young girl's inner thigh. This image of red blood on virginal white skin and its symbolic frame of purity and impurity is both an originating center and an interior duplication of the proliferation of similar images through the work.

It is Angèle herself who tells confidential "cruel" stories with "greedy horror" (p. 239) of the rape and murder of young girls, whose bodies are found still warm and bleeding in the local thickets. These "stories" or mises en scène of secret fears and desires are the hidden content of a certain adolescent heroic-masochistic feminine imagination. They stage a fascination with the domination, blood, hurt, and pain that seem to be a necessary part of sexual self-discovery, the pleasure of sexual danger, and of the intense feeling produced by abjection, humiliation, and shame.

Are these "really" female phantasies? Or is the male, as in so much pornographic representation, projecting his own desires, his own stories into the female's silence? The simple answer that this is the writer's self-indulgent direct confession of personal sexual "difference" (affinity with the sadomasochistic world) or of an experience of a childhood sexual imprinting or a fixating on an early erotic context, which alone can provoke later sexual response, cannot be verified. Even if it could be, would it have much explanatory power? I did, somewhat indiscreetly, ask Robbe-Grillet on more than one occasion whether what he called his sexual "difference" in *Angélique* is, in his opinion, a product of particular childhood experiences and fixations. His answer was invariably that he did not know but wrote to know the nature or the knowability of personal monsters he felt compelled to explore. And these images are indeed also the images of detective, spy, and thriller genres, from Hitchcock through James Hadley Chase to *Histoire d'O,* or again, metaphors of the "perversion," the "extremities of meaning" toward which "writing" must move for Roland Barthes.[17]

Still organizing the scene and imposing the sexual rules, troubling for the male in both her power and her apparently assumed power-lessness, Angèle/Angelica/Violet tells the adolescent Alain triumphantly that he will be punished, indeed "cursed," for deflowering her; then she disappears. The reader, moved by this apparently very personal and explicit account of sexual initiation, is also disturbed by the feeling of having passed many times along this textual path before. The adventurous and dangerously uninhibited adolescent Violet of *Le Voyeur,* the ingenuous freedom in sexual adventure and duplicity of an Alice in the film *Glissements progressifs du plaisir,* like the cultural story of the dangerous "impurity" of the bleeding woman, or the images of red blood on virginal white and of female sexual bondage have already worn a track through the creative work.

The ending of Angèle's story is almost a retelling of *Le Voyeur,* as the missing Angelica's young body is washed up at the foot of a particularly dangerous cliff in the Léon region, apparently drowned but, like Violette's body, inexplicably naked. The reader, caught in the "realist illusion" and the autobiographical "pact," may have the uneasy feeling that the French police should reopen all their files on accidental drownings along the Léon coast in 1934.

As Vareille writes of the "Fragment autobiographique," which appeared in *Minuit* in 1979,[18] well before its republication in *Le Miroir qui revient* (1986), the slippage between the frames of the young adolescent's experiences and those of the writing makes it impossible to situate an original. The childhood bedroom with its red curtains through whose openings the maternal gaze watches over solitary pleasures tinged with sadism metamorphoses directly into the writer's room and the sadomasochistic relations with the text.[19]

Little public sympathy is felt for Angèle in conservative and isolated Brittany. This child of a "witch" (a stranger from Paris to boot!) is seen as precociously and dangerously sensually attractive. But the striking resemblance to her provocative, adolescent fictional sister Violette, who would have been burned as a witch "for less than that, not so long ago" [on l'aurait brûlée comme sorcière "pour moins que ça, il n'y a pas si longtemps"] (p. 85) is as troubling as this representation of apparently personally experienced adolescent female sexuality. The writer/Robbe-Grillet's own fascination with the preadolescent girl's resistance to authority, with her freedom of body and spirit, and with the "precociousness" of an Alice-Lolita who orders the story is evident in much of his work. In a 1985 interview with me, Robbe-Grillet claimed with some vivacity that his Alice was much more interesting than Nabokov's limited and unimaginative nymphet Lolita.

At the level of social reality such independence in "real" young girls in contemporary Western culture is being confirmed by a long-term psychosocial study of twelve-year-old American girls. Carol Gilligan[20] postulates the potential power of the disruptive presence, the questions, the determination to look, to see, and to remember of these adolescent females. Their knowledge, she claims, is still based on experience rather than on the stories society inculcates. While she finds the focus on love and connection to be more important in girls' ego development than in that of boys at this stage, the parallel thread of feminine resistance to the social and family codes is, for her, a promise that one day women will find their own and different voice. The story of Psyche's rebellion against the prohibition of seeing or knowing her lover Eros and her refusal of her mother and sister's stories of love, rebellion that gives birth to knowledge, to a more just and truer love and to the birth of a daughter named Pleasure offers, for Gilligan, an alternative to the "love" that within the dominant Oedipus story is a silencing and a blinding.[21] What is noteworthy here is the very different nature of Gilligan's and Robbe-Grillet's respective recastings of classical myth. Robbe-Grillet's texts seem to take as much interest and pleasure in the resistance to authority of the prepubescent girl as Gilligan's. But rather than suggest a new reading of Psyche's rebellion and of male-female relations, Robbe-Grillet ultimately translates this female resistance as sexual provocation and dwells on the young girl's apparent consent to her subsequent "deserved" punishment.

The old-fashioned wooden cart that takes Angèle's body to its final resting place in *Angélique* has rumbled empty, accompanied by Death (the Breton Ankou), or as transport for the captured spy Carmina (the operatic heroines Carmen and Mina), through stories from romantic opera, or from medieval romances and the father's tales of death and danger on the Franco-German frontier in the Great War. We cannot say that this story/personal history, dramatically and even poignantly recounted and with the ring of authenticity and emotion, is falsehood. Indeed the identity between writer, narrator, and character that is required by Lejeune's "autobiographical pact" seems to be respected, and the story of Angèle appears to be the retrospective account of the formation of the writer's personality that characterizes the autobiographical project. But the golden ring is hollow, and it is the void at its heart, an unfulfilled desire, an untold story, that is most clearly seen. This untold story or desire may include an early history and conditioning of Robbe-Grillet's childhood (sexual) body and a staging of adult orientations, obsessions, paranoias, and feelings of literary imposture. But given the deconstructing, polysemic texture of Robbe-Grillet's writing, a childhood experience and an adult sense of imposture do not seem likely to be the work's single "truth."

Whether it is an individuated childhood experience or a more obscure collective enchantment that is imprisoned and interrogated in Robbe-Grillet's sacrificial "secret room," flattened in fragmented Sadean tableaux, punished and suppressed, the chaotic Angélique, like the Phoenix, continues to rise from her ashes, object of a psychic pleasure principle but also of a (similarly Freudian) destructive biological compulsion to repeat. In the preface of L'Image,[22] the hero-protagonist sees himself as enslaved by the goddess Vanadé, voluptuous or vanquished or vampire, giving herself to be seen and provoking the Other to an encounter that gives her pleasure. (The Lacanian analyst Lemoine-Luccioni[23] argues that feminine desire functions in such a provocative, passive fashion.) Like Angèle, Vanadé observes her own victory in her very violation, in a subtle game of mirrors that renders the male's vertiginous, violent aspiration to fusion quite vain. Angélique or Vanadé's parted lips as inaccessible or as enchantment are therefore made to assume or inscribe the observer's own insecure positions, become fatal and guilty of their own violation.

From a fascination with linguistic generators and with Tel Quel writings in the sixties and early seventies, Robbe-Grillet has moved in the recent theoretical justifications of his writing practice (back) toward a position he labels with the imprecise term of subjective reality. This subjective reality is not the old timeless philosophical identity. Nor is it an essence or an individuated, full (presence to it)self. But it is at least as close to individual mental life as it is to language alone. Michel Contat notes in an interview with the writer[24] following the appearance of *Angélique* that although Rybalka, notable Sartre scholar, pointed out to Robbe-Grillet, while the latter was still working on the manuscript, that Sartre had never attended Kojève's seminar on Hegel in the thirties with Bataille, Aron, Queneau, and Lacan as Robbe-Grillet's text claimed, the detail was not changed before publication. The writer's explanation was, astonishingly, that it was the mental reality of his own link with the Sartrean world that is significant and not a physical truth. ("For me", the writer claims in *Le Miroir qui revient,* "Sartre a assisté à ce séminaire" [Sartre was present at this seminar].) Despite the anguish of the void of self, beyond the postmodern prison walls of readymade languages and structures, the writer can attempt to reinvent his life.

Within the creative text, it is by a semantic slippage that a photograph of Jacqueline/Angélique becomes bound Violette, hands attached behind her back, twisting, burning at the stake in *Le Voyeur*; by a slippage of verb form that a description of an Ingres painting, *Roger délivrant Angélique* is transformed into aggressive narrative action as a threatening male "monster" or "giant" approaches. As representation becomes "real," and "real" is shown to derive from the represented, the reader is "always, already" within the circularity of logical paradox, in postmodern aporia, or in a "strange loop." The question becomes how we situate what Robbe-Grillet labels "mental reality" or psychological truth—a strange reality or truth that transforms an innocent photograph of an adolescent into that of a bound and tortured victim/witch. Does the mental reality derive from inside or outside this loop?

Robbe-Grillet himself gives the answer that the real must always pass through the imaginary. In an interview with Claude Du Verlie, Robbe-Grillet sets himself apart from Ricardou's hard-line poststructuralist position, which "completely denies the representational effects of literature." "I don't," he asserts; "that is, I do agree that literature does try to represent, cannot hope to represent, even scorns any attempt to represent. But where I disagree is in knowing that the representational effects constantly are there and probably affect the understanding of the text" (p. 534).[25]

What are these somewhat vague "representational effects"? The term
suggests the reservations Robbe-Grillet has always felt about the limitations of postmodernism or deconstruction. These reservations return
us to the consideration of the question of postmodernism versus essentialism (construction versus nature), tangled with throughout this study
but never entirely negotiated.

Postmodernism and Essentialism

In a controversial 1989 article entitled "The Essence of the Triangle
or, Taking the Risk of Essentialism Seriously," Teresa de Lauretis
espouses the Italian feminist case for essential difference(s) between, for
example, postmodernism and feminism as between male and female.
These differences derive, according to de Lauretis, both from originary
sexual difference (a female or male body) and from an "essence" no
longer defined as the thing in itself, or the nature of the thing, but as
the essential qualities or attributes (the effects?) of the thing determined
by its historical specificity. Like Robbe-Grillet, de Lauretis does not
negate the dominant postmodern theoretical positions that gender, like
identity, is discursively and socially produced. But much as Robbe-Grillet
does, and for personal-political as well as intellectual purposes, the
theorist introduces polysemous functioning and disorder into her universe; a new logic of chaos and of complementarity, necessarily argued
logically. De Lauretis's chaotic rethinking of the "essential essence of
the triangle," (woman) has as its corollaries equally risky and unfash-
ionable doctrines—consciousness-raising to gender difference as an alternative to struggle for gender equality, entrustment and accountability
to other women rather than vindication of women's rights under patriarchal law, acceptance of disparity of power and of the erotic dimension
of relationships among women within difference and inequality and not
only within idealized sameness and equality. Gender difference, entrustment, or at least complicity within inequality rather than equal rights,
and disparity of power as constitutive of the erotic can also be seen to
characterize Robbe-Grillet's investigation of his sadomasochistic "memories of the golden triangle." Is this risk of standing on common ground

with Robbe-Grillet (the common ground of the parti pris for sexual difference) a risk that the feminist de Lauretis indeed meant to take?

The need for a rethinking of essentialism, claims de Lauretis, arises from the paradox on which woman is founded and which has been the first task of feminist thought to disentangle: "the paradox of woman, a being that is at once captive and absent in discourse, constantly spoken of but itself inaudible or inexpressible, displayed as spectacle and yet unrepresented; a being whose existence and specificity are simultaneously asserted and denied, negated and controlled."[26]

De Lauretis might be describing Robbe-Grillet's figures of the feminine. If these figures in their absent, captive character are, in some way, and paradoxically, exemplary, and perhaps more so again in their open embodiment of the erotic, of power, and of phantasy, could their role, then, be seen to be a feminist one? De Lauretis continues, "And hence the task of feminist philosophy, as Cavareo puts it: 'thinking sexual difference through the categories of a thought that is supported by the non-thinking of difference itself'" (p. 26).

If language is male-conceived and paternalistic or patriarchal and there is no feminine access to the symbolic, nonetheless something in the quality of absence, in phantasy, or in the power of the erotic may provide insights into the unspoken other, the nondiscourse, or the primal connection with intense, self-dissolving, maternal love, the cyclical mère/mer. In an article on the fragment "L'Horreur d'un pareil amour" in Marguerite Duras's *Outside,* which juxtaposes evocations of the writer's loss of her first stillborn child and her avid watching of her second baby's signs of life, Robert Greene[27] puzzles over the typology of an analogous core or substance he senses in the organic blackness, the blank spots, the hole in being or "unnameable affect" out of which Duras attempts to write in an "irresolvable ambiguity." As it is for her heroine Lol V. Stein, this is the indeterminacy of being "ravished," that is, simultaneously swept away and annihilated and enthralled (or could we say, in Robbe-Grillet's vocabulary, enchanted?).

It may be, as de Lauretis has suggested, that the personal (narrative) is political. Laura Mulvey contends that "sadism," deep structure of narrative or at least coextensive with it, "demands a story":[28] the male text in power is characterized by sadistic desire. Robbe-Grillet's textual tracing of the erotic as deriving from a bi-polar (I would argue rather for the designation "complementary") psychosexual structure of masculine will to power and feminine desire for powerlessness and abnegation echoes the power scenarios of many other texts of modernity. Among Bunuel's surrealist films, which draw on the subversive power of desire and violence, *Belle de jour* recounts the story of a beautiful middle-class woman who seeks fulfillment in sadomasochistic phantasies and in her secret life as a prostitute. The sex war is made explicit in Philippe Sollers's *Femmes,* in which Sollers claims that "the world belongs to women, that is, to death." The feminine is natural disorder, dissolution, and time against the background of the saga of military battles that constitutes Western history in the work of Claude Simon. Again, the close sadomasochistic relationships of Beckettian pairs—Pozzo and Lucky as master and slave, the sadistic relation of rejection and acceptance between Vladimir and Estragon, for example—share something of this battle of the sexes. There are, as we have observed, similar convergences with currents in "low" culture, evident particularly in a certain kind of pornographic production and in horror, detective, slasher, or monster genres.

As these texts have become more visible in society—the commercial success in France of the film *Histoire d'O* being an obvious example—they have provoked a variety of complex interactions and reactions. The film *The Night Porter,*[29] which depicts the passionate sadomasochistic relationship between a Jewish concentration camp victim and a German guard dominator, which revives compulsively when the two meet again by chance after the war, profoundly disturbs a generation passionately questioning the totalitarian impulses of their recent past. Christiane Rochefort's *Quand tu vas chez les femmes,*[30] inversion of Nietzsche's misogynist prescription ("When you go to women, take your whip along") in its casting of male as extreme masochist and female as dominator, is no less discomforting in spite of its reversal of the dominant cultural gendering of masochism. The French film *Maîtresse* (Barbet Schroeder, 1976) was a study of the masochistic universe and the difficulties and contradictions, the strength required for a woman to sustain the role of dominatrix. The film was acted by volunteers from the Paris sadomasochistic community. *Attache-moi,* a box office success in 1990, returns to the more easily exploitable bondage of the female. In the United States during a period when Robbe-Grillet has spent a significant

amount of time writing and lecturing within the university system, there
has been a controversial emergence in the eighties, particularly within
the gay subcultures, of such s&m publications as the lesbian *Off Our
Backs* by the Samois group.[31] The publication of the Kinsey Institute's
serious statistics and Nancy Friday's collections of phantasies confirm
that masochistic phantasies are prevalent, more common still in men
than in women.

Raising the question again as the somewhat different one of the
relation between narrative and our lives, and particularly of female
consent in narrative, de Lauretis has found examples of the presence of
aggressive male desire recurring in very different kinds of stories. These
range from "the attack launched by the army of sperm on the hiding
place of the ovum" in the medical epic of *The Everyday Miracle,* to
the "battle" waged by the Shaman's phallic spirits inside the pregnant
woman's body to ensure safe passage of the son of man, to the "slaying"
of the Medusa, and to the "penetration" of Lotman's (male) hero of
folktale into the other space to "overcome" the female obstacle/death.
De Lauretis, like Duras, is undertaking through her investigation of
preverbal and verbal desire to escape both from biology as destiny or
from cultural sexual determinations of her time through aware rereadings or reinscriptions of her body. Should she/we allow Robbe-Grillet
the scope to do the same? Or are the projects and the stakes too different?

Both the thematics and semiotics of Duras's feminine and Robbe-
Grillet's masculine constructions of desire have, as we have seen, parallels
in mainstream feminine romance fiction. (Femininity and masculinity,
in Freud's story, for example, as de Lauretis defines them, are positions
occupied by the subject in relation to desire, corresponding respectively
to the passive and active aims of the libido, active desire for the other
and passive desire to be desired by the other.)[32] The strong, dark, fiercely
independent corsair sweeping his enjoyably helpless victim from her feet,
her taming of her brutal aggressor to her service or to marriage, tales
of lust and savagery, of repentance and regressive phantasy that have
made Delly, Mills and Boon, Barbara Cartland, and Harlequin such
supermarket successes are the other face, another more romantic coloring
with a more desirable real-life ending, of the same imagination of beauty
and the beast, the siren and the sadist. Helen Hazen's analysis of this
fiction shows the female sexual imagination firmly situated in an eroticization of power.[33] Joanna Russ, refusing positions of censorship for

feminism, points out that phantasy does not simply translate into behavior but conceals useful compromise.[34] The protagonist is "harmed" in order for her to be subsequently satisfyingly consoled and saved. In a female pornographic production that she calls "K/S fanzines" Russ examines this ambiguous but apparently unselfconscious "harming," which then makes it necessary for the heroine to be comforted and controlled. "K/S fanzines" arose out of the TV program *Star Trek* and the sensing by the women writers of a "feminine" in the caring, non-competitive, self-effacing, stoical, and self-sacrificially passionate relationship between K & S (Kirk and Spock), who can also save the universe on a regular basis without becoming victims or tyrants. Russ reads these fanzines as a postromance female production, marked by the inflicting of heroic difficulties and pain in order to permit devotion and quiet heroism. This "feminine" pornography, for Russ, a nurturing that also calls up a battering, is a sexualization of female training and is characteristically, if totally unselfconsciously, sadomasochist. (*Star Trek: The Next Generation* loses Kirk and Spock, but Lieutenant Worf of the race of Klingons continues to represent both the dark warrior forces within and the heroic merit in enduring pain and death. In the June 18, 1990, episode his "mating" with a half-human, half Klingon observes a distinctively sadomasochistic conventional code of pain as pleasure, but it is the woman, nails piercing the palms of her hands, who must bleed to seal their sexual union.) Russ explains the prevalence of s&m and female masochism in women's sexuality in the following way: "What seems to be happening in sexual fantasies is that any condition imposed or learned with sexuality, either as sex or as a substitute for sex or an indispensable condition of it is capable of being sexualized" (p. 89).

Women, Russ claims, have sexualized their female situation, their waiting, their training to enchant or provoke rather than to initiate. They have sexualized their powerlessness and dependency in the heterosexual dominance-submission model and even the models of polluted or guilty and angelic or self-sacrificing sex, of pure and impure blood. In the "'K/S fanzines," according to Russ, the commitment, delay, nurturing, and empathy that characterize the "feminine" hero(ine) and the redirection of the ideals of heroic service and self-sacrifice that characterized the old love comics go hand in hand with hurt and battering.

The loved one cannot be rescued and comforted without the evocation of humiliation or pain. The knight in shining armor requires the devouring dragon; the young Jean-Paul Sartre in *Les Mots*[35] must first daydream his young female neighbor's torture and her helplessness in order to fly, heroic and powerful, to her aid.

While Duras identifies the war with the emotions experienced in a feminine waiting for her deported husband to return from Dachau and, somewhat problematically, with the cries of her own giving birth in her pseudodiary, *La Douleur,*[36] Robbe-Grillet, like Sade as Barthes interprets him, locates the scream of pain/pleasure outside the "masculine" self in the "feminine" other. Women, too, are prisoners of the representations of the relations of sexual power and powerlessness on the "walls of the city" around them, fixed predominantly at the masochistic pole of the masochistic-sadistic frame in power. Is their production also an eroticization of power (the power relations in place)? Or does it too suggest a power of the erotic; something "deeper" or more "structural," something noncontingent concealed behind the phantasy life of male and female alike? Is it the case, as Freud believed, that woman's superego is never so inexorable and independent of its emotions as it is required to be in men, and is this because of biology? Or, as Helene Deutsch has argued, are rape phantasies archetypal rather than individual? Are they an evolutionary consequence of women's adaptation to men's prehistoric sexual nature? The writings of Stekel, Krafft-Ebbing, Havelock Ellis, Freud, Gear and Hill, Benjamin, Deleuze, Silverman, and Adams, discussed in earlier chapters, cast some light on the psychoanalytical aspects of these questions. Studies of the politics of sadomasochistic phantasies that the scope of this book allows us to mention only briefly (Robin Morgan's work, for example) seek the origins of these phantasies in such social experiences as longing for the absent father, self-loathing, or fear of sex.

In Robbe-Grillet's sadomasochistic scenario, Angèle adopts the position of consenting passive slave and protects herself from initiating forbidden activity by manipulating her active partner to realize her pleasure. Her transgression of taboo (manual defloration) is a source of strong sensations (pleasure and guilt), which are subsequently projected on the violent other. The young male, for his part, feels that the Christian slave she plays at, naked and bound before him, is the real mistress of the game, free and elusive, mobile and fluid in a way the spell-bound and abusive male cannot be.

In the work of both Robbe-Grillet and Duras we are in representations not of real experience but of phantasies, which, like our sexuality, are related as much to a world of "false" symbols as to our bodies. And we are in literary texts. Rape, ugly and frightening in its implications and consequences in life, is also one of the more powerful myths. In the collective Western literary imaginary, rape is an act of the gods (Leda, Europa), or the founding of the city (the rape of the Sabines), or grand dishonor, the fate worse than death (Lucretia who commits suicide to save her husband's honor after being raped by her brother-in-law), or the capturing of the young maiden/the nymph by the satyrs (Tiepolo's allegorical "Conquête de l'éternelle jeunesse"). Such phantasies are not derived from "real" desires and behavior in any simple one-to-one way. As Freud has also indicated, they work by indirection, disguise, and often inversion, not an attenuated reality, but themselves a language that does not transmit desire directly.

In Robbe-Grillet's work, there is a conscious rejection of feminist pretentions and a less conscious defense of male separateness and cultural power against the swirling tides and rising waters that signify the dangerous attraction of the feminine. Robbe-Grillet's texts are marked by a desire to retain power; in Duras's writing, there is a predilection for a feminine erotic of nature, flow, and loss of self in the other and a fascination with the weakness, male or female, that, for her, also characterizes the feminine power of desire or desire to go beyond the power in place. Both thematic modes of representation of women may seem politically suspect to feminism, although Parveen Adams defends a lesbian sadomasochism played out as conscious travesty of a dominant ideology. (Gaylyn Studlar's[37] argument for the acceptability of a masochism that involves a submission to the authority of the mother to offer women some empowerment seems less convincing.) Yet, in the final instance, the thematics of domination and submission, sadism and masochism are staged by new textual forms that work against the oppositions they examine. The textual mechanisms subvert binary oppositions and operate nonexclusive contradiction (both . . . and), suggesting the possibility of transformation of one pole into the other. Polysemic play and "polymorphous diversity" replace binarism. There are not just two coexisting and mutually contradictory eternally fixed poles, sadism and masochism; the poles are interchangeable. The plurality and "productivity" of the sign replace any single logic; uncertainty, mobility, and virtuality question any permanent given. At the same time, Robbe-Grillet's and Duras's open texts seek knowledge in infinite duplication of their origins and imprisonments, tracing concentric or double circles around an absent center and shaping infinitely repeating self-similar forms within new complementary and chaotic narrative structures.

Robbe-Grillet's representations of gender, which situate the feminine in the dangerous but promising void and which figure the seduction of the feminine other as duality (angel/devil) to subsequently interrogate or suppress her, are clearly imprisoned within the ideology in power, as are Marguerite Duras's representations of violence against the boundaries of the feminine self. Yet, however reluctant one is to relinquish or the other is to assume gender, identity and power, however suspect their thematics and fraught with difficulties the necessary questions of the relations between life and text, both writers are also carried beyond the gendered social self in their new textual organizations; organizations that are perhaps indeed revolutionary in a feminist sense.

Robbe-Grillet's open text seeks knowledge in infinite duplication of its sexual origins and its imprisonments. Yet figured in the flaws, the holes, the hollows in these flat surfaces, we catch glimpses of the unseen/unsaid vertigoes in our discourses and in ourselves, the (im)possibility of (self) knowledge at the margins. The images of the male giant and his frail female victim are no longer human "nature" and "destiny." But, whether they are two-dimensional cultural products, or perhaps products of the structuring mechanisms of mind, or, rather, constants of human phantasy life, of psychosexual development, and a sado-masochistic structure of the psyche, they are not completely exorcised. Violence and will to power continue to echo through Robbe-Grillet's work to the sound of marching boots. Sexual obsession, guilt, fear, and the fascination of abjection or self-loss implode as the anxious narrator attempts to make his way along the ever-narrowing corridors. The criminal voyeur-sadist and subversive, alter ego of the male postmodern writer, is in the final instance at risk from cataclysm (the falling stone), at risk of being not empowered by the display/free play of this erotic (the ascent of the phoenix) but overpowered by it. Although God and

Truth are absent from these texts, replaced by scientific analyses of language, although virtue and sin are under erasure, a disquieting power remains. Disquiet comes to lodge in the choices of material, in the narrowing of focus to a potentially destructive erotic power that suggests that the central problems of writing, which for Balzac and Dostoevski were humanist and metaphysical, have not been resolved by twentieth-century paradigm shifts. The writing of sado-eroticism, violence, and death resonates beyond the play and pleasure of the text.

The texts of Robbe-Grillet attempt to flatten and deconstruct the sacred and absolute character of Girardian "sacrificial" ceremonies, to lay bare the functioning of what Twitchell labels "preposterous violence" while examining and exposing the power of the mechanisms that under-lie the latter. The "victim"/guardian angel that he chooses to stage is sexualized and inevitably feminized. His own phantasmatic productions reveal forms of intense inter- and intrapsychic identification between victim and executioner (self and other, ego and superego), which suggest that the voyeur-sadist, like his blindfolded victim, may only fear and feel, experience his/her own body fully, through the feelings of the "other" on whom he/she acts/by whom he/she is acted upon. Girard's thesis would suggest that it is the desire to maintain sexual differenti-ation, the fear of assimilation by the female principle, that leads the male group to suppress the female. It is the conscious staging of the obsession with the capture and suppression of this dangerous sexual attraction that becomes, for Robbe-Grillet, the only possible space of freedom.

Such a "freedom" is limited. It retains the acceptance of the use of the feminine scapegoat, the necessity for a victim, and the war of the sexes that is both the mark and the instrument of the differentiation that Girard finds so essential to the survival of a society. It might also indicate an impotence, an inability to make any other kind of connection or inclusion with the "other" except through the abuse that assures domination.

To sum up, then, at the level of Robbe-Grillet's thematics and semi-otics of sex there is both male domination and an implicit reinforcement of the thesis of biological aggressivity of the male confronted with the nonaccessible desired body or with sexual difference. The theses of Darwin, Marx, Engels, and Lorenz that the laws of nature and society are those of struggle, cruelty, and competition for power lurk close enough to the text's surface and to its mise en scène of the desires behind sadomasochism to be perceptible. Sadomasochism is both game, text, and the shadow side of idealized romantic love or of the asceticism of the religious mind. There is clearly also a certain predilection for an erotic of power in Robbe-Grillet's narrative. This predilection can be characterized by the fear of the female other who may paralyze or castrate the strength of the male, as in Leiris's work, and the punishment meted out to the object (the female body) that entraps or holds. The projection onto that object of her own complicity with or desire for this punishment makes the erotic object subsequently "guilty of her own violation." The objectifying "scientific" impulse is inextricably implicated in the will to separateness and control of the dangerous other (or everything that man denies in himself), to defense against identification with a disordering female nature and a seeking of solutions in culture.

At the deepest unconscious level, however, it has been argued, these conflicting structures coexist, ungendered. Lacan's concept is of a split consciousness that becomes fascinated by the image of the ego reflected by the other and no longer sees what the ego is. Melanie Klein's elaboration of the Freudian thesis insists that the conflict with the monsters or the power of monstrosity (more central to psychoanalysis for her than the problems of splitting and the decentered self) is ultimately played out between Thanatos and the Ego. Robbe-Grillet, who has claimed that his themes derive from the collective unconscious, entitled his first film L'Immortelle in a replay of the myth of Orphic descent (dissolution, return to the womb, transmutation and rebirth). To the various versions of Angelica swallowed by a monster he has added apparent rituals of burial, such as Temple wrapped in an animal skin (although this is also the "peau d'âne" [donkey's skin] of fairy tale, and she is a potential incest victim). Jacqueline Piatier, who reviewed Djinn for Le Monde, observed that behind the cover of the grammatical structures, Simon Lecoeur, alias Boris, alias the writer, was discovering in the photograph of a sailor "péri en mer" [perished at sea/in the mother] the image of "the absent person he will someday be."[38] With her usual acumen, Piatier saw that Robbe-Grillet's work is increasingly an encounter with the figure of death.

Yet, once again I conclude from the overall texture of the Robbe-Grillet texts, as from the manner of their weaving, that beyond the

abusive eroticization of a defended male power, in their staging and
their subsequent reorganization of relationships between opposite poles
in terms of complementary and chaotic structures, these forms of disruption of traditional discursive power may indeed prove to be revolutionary even in a feminist sense. The use of Angélique goes beyond
the dialectical thematic movement between opposites (love and death)
of which her figure is emblematic: the strategies of the text situate her
in a "complementary" relation to Enchantment, as in the title *Angélique
ou l'enchantement,* her uses function in a "complementary relation" to
her sadomasochistic abuse. (In a similar fashion, Angelique embodies
the complexities of the strange loop between real and representation,
between autobiography and fiction with its proliferating selves.) It has
been powerfully argued in this century in linguistic, psychoanalytic,
literary, and feminist theory that identity acquires meaning only through
opposition, through relations of sameness and alterity. And in the water
mirrors in *Le Miroir qui revient* and *Angélique* (a garden pool and
reflected statue in Robbe-Grillet's classical garden at Mesnil), Angélique
is used to allow the narcissistic writer to see both death (self-loss) and
renewal (rebirth) in identification with the nymph Echo. The beautiful
paper captive—like sexuality itself, at once both pleasure and danger,
escape from self and feared impotence, weakening of self by other—
allows both a vicarious identification and a distancing. Where Angélique
is abused is that what she is made to see in the magic mirror is not the
other but herself being seen, her provocation of the other to her own
brutal ravishing-enchantment, pleasure-pain.

Robbe-Grillet's theoretical discourse in/on *Angélique* does come
close to what Kaja Silverman would describe as the "discursive fellow-
ship" of Jean Paulhan, an eroticizing of the male power in place.[39] In
his preface to *Histoire d'O,* Paulhan wrote "Rare is the man who has
not dreamed of possessing Justine,"[40] thus presenting such phantasies
as collective representation or biological givens fixed beyond choice or
change. (Robbe-Grillet, for his part, has insisted that all women phantasize rape.)[41] Robbe-Grillet's arguments are at moments close to Paulhan's subsequent presentation of O (that is, the masochistic bases of
female desire) as women's "nature," "the call of their blood."[42] Yet Paulhan also claims that enslavement is always self-enslavement, and, like
O, Angélique appears to choose her subjugation as a matter of individual

psychic needs and sexual liberation. Subjugation for Paulhan, as Kaja Silverman reads him, is "entirely a matter between an individual (black or female) and his or her psychic/biological needs" (p. 329). One suspects that this is a position for individual freedom that Robbe-Grillet shares. But the notions of "givens," "needs," and "choice" and their interrelationships require a finer analysis than this. Back in the strange loops of real and representation, we recall that this "call of the blood" fixing women at the masochistic pole—or women's so-called psychic and biological needs—maintains the power relations protected by the discourses in power.

However, this abuse has a second (complementary) face. In the multiple functioning of this figure, in the psychic and structural forms she (re-)organizes, there may indeed be a certain revelation of secrets analogous to the secrets of psychosexual development and the life of the unconscious that Bettelheim's *Uses of Enchantment*[43] finds in the fairy tale. Bettelheim saw certain primitive rites of male puberty such as Aboriginal self-wounding or creation of a vagina, for example, as ways of representing the feminine traits and desires of men and symbolically helping to cope with an unconscious hatred or envy toward women. The divinity of feminized suffering and death in submission and humility in Western Christian culture could be inscribed in a similar frame.

Marx began to shift emphasis from Hegel's philosophical and static ahistorical master-slave dialectic to a more dynamic historical model that would permit change. While the surfaces of the Robbe-Grillet text continue to situate Angélique as object of control, a position that corresponds, not coincidentally, to women's socialization to censor resistance or competition in favor of self-sacrifice and connection, the mobile complementary and chaotic structures of his work suggest the necessity of movement beyond any model of gender-specific content of psychic structure fixed at opposite poles. This exploration of the multiple chaotic structures that might take us beyond traditional binary operation in the enigma of the relations between the sexes, beyond the hidden but widespread fear of profane and devouring (female) sexual organs (the desire to be absorbed by a woman) seems to be a justifiable use of Angélique. There is, then, also a probing of the self and of the "essential" difference of the triangle as defined by de Lauretis behind the writing out of the power of the erotic, a production of desire that is a revolutionary and individual re-creation of the old questions of nature, that brings me to conclude that Robbe-Grillet's ex-posing of the abused body of Angélique may, in the final analysis, be of subversive use.

Interview

The following interview with Alain Robbe-Grillet and fragments from his lectures in New Zealand in April 1986 are the embryo of much of the present book. For this reason, I have decided to reprint, virtually unchanged, the following text, which appeared in *Landfall: A New Zealand Quarterly,* a journal of literary studies, in June 1986. In 1986 Robbe-Grillet was in New Zealand on a lecture tour as the Vice-Chancellors' Visitor and, concurrently, as an invited participant at the Writers' Week Festival in Wellington, where I served as his translator and presenter. At that time I was in my eighth year of teaching at Massey University, an institution that figured on the writer's tour. I had previously interviewed Robbe-Grillet at the Grand Hotel in Toulouse in 1972 on the occasion of a first screening of *L'Eden et après* and again in early 1985 at the Editions de Minuit in Paris. The earlier interviews feed into and color these texts of 1986.

With the permission of the writer and theoretician of the French "New Novel," this portrait is my assemblage and translation. The first face is from fragments of Robbe-Grillet's public lecture performances in New Zealand and from informal discussions during Writers' Week; the second face is a transcription of a formal interview at Massey University in 1986.

The portrait is colored for me by an immediate, intense, intellectually powerful if somewhat egocentric presence, surprising warmth and naturalness in personal contact and a curious mixture of direct, even provocative, honesty and of defensive ratiocination. It is softened by my observance of striking interaction with his wife, Catherine, with whom he has a living and close relationship (reversibly protective-dependent) although both now live their own sexual lives, independently.

This portrait is colored also by the mirror of my own mind, academic and female, by the attempt to understand intellectually, without foreclosure, the insistent, deliberately excessive stories of the domination,

[Note: "An Identikit Portrait" was published under my married name, Raylene O'Callaghan. The interviewer is referred to as R.O'C. These initials have been replaced in the present text by R.R., as I now use my birth name professionally.]

humiliation, fragmentation, and suppression of the eternally young and beautiful female body, naked for the most part, fragile and consenting; stories that proliferate in the later texts and films. By the disquiet as would-be female subject that this demonstration of the violence latent in the sexually based "objectivization" of young women in our culture provokes within me.

Such a conflict is resolved provisionally by the recognition that, in the relationship sadist and siren, masculine writer and myth of the feminine, signs are exchanged ludically, textually, in what might be accepted, certainly examined, as a project of liberation. If inversions there are, provocative, theoretical self-justifications of untenable phallocratic positions, the clear honesty and vulnerability of the explicitly seeking approach command attention. And above all, the operations of the text itself engage in their own complex contest with the sado-erotic ready-mades, put into play as 'building material', unmade and remade.

An Identikit Portrait (*Face One*)

This Text is a Pre-Text. (An inter-text; self quotation.) The stories we tell, from civilization to civilization, are the same. Only their forms change. I am constituted by Greek mythology, Germanic legend, Celtic lore, the Old and New Testaments. . . . The poetic fact comes from a distance. . . . It is always there . . . and, once again suddenly, it erupts . . . The Phoenix . . . The Firebird. . . . Writing is a re-writing.

The consciousness of modern man is on the walls of the city . . . chased outside . . . in the pre-text. The meanings of my texts are in the movement of the writing, the structures of the work, not in their stories.

I Speak Because I Do Not Know. . . . It doesn't 'mean' anything. Linear chronology, intrigue, causality, narrator are still present in my work but at war with subversions from within. The narration is incompetent; the world is incoherent. . . . Different narrative instances struggle for power. The text is the movement toward the text. The return re-written ("Retour raturé").

The Gap as Textual Generator. Uncertainty, virtuality, multiplicity, discontinuity, and repetition characterize the world; tiny islets of knowledge set in a vast space of void, gaps, the unknown.

The Real Is Everything Outside Meaning. The familiar, the constituted (world/text), is ideological, a cultural and linguistic construction. The real is what is outside this. . . .

Topology of the Phantom City. Non-plane surfaces, non-Euclidean geometry . . . the surfaces of the Möbius strip, the Klein bottle . . . Inside and outside, interior and exterior are interchangeable, reverse . . . The surfaces of dream . . .

The Assassin on His Own Track. The writer is both the King and his divine text, order, and the Prophet who contests this text, this order. The Prophet of he who *is to come.* He is the criminal and the poet, both chased from Plato's Republic for the disorder they threaten. . . . The writer is at once the criminal and the detective.

Order and Disorder. "Two dangers threaten the world. Order and Disorder." (Claude Simon and Stéphane Mallarmé.) The text is the movement between order and disorder.

Project for a Revolution . . . Artistic revolution is the contesting of the established Truth. Not the elaboration of a new Truth to replace the old. . . . Not Stalin replacing the Tsar. One Truth is the same as another. . . . In China, on the walls of the university auditorium, the students had replaced the title of my book "Toward a New Novel" by the words "Toward a New Sexuality." . . . Text, sex, and criminal project are metaphors, one of the other in my work.

The Movement of the Text. Being is the movement between Void and Being. (Heidegger) (If consciousness is free, it must be empty.)

The text is the movement toward the text. (The constituted text is a fossilized form.)

Freedom is the movement toward freedom. (Constituted it becomes a Truth.)

The World Is . . . The world is neither meaningful nor absurd. It *is . . .* quite simply. But it is not the familiar world of the humanist text and anthropomorphic metaphor. The world is . . . the strange ("étranger").

Anguish . . . arises from this meaning in ruins. Anguish that it is necessary to face to reach the spaces of a possible freedom of the mind.

The War of the Sexes . . . The sex-struggle is the motive force of History/ Story ("Histoire.") (Homage to Marx.)

Temple in Ruins to the Goddess Vanadé. . . . Victorious/Vanquished. Woman as dual sign Angel/Devil, Salvation/Siren . . . Marie-Ange/Eve, Blanche/Violette . . .

The Monsters of the Creative Text . . . Why did I, a successful agronomist/researcher begin to write novels, give up a career . . .?
Perhaps the monsters of my own sexual difference . . .?
Perhaps the gap between language and the world . . . the language of blond, clean, ordered, National Socialism and the hidden Holocaust . . .?

The Text is a Pre-Text? Robbe-Grillet's theoretical text thus bites its tail . . . like Ouroboros, the mythical serpent . . . or almost. For we end this assemblage with the words of another performer at the Wellington Arts Festival during Writers' Week, performer of the next generation— Laurie Anderson—herself using the words of William Burroughs transformed in song. . . . "Suspicious of language . . . Nothing is 'natural' . . . Speaking you think you are saying . . . You say nothing. Naming you think you know, . . . You know nothing. Language is a virus, from outer space."

Sex, Text, and Criminal Project (*Face Two*)

R.R.   "Fragility," "Finesse," "Fear,"—"Captive," "Curve," "Compliance"—Is there a feminine 'nature' implicit in your images and in your language?

A.R-Grillet   I believe . . . that if anything feminine exists in this world, it is this feminine something that writes, even in male writers. That is, Flaubert, whose virility cannot be questioned and who adored stories of the bordello . . . admitted that what was writing through him was a fable of himself, a woman, and that when he chose Charles Bovary to represent stability and to some extent vulgarity and Emma, on the other hand, to represent aspiration toward something else . . . lack, . . . need for freedom, etc., I believe it was to represent the double nature that he must have had. He is both Charles and Emma. The critics say that he is very hard on Charles and Emma. I believe that he was talking about himself and that when he says, I am Mme Bovary, it is meant sincerely; that she is something like an image of the writer. Proust also said that it was their feminine nature which was speaking in male writers. Perhaps one could even say [laughter] that it is their masculine nature which speaks in woman writers; in Marguerite Duras and Nathalie Sarraute. For example, that the writer is someone who has a kind of double nature and that it is not the appearance speaking in the text, but on the contrary, the Other. In Joyce, it's the woman speaking; in Virginia Woolf, the man!

R.R.   You stated in an interview with Germaine Brée that "what interests me is eroticism." Is eroticism a means, for you, of approaching the unknown body, the Other, of suppressing this difference, or is this difference also you, the potential femininity of any male? To what extent does sadism imply identification with the victim and her humiliation . . . ?

A.R-Grillet   Probably true eroticism can only be obtained by the

individual whose nature is not too massively at one pole
or the other. . . . I am a biologist by training, and for biology male and female are statistical characteristics; that is,
we know that both hormones exist in both sexes. They
are simply present in different proportions and it is only
statistically that we can say: "This characteristic belongs
to the male side, this characteristic to the female side. . . ."
Eroticism, like literature, could develop in those in whom
the preponderance is uncertain . . . that is, that Charles
Bovary is too massively on the male side, but what we
know of writers indicates that they are not at all 'massive'
in their sexual predominance.

R.R.   Yet the dominant figure of eroticism is masculine violence
                and domination exerted against the weakness/need for
                domination of the woman, prisoner of man's desire and of
                her own need of this desire. Can eroticism be seen as sexual
                liberation for woman, or does it, at a point in history
                where, for the first time, they have the possibility of dis-
                posing of their own body without control by father,
                brother, or husband, constitute a new servitude, a sexual
                (passive) 'nature'?

A.R-Grillet   Have you read my wife's books . . .? [written under the
                pseudonym of Jeanne de Berg]

R.R.   Yes. . . . But is the contrary representation—capture, humil-
                iation, fragmentation of the male body by the dominating
                female, that is beginning to make an appearance—really
                female eroticism, or is this eroticism equally the satisfying of
                other male desires by women, compliant, desiring to please?

A.R-Grillet   We don't know. This is a question we can't yet answer.
                The civilization in which we live, from its Jewish origins,
                has been a civilization dominated by man. Woman has not
                had the power to speak. It is very difficult to ascertain
                what goes on in a woman's head. She has always spoken
                the language of the other. Without really suffering from
                this. She completely adapted. . . . And men who confess

their masochism . . . meet enormous difficulties. . . . They attempt to induce in the other a willingness to participate in what shall I say, a creative situation, and they meet refusal, often shocked refusal. This is not the traditionally assigned role.

R.R.   Mythological woman is woman seductive and fatal, serpent and siren, dangerous, associated with blood, the Angel of Death in your work. Yet she is also doll, object of exchange and consumption, glossy representation, object. And paradoxically, perverse, spirit of disorder, of revolution, witch, nature, subject, who threatens male order. . . .

A.R-Grillet   These are the stereotypes of the world around us . . . on the walls of the Western city, the texts of our civilization . . .

R.R.   The narrators of some of your recent works are in fact 'subjects'—sexually 'liberated' women but at the same time victims of the scenarios and the persuasions of your texts. What freedom do they really have? Will liberated female narration not, in fact, be completely different from your attempt to identify with a female narrator?

A.R-Grillet   It is too soon to know. . . . What I currently believe is that phantasies are not male or female; phantasies are places of interaction. . . . It is difficult to say, as it has always been the male who has spoken; he has contaminated everything . . . but nonetheless, I believe that we will find that, for example, the phantasy of rape is a shared one, that even when women are free, they will still be capable of playing at being raped.

R.R.   Where does this image of rape, the crime that stalks all strata of your phantom city—and crime stalks all literature in your view—come from?

A.R-Grillet   It is, quite evidently, biological. . . . Since you find it in all animals. Ah . . . What I wanted to say about the struggle for power between the sexes . . . Generally speaking, what bothers me most about the M.L.F. [Movement for Women's Liberation] is that they have sought with much greater ardor to castrate male phantasies than to develop female phantasies, and certain women have said that phantasies are unclean and, in fact, belong to the male who is himself an unclean individual. . . . And other things complicate the problem. . . . Psychoanalysis, which incredibly sees women as lacking a sex, as truncated sexually. . . . And if the mediaeval world denied women a soul, a Philippe Sollers now makes the preposterous claim that women have no Eros . . . that Eros which in some ways replaces the modern soul. . . . Women are free to develop their own eroticism . . . to create their own texts. . . . That is what we are doing in my family.

R.R.   And Censorship? With satellites, modern mass communications, New Zealand will no longer be able to protect her order by censorship. Is the ability to critically assess the representations that will flood in, pornographic, sexist, and other, to see their nature as 'construction' and not as 'real', to establish distances . . . is this ability accessible to all?

A.R-Grillet   What a good thing for New Zealand! You know that that idiotic Simone de Beauvoir—you can leave the term in your text—wanted quite simply, to censure Sade with his ambivalent fantasy world* [*Author's note: This is, of course, a misconception on Robbe-Grillet's part], Justine and Juliette at opposite poles . . . that the Grove Press who publish my work in translation in the U.S.A. are still defending cases in some states against the publication of D. H. Lawrence's work. Just imagine . . . In Denmark it is quite clear that the proliferation of pornographic literature has brought about a decrease in sex crimes. . . . And Nixon's senatorial commission, investigating sex crimes by the American soldiers isolated from the moral orders of home in the Vietnamese jungles, concluded that these horrific excesses were *not* a result of previous representations, of exposure to pornography . . . even if Nixon took no notice of these findings and simply responded with more censure and repression!

R.R.   But your sado-erotic representations are so insistent, so excessive—scenes of aristocratic male hunting parties chasing a young girl, then served up for the hunt dinner, sacrilegious scenes of female crucifixion, with candles put to sadistic purposes with long scenes of rape and torture of delicate female flesh saturating the text, provoking whom . . . what?

A.R-Grillet   I observe these phantasies in myself. That is, masturbation in my early childhood was linked to such representations. But my childhood was a happy one, loved by my father, by my mother, very close to both of them. There was thus something in my childhood not linked to my childhood situation. I grew more and more aware of these phantasies which may have had something to do with my decision to write. I began by concealing them in my text, then concealing-revealing them, and then I decided that I would show them openly and go beyond them . . . make them the object of the text. These phantasies are my own . . . as they were the phantasies of Michelet and of many other writers, and I belong to a time when one should be able to tell them, without fear of shocking, perhaps even thinking that shocking is a necessary part of this conscious awareness . . . the more visible they are, the more clearly can they be designated as phantasies, that is, as stereotypes. . . .

R.R.   You claim in an interview that "virtue leads to crime" and not the open expression of violent sexual phantasies. But can awareness of these phantasies, their open expression, the removal of their hidden depth, the mystery of transgression, and their distancing in fact solve the problem of crime?

A.R-Grillet   In any case, crime is in our heads. And any book can trigger a crime. Do you know the story of the student at the University of Texas, Austin, who climbed up into a tower with a machine gun and shot at his fellow students . . . he killed fourteen. When he was asked, why, he said that he had been reading Camus's *The Outsider*— Camus, a moralist. . . . We perhaps need to protect children who are impressionable. . . . And yet, phantasies can be fed from anywhere . . . mine as a child, were fed by the classical paintings I found in the two volumes of the illustrated *Larousse Universel . . .* * [*discussion on the nineteenth-century paintings of Ingres *Roger Freeing Angelique,* chained to the rock before the approaching sea monster, discussion of Delacroix . . .]. But statistically normal minds. . . . There are different responses possible. Puritanism believes everything must be hidden. I believe this leads to crime. Excess, on the other hand, may play a liberating role. Greek theater was excessive. All the most horrible atrocities—parricide, infanticide, incest—were represented on the stage but with the actors wearing masks, by a *Verfremdungseffekt,* to prevent mimesis, to distance the actions portrayed. Mimesis is more likely to occur, in fact, with books seriously depicting Nazi crime or documentaries on pornography, than for example with the work of Sade with its constant play of distancing, alienating devices. . . . I do not claim to be the holder of the truth, but I believe that it is preferable to 'play' with one's own phantasies than to mask them with an appearance of virtue. Ingres seemed totally unaware of the messages of his paintings . . . claimed innocence. . . .

R.R.   Why is 'innocence' such a key word in your theoretical work . . . even though you claim that language is never innocent?

A.R-Grillet   Don't you know the old Chinese proverb: The bleating of the lamb excites the tiger . . . (laughter)

R.R.   Food for love or food for thought . . . ?

Notes

Introduction

1. These terms that suggest the intergeneric and interdisciplinary character of the narrative and cinematic techniques used by Robbe-Grillet are employed by Inge Crosman Wimmers in her study of *Projet,* "Towards a Reflexive Act of Reading: Robbe-Grillet's *Projet pour une révolution à New York.*" The terms "illusion-making" and "illusion-breaking" are also used by this critic.

2. This is the term used by Roch Smith in his study of imagistic generators or game with a visual lexicon: "Generating the Erotic Dream Machine: Robbe-Grillet's *L'Eden et après* and *La Belle Captive.*"

3. Simone de Beauvoir, *Faut-il brûler Sade?*

Chapter 1

1. All references to novels by Robbe-Grillet are to the Editions de Minuit editions except for *Les Gommes* and *Dans le labyrinthe* where page references are to the U.G.E. 10/18 paperback editions of 1964 and 1969 respectively and *Pour un nouveau roman* where the 1964 Gallimard paperback edition was used. All of the translations from French in this book are my own unless otherwise stated.

2. See for example G. Gale, *The Theory of Science,* and A. March, *La Physique moderne et ses idées.*

3. *Pour un nouveau roman,* hereafter *PNR,* is a collection of reprinted articles on the art of the novel.

4. Although the term "nouveau roman" has come to be widely used, Robbe-Grillet is himself the first to admit its fortuitous character and unjustifiable pretensions. "Personne n'aurait l'idée de louer un musicien pour avoir, de nos jours, fait du Beethoven ... Beaucoup de romanciers savent qu'il en va de même en littérature, qu'elle aussi est vivante, et que le roman depuis qu'il existe a toujours été nouveau" [Nobody would think of praising a musician for having, in our time, composed Beethoven. ... Many novelists know that this is also true in literature, that it too is alive, and that since it has been in existence the novel has always been new] (*PNR,* pp. 9–10).

5. Reprinted in Roland Barthes, *Essais Critiques,* pp. 29–40.

6. Erwan Rault, *Théorie et expérience romanesque chez Robbe-Grillet: "Le Voyeur" (1955).*

7. Barthes, *Essais critiques,* p. 39.

8. Gaston Bachelard, *L'Activité rationaliste de la physique contemporaine,* p. 7.

9. Ibid., p. 10.

10. Ibid., p. 13.

11. Alain Robbe-Grillet, "Sur le choix des générateurs," in *Nouveau roman: hier, aujourd'hui,* 2, p. 160.

12. D. Wendt, "Language, Scientific Theories, and the Arts as Mappings of Reality," *Degrés* 3 (1973): 1.

13. Jacques Dhaenens, *"La Maison de rendez-vous" d'Alain Robbe-Grillet*; Jacques Leenhardt, *Lecture politique du roman: "La Jalousie" d'Alain Robbe-Grillet*; Lucien Goldmann, *Pour une sociologie du roman.*

14. Bachelard, *L'Activité rationaliste,* p. 35.

15. In "Order and Disorder in Film and Fiction," translated by Bruce Morrissette, p. 19.

16. Arthur Eddington, *The Philosophy of Physical Science.*

17. Ben Stoltzfus, "Robbe-Grillet's Dialectical Topology."

18. Edward De Bono, *The Mechanism of Mind.*

19. Rachel Garden, *Modern Logic and Quantum Mechanics.*

20. My own attempt to present the theories of contemporary physics in everyday language is, of course, open to similar criticism, and only partially vindicated by its heavy dependence on the writings (also vulgarizations) of the physicists involved in the elaboration and refutation of theories of "complementarity."

21. André Brink, "Transgressions: A Quantum Approach to Literary Deconstruction."

22. Stéphane Lupasco, *Les Trois matières,* p. 24.

23. Morrissette, "Order and Disorder," p. 16.

24. Jean Ricardou, "La Fiction flamboyante," in *Pour une théorie du nouveau roman,* p. 230.

25. Bruce Morrissette, *Les Romans de Robbe-Grillet*; *Intertextual Assemblage in Robbe-Grillet from "Topology" to the "Golden Triangle"*; "Postmodern Generative Fiction," in *Novel and Film: Essays in Two Genres.*

26. My unpublished doctoral thesis (1972, L'Université de Poitiers), entitled "La Complémentarité multiple: Une étude de l'oeuvre d'Alain Robbe-Grillet," argued that there were connections between the theories emerging in the contemporary scientific world and the structures of Alain Robbe-Grillet's work. French literary criticism, at that time, was emerging out of existentialism, phenomenology, and structuralism into a poststructuralist era. The relational nature of meaning and reality that poststructuralism was to foreground figured the new epistemological questions that Derridean deconstruction, and various postmodernisms were beginning to formulate. Robbe-Grillet's work has interacted with, or espoused experimentally, all of these new approaches but settled in none.

27. Louis de Broglie, "Qu'est-ce que la vibration," in *Sur les sentiers de la science.*

28. Stephen Heath, *The Nouveau Roman: A Study in the Practice of Writing*, p. 147.

29. Alain Robbe-Grillet, "La Littérature aujourd'hui," *Tel Quel*, no. 14 (1963): 14.

30. Ilya Prigogine and Isabelle Stengers, *La Nouvelle Alliance: Métamorphose de la science*, p. 16.

31. Umberto Eco, *Foucault's Pendulum*.

32. For example, the disintegration of radium is without known cause, but the statistical time that marks the evolution of disintegration of large numbers of radium atoms can paradoxically be taken as the most perfect model of regular time. This innumerable host of accidents (as, for an individual nucleus of radium, disintegration is an accident) provides a time almost without accident.

33. Richard Feynman, *The Character of Physical Law*.

34. Prigogine, *La Nouvelle Alliance*, p. 29.

35. Morrissette, "Postmodern Generative Fiction," in *Novel and Film*, p. 8.

36. Morrissette, *Novel and Film*, pp. 169–70. Morrissette quotes Jean Alter's early work *La Vision du monde d'Alain Robbe-Grillet*.

37. In *Etudes* (March 1966). Quoted by Morrissette in *Novel and Film*, p. 176.

38. G. Rattray-Taylor, "Science in the Seventies," review article in *The Listener*, December 20, 27, 1979.

39. A brief indication of the kinds of personal choice my translations of Robbe-Grillet's French text make is perhaps called for. For example, Jo Levy's translation of *Le Miroir qui revient* as *Ghosts in the Mirror* (New York: Grove Weidenfeld, 1988) gives "uneasily" as a translation of "sans repos" and cleverly suggests the feelings of difficulty and uncertainties Robbe-Grillet's enterprise inspires in the writer. I have preferred to use the word "restlessly" to identify Robbe-Grillet with the wandering phantoms of self that Weidenfeld's translation of the French title in fact insists on. "Ceaselessly" or "without rest" would also be possible translations.

40. Jean-Claude Vareille, *Alain Robbe-Grillet l'étrange*.

41. "Le style, c'est l'homme," *Apostrophes* (a literary television program hosted by Bernard Pivot), Antenne 2, June 1981.

Chapter 2

1. Pierre de Boisdeffre, *La Cafetière est sur la table ou contre le nouveau roman*.

2. Vladimir Propp, *Morphology of the Folktale*.

3. Claude Lévi-Strauss, *Structural Anthropology*.

4. John Sturrock, *The French New Novel*.

5. I had the interesting experience of personally verifying Robbe-Grillet's reputation in this domain during his participation at a Writers' Week Festival in Wellington, New Zealand in March 1986, and subsequently on his lecture tour of the New Zealand universities. As translator on some of these occasions and occasional host and driver, I was able to note at leisure his passionate and taxonomic botanical curiosity, his desire to stop the car to photograph the fine detail of play of light and shadow on hillside and forest, and his disappearances during an official reception into the Vice-Chancellor's garden to examine varieties of rose of which he invariably knew the botanical name.

6. Italo Calvino, *Invisible Cities,* pp. 45–46.

7. Ronald Bogue, "A Generative Phantasy: Robbe-Grillet's 'La Chambre secrète.'" Bogue's thoughtful reading sees this text as a self-generating verbal structure and emplotment of the inextricability of violence, desire, and the unfolding of the writing. However, he also notes that such self-conscious textuality may protect personal phantasy in a defensive process similar to that which Freud called *Verleugnung* (disavowal).

8. Jorge Luis Borges, "The Circular Ruins."

9. Ronald Schleifer, "Narrative Analysis and the Psychology of Meaning: A. J. Greimas at the Limits of Science." Schleifer quotes Derrida, "Structure, Sign, and Play in the Discourse of the Human Sciences," p. 272.

10. Stanley Fish, *Doing What Comes Naturally.*

11. Jacques Derrida, "Structure, Sign, and Play in the Discourse of the Human Sciences." Quoted by Schleifer, p. 10.

12. Schleifer, "Narrative Analysis," pp. 13–14.

13. Ibid., p. 14.

14. Teresa de Lauretis, "Desire in Narrative," p. 104. De Lauretis quotes Barthes's preface to the 1966 volume of the journal *Communications.*

15. Roland Barthes, "Introduction to the Structural Analysis of Narratives," in *Image-Music-Text,* p. 124.

16. Barthes, *The Pleasure of the Text,* p. 10. Quoted in de Lauretis, "Desire in Narrative," pp. 107–8.

17. Robert Scholes, *Fabulation and Metafiction,* p. 26. Quoted in de Lauretis, "Desire in Narrative," p. 108.

18. De Lauretis, "Desire in Narrative," p. 143 draws in particular from the essay by Freud that I discuss in greater detail in chapter 6; Sigmund Freud, "A Child is Being Beaten."

19. Marie Gear and Melvyn Hill, *Working through Narcissism. Treating Its Masochistic Structures.*

20. Emile Benveniste, *Problèmes de linguistique générale,* p. 260.

21. John Berger, *Ways of Seeing.*

22. Laura Mulvey, "Visual Pleasure and Narrative Cinema." De Lauretis quotes passages from Mulvey's thought-provoking article in which sadism and narrative are situated in a relation of reversibility: "Sadism demands a story,

depends on making something happen, forcing a change in another person, a battle of will and strength, victory/defeat . . ." ("Desire in Narrative," p. 103).

23. De Lauretis, "Desire in Narrative," p. 109.

24. The interior and exterior surfaces of the Klein bottle (like the Möbius strip) are so ingeniously melded that it is impossible to say which is container and which is contained. Liquid in such a bottle could thus be seen to flow from outside in. In *Nouveau roman: hier, aujourd'hui*, (2: 132), Morrissette examined the closed spaces inverted subsequently through windows or keyholes, the interior duplications (novel within a novel or tape recording), not clearly container or contained that are analogous to these mathematical forms. He posed the question of the significance of the shock of this meeting between the creative literary imagination and the formal mathematical domain. Would structuralist thought, he asked, see in the coincidence between abstract thinking and the literary text a proof of universal modes of thought?

25. N. Katherine Hayles, *The Cosmic Web: Scientific Field Models and Literary Strategies in the 20th Century*.

26. Joan DeJean, *Literary Fortifications: Rousseau, Laclos, Sade*.

27. François Jost, "From the 'New Novel' to the 'New Novelists.'"

28. Ben Stoltzfus pointed out to me the possible connections between Magritte's *The Difficult Crossing* and the rite of passage of the crossing of the limen and founding of distinctions that Robbe-Grillet incorporates in his text.

29. Gödel's incompleteness theorem proved that for any axiomatized theories strong enough for arithmetic, the theory will be inconsistent or contain propositions whose truth (or falseness) cannot be clearly demonstrated. Mathematics, not demonstrably false, intuitively consistent, could therefore not be demonstrably true, or proven to be consistent. Discussing formally undecidable propositions (*The Cosmic Web*, pp. 31–33), Katherine Hayles gives the following example of this kind of paradox, which Douglas Hofstadter calls a "strange loop" in his path-setting book, *Gödel, Escher, Bach: An Eternal Golden Braid*: "On one side of the paper write the words. 'The statement on the other side is true.' Now turn the paper over and write 'The statement on the other side is false.' . . . Such statements can be neither true nor false; they are inherently undecidable" (Hayles, p. 34). Hayles also discusses the "Halting Problem" in computational theory as similarly indeterministic. It seems that it is not possible to determine in advance whether a computer will be able to come to a halt, that is, be able to find a solution for any given problem. For Hayles, strange loops appear because the analysis is inseparable from the object to be analyzed, that is, precisely because of the problem of self-reference.

30. Laura Mulvey, "Changes: Thoughts on Myth, Narrative and Historical Experience," *History Workshop Journal* (1986): 12. Mulvey quotes from Juliet Mitchell's "Psycho-analysis, Narrative, and Femininity," in *Woman, the Longest Revolution* (London: Virago, 1984).

31. Mulvey, "Changes," p. 15.

32. Jacques Derrida, *Positions*.

33. "Alain Robbe-Grillet," in Lois Oppenheim, *Three Decades of the French New Novel*, pp. 29–30.

34. John Barth, "Lost in the Funhouse."

35. Susan Rubin Suleiman, "Reading Robbe-Grillet: Sadism and Text in *Projet pour une révolution à New York.*"

36. Suleiman, "Reading Robbe-Grillet: Sadism and Text," republished and represented in *Subversive Intent: Gender, Politics and the Avant-Garde*, p. 51.

37. Ibid., p. 13.

38. Jean Ricardou, *Problèmes du nouveau roman*.

39. Martin Eger, "The New Epic of Science and the Problem of Communication," p. 15.

40. *Robbe-Grillet: analyse, théorie*, Colloque de Cérisy, edited Jean Ricardou, vol. 1, p. 312.

41. James Gleick, *Chaos: Making a New Science*, p. 19.

42. Ibid., p. 123.

43. A. K. Dewdney, "Computer Recreations. A Tour of the Mandelbrot Set Aboard the Mandelbus."

44. E. Wilson, *On Human Nature*.

45. Eger, "The New Epic of Science," p. 15.

46. Hofstadter, *Gödel, Escher, Bach*.

47. Thomas Kuhn, *The Structure of Scientific Revolutions*.

48. Peter Stoicheff, "The Chaos of Metafiction," unpublished paper given on a panel entitled "Chaos and Systems Theory" organized by Katherine Hayles with Peter Stoicheff and Eric White at the Conference of the Society for Literature and Science. Rensselaer Polytechnic, Oct. 7, 1988. My own paper on this panel was an early version of this section of my chapter.

49. It would require another book-length study to do justice to other significant work defining and rethinking postmodern self-conscious writing. My own rereading of Linda Hutcheon's *A Poetics of Metafiction* preceded the writing of this chapter. A subsequent reading of other recent works on metafiction, Patricia Waugh's *Metafiction*, Brian McHale's *Postmodernist Fiction*, and Alan Thiher's *Words in Reflection* among them, raised a number of other questions that would also be pursued with profit in a more developed study of postmodernism.

50. Eger, "The New Epic of Science," p. 15.

51. Eric White, "Negentropy, Noise and Emancipatory Thought," p. 8.

52. Felman, "Beyond Oedipus: The Specimen Story of Psychoanalysis."

53. Ibid., p. 1034.

54. Ibid., p. 1032.

55. Ibid., p. 1050.

56. Ibid., pp. 1050–51.

Chapter 3

1. Jean-Pierre Valabréga, et al., *Le Désir et la perversion,* p. 8.
2. For example, Bruce Morrissette, "Oedipe ou le cercle fermé," in *Les Romans de Robbe-Grillet,* pp. 37–75; C. Astier, "*Les Gommes* d'Alain Robbe-Grillet: Un Avatar moderne du mythe d'Oedipe dans la littérature," in *Le Mythe d'Oedipe* (Paris: Colin, 1974), pp. 191–215; L. Roudiez, "The Embattled Myths," in *Héréditas* (Austin, Texas: Ayer Co. pubs., 1964), pp. 75–94; M. Spencer, "Avatars du mythe chez Robbe-Grillet et Butor," in *Robbe-Grillet: analyse, théorie,* vol. 1, pp. 64–84; Betty Rahv, "The Labyrinth as Archetypal Image of the New Novel," in *From Sartre to the New Novel,* pp. 99–148; H. Ronse, "Le Labyrinthe, espace significatif," in *Cahiers internationaux de Symbolisme,* no. 9–10 (1965–66): 27–43; P. Sturdza, "The Rebirth Archetype in Robbe-Grillet's *L'Immortelle,*" *French Review,* vol. 48, no.6 (1975): 990–95.
3. Leigh S. M. Bridge, "Robbe-Grillet's *Djinn:* Le Coeur a ses raisons que la raison ne connaît pas," *French Studies Bulletin,* No. 13 (Winter 1984/5): 9–11.
4. Ibid., p. 10.
5. Ben Stoltzfus points out this example of a juxtaposition of Jungian and Lacanian images in "Robbe-Grillet's Mythical Biography: Reflections of *La Belle Captive* in *Le Miroir qui revient.*"
6. Ibid., p. 399.
7. K. Ruthven in *Myth* discusses E. Cassirer's *Mythical Thought: The Philosophy of Symbolic Forms,* vol. 2, translated by Ralph Manheim (New Haven: Yale University Press, 1953–57); Joseph Campbell's *The Hero with a Thousand Faces* (New York: Princeton University Press, 1949); *The Golden Bough,* edited by James Frazer (London: Martin, 1911). This kind of myth criticism, for Ruthven, can be seen as influenced by the overtly symbolic or allegorical mode of nineteenth-century American literature.
8. Bruno Bettelheim, *The Uses of Enchantment: The Meaning and Importance of Fairy Tales.*
9. Claude Lévi-Strauss, *Mythologiques IV. L'Homme nu,* p. 571.
10. "Le propre de la pensée mythique est de s'exprimer à l'aide d'un répertoire dont la composition est hétéroclite . . . Elle apparaît ainsi comme une sorte de bricolage intellectuel, ce qui explique les relations qu'on observe entre les deux. Comme le bricolage sur le plan technique, la réflexion mythique peut atteindre, sur le plan intellectuel, des résultats brillants et imprévus" [What characterizes mythical thought is the way it expresses itself with the help of a repertory of objects of mixed composition. . . . It thus seems to be a kind of intellectual *bricolage,* which explains the relations one observes between the two. Like bricolage on the technical level, mythical reflection can achieve, on the intellectual level, brilliant and unexpected results] (Claude Lévi-Strauss, *La Pensée sauvage,* p. 26).
11. Joan DeJean, *Literary Fortifications: Rousseau, Laclos, Sade.*

12. Roland Barthes, *Mythologies,* pp. 215–68.

13. Ibid., p. 216.

14. *Obliques,* No. 16–17 (Paris: Borderie, 1978), pp. 169–72.

15. Barthes, *Mythologies,* p. 233.

16. Peter Tremewan, "Allusions to Christ in Robbe-Grillet's *Les Gommes.*"

17. Bruce Morrissette, *Les Romans de Robbe-Grillet,* pp. 37–75.

18. Claude Lévi-Strauss, *La Pensée sauvage,* p. 26.

19. Jean-Jacques Brochier, "Oedipe à Cologne," *Magazine Littéraire* (Avril 1981): 53.

20. René Girard, *La Violence et le sacré* (Paris: Grasset, 1972).

21. Gilles Deleuze and Félix Guattari, *L'Anti-Oedipe.*

22. Jean Ricardou, "Inquiète métaphore," in *Problèmes du nouveau roman,* pp. 145–57. "La Fiction flamboyante," in *Pour une théorie du nouveau roman,* pp. 211–33, is also a study of the phonological generators of violence and revolution in *Projet*. The organization of *Projet*'s "mythologies" seems, however, to be predominantly "thematic," based on semantic and cultural associations such as "revolution"—political change with violence and red as in murder/ fire/sex/blood/rape, and the return to the point of departure of the text.

23. Sigmund Freud, "Delusions and Dreams in Jensen's *Gradiva.*"

24. André Gardies, "L'Érotuelle."

25. Roland Barthes, *Le Plaisir du texte,* p. 60.

26. Susan Winnett, "Coming Unstrung: Women, Men, Narrative, and Principles of Pleasure."

27. Robert Scholes, *Fabulation and Metafiction,* p. 26. Quoted in de Lauretis *Alice Doesn't,* p. 108; quoted in Winnett, p. 506.

28. Peter Brooks, *Reading for the Plot: Design and Intention in Narrative.*

29. Winnett, "Coming Unstrung," p. 507.

30. Ibid., p. 512.

31. Richard Levin, "The Poetics and Politics of Bardicide."

32. Ronald Bogue, "Meaning and Ideology in Robbe-Grillet's *Topologie d'une cité fantôme.*"

33. Michel Foucault, "Maurice Blanchot: The Thought from Outside" in *Foucault/Blanchot,* translated by Brian Massumi, (Zone Books: New York, 1987), p. 17.

34. Vicki Mistacco, "Interview with Robbe-Grillet," p. 40.

Chapter 4

1. Carole Deutsch and Lisa Steinbrugge, "Le démontage de la bonne conscience. La fonction de l'image de la femme dans *Projet pour une révolution à New York.*" *Lendemains* 20 (5 November 1980): 35.

2. "Piège à fourrure" was the title of a projected Robbe-Grillet film.

3. "La Cover-girl du diable." Interview with M. Grisolia.

4. "La Cover-girl du diable," p. 55

5. "L'Organisation structurelle des éléments thématiques travaille de façon délibérée dans tous mes romans et mes films, contre les contenus idéologiques véhiculés par ces éléments" [The structural organization of the thematic elements works deliberately, in all my novels and my films, against the ideological content carried by those elements] (interview with François Jost, *Obliques;* no.16–17, p. 2).

6. Discussed by Gardies in "L'Erotuelle."

7. Diane Crowder, "Narrative Structures and the Semiotics of Sex in the Novels of Alain Robbe-Grillet," (dissertation, University of Wisconsin, Madison, 1977). The quotation is from Crowder's summary in Dissertation Abstracts International, vol. 38, no. 10 (April 1978), 6156–6157 A.

8. Suzanne Kappeler, *The Pornography of Representation,* p. 98.

9. Ibid., p. 103.

10. Roland Barthes, "The Death of the Author." Cited in Kappeler, pp. 114, 142.

11. Kappeler, *The Pornography of Representation,* p. 136.

12. Ibid., p. 141.

13. Jules Michelet, *La Sorcière,* p. 50.

14. Roland Barthes, *Michelet par lui-même.*

15. Roland Barthes, "La Sorcière," in *Essais Critiques,* p. 131.

16. Jules Michelet, *La Femme.*

17. Alain Robbe-Grillet, "La Cover-girl du diable," p. 54.

18. In the "Documentation pour la presse" for *Glissements,* Robbe-Grillet claims, as he has for his wife's own sado-masochistic texts, that " . . . Alice veut briser le carcan de l'ordre établi (le pouvoir, la justice répressive, l'Eglise, la Sorbonne . . .) en se tournant du côté de l'interdit, de l'anti-naturel" [Alice wants to break the chains of the established order (power, repressive justice, the Church, the University . . .) by turning toward the forbidden and the anti-natural].

19. John Michalczyk, "Robbe-Grillet, Michelet, and Barthes: From *La Sorcière* to *Glissements progressifs du plaisir,*" p. 236.

20. This is the account given by Ben Stoltzfus in "Robbe-Grillet's Mythical Biography: Reflections of *La Belle Captive* in *Le Miroir qui revient.*"

21. Ibid., p. 391.

22. Ibid.

23. Ibid., p. 396.

24. Ibid., p. 389.

25. Ibid., pp. 389–90.

26. Ibid., p. 402.

27. John Fletcher, *Alain Robbe-Grillet,* p. 8.

28. Laura Mulvey, "Visual Pleasure and Narrative Cinema."

29. Henri Laborit, *L'Agressivité détournée.*

30. Alain Robbe-Grillet, "Le Sadisme contre la peur," interview with Guy Dumur.

31. Alain Robbe-Grillet, "Histoire de rats' ou La vertu c'est ce qui mène au crime," *Obliques,* no.16–17, p. 172.

32. Monique Wittig, *Les Guérillères.*

33. Andrea Cali, *Sémio/Thématique du sexe chez Alain Robbe-Grillet.*

34. Ibid., p. 35.

35. Susan Rubin Suleiman, "Reading Robbe-Grillet: Sadism and text in *Projet pour une révolution à New York,*" in *Subversive Intent: Gender, Politics and the Avant-Garde,* p. 66.

36. John Clayton, "Alain Robbe-Grillet: The Aesthetics of Sado-Masochism."

37. Crowder, "Narrative structures and the Semiotics of Sex in the Novels of Alain Robbe-Grillet " (Dissertation Abstracts International vol. 38, no. 10), 6157 A.

38. Alain Robbe-Grillet, "What Interests Me is Eroticism," interview with Germaine Brée, p. 92.

39. Ibid., p. 92.

40. Alain Robbe-Grillet, "J'aime éclairer les fantasmes," interview with J. Duranteau, p. 18.

41. M. Calle Grube, "Survivre à sa mode. Entretien avec Alain Robbe-Grillet," pp. 7–15. "J'ai dénoncé les stéréotypes et joué avec les stéréotypes; c'est-à-dire que je m'en suis servi comme matériau. Or, dans ces *Fragments,* passent quelquefois des morceaux de souvenirs qui sont absolument des stéréotypes dont je me soupçonne d'être dupe au moment de l'écriture.... L'histoire de mon grand-père ... Cela pourrait, par moment, être du Gide ... Cela m'a formé; c'est sûrement là encore" [I denounced stereotypes and played with them; that is, I used them as raw materials. Yet, bits and pieces of memories that are absolute stereotypes pass into these *Fragments,* memories by which I suspect I was deceived at the time of writing.... The story of my grandfather.... That could, at moments, be Gide.... That formed me; it's certainly still there] (pp. 14–15). The uneasiness of Robbe-Grillet's relationship with the meanings of the stereotypes he selects and reuses is intimated here.

Chapter 5

1. This chapter has its origins in a paper given at a symposium on the films of Alain Robbe-Grillet organized by Annette Michelson and Tom Bishop at New York University, April 28, 1989, on the occasion of a Retrospective of the Films of Alain Robbe-Grillet.

2. Dominique Chateau and François Jost, *Nouveau Cinéma, nouvelle sémiologie.*

3. Dominique Chateau, "La question du sens dans l'oeuvre d'Alain Robbe-Grillet," pp. 320–35.

4. Raylene O'Callaghan, "Alain Robbe-Grillet: An Identikit Portrait." *Landfall: A New Zealand Quarterly of Literary Studies* 158 vol. 40, no. 2 (June 1986): 180–187. The interview is reprinted in the present book as an appendix.

5. Helen Hazen, *Endless Rapture: Rape, Romance, and the Female Imagination.*

6. Michel Rybalka, "Alain Robbe-Grillet: At Play with Criticism," p. 35.

7. Susan Rubin Suleiman, "Pornography, Transgression and the Avant-garde: Bataille's *Story of the Eye*," p. 131.

8. Susan Sontag, "The Pornographic Imagination."

9. Jessica Benjamin, "Master and Slave: The Fantasy of Erotic Domination."

10. Ibid., p. 282.

11. Ibid., p. 283. Benjamin discusses G. W. F. Hegel, "The Independence and Dependence of Self-Consciousness: Master and Slave," chapter 4 of *The Phenomenology of Spirit* (Hamburg: Felix Meiner, 1952), pp. 141–50, and Georges Bataille, *Death and Sensuality.*

12. Daniel Deneau, "Bits and Pieces Concerning One of Robbe-Grillet's Latest Verbal Happenings," p. 42.

13. Nancy Chodorow, *The Reproduction of Mothering: Psychoanalysis and the Sociology of Gender.*

14. Suleiman, "Pornography, Transgression and the Avant-garde," p. 125.

15. Anne-Marie Dardigna, *Les Châteaux d'éros ou l'infortune du sexe des femmes.*

16. Jean de Berg, *L'Image.* Catherine Robbe-Grillet admits to being the author of this work published under a pseudonym. Although Alain Robbe-Grillet has not openly admitted his collaboration, it seems clear to me that, at the least, he contributed to the preface. P. R. refers to Pauline Réage, alias Dominique Aury, author of *Histoire d'O* and former mistress of Jean Paulhan. Aury continues to be a figure in French intellectual life.

17. John Fletcher, *Alain Robbe-Grillet*, p. 78.

18. Julia Kristeva, *Pouvoirs de l'horreur.*

19. Kaja Silverman, "Masochism and Male Subjectivity."

20. Ibid., p. 32.

21. Sigmund Freud, *The Ego and the Id,* translated by Joan Riviere and James Strachney (New York: Norton, 1962), p. 31. Quoted in Silverman, p. 34.

22. Richard Krafft-Ebing, *Psychopathia Sexualis: A Medico-Forensic Study,* translated by Harry E. Wedeck (New York: Putnam's Sons, 1965).

23. Theodor Reik, *Masochism in Sex and Society,* translated by Margaret H. Beigel and Gertrud M. Kurth (New York: Grove Press, 1962).

24. Sigmund Freud, "The Economic Problem of Masochism," and "A Child Is Being Beaten."

25. Silverman, "Masochism and Male Subjectivity," p. 51.

26. Gilles Deleuze, *Masochism: An Interpretation of Coldness and Cruelty,* 1971.

27. Parveen Adams, "Per Os(cillation)."

28. Julia Kristeva, "The Pain of Sorrow in the Modern World: The Works of Marguerite Duras."

29. Marguerite Duras, *Emily L.*

30. Marie Bonaparte, *Sexualité de la femme* (Paris: P.U.F., 1967).

31. Nathalie Sarraute, *Tu ne t'aimes pas* (Paris: Gallimard, 1989).

32. Marianne Hirsch, "Gender, Reading, and Desire in *Moderato Cantabile,*" *Twentieth Century Literature,* vol. 28 no. 1 (Spring 1982): 69–85.

33. Julia Kristeva, *Des Chinoises.*

34. Emily Apter, "The Story of I: Female Masochism in Irigaray." Circulated paper discussed in a seminar of the Women's Studies group at the Center for Cultural and Literary Studies, Harvard University, 1989.

35. Luce Irigaray, *Passions élémentaires,* p. 9. The translation is Emily Apter's.

36. Ibid., p. 12.

37. Apter, "The Story of I: Female Masochism," p. 6.

38. Apter (p. 4) quotes from Jane Gallop's *The Daughter's Seduction,* p. 79.

39. *A Lesbian S/M Sexuality Reader* and *Coming to Power: Writing and Graphics on Lesbian S/M* published by members of Samois. The preferences listed—military uniforms, bondage, golden showers, piercing—and the separation into active (handkerchief on one side) and passive (handkerchief on the other) organize a sexual universe not dissimilar to that which Robbe-Grillet evokes in more aestheticized and intellectual modes.

40. Apter, "The Story of I: Female Masochism, " p. 10.

41. René Girard, *La Violence et le sacré.*

42. William Stekel, *Sadism and Masochism: The Psychology of Hatred and Cruelty.*

43. Richard von Krafft-Ebbing, *Psychopathia Sexualis. A Medico-Forensic Study.*

44. Havelock Ellis, *Studies in the Psychology of Sex.*

45. Sigmund Freud, *Three Essays on the Theory of Sexuality,* pp. 48, 50.

46. Marie Gear and Melvyn Hill, *Working through Narcissism: Treating Its Masochistic Structure.*

47. Ibid., p. 301.

48. Alice Jardine, "Opaque Texts and Transparent Contexts: The Political Difference of Julia Kristeva."

Chapter 6

1. Benoîte Groult, *Ainsi soit-elle* (Paris: Grasset, 1975).
2. Anne-Marie Dardigna, *Les Châteaux d'éros ou l'infortune du sexe des femmes*.
3. See Alice Jardine, *Gynesis: Configurations of Woman and Modernity*, for a major contribution to the debate on woman and the postmodern or "modernity."
4. Luce Irigaray, *Le Corps à corps avec la mère*, p. 136.
5. Luce Irigaray, "Une Lacune natale" in *Le Nouveau Commerce*, Cahier 55 (1984): 41–47.
6. Jacqueline Lévi-Valenski, "Figures féminines et création romanesque chez Alain Robbe-Grillet."
7. Françoise Bech, "Imagination et images de femmes."
8. Ibid., pp. 42–43.
9. Ibid., p. 41.
10. Ibid., p. 44.
11. Daniel P. Deneau, "Bits and Pieces Concerning One of Robbe-Grillet's Latest Verbal Happenings."
12. Leon Roudiez, *French Fiction Today: A New Direction*, p. 228.
13. Deneau, "Bits and Pieces," p. 38.
14. Antony Pugh, "Robbe-Grillet in New York," *International Fiction Review*, no. 1 (1974): 122.
15. Joseph Bentley, "Notes on Pornography."
16. Deneau, "Bits and Pieces," p. 39.
17. Ibid., p. 44.
18. Ibid., p. 52.
19. John Sturrock, *The French New Novel*, p. 234.
20. Bruce Morrissette, "Postmodern Generative Fiction," in *Novel and Film: Essays in Two Genres*, p. 9.
21. Raymond Jean, "Robbe-Grillet, le sexe et la révolution," p. 47.
22. Ben Stoltzfus, "*Souvenirs du triangle d'or*: Robbe-Grillet's Generative Alchemy."
23. Thomas O'Donnell, "Thematic generation in Robbe-Grillet's *Projet pour une révolution à New York.*"
24. Ronald Bogue, "Meaning and Ideology in Robbe-Grillet's *Topologie d'une cité fantôme.*
25. Michael Nerlich, "Alain Robbe-Grillet Pornographe? Notes sur la difficulté de traiter la réalité," *Lendemains* vol. 20 (5 November 1980). See also *Apollon et Dionysos ou la science incertaine des signes: Montaigne, Stendhal, Robbe-Grillet* (Marburg: Hitzeroth, 1989).
26. Michel Rybalka, "Alain Robbe-Grillet: At Play with Criticism," p. 38.
27. Jean-Claude Vareille, *Alain Robbe-Grillet l'étrange*. "La supliciée ne se tord harmonieusement que parce-qu'elle est entravée," [The tortured prisoner twists harmoniously only because she is bound] (p. 184).

28. Ben Stoltzfus, "The Body of Robbe-Grillet's Text: Sex, Myth, and Politics in the Nouveau Nouveau Roman," p. 196.

29. John Fletcher, *Alain Robbe-Grillet*, p. 65.

30. Franklin Mathews, postface to the paperback edition of *La Maison de rendez-vous* (Paris: Union Générale d'Editions, 1965), entitled "Un Ecrivain non-réconcilié," p. 178.

31. Fletcher, *Alain Robbe-Grillet*, p. 59.

32. Nancy Miller, "Autobiographical Criticism," paper read at MLA Convention, Chicago, December 28, 1990.

33. Alexandrian, ed., *Les Libérateurs de l'amour*.

34. John Clayton, "Alain Robbe-Grillet: The Aesthetics of Sado-Masochism," p. 118.

35. Ingeborg Kohn discussed the sado-erotic thematics of the works of Guibert, Wittig, and Robbe-Grillet in a paper entitled "Sadism and the Nouveau Roman" at the MLA 1990 Colloquium in a special session I organized on the theme of "Violence and Sexuality in French texts of *modernité*."

36. Michel Foucault, *Histoire de la sexualité*.

37. "Robbe-Grillet commenté par lui-même," interview with Michel Rybalka, *Le Monde des Livres*, no. 1340465 (22 September 1978) pp. 17, 22.

38. Colette Goddard, "Robbe-Grillet et le mythe de la Cover-Girl," *Le Monde*, no. 9367 (26 February, 1975): 23.

39. Suzanne Kappeler, *The Pornography of Representation*, p. 53.

40. Roland Barthes, *Sade, Fourier, Loyola*.

41. "*Report of the Commission on Obscenity and Pornography,*" 1970; *Report of the Commission on Pornography,* 1986.

42. Edward Donnerstein, *The Question of Pornography: Research Findings and Policy Implications;* and Neil M. Malamuth and Edward Donnerstein, eds. *Pornography and Sexual Aggression*.

43. *Report of the Committee on Obscenity and Film Censorship,* 1979. *Pornography: The Longford Report,* 1972.

44. Andrea Dworkin, *Pornography: Men Possessing Women;* Laura Lederer, editor, *Take Back the Night: Women on Pornography;* Mary Daly *Gyn/Ecology: The Metaethics of Radical Feminism;* Kathleen Barry, *Female Sexual Slavery*. For the other side of the debate, see *Caught Looking: Feminism, Pornography and Censorship,* edited by Kate Ellis et al.

45. Christine Pickard, "Perspective on Female Responses to Sexual Material."

46. There have been a number of recent collections of essays such as *Pleasures* (London: Futura, 1986) or *Erotic Interludes: Tales Told by Women* (London: Futura, 1988), both edited by Lonnie Barbach, which seek to produce creative female "erotic" material and explore and liberate female sexuality.

47. Susan Sontag, "The Pornographic Imagination," *Partisan Review*, no. 34 (1967): 200; quoted in Deneau, "Bits and Pieces," p. 52.

48. Rybalka, "Alain Robbe-Grillet: At Play with Criticism, p. 35.

49. Jean-Jacques Brochier, *Alain Robbe-Grillet: qui suis-je?*, pp. 61–2.

50. For Mary Daly, in *Gyn/Ecology*, pornography is the form of resistance that the ego takes when the nude body of woman evokes its infancy and thus the possibility of its own death.

51. Alain Robbe-Grillet, "'Histoire de rats' ou La vertu c'est ce qui mène au crime," p. 172.

52. Lautréamont, *Les Chants de Maldoror*, Chant VI.

53. "Pour Sibylle Ruppert," preface to the limited edition artwork by Sibylle Ruppert, *Dessins pour Lautréamont* (Paris: Editions Notiris, 1980). 1,300 signed copies of Ruppert's illustrations of Lautréamont's text were produced by the Galerie Bijan Aalam.

54. Ibid., last page of preface.

55. Edward Lachman and Elieba Levine, *Chausse-trappes*, ("Roman-photo"); preface by Alain Robbe-Grillet, "Pour le roman-photo," pp. I–V (Paris: Editions de Minuit, 1981).

56. Alain Robbe-Grillet, *Le Magicien*, Film Synopsis in *Obliques*, no. 16–17, pp. 259–61.

57. Alain Robbe-Grillet, preface to *La Nouvelle Justine*, p. i.

58. Ibid., preface, p. i.

59. "Ils ont . . . dans cet exercice . . . un souci de netteté, de propreté du texte que Gilbert Garnon retrouve avec bonheur dans son dessin. Produire une forme aux contours sans bavures, n'est-ce pas là le projet majeur du criminel au fond de sa cellule? Et dans quel but? Dans celui, précisément de prouver son innocence à ses persécuteurs. On l'accuse de Satanisme? Il va démontrer au contraire sa pureté, telle son héroïne, en mettant au monde sous les yeux du juge ébloui un trait de plume si parfait, des objets cernés de façon si ferme et définitive, des architectures tellement incontestables que la malignité de ses détracteurs n'y aura plus aucune prise" [In this exercise . . . they show a concern for the sharpness, the cleanness of the text that Gilbert Garnon reproduces with felicity in his drawings. Is not the production of a form whose outline is faultless not the major project of the criminal in the depths of his cell? And with what goal in mind? Precisely the goal of proving his innocence to his persecutors. Is he accused of Satanism? Like his heroine, he will demonstrate, to the contrary, his purity, bringing into the world beneath the gaze of the bedazzled judge a pen-stroke so perfect, objects grasped in such a firm and definitive way, architectures that are so unquestionable that the spitefulness of his detractors will no longer have any hold] (preface, p. i).

60. Jean de Berg, *L'Image*.

61. Jeanne de Berg, *Cérémonies de Femmes*.

Chapter 7

1. Françoise Gaillard, "Post-Modernism: Angst or Agony of Modernism?" translated by Jennifer Cage. Circulated paper discussed at a seminar at

the Center for Cultural and Literary Studies, Harvard University, 7 November 1990, p. 14.

2. Deborah Lee, "Figuring Violence. Postmodern Meanings of Robbe-Grillet's Metalepsis." Unpublished paper read at the MLA convention, 30 December 1990, in Chicago in a special session I organized on "Gender, Writing and Violence in the Recent Texts of the French New Novelists."

3. Inge Crosman Wimmers, "Towards a Reflexive Act of Reading. Robbe-Grillet's *Projet pour une révolution à New York.*"

4. Susan Rubin Suleiman, *Subversive Intent: Gender, Politics and the Avant-Garde.*

5. Raylene O'Callaghan, "Reading Nathalie Sarraute's *Enfance.*"

6. James Twitchell, *Preposterous Violence: Studies of Fables of Aggression in Modern Culture.*

7. Bruce Morrissette, "Robbe-Grillet No. 1, 2, . . . , X," p. 128.

8. Bruce Morrissette, "Clefs pour *Les Gommes.*" Added in the form of an epilogue to the 10/18 edition of *Les Gommes* (Paris: Union Générale d'Editions, 1964).

9. Ruth Holzberg, "Décryptage du *Voyeur*: le contrepoint et les répliques du 'voyant.'"

10. This is John Sturrock's often-quoted phrase from a study of *Projet* entitled "The Project of A l'aine robe grillée."

11. Jean Dufy. "Les Codes narratifs dans *Djinn* d'Alain Robbe-Grillet."

12. Laure Adler, *Misérable et glorieuse la femme du XIXe siècle* and *Secrets d'alcôves: histoire du couple de 1830 à 1930.*

13. Georges Bataille, *L'Erotisme.*

14. Ronald Bogue, "Meaning and Ideology in Robbe-Grillet's *Topologie d'une cité fantôme.*"

15. Ben Stoltzfus, "*Souvenirs du triangle d'or.* Robbe-Grillet's Generative Alchemy."

16. Philippe Lejeune, *Le Pacte autobiographique.*

17. Roland Barthes, *Roland Barthes par Roland Barthes,* p. 22.

18. Alain Robbe-Grillet, "Fragment autobiographique imaginaire."

19. Jean-Claude Vareille, "Alain Robbe-Grillet et l'écriture: Délice et Supplice."

20. Carol Gilligan, *In a Different Voice: Psychological Theory and Women's Development.*

21. Carol Gilligan, "Oedipus and Psyche," Werner Herzog memorial lecture at Clark University, 18 November 1988.

22. Jean de Berg, *L'Image.*

23. Laura Mulvey, in "Visual Pleasure and Narrative Cinema," quoted by Teresa de Lauretis, *Alice Doesn't: Feminism, Semiotics, Cinema,* p. 135.

24. Michel Contat, "Portrait de Robbe-Grillet en châtelain," *Le Monde,* 12 February 1988, p. 15.

25. Claude du Verlie, "Beyond the Image."

26. Teresa de Lauretis, "The Essence of the Triangle or, Taking the Risk of Essentialism Seriously: Feminist Theory in Italy, the U.S. and Britain."

27. Robert Greene, "Words for Love in Marguerite Duras: *L'Après-midi de Monsieur Andesmas* (1962) and *Le Ravissement de Lol V. Stein* (1964)."

28. Mulvey, "Visual Pleasure and Narrative Cinema," quoted in de Lauretis, "Desire in Narrative," p. 135.

29. A Lotar Film production directed by Joseph Levine with Charlotte Rampling and Dirk Bogarde, Vienna, 1957.

30. Christiane Rochefort, *Quand tu vas chez les femmes.*

31. See also *Coming to Power,* members of Samois.

32. De Lauretis, "Desire in Narrative," p. 143.

33. Helen Hazen, *Endless Rapture: Rape, Romance, and the Female Imagination.*

34. Joanna Russ, *Magic Mommas and Trembling Sisters. Puritans and Perverts: Feminist Essays.*

35. Jean-Paul Sartre, *Les Mots* (Paris: Gallimard, 1964).

36. Marguerite Duras, *La Douleur.*

37. Gaylyn Studlar, *In the Realm of Pleasure: Von Sternberg, Dietrich and the Masochistic Aesthetic.*

38. Jacqueline Piatier, "Robbe-Grillet ensorcelle la grammaire," *Le Monde,* 20 March 1981. "Simon Lecoeur, alias Boris, alias Robbe-Grillet, découvre l'image de l'absent qu'il sera un jour" [Simon Lecoeur, alias Boris, alias Robbe-Grillet, discovers the image of the absent person that he will one day be].

39. Kaja Silverman, "Histoire d'O."

40. Jean Paulhan, preface to Pauline Réage, *Histoire d'O,* translated by Sabine d'Estrée, *Story of O,* p. xxv. Quoted by Silverman in *Pleasure and Danger,* p. 330.

41. Raylene O'Callaghan, "An Identikit Portrait" and "Text, Sex, and Criminal Project." Interviews with Robbe-Grillet. Reprinted in this work as an appendix.

42. Paulhan, preface to *Story of O,* p. xxv.

43. Bruno Bettelheim, *The Uses of Enchantment: The Meaning and Importance of Fairy Tales.*

Works by Alain Robbe-Grillet

Novels

Un Régicide (published 1978)	1949
Les Gommes	1953
Le Voyeur	1955
La Jalousie	1957
Dans le labyrinthe	1959
La Maison de rendez-vous	1965
Projet pour une révolution à New York	1970
Topologie d'une cité fantôme	1976
Souvenirs du triangle d'or	1978
Djinn: un trou rouge entre les pavés disjoints	1981
Le Miroir qui revient	1984
Angélique ou l'enchantement	1987

Paris: Editions de Minuit. Translations are my own. Translations exist in English for all of the above works except *Un Régicide, Souvenirs,* and *Angélique.*

Paperback editions cited. (My quotations from *Les Gommes* and *Dans le labyrinthe* are from these paperback editions.)

Les Gommes. Paris: Union Générale des Editions 10/18, 1964. Followed by "Clefs pour *Les Gommes*" by Bruce Morrissette.

Dans le labyrinthe. Followed by "Dans les couloirs du Métropolitain" and "La Chambre secrète" from *Instantanés* and "Vertige fixé" par Gérard Genette. Paris: U.G.E. 10/18, 1969.

Short Fiction

Instantanés. Paris: Editions de Minuit, 1962.

Critical Essays

Pour un nouveau roman. Paris: Editions de Minuit, 1963. Paris: Gallimard, Collection Idées, 1964. My quotations are taken from the Gallimard paperback edition.

Films and Ciné-novels

L'Année dernière à Marienbad (Last Year at Marienbad). Script and dialogue by Alain Robbe-Grillet, directed by Alain Resnais, 1961. Ciné-novel, Paris: Editions de Minuit, 1961.

Films Directed by Alain Robbe-Grillet

L'Immortelle. 1963. Ciné-novel, Paris: Editions de Minuit, 1983. Translated by A. M. Sheridan Smith as *The Immortal One.* London: Calder and Boyars, 1971.

Trans-Europ-Express. 1966.

L'Homme qui ment. 1968.

L'Eden et après. 1970.

N a pris les dés. 1971.

Glissements progressifs du plaisir. 1974. Ciné-novel, Paris: Editions de Minuit, 1974.

Le Jeu avec le feu. 1975.

La Belle Captive. 1983.

Other Texts by Robbe-Grillet

"L'Ange gardien." In *Minuit;* republished in *Obliques,* no. 16–17, p. 93.

La Belle Captive. Alain Robbe-Grillet (text). René Magritte (paintings). Lausanne: Bibliothèque des Arts, 1975. Written texts later collected in *Souvenirs du triangle d'or* and *Topologie d'une cité fantôme.*

Chausse-trappes. (Roman-photo). Edward Lachman and Elieba Levine. Preface, "Pour le roman-photo," (pp. i-iv), by Alain Robbe-Grillet. Paris: Editions de Minuit, 1981.

(Interventions in) Colloque de Cérisy. *Nouveau roman: hier, aujourd'hui;* ed. Ricardou. 2 vols. Paris: U.G.E. 10/18, 1972.

(Interventions in) Colloque de Cérisy. *Robbe-Grillet: analyse, théorie;* ed. Ricardou. 2 vols. Paris: U.G.E. 10/18, 1976.

Construction d'un temple en ruine à la déesse Vanadé. Alain Robbe-Grillet (text) and Paul Delvaux (etchings). Paris: Le Bateau-Lavoir, 1975. Limited edition. (Written texts later appeared in *Topologie d'une cité fantôme.*)

Les Demoiselles d'Hamilton. Alain Robbe-Grillet (texts) and David Hamilton (photographs). Paris: Robert Laffont, 1972. Texts collected in *Topologie d'une cité fantôme).*

"Fragment autobiographique imaginaire." *Minuit,* no. 31 (November 1978): 2–8.

"Histoire de rats' ou La vertu, c'est ce qui mène au crime." *Obliques,* no. 16–17, p. 172.

"Images and Texts: A Dialogue." In *Generative Literature and Generative Art: New Essays,* edited by David Leach, 38–47. Fredericton, New Brunswick: York Press. 1983.

Le Magicien. (Film Synopsis). In *Obliques,* no. 16–17, pp. 259–61.

La Nouvelle Justine. Donatien Alphonse François de Sade. Illustrations by Gilbert Garnon. Préface d'Alain Robbe-Grillet. Nyons: Editions Borderie, 1979.

Obliques no. 16–17. Paris: Borderie, 1978. There are a number of minor unpublished texts by Alain Robbe-Grillet in this special issue devoted to critical articles, commentaries and bibliographies on Robbe-Grillet's work.

Oeuvres cinématographiques. Edition vidéographique critique. Paris: Ministère des relations extérieures / Cellule d'animation culturelle, 1982. Video cassettes of first five films and transcripts of interviews with Robbe-Grillet.

"Order and Disorder in Film and Fiction." Translated by Bruce Morrissette. *Critical Inquiry,* vol. 4, no. 1 (Autumn 1977): 1–20.

"Pour Sibylle Ruppert." Preface to the limited edition artwork by Sibylle Ruppert, *Dessins pour Lautréamont.* Paris: Editions Notiris, 1980. 1,300 signed copies of Ruppert's illustrations of Lautréamont's text were produced by the Galerie Bijan Aalam.

"Pourquoi j'aime Barthes" (essai). Paris: Christian Bourgois, 1978.

Rêves de jeunes filles. Alain Robbe-Grillet (text) and David Hamilton (photographs). London: Collins, 1971. (Texts later appeared in *Topologie d'une cité fantôme.*)

Temple aux miroirs. Alain Robbe-Grillet (text) and Irina Ionesco (photographs). Paris: Seghers-Laffont, 1977. (Texts later appeared in *Souvenirs du triangle d'or.*)

Traces suspectes en surface. Alain Robbe-Grillet (text) and Robert Rauschenberg (lithographs). New York: Tatyana Grosman, Universal Limited Art Editions, 1978. (Texts collected in *Topologie d'une cité fantôme* and *Souvenirs du triangle d'or.*)

Interviews

"J'aime éclairer les fantasmes." Interview with J. Duranteau. *Le Monde* (30 October, 1970): 18.

"La Cover-girl du diable." Interview with M. Grisolia. *Le Nouvel Observateur* (18 February, 1974): 54–55.

"Le Sadisme contre la peur." Interview with G. Demur. *Le Nouvel Observateur* (19 October, 1970): 47–49.

"What Interests Me Is Eroticism." Interview with Germaine Brée. In *Homosexualities and French Literature: Cultural contents, Critical texts,* edited by Georges Stambolian and Elaine Marks. Ithaca, N.Y.: Cornell University Press, 1979.

Selected Bibliography

Adams, Parveen. "Per Os(cillation)." *Camera Obscura,* no. 17 (1988): 8–29.

Adler, Laure. *Misérable et glorieuse la femme du XIXe siècle.* Paris: Fayard, 1980.

———. *Secrets d'alcôve: histoire du couple de 1830 à 1930.* Paris: Hachette, 1983.

Alexandrian, ed. *Les Libérateurs de l'amour.* Paris: Editions du Seuil, 1977.

Allott, Ken and Peter Tremewan. *"Les Gommes" d'Alain Robbe-Grillet: Index verborum et table des fréquences.* Geneva: Slatkine, 1985.

Alter, Jean. *La Vision du monde d'Alain Robbe-Grillet.* Geneva: Droz, 1966.

Altermeyer, Bob. "Marching in Step." *The Sciences* (April 1988): 30–38.

Armes, Roy. *The Films of Alain Robbe-Grillet.* Amsterdam: John Benjamins, 1981.

Astier, C. *Le Mythe d'Oedipe.* Paris: Colin, 1974.

Bachelard, Gaston. *L'Activité rationaliste de la physique contemporaine.* Paris: Presses Universitaires de France, 1951.

Barry, Kathleen. *Female Sexual Slavery.* Englewood Cliffs, N.J.: Prentice Hall, 1979.

Barth, John. "Lost in the Funhouse." In *Lost in the Funhouse: Fiction for Print, Tape, Live Voice.* New York: Doubleday, 1988.

Barthes, Roland. *La Chambre claire. Notes sur la photographie.* Paris: Seuil, 1980. Translated by Richard Howard as *Camera Lucida: Reflections on Photography.* New York: Hill & Wang, 1981.

———. "The Death of the Author." In *Image-Music-Text,* edited by Stephen Heath. New York: Hill & Wang, 1977.

———. *Essais critiques.* Paris: Editions du Seuil, 1964.

———. *Michelet par lui-même.* Paris: Editions du Seuil, 1954.

———. *Mythologies.* Paris: Editions du Seuil, 1957.

———. *Le Plaisir du texte.* Paris: Editions du Seuil, 1973. Translated by Richard Miller as *The Pleasure of the Text.* New York: Hill & Wang, 1975.

———. *S/Z.* Paris: Editions du Seuil, 1970. Translated by Richard Miller as *S/Z.* New York: Hill & Wang, 1974.

———. *Sade, Fourier, Loyola.* Paris: Editions du Seuil, 1971.

Bataille, Georges. *Death and Sensuality.* New York: Walker, 1962.

———. *L'Erotisme.* Paris: Editions de Minuit, 1957.

Beauvoir, Simone de. *Faut-il brûler Sade?* (Original edition, *Les Temps Modernes,* 1952.) Paris: Gallimard, 1955.

Bech, Françoise. "Imagination et images de femmes." *Lendemains* 20 (November 1980): 37–44.

Benjamin, Jessica. *The Bonds of Love: Psychoanalysis, Feminism, and the Problem of Domination*. New York: Pantheon Books, 1988.

———. "Master and Slave: The Fantasy of Erotic Domination." In *Powers of Desire*, edited by Ann Snitow, Christine Stansell, and Sharon Thompson, pp. 280–99. New York: Monthly Review Press, New Feminist Library, 1983.

Bentley, Joseph. "Notes on Pornography." In *The Pornographic Imagination: Sexuality and Literary Culture*, edited by Irving Buchen, pp. 132–33. New York: New York University Press, 1970.

Benveniste, Emile. *Problèmes de linguistique générale*. Paris: Gallimard, 1966.

Berg, Jean de. *L'Image*. Paris: Editions de Minuit, 1956. (Reprinted by Editions J'ai Lu, 1984).

Berg, Jeanne de. *Cérémonies de Femmes*. Paris: Editions J'ai Lu, 1986.

Berger, John. *Ways of Seeing*. London: B.B.C. and Penguin Books, 1972.

Bettelheim, Bruno. *The Uses of Enchantment: The Meaning and Importance of Fairy Tales*. New York: Knopf, 1976.

Bishop, Michael, ed. *De Duras et Robbe-Grillet à Cixous et Deguy*. Dalhousie French Studies, special issue, vol. 17 (Fall-Winter 1989).

Blanchot, Maurice. *Lautréamont et Sade*. Paris: Editions de Minuit, 1963.

Bogue, Ronald. "A Generative Phantasy: Robbe-Grillet's 'La Chambre secrète.'" *South Atlantic Review*, vol. 46, no. 4 (November 1981): 1–16.

———. "Meaning and Ideology in Robbe-Grillet's *Topologie d'une cité fantôme*." *Modern Language Studies*, vol. 14, no. 1 (Winter 1984): 33–46.

Bohr, Niels. *Atomic Theory and the Description of Nature*. New York: John Wiley, 1958.

Boisdeffre, Pierre de. *La cafetière est sur la table ou contre le nouveau roman*. Paris: Editions de la Table Ronde, 1967.

Borges, Jorge Luis. "The Circular Ruins." In *Labyrinths: Selected Stories and Other Writings*, edited by Donald A. Yates and James E. Irby. New York: New Directions, 1964.

———. *Ficcions*. Buenos Aires: Emecé Editores, 1956.

———. "The Library of Babel." In *Labyrinths: Selected Stories and Other Writings*, edited by Donald A. Yates and James E. Irby. New York: New Driections, 1964.

Brée, Germaine. Interview with Robbe-Grillet. "What Interests Me Is Eroticism." In *Homosexualities and French Literature: Cultural Contents, Critical Texts*, edited by George Slambolian and Elaine Marks. Ithaca, N.Y.: Cornell University Press, 1979.

Brink, André. "Transgressions: A Quantum Approach to Literary Deconstruction." *Journal of Literary Studies*, vol. 1, no. 3 (1985): 10–26.

Brochier, Jean-Jacques. *Alain Robbe-Grillet: qui suis-je?* Lyon: La Manufacture, 1985.

Broglie, Louis de. *Sur les sentiers de la science*. Paris: Albin Michel, 1960.

Brooks, Peter. *Reading for the Plot: Design and Intention in Narrative.* New York: Knopf, 1984.

Brown, Royal. "Robbe-Grillet: Sexist or Feminist?" Paper read at a symposium on the films of Alain Robbe-Grillet, New York University, 28 April 1989.

Cali, Andrea. *Semio/Thématique du sexe chez Alain Robbe-Grillet.* Leece: Adriatica Editrice Salentina, 1982.

Calle Gruber, M. "Survivre à sa mode. Entretien avec Alain Robbe-Grillet." *Micromégas* (1982): 7–15.

Calvino, Italo. *Invisible Cities.* 1972. Translated by William Weaver. San Diego: Harcourt Brace Jovanovich, 1974.

Chateau, Dominique. "La Question du sens dans l'oeuvre d'Alain Robbe-Grillet." In *Robbe-Grillet. Colloque de Cérisy,* vol. 2, Ciné/Roman, pp. 320–35. Paris: Union Générale d' Editions, 1976.

Chateau, Dominique, and François Jost. *Nouveau cinéma, nouvelle sémiologie.* Paris: 10/18 Union Générale d'Editions, 1979.

Chodorow, Nancy. *The Reproduction of Mothering: Psychoanalysis and the Sociology of Gender.* Berkeley: University of California Press, 1978.

Cixous, Hélène. "Le Rire de la Méduse." *L'Arc* 61 (1975): 39–54. Translated by Keith Cohen and Paula Cohen as "The Laugh of the Medusa," in *New French Feminisms,* edited by Elaine Marks and Isabelle de Courtivron. New York: Schocken Books, 1981.

Clayton, John. "Alain Robbe-Grillet: The Aesthetics of Sado-Masochism." *Massachusetts Review* 18 (1977): 106–19.

Conley, Tom. "Le Texte iconique/The Iconic Text." Unpublished paper. Symposium on the Films of Alain Robbe-Grillet, New York University, 28 April, 1989.

Crosman, Inge K., and Susan R. Suleiman, eds. *The Reader in the Text: Essays on Audience and Interpretation.* Princeton: Princeton University Press, 1980.

Crosman Wimmers, Inge. "Towards a Reflexive Act of Reading Robbe-Grillet's *Projet pour une révolution à New York.*" In *Poetics of Reading: Approaches to the Novel,* pp. 121–53. Princeton: Princeton University Press, 1988.

Crowder, Diane. "Narrative Structures and the Semiotics of Sex in the Novels of Alain Robbe-Grillet." Dissertation, University of Wisconsin, 1977.

Culler, Jonathan. *Structuralist Poetics.* London: Routledge and Kegan Paul, 1975.

Daly, Mary. *Gyn/Ecology: The Metaethics of Radical Feminism.* Boston: Beacon Press, 1978.

Dardigna, Anne-Marie. *Les Chateaux d'éros ou les infortunes du sexe des femmes.* Paris: Maspero, 1981.

———. *Pierre Klossowski: l'homme aux simulacres.* Paris: Navarin, 1986.

De Bono, Edward. *The Mechanism of Mind.* Harmondsworth: Pelican, 1971.

DeJean, Joan. *Literary Fortifications: Rousseau, Laclos, Sade.* Princeton: Princeton University Press, 1984.

De Lauretis, Teresa. "Desire in Narrative." In *Alice Doesn't: Feminism, Semiotics, Cinema*, pp. 103–211. Bloomington: Indiana University Press, 1984.
———. "The Essence of the Triangle or, Taking the Risk of Essentialism Seriously: Feminist Theory in Italy, the U.S., and Britain." *Differences* 1 (Summer 1989): 3–35.
Deleuze, Gilles. *Présentation de Sacher-Masoch: le froid et le cruel*. Paris: Editions de Minuit, 1967. Translated as *Masochism: An Interpretation of Coldness and Cruelty*. London: Georges Braziller, 1971.
Deleuze, Gilles, and Félix Guattari. *L'Anti-Oedipe*. Paris: Editions de Minuit, 1972.
Deneau, Daniel. "Bits and Pieces Concerning One of Robbe-Grillet's Latest Verbal Happenings." *Twentieth-Century Literature,* vol. 25, no. 1 (Spring 1979): 33–53.
Derrida, Jacques. *L'Ecriture et la différance*. Paris: Editions du Seuil, 1967.
———. *Positions*. Paris: Minuit, 1972.
———. "Structure, Sign, and Play in the Discourse of the Human Sciences." In *The Structuralist Controversy: A Discourse on the Human Sciences,* edited by Richard Macksey and Eugenio Donato, pp. 247–72. Baltimore: John Hopkins University Press, 1972.
Dewdney, A. K. "Computer Recreations. A Tour of the Mandelbrot Set Aboard the Mandelbus." *Scientific American* (February 1989): 108–11.
Dhaenens, Jacques. *"La Maison de rendez-vous" d'Alain Robbe-Grillet*. Paris: Archives des Lettres Modernes, no. 113, 1970.
Donnerstein, Edward. *The Question of Pornography: Research Findings and Policy Implications*. New York: Free Press, 1987.
Dufy, Jean. "Les Codes narratifs dans *Djinn* d'Alain Robbe-Grillet." *Degré Second* 10 (September 1986): 39–49.
Duras, Marguerite. *L'Amant*. Paris: Editions de Minuit, 1984.
———. *La Douleur*. Paris: P.O.L., 1985.
———. *Emily L.* Paris: Editions de Minuit, 1987.
———. *Hiroshima mon amour*. Scénario et dialogues. Paris: Gallimard, 1960.
———. *L'Homme assis dans le couloir*. Paris: Editions de Minuit, 1980.
Dworkin, Andrea. *Pornography: Men Possessing Women*. New York: Perigee, 1981.
Eddington, Arthur. *The Philosophy of Physical Science*. Cambridge: Cambridge University Press, 1939.
Eco, Umberto. *Foucault's Pendulum*. Translated by William Weaver. San Diego: Harcourt Brace Jovanovich, 1989.
Eger, Martin. "The New Epic of Science and the Problem of Communication." Paper presented at the 1988 Conference of the Society for Literature and Science, Rensselaer Polytechnic Institute, October 6–9.
Eigen, M. and R. Winkler. *Laws of the Game* (1975). Translated by R. Kimber. New York: Harper & Row, 1981.

Ellis, Havelock. *Studies in the Psychology of Sex.* Vol. 1, part 2, *Love and Pain.* 1903. New York: Random House, 1942.

Ellis, Kate, et al., eds. *Caught Looking: Feminism, Pornography and Censorship.* Seattle: The Real Comet Press, 1986.

Felman, Shoshana. "Beyond Oedipus: The Specimen Story of Psychoanalysis." *Modern Language Notes,* vol. 98, no. 5 (1983): 1021–53.

Feynman, Richard. *The Character of Physical Law.* Cambridge: MIT Press, 1967. Translated as *La Nature des lois physiques.* Paris: Laffont, 1970.

Fish, Stanley. *Doing What Comes Naturally.* Durham: Duke University Press, 1989.

Fletcher, John. *Alain Robbe-Grillet.* London: Methuen, 1983.

Foucault, Michel. *Le Souci de soi* and *L'Usage des plaisirs.* In *L'Histoire de la sexualité.* Paris: Gallimard, 1984–88.

Freud, Sigmund. *Beyond the Pleasure Principle.* New York: Norton, 1989. Translation of *Jenseits des Lust Prinzips, 1920.*

———. "A Child is Being Beaten." In *Collected Papers of Sigmund Freud,* translated by James Strachey and Alice Strachey, pp. 172–201. London: Hogarth Press, 1924.

———. *Délires et rêves dans la "Gradiva" de Jensen.* Paris: Gallimard, 1949; Collection Idées, 1982. Translated from the German *Der Wahn und die Träume in W. Jensen's "Gradiva."* English translation "Delusions and Dreams in Jensen's 'Gradiva.'" In *Jensen's "Gradiva" and Other Works,* vol. 9 of *The Standard Edition,* translated by James Strachey, pp. 1–95. London: Hogarth Press, 1959.

———. "The Economic Problem of Masochism." In *The Standard Edition of the Complete Psychological Works of Sigmund Freud,* translated by James Strachey, vol. 19, no. 177. London: Hogarth Press, 1953.

———. *Three Essays On the Theory of Sexuality.* 1905. New York: Avon Books, 1965.

Gale, G. *The Theory of Science.* New York: McGraw-Hill, 1979.

Garden, Rachel. *Modern Logic and Quantum Mechanics.* Bristol: Adam Hilger, 1984.

Gardies, André. *L'Erotuelle,"* in *Obliques,* no. 16–17, pp. 112–19. Paris: Borderie, 1978.

Gear, Marie, and Melvyn Hill. *Working through Narcissism. Treating its Masochistic Structures.* New York: Aronson, 1982.

Genette, Gérard. "Vertige fixé," preface to the 10/18 paperback edition of *Dans le labyrinthe (1969).* Republished in *Obliques,* 16–17 (October 1978).

Gilligan, Carol. *In a Different Voice: Psychological Theory and Women's Development.* Cambridge, Mass.: Harvard University Press, 1982.

Girard, René. *La Violence et le sacré.* Paris: Grasset, 1972.

Gleick, James. *Chaos: Making a New Science.* New York: Viking, 1987.

Goldmann, Lucien. *Pour une sociologie du roman.* Paris: Gallimard, 1964.

Goulet, Alain. *Le Parcours möbien de l'écriture: Le Voyeur d'Alain Robbe-Grillet.* Paris: Archives des Lettres Modernes, 1982.

Greenblatt, Stephen. "Towards a Poetics of Culture." In *The New Historicism,* edited by H. Veeser. New York: Routledge, 1989.

Greene, Robert. "Words for Love in Marguerite Duras: *L'Après-midi de Monsieur Andesmas* (1962) and *Le Ravissement de Lol V. Stein* (1964)." *Romanic Review,* vol. 80, no. 1 (January 1989): 131–48.

Griffin, Susan. *Pornography and Silence: Nature's Revenge against Culture.* New York: Harper & Row, 1986.

Hayles, N. Katherine. *The Cosmic Web: Scientific Field Models and Literary Strategies in the 20th Century.* Ithaca, N.Y.: Cornell University Press, 1984.

Hazen, Helen. *Endless Rapture: Rape, Romance, and the Female Imagination.* New York: Charles Scribner's Sons, 1983.

Heath, Stephen. *Image-Music-Text.* New York: Hill & Wang, 1977.

———. *The Nouveau Roman: A Study in the Practice of Writing.* London: Elek, 1972.

Heisenberg, Werner. *La Nature dans la physique contemporaine.* Paris: Gallimard, 1968: Translated as *Across the Frontiers.* New York: Harper & Row, 1974.

Hofstadter, Douglas. *Gödel, Escher, Bach: An Eternal Golden Braid.* New York: Basic Books, 1979.

Holzberg, Ruth. "Décryptage du *Voyeur*: le contrepoint et les répliques du voyant." *French Review,* vol. 52, no. 6 (May 1979): 848–55.

Houque, Patrick. *Eve, éros, élohim: la femme, l'érotisme, le sacré.* Paris: Denoël Gonthier, 1982.

Huston, Nancy. *Mosaïque de la pornographie.* Paris: Denoël Gonthier, 1982.

Hutcheon, Linda. *Narcissistic Narrative: The Metafictional Paradox.* New York: Methuen, 1984.

———. *A Poetics of Postmodernism: History, Theory, and Fiction.* New York: Routledge, 1988.

Irigaray, Luce. *Ce sexe qui n'est pas un.* Paris: Editions de Minuit, 1977.

———. *Le Corps à corps avec la mère.* Montreal: Pleine Lune, 1981.

———. *Passions élémentaires.* Paris: Editions de Minuit, 1982.

Jacob, François. *Le Jeu des possibles.* Paris: Fayard, 1981.

Jardine, Alice. *Gynesis: Configurations of Women and Modernity.* Ithaca, N.Y.: Cornell University Press, 1985.

———. "Opaque Texts and Transparent Contexts: The Political Difference of Julia Kristeva." In *The Poetics of Gender,* edited by Nancy Miller, pp. 96–116. New York: Columbia University Press, 1986.

Jean, Raymond. *Lectures du désir.* Paris: Editions du Seuil, 1977.

———. "Robbe-Grillet, le sexe et la révolution." In *Pratique de la littérature.* Paris: Editions du Seuil, 1978.

Jefferson, Ann. *The Nouveau Roman and the Poetics of Fiction.* Cambridge: Cambridge University Press, 1980.

Jost, François. "From the 'New Novel' to the 'New Novelists.'" In *Three Decades of the French New Novel,* edited and translated by Lois Oppenheim, pp. 44–56. Urbana: University of Illinois Press, 1986.

———. "Les Eclats de la représentation." Paper read at the Symposium on the Films of Alain Robbe-Grillet, New York University, 28 April 1989.

Kappeler, Suzanne. *The Pornography of Representation.* Cambridge: Polity Press, 1984.

Krafft-Ebbing, Richard von. *Psychopathia Sexualis. A Medico-Forensic Study.* 1886. Translated by Harry Wedeek. New York: G.P. Putnam's Sons, 1965.

Kristeva, Julia. *Des Chinoises.* Paris: Editions des Femmes, 1974.

———. "The Ethics of Linguistics." In *Desire in Language,* edited by Leon Roudiez. New York: Columbia University Press, 1980.

———. *Histoires d'amour.* Paris: Denoël (folio), 1983.

———. "The Pain of Sorrow in the Modern World: The Works of Marguerite Duras." Translated by Katherine Jensen. *PMLA,* vol. 102, no. 2 (March 1987): 138–52. From *Soleil noir: dépression et mélancolie.* Paris: Gallimard, 1987.

———. *Pouvoirs de l'horreur.* Paris: Seuil, 1980.

———. *Séméiotiké: recherches pour une sémanalyse.* Paris: Editions du Seuil, 1969.

Kuhn, Thomas. *The Structure of Scientific Revolutions.* Chicago: University of Chicago Press, 1962.

Laborit, Henri. *L'Agressivité détournée.* Paris: Union Générale d'Editions, 1970.

———. *Biologie et structure.* Paris: Gallimard, 1968.

Lautréamont. *Les Chants de Maldoror.* Clermond-Ferrand: G. de Bussac, 1920.

Leach, David, ed. *Generative Literature and Generative Art: New Essays.* Fredericton, New Brunswick: York Press, 1983.

Lederer, Laura, ed. *Take Back the Night: Women on Pornography.* New York: William Morrow, 1980.

Leenhardt, Jacques. *Lecture politique du roman: "La Jalousie" d'Alain Robbe-Grillet.* Paris: Minuit, 1973.

Lejeune, Philippe. *Le Pacte autobiographique.* Paris: Editions du Seuil, 1975.

Levin, Richard. The Poetics and Politics of Bardicide. *PMLA,* vol. 105, no. 3 (May 1990): 491–504.

Lévi-Strauss, Claude. *L'Homme nu.* Paris: Plon, 1971.

———. *La Pensée sauvage.* 1958. Paris: Plon, 1962.

———. *Structural Anthropology.* Translated by C. Jakobson and B. Schoepf. New York: Doubleday, 1967.

Lévi-Valenski, Jacqueline. "Figures féminines et création romanesque chez Alain Robbe-Grillet." In *Figures féminines et roman,* edited by Jean Bessière, pp. 125–41. Paris: Presses Universitaires de France, 1982.

Lupasco, Stéphane. *Les Trois matières.* Paris: Union Générale d'Editions, Collection 10/18, 1970.

Lyotard, Jean-François. *La Condition postmoderne: rapport sur le savoir*. Paris: Editions de Minuit, 1979.

McHale, Brian. "Change of Dominant from Modernist to Postmodernist Writing." In *Approaching Postmodernism,* edited by Douwe Fokkema and Hans Bertens, pp. 53–79. Amsterdam: Benjamins, 1986

———. *Postmodernist Fiction*. New York: Methuen, 1987.

Malamuth, Neil M., and Edward Donnerstein, eds. *Pornography and Sexual Aggression*. Orlando: Academic Press, 1984.

March, A. *La Physique moderne et ses idées*. Paris: Gallimard, 1965.

Michalczyk, John. "Robbe-Grillet, Michelet, and Barthes: From *La Sorcière* to *Glissements progressifs du plaisir.*" *French Review*, vol. 51, no. 2 (December 1977): 233–44.

Michelet, Jules. *La Femme*. 1859. Paris: Garnier-Flammarion, 1981.

———. *La Sorcière*. 1862. Paris: Garnier-Flammarion, 1966.

Mistacco, Vicki. "Interview with Robbe-Grillet." *Diacritics,* vol. 6, no. 4 (1976): 35–43.

———. "The Theory and Practice of Reading Nouveaux Romans: Robbe-Grillet's *Topologie d'une cité fantôme.*" In *The Reader in the Text,* edited by Susan R. Suleiman and Inge K. Crosman, pp. 371–400.

Mitchell, Juliet. "Psycho-analysis, Narrative, and Femininity." In *Woman: The Longest Revolution*. London: Virago, 1984.

Monod, Jacques. *Chance and Necessity*. Translated by A. Wainhouse. New York: Random House, 1971.

Morrissette, Bruce. *Intertextual Assemblage in Robbe-Grillet From "Topology" to "The Golden Triangle."* Fredericton, New Brunswick: York Press, 1979.

———. *Novel and Film: Essays in Two Genres*. Chicago: University of Chicago Press, 1985.

———. "Order and Disorder in Film and Fiction." *Critical Inquiry,* vol. 4, no. 1 (Autumn 1977): 1–20.

———. "Robbe-Grillet no. 1, 2 . . . X." In *Nouveau roman: hier, aujourd'hui,* vol. 2. Proceedings of Colloque de Cérisy. Paris: Union Générale d' Editions, Collection 10/18, 1972.

———. *Les Romans de Robbe-Grillet*. Paris: Editions de Minuit, 1963. Translated and revised as *The Novels of Robbe-Grillet*. Ithaca, N.Y.: Cornell University Press, 1975.

Mulvey, Laura. "Visual Pleasure and Narrative Cinema." In *Feminism and Film Theory,* pp. 57–68. New York: Routledge, 1988.

Nerlich, Michael. *Apollon et Dionysos ou la science incertaine des signes: Montaigne, Stendhal, Robbe-Grillet*. Marburg: Hitzeroth Verlag, 1989.

Nicholson, Linda, ed. *Feminism/Postmodernism*. New York: Routledge, 1990.

Nicolescu, Basarab. *Nous, la particule et le monde*. Paris: Editions le Mail, 1985.

O'Callaghan, Raylene. [*see also* Ramsay, Raylene]. "The Art of the (Im)possible. The Autobiography of the French New Novelists." *Australian Journal of French Studies,* vol. xxv, no. 1 (1988): 71–91.

———. "Alain Robbe-Grillet. An Identikit Portrait" and "Text, Sex, and Criminal Project." Interviews with Robbe-Grillet. *Landfall: A New Zealand Quarterly* 158 (June 1986): 180–87. Reprinted in the Appendix of this volume.

———. "La Complémentarité multiple: une étude de l'oeuvre d'Alain Robbe-Grillet." Unpublished doctoral thesis, Université de Poitiers, 1972.

———. "Reading Nathalie Sarraute's *Enfance.* Reflections on Critical Validity." *Romanic Review,* vol. lxxx, no. 3 (May 1989): 445–62.

———. "The Sadist and the Siren. Modern Myth in the Writing of Alain Robbe-Grillet." *The New Zealand Journal of French Studies* (May 1986): 45–72.

———. "The Sense of Science in the Work of Alain Robbe-Grillet." *Romance Studies,* no. 9 (Winter 1986): 97–115.

———. "The Uses and Abuses of Enchantment in *Angélique et l'enchantement.*" In *De Duras et Robbe-Grillet à Cixous et Deguy.* Special number of *Dalhousie French Studies,* vol. 17 (Fall-Winter 1989): 109–16.

O'Donnell, Thomas. "Thematic generation in Robbe-Grillet's *Projet pour une révolution à New York.*" In *Twentieth-Century French Fiction: Essays for Germaine Brée,* edited by Henri Peyre, pp. 184–97. New Brunswick: Rutgers University Press, 1975.

Ollier, Claude. *Déconnection.* Paris: Flammarion, 1988.

Oppenheim, Lois, ed. and trans. *Three Decades of the French New Novel.* Urbana: University of Illinois Press, 1986.

Oppenheimer, J. *Science and the Common Understanding.* New York: Simon & Schuster, 1966. There is a French version of this work: *La Science et le bon sens.* Paris: Gallimard, 1955.

Pickard, Christine. "Perspective on Female Responses to Sexual Material." In *The Influence of Pornography on Behavior,* edited by Edward Nelson and Maurice Yaffe, 92–117. London: Academic Press, 1982.

Poirot-Delpech, Bernard. "*Angélique ou l'enchantement.* Robbe et Grillet." Review article in *Le Monde* (5 février, 1988): 11, 15.

Pornography: The Longford Report. London: Coronet Books, 1972.

Prigogine, Ilya, and Isabelle Stengers. *Order out of chaos.* New York: Bantam Books, 1984. Translated from *La Nouvelle Alliance: métamorphose de la science.* Paris: Gallimard, 1982.

Propp, Vladimir. *Morphology of the Folktale.* Austin: University of Texas Press, 1968.

Rahv, Betty. *From Sartre to the New Novel.* Port Washington, N.Y.: Kennikat Press, 1974.

Ramsay, Raylene [*see also* O'Callaghan, Raylene]. "Autobiographical Fictions: Duras, Sarraute, Simon, Robbe-Grillet Rewriting History, Story, Self." *The International Fiction Review,* vol. 18, no. 1 (Fall 1991). In press.

————. "Chaos Theory, the Work of Alain Robbe-Grillet, and the Female Body." *Language Quarterly,* vol. 29, no. 3–4 (Fall 1991): 57–69.

————. "The Sado-Masochism of Representation in French Texts of Modernity: The Power of the Erotic and the Eroticization of Power in the Work of Marguerite Duras and Alain Robbe-Grillet." *Literature and Psychology,* vol. 37, no. 3 (Fall 1991): 18–28.

————. "The Second World War as History and Story, Text and Pre-text, Order and Chaos in Alain Robbe-Grillet's Autobiography, *Le Miroir qui revient.*" *Literature and History,* vol. 2, no. 2 (Autumn 1991): 54–69.

————. "Through a Textual Glass, Darkly: Masochism in the Feminine Self in Duras's *Emily L.*" *Atlantis: Revue d'Etudes sur la Femme,* vol. 17, no. 1 (Fall 1991): 91–104.

Rault, Erwan. *Théorie et expérience romanesque chez Robbe-Grillet: "Le Voyeur" (1955).* Paris: La Pensée Universelle, 1975.

Réage, Pauline. *Histoire d'O.* Paris: Jean-Jacques Pauvert, 1954. Translated by Sabine d'Estrée as *Story of O.* New York: Grove Press, 1965.

Reik, Theodor. *Masochism in Sex and Society.* Translated by Margaret H. Beigel and Gertrud M. Kurth. New York: Grove Press, 1962.

Report of the Commission on Obscenity and Pornography. Washington, D.C.: USGPO, 1970. Reprinted, New York: Bantam Books, 1970.

Report of the Commission on Pornography. Washington, D.C.: USGPO, 1986.

Report of the Committee on Obscenity and Film Censorship. London: HMSO, 1979.

Ricardou, Jean. *Le Nouveau roman.* Paris: Editions du Seuil, 1973.

————. *Nouveaux problèmes du roman.* Paris: Editions du Seuil, 1978.

————. *Pour une théorie du nouveau roman.* Paris: Editions du Seuil, 1971.

————. *Problèmes du nouveau roman.* Paris: Editions du Seuil, 1967.

————, ed. *Robbe-Grillet: Colloque de Cérisy.* 2 vols. Paris: Union Générale d'Editions, Collection 10/18, 1976.

Ricardou, Jean, and Françoise von Rossum-Guyon, eds. *Nouveau roman: hier aujourd'hui.* 2 vols. Paris: Union Générale d'Editions, Collection 10/18, 1972.

Rochefort, Christiane. *Quand tu vas chez les femmes.* Paris: Grasset, 1972.

Roudiez, Leon. *French Fiction Today: A New Direction.* New Brunswick, N.J.: Rutgers University Press, 1972.

Russ, Joanna. *Magic Mommas and Trembling Sisters. Puritans and Perverts: Feminist Essays.* Freedom, Calif.: Crossing Press, 1985.

Ruthven, K. K. *Myth.* London: Methuen, 1976.

Rybalka, Michel. "Alain Robbe-Grillet: At Play with Criticism." In *Three Decades of the French New Novel,* edited and translated by Lois Oppenheim. Urbana: University of Illinois Press, 1986.

Sacher-Masoch, Leopold von. *La Vénus à la fourrure.* Paris: Presses Pocket, 1985.

Saïd, Edward. *Beginnings: Intention and Method*. New York: Basic Books, 1975.

Samois, members of. *Coming to Power: Writing and Graphics on Lesbian S/ M*. Berkeley: Samois, 1981.

———. *A Lesbian S/M Sexuality Reader*. Berkeley: Samois, 1979.

Schleifer, Ronald. "Narrative Analysis and the Psychology of Meaning: A. J. Greimas at the Limits of Science." Unpublished paper read at the 1988 Conference of the Society for Literature and Science, Rensselaer Polytechnic Institute, October 6–9.

Scholes, Robert. *Fabulation and Metafiction*. Urbana: University of Illinois Press, 1979.

Serres, Michel. *Le Parasite*. Paris: Grasset, 1980.

Silverman, Kaja. "Histoire d'O." In *Pleasure and Danger: Exploring Female Sexuality*, edited by Carole Vance, 320–49. Boston: Routledge & Kegan Paul, 1985.

———. "Masochism and Male Subjectivity." *Camera Obscura*, no. 17 (1988): 31–68.

Smith, Keren. "Voyeurism and the Void of Self: The Problem of Human Identity in Robbe-Grillet's *Le Voyeur* and Dostoevsky's *Crime and Punishment*." In *New Zealand Journal of French Studies*, vol. 9, no. 2 (1988): 34–41.

Smith, Roch. "Generating the Erotic Dream Machine: Robbe-Grillet's *L'Eden et après* and *La Belle Captive*." *The French Review*, vol. 63, no. 3 (February 1990): 492–502.

Snitow, Ann, et al., eds. *Powers of Desire: The Politics of Sexuality*. New York: Monthly Review Press, 1983.

Sontag, Susan. "The Pornographic Imagination." In *Styles of Radical Will*, pp. 35–73. New York: Delta, 1981. Previously in *Partisan Review*, no. 34 (1967).

Stekel, William. *Sadism and Masochism: The Psychology of Hatred and Cruelty*, translated by Louise Brink. New York: Liveright, 1939.

Stoicheff, Peter. "The Chaos of Metafiction." Paper read at the 1988 Conference of the Society for Literature and Science, Rensselaer Polytechnic Institute, October 6–9.

Stoltzfus, Ben. *Alain Robbe-Grillet. Life, Work and Criticism*. Fredericton, New Brunswick: York Press, 1987.

———. "*La Belle Captive*. Magritte et Robbe-Grillet." *Comparatist* 2 (May 1987): 64–75.

———. "The Body of Robbe-Grillet's Text: Sex, Myth, and Politics in the Nouveau Nouveau roman." *Neophilologus*, vol. 68, no. 2 (April 1984): 192–205.

———. "Dead, Desacralized, and Discontent: Robbe-Grillet's New Man." *Modern Fiction Studies*, vol. 27, no. 4 (Winter 1981–1982): 543–53.

———. "Mirror, Mirror on the Wall . . . : Inescutcheon in Art and Robbe-Grillet." *Stanford French Review*, vol. 5, no. 2 (Fall 1981): 229–45.

———. "Robbe-Grillet's Dialectical Topology." *The International Fiction Review, no. 9 (1982): 83–92.*

———. "Robbe-Grillet's Mythical Biography: Reflections of *La Belle Captive* in *Le Miroir qui revient.*" *Stanford French Review* (Fall–Winter 1988): 387–404.

———. "*Souvenirs du triangle d'or*: Robbe-Grillet's Generative Alchemy." *Romance Quarterly,* vol. 29, no. 4 (1982): 331–45.

———. "Towards Bliss. Barthes, Lacan, and Robbe-Grillet." *Modern Fiction Studies,* vol. 35, no. 4 (Winter 1989): 699–706.

Studlar, Gaylyn. *In the Realm of Pleasure: Von Sternberg, Dietrich, and the Masochistic Aesthetic.* Urbana: University of Illinois Press, 1988.

Sturrock, John. *The French New Novel.* London: Oxford University Press, 1969.

Suleiman, Susan Rubin. "Pornography, Transgression and the Avant-Garde: Bataille's *Story of the Eye.*" In *The Poetics of Gender,* edited by Nancy Miller. New York: Columbia University Press, 1986.

———. "Reading Robbe-Grillet: Sadism and Text in *Projet pour une Révolution à New York.*" *Romanic Review,* vol. 68, no. 1 (1977): 43–62. Republished in *Subversive Intent: Gender, Politics and the Avant-Garde,* 51–71. Cambridge, Mass.: Harvard University Press, 1990.

———, ed. *The Female Body in Western Culture.* Cambridge, Mass.: Harvard University Press, 1986.

Sunday, Suzanne, and Ethel Tobach, eds. *Violence Against Women: A Critique of the Sociobiology of Rape.* New York: Gordian Press, 1985.

Thiher, Alan. *Words in Reflection.* Chicago: University of Chicago Press, 1984.

Tremewan, Peter. "Allusions to Christ in Robbe-Grillet's *Les Gommes.*" *AUMLA,* no. 51 (May 1979): 40–48.

Twitchell, James. *Preposterous Violence: Studies of Fables of Aggression in Modern Culture.* New York: Oxford University Press, 1989.

Valabréga, Jean-Pierre, et al. *Le Désir et la perversion.* Paris: Editions du Seuil, 1967.

Vance, Carole, ed. *Pleasure and Danger. Exploring Female Sexuality.* Boston: Routledge & Kegan Paul, 1985.

Vareille, Jean-Claude. *Alain Robbe-Grillet l'étrange.* Paris: Nizet, 1981.

———. "Alain Robbe-Grillet et l'écriture: Délice et Supplice." *Critique,* no. 381 (février 1979): 151–61.

Verlie du, Claude. "Beyond the Image." *New Literary History,* vol. 2, no. 3 (1980): 527–34.

Waugh, Patricia. *Metafiction.* London: Methuen, 1984.

Weinberg, Stephen. *The First Three Minutes.* New York: Bantam 1979.

White, Eric. "Negentropy, Noise and Emancipatory Thought." Paper read at the 1988 Conference of the Society for Literature and Science, Rensselaer Polytechnic Institute, October 6–9.

Wilson, E. *On Human Nature.* New York: Bantam Books, 1978.

Winnett, Susan. "Coming Unstrung: Women, Men, Narrative, and Principles of Pleasure." *PMLA,* vol. 105, no. 3 (May 1990): 505–18.

Winnicott, D. W. *Playing and Reality.* New York: Basic Books, 1971.

Wiseman, Mary Bittner. *The Ecstasies of Roland Barthes.* London: Routledge & Kegan Paul, 1989.

Wittig, Monique. *Le Corps lesbien.* Paris: Editions de Minuit, 1973.

———. *Les Guérillères.* Paris: Editions de Minuit, 1969.

———. *Virgile, non.* Paris: Editions de Minuit, 1985.

Index

Library of Congress Cataloging-in-Publication Data

Ramsay, Raylene L.
    Robbe-Grillet and modernity: science, sexuality, and subversion /
Raylene L. Ramsay.
        p. cm. — (University of Florida humanities monograph; no
66)
    Includes bibliographical references and index.
    ISBN 0-8130-1145-0 (alk. paper)
    1. Robbe-Grillet, Alain, 1922– —Criticism and interpretation.
2. Literature and science—France—History—20th century.
3. Modernism (Literature)—France.   4. Sex in literature.
5. Deconstruction.   I. Title   II. Series: University of Florida
monographs.   Humanities: 66.
PQ2635.O117Z778   1992   92–12415
843'.914—dc20   CIP